Colonial Delaware Soldiers and Sailors

1638-1776

Henry C. Peden, Jr.

HERITAGE BOOKS
2008

HERITAGE BOOKS
AN IMPRINT OF HERITAGE BOOKS, INC.

Books, CDs, and more—Worldwide

For our listing of thousands of titles see our website at
www.HeritageBooks.com

Published 2008 by
HERITAGE BOOKS, INC.
Publishing Division
100 Railroad Ave. #104
Westminster, Maryland 21157

Copyright © 1995 Henry C. Peden, Jr.

All rights reserved. No part of this book may be reproduced or transmitted in any form or by any means, electronic or mechanical, including photocopying, recording or by any information storage and retrieval system without written permission from the author, except for the inclusion of brief quotations in a review.

International Standard Book Numbers
Paperbound: 978-1-58549-376-0
Clothbound: 978-0-7884-7175-9

INTRODUCTION

Late in August, 1609, Henry Hudson, a British sea captain and adventurer in the service of the Dutch West India Company, visited the Delaware area in search of a northwest passage.

Subsequently, between 1614 and 1620, Cornelius Hendricksen, a Dutch captain and navigator, visited the area. As a result of these visits and the information they provided, a charter was granted to the Dutch West India Company to grant land in the New World in 1629.

The following year the company bought land adjoining the Delaware River and in 1631 David Pietersen de Vries established a colony at the Whorekill (now Lewes). This whaling colony only lasted two years, but it was actually the first settlement in what is now the State of Delaware.

Not to be outdone by these other European expeditions, Swedish rulers encouraged settlement and outfitted the New Sweden Company with two ships, *Kalmar Nyckel* and *Grip*, to go to the New World and colonize it. They arrived at Jamestown, Virginia, in March, 1638, where they remained a few days and then continued on to Delaware. They established settlements south of the area that later became Wilmington. The Swedes were attacked continuously by the Dutch between 1651 and 1655. As a result, a number of forts were built in the area, such as Fort Christina, Fort Casimir and Fort Elfsborg, some of which were in what is now Pennsylvania and New Jersey, as well as Delaware. The first Finnish colonists arrived in 1656.

The British next took charge of the Delaware colony, as well as New Amsterdam (now New York) in 1664. Two years later a large influx of English people from Virginia, Maryland, New Jersey, New York, and Europe made their homes among the Swedes and the Dutch in Delaware. In turn, many of these settlers spread into Pennsylvania, Maryland, and New Jersey.

Many of these early settlers and their descendants were civilians who had to become soldiers and sailors out of necessity, as they were called upon constantly to fight the enemy. They fought in King William's War, 1689-1697, in Queen Anne's War, 1702-1713, in the War of Jenkins' Ear, 1739-1742, in King George's War, 1744-1748, and the French and

Indian Wars, 1754-1763. Many also served in the American Revolution, 1775-1783.

Most records of the colonial militia have not survived; however, those that have survived are scattered among the governing bodies of colonial Delaware, Pennsylvania, New Jersey and New York.

It is the intent to present in this one book, from available sources, as many of the colonial soldiers and sailors as possible who served in the area that is now Delaware beginning on March 29, 1638, when the first colonists arrived in New Sweden, and continuing up to July 4, 1776, when their descendants declared their independence from Great Britain.

Also, in order to make this book as complete as possible, and not to leave anyone out who may have served, the names of soldiers, sailors, mariners, pilots, and other "officers" have been included. The reader should keep in mind that this list is not complete and some of those mentioned could have been civilians, or governmental in nature, rather than military men. In some instances persons living in nearby areas have been included.

Every entry in this book is documented and one will find a code consisting of letters and numbers representing sources and pages within the stated source. Those sources are as follows:

DA = *Delaware Archives, Military, Volume I* (Wilmington: Mercantile Printing Company, 1911).

DB = Virdin, Donald O. *Delaware Bible Records, Volume 2* (Bowie, Maryland: Heritage Books, Inc., 1992).

DC = Horle, Craig W., ed. *Records of the Courts of Sussex County Delaware 1677-1710* (Philadelphia: University of Pennsylvania Press, 1991).

DD = Mason, Elaine Hastings, and Wright, F. Edward. *Land Records of Sussex County, Delaware, 1782-1789* (Westminster, Maryland: Family Line Publications, 1990).

DF = Clark, Raymond B., Jr. *Delaware Families* (St. Michael's, Maryland: Published by the Author, 1988).

DH = Scharf, J. Thomas. *History of Delaware, 1609-1888, Volume I* (Philadelphia: L. J. Richards & Company, 1888).

DJ = Johnson, Amandus. *The Swedish Settlements on the Delaware, Volume II* (Baltimore: Genealogical Publishing Company, 1969).

DK = de Valinger, Leon, Jr. *Calendar of Kent County, Delaware, Probate Records, 1680-1800* (The Public Archives Commission, State of Delaware, 1944).

DM = de Valinger, Leon, Jr. *Colonial Military Organization in Delaware, 1638-1776* (Delaware Tercentenary Commission, 1938).

DN = *A Calendar of Delaware Wills, New Castle County, 1682-1800.* Abstracted by the Historical Research Committee of the Colonial Dames of Delaware in 1911. (Baltimore: Clearfield Company, 1989, as reprinted by Genealogical Publishing Co.).

DP = Gehring, Charles T., ed. *New York Historical Manuscripts, Dutch, Volumes XX-XXI,* "Delaware Papers (English Period), 1664-1682." (Baltimore: Genealogical Publishing Co., 1977).

DR = Bendler, Bruce A. *Colonial Delaware Records, 1681-1713.* (Westminster, Maryland: Family Line Publications, 1992).

DS = de Valinger, Leon, Jr. *Calendar of Sussex County, Delaware, Probate Records, 1680-1800* (The Public Archives Commission, State of Delaware, 1964).

DY = *The Duke of York Record, Delaware Land Titles, 1646-1679.* (Westminster, Maryland: Family Line Publications, 1988).

One should consult any of the above sources for more information on the colonists and their lifestyle in the land we now call Delaware.

Henry C. Peden, Jr.
Bel Air, Maryland
February 1, 1995

COLONIAL DELAWARE SOLDIERS AND SAILORS, 1638-1776

ABBOTT, James. Private. Enlisted on May 20, 1758, in Capt. French Battell's Company of Lower County Provincials, during the French and Indian Wars. [Ref: DA-16].
ABEL, Lucas. Soldier. Planter in Delaware who paid his quit-rent to the governor in 1671, having received a land grant on west side of Delaware Bay on June 17, 1671. [Ref: DP-29, DY-151].
ADAIR, Jane. See "William Faries," q.v.
ADAIR, John. Private. Served in Capt. Henry Darby's Company of the Delaware Regiment of Continental Troops. Enlisted on January 18, 1776, and was on duty (in barracks) at Dover on April 12, 1776. [Ref: DA-46].
ADAMS, John. Mariner. Lived in Sussex County on the west side of the Indian River by November 7, 1771, at which time he conveyed part of the tract *Long Neck* to John Holloway. He was a grandson of William Bagwell, who had obtained the land from his father, Thomas Bagwell, prior to 1690. John Adams and wife Cornilea were living in Indian River Hundred in 1772. [Ref: DD-48, 49].
ADAMS, Nathan. Captain. Served in the 6th Company of Delaware State Troops in Continental Service. Commissioned January 19, 1776, and was on duty (in barracks) with the Delaware Regiment of Continental Troops at Dover on April 12, 1776. [Ref: DA-34, 36, 52].
ADAMS, Peter. Private. Served in Capt. David Hall's Company of the Delaware Regiment of Continental Troops. Enlisted on March 15, 1776 and was on duty (in barracks) at Lewis Town on April 11, 1776. [Ref: DA-43].
ADAMS, Samuel. See "John Shannon," q.v.
ADDAM, John. Drummer. Born 1738, Holland. Served in Capt. John Wright's Company on May 11, 1759, during the French and Indian Wars. [Ref: DA-25].
ADLEY, George. Private. Served in Capt. Joseph Vaughan's Company, Delaware Regiment of Continental Troops. Enlisted on January 20, 1776, and was on duty (in barracks) at Dover on April 12, 1776. [Ref: DA-59].
AKERMAN, Hakan Persson. Soldier. Arrived in New Sweden on the ship *Orn* in 1654. He returned to Europe with Director Rising in 1655. [Ref: DJ-717, 724].

AKIN, Alexander. Private. Born 1739 (place not stated). Laborer. Enlisted May 14, 1759, in the French and Indian Wars, Capt. James Armstrong's Company in the Pennsylvania Regiment. [Ref: DA-25].

ALBERTS, Dirck. Soldier. Planter in Delaware who paid his quit-rent to the governor in 1670. [Ref: DP-29]. "Derrick Alberts" received a grant for some land near the fort at New Castle on August 11, 1670. [Ref: DY-145].

ALBRECHTSEN, Jacob. Sailor. Mate on the ship *Gyllene Haj* during the seventh expedition to New Sweden between 1646-1647. [Ref: DJ-760].

ALDRICKS, Peter. See "Pieter Alricks," q.v.

ALEXANDER, James. Cornet. Born 1690. Died 1779. Son Amos Alexander married Sarah Sharpe and he became a Justice of the Peace in Cecil County, Maryland during the American Revolution. He is buried in Head of Christiana near Newark, Delaware. [Ref: DB-1].

ALEXANDER, John. Private. Served in Capt. Samuel Smith's Company, Delaware Regiment of Continental Troops. Enlisted on February 16, 1776, and was on duty (in barracks) at Dover on April 12, 1776. [Ref: DA-54].

ALFORD, John. Private. Served in Capt. Joseph Stedham's Company, Delaware Battalion of Continental Troops. Enlisted on February 24, 1776, and was in quarters at Dover on April 12, 1776. [Ref: DA-40].

ALFORD, Mary and Thomas. See "Mary and Thomas Allfoard," q.v.

ALFREE, Paul. Lieutenant. Served in Capt. Henry Dyer's Company, New Castle County, in 1747-1748, in King George's War against Canada. [Ref: DA-7].

ALL, William. Private. Born 1724, Ireland. Laborer. Enlisted on May 1, 1758, in the French and Indian Wars, by Capt. Benjamin Noxon. [Ref: DA-18]. (Name also spelled "Awl").

ALLARD, John. Land patentee and probable militiaman in Delaware in November, 1677. [Ref: DP-167, 168]. (Name also spelled "Alward").

ALLEE, Jacob. Lieutenant. Served in Capt. George Martin's Company, Kent County, 1747-1748, in King George's War against Canada. [Ref: DA-8]. One "Jacob Allee, yeoman," died testate in Kent County and his will was probated October 13, 1766, mentioning his wife (no name given), son John Jr. [sic], daughter Rebecca Killen (wife of William Killen), and his granddaughters Elizabeth and Mary Killen (daughters of William and Rebecca Killen). [Ref: DK-223].

ALLEE, Sarah and Abraham. See "Thomas Tilton," q.v.

ALLEN, David. Private. Enlisted on May 5, 1759, in the French and Indian Wars, and appeared on a return of Capt. Henry Van Bibber's

Company of the Lower Counties on Delaware Troops, at New Castle, on June 4, 1759. [Ref: DA-26].

ALLEN, John. Private. Served in Capt. Jonathan Caldwell's Company, Delaware Regiment of Continental Troops. Enlisted on January 13, 1776, and was on duty (in barracks) at Dover on April 12, 1776. [Ref: DA-41].

ALLFOARD, Mary and Thomas. See "Alexander Bryan," q.v.

ALLIN, Moses. Pilot. Lived in Sussex County by March 25, 1772, at which time he purchased a lot on 2nd Street in Lewes. [Ref: DD-50].

ALLWINKLE, Joseph. Private. Born 1736, Maryland. Laborer. Enlisted on April 21, 1758, in the French and Indian Wars, by Capt. Benjamin Noxon. [Ref: DA-18]. Also, one Joseph Allwinkle enlisted on May 1, 1759, and his name appeared on a return of Capt. Henry Van Bibber's Company of the Lower Counties on Delaware Troops at New Castle on June 4, 1759. [Ref: DA-26].

ALMOND, John. Captain. New Castle County Company, 1747-1748, and served in King George's War against Canada. [Ref: DA-7].

ALRICKS, Jacob. Commissary General. Uncle of Pieter Alricks. Jacob is buried in Old Drawyers Cemetery in Odessa in New Castle County, Delaware. He was director and commissary general of a force of 50 soldiers and 160 civilians who came to New York in March, 1657, where they received their commissions and orders from Gov. Peter Stuyvesant. They sailed to New Amstel. Jacob Alricks died December 30, 1659, without issue. [Ref: DB-2].

ALRICKS, Pieter. Soldier. Planter in Delaware who paid his quit-rent to the governor in 1670. "Peeter Aldricks" appeared on a nomination list for officers in New Castle, Delaware, circa 1675 (list not dated). He was born circa 1631 and was the son of Pieter Alricks "of Nijkerck, Groninger, in the Nederland." His wife was Marie Wessells and they were married in the Dutch Church in New York City on February 9, 1664. They had four sons: Peter Sigfridus, Harmanus, Jacobus, and Wessells. "Peter Alricks" was one of the most prominent men of the Delaware Colony and was selected by the Dutch and the English for many civic activities. "Peter Alrichs" wrote his will in the Town of New Castle, Delaware, on January 25, 1694 (and died in 1697), naming his "eldest son Sigfridus Aldrichs, sons Hermanns Alrichs, Jacobus, and Wessell." [Ref: DP-29, DP-170, DB-2, DB-3, DN-9]. "Peter Alricks" received a grant on February 15, 1667, "for two certain islands in Delaware River situate, lying and being on ye west side of ye said river and about south west from ye island commonly called Matiniconck, the which [sic] is the biggest of the two islands having been formerly known by the name of Kipps Island and by the Indian name *Koomenakineknock*." [Ref: DY-125].

ALRICKS, Samuel. Lieutenant. Served as an ensign in Capt. Alexander Porter's Company, New Castle County, 1747-1748 in King George's War and a lieutenant in Capt. Alexander Porter's Company in the Upper Regiment, New Castle Hundred, 1756, in the French and Indian Wars. [Ref: DA-7, 11]. Son of Peter Alricks and Dorcas Land. [Ref: DB-3].

ALTUM, James. Private. Enlisted on May 28, 1758, in Capt. French Battell's Company of Lower County Provincials, during the French and Indian Wars. [Ref: DA-16].

AMUNDSSON, Hans. Commander. Served on the ship *Katt* during the ninth expedition to New Sweden in 1649. [Ref: DJ-761].

ANDERSON, Ann. See "Samuel Platt," q.v.

ANDERSON, Edward. Private. Born 1735, Virginia. Enlisted in Capt. John Wright's Company and was on the muster roll of May 11, 1759, during the French and Indian Wars. [Ref: DA-25].

ANDERSON, Edward. Private. Born 1738, Sussex, Delaware. Laborer. Enlisted on May 9, 1758, during the French and Indian Wars, as a private by Capt. John McClughan "for the campaign in the lower counties." [Ref: DA-17].

ANDERSON, Enoch. Second Lieutenant. Served in 1st Company of the Delaware State Troops in Continental Service. Commissioned on January 13, 1776. [Ref: DA-34, 36].

ANDERSON, Herdman. Fifer and drummer. Served in Capt. Joseph Stedham's Company of the Delaware Battalion of Continental Troops. Enlisted on January 22, 1776, and was in quarters at Dover on April 12, 1776. [Ref: DA-39].

ANDERSON, John. Ensign. Served in Capt. John Vance's Company, St. George's Hundred, Lower Regiment, New Castle County, 1756, during the French and Indian Wars. [Ref: DA-11].

ANDERSON, John. Private. Served in Capt. Richard McWilliams' Company, New Castle County. Enlisted on December 28, 1757, during the French and Indian Wars. [Ref: DA-15].

ANDERSON, Mary and Samuel. See "Samuel Platt," q.v.

ANDERSON, Thomas. Corporal. Served in Capt. Joseph Stedham's Company, Delaware Battalion of Continental Troops. Enlisted on January 27, 1776, and was in quarters at Dover on April 12, 1776. [Ref: DA-39].

ANDERSON, William. Private. Served in Capt. Joseph Vaughan's Company, Delaware Regiment of Continental Troops. Enlisted on January 19, 1776, and was on duty (in barracks) at Dover on April 12, 1776. [Ref: DA-59].

ANDERSSON, Anders. Soldier. Arrived in New Sweden in 1643 "from the Castle of Elfsborg as a punishment." Served as a soldier (*saldater*) at Fort Elfsborg during 1643-1644 and was one of the men "who daily followed and served the governor" [Johan Printz] at Fort Tinicum, until he returned to Sweden in 1653. [Ref: DJ-703, DJ-706, DJ-714]. (Also referred to as "Anders Andersonn, the Finn").

ANDERSSON, Erick. Trumpeter (*trumbetarenn*). An "officer" at Fort Christina in New Sweden, having arrived there in 1643. He served until July 1, 1645, when he became a freeman. On February 1, 1647, he again entered "the service of the Crown" and remained in service until April 1, 1648 when he returned to Sweden. He came again to New Sweden as a soldier on the ship *Orn* in 1654. He died either on the journey or in New Sweden before June 9, 1654, leaving a widow. [Ref: DJ-701, 715, 717]. (Name also spelled "Erich Andersonn").

ANDERSSON, Herman. Sailor. Served on the ship *Kalmar Nyckel* during the first expedition to New Sweden between 1637-1639. He was dead by 1640, leaving a widow in Stockholm. [Ref: DJ-758].

ANDERSSON, Johan. Boatswain. Served on the ship *Swan* during the fifth expedition to New Sweden in 1642-1643. [Ref: DJ-759].

ANDERSSON, Johan. Soldier. From Strangnas, he was hired by Mans Kling as farm hand in 1641 and arrived in New Sweden that year. He was a common soldier (*saldater*) "who daily followed and served the governor" [J. Printz] at Fort Tinicum in 1643. On October 1, 1646, "he was hired as a soldier and seems to have left with Printz" and returned to Sweden in 1648. [Ref: DJ-706, DJ-712, DJ-716, DH-45].

ANDERSSON, Lars. Soldier (*saldater*). He "daily followed and served the governor" [Johan Printz] at Fort Tinicum in 1643. [Ref: DJ-705, DJ-706, DH-47]. There appears to be several men by this name. Lars Andersson (from Gothenburg) was "cook on the sloop" in 1641. [Ref: DJ-712]. Also, Lars Andersson, a soldier (from Saltuna, Stockholm), arrived in New Sweden in 1643, served until September 1, 1653, and returned to Sweden with Governor Johan Printz. [Ref: DJ-713]. Lars Andersson, the peasant (from Aland) died on July 31, 1643, at Fort Elfsborg. [Ref: DJ-708]. Lars Anderson (Andersson), muster clerk (*munsterschreiber*), was an "officer" who arrived in New Sweden on the ship *Orn* in 1654. [Ref: DJ-716]. Lars Andersson, the Finn, was a soldier in New Sweden in 1654. [Ref: DJ-717].

ANDERSSON, Nils. Soldier. From Mallpa in Kinna Hundred in the Ostergotlands, he arrived in New Sweden in 1643, and served as a soldier (*saldater*) "who daily followed and served the governor" [J. Printz] at Fort Tinicum in 1643. He was a soldier "until the middle of 1649 when he died owing the company 35.42 *riksdalers*." His widow was still in New Sweden in 1654. Nils Andersson, a freeman, died on the ship *Orn* circa June 9, 1654. [Ref: DJ-705, DJ-706, DJ-714, DJ-717, DH-47]. Also, "Nils Andersson, cabinet maker (*snickare*)," was a soldier who was hired at Stockholm in 1653 and may have arrived in New Sweden after 1655. [Ref: DJ-723].

ANDERSSON, Peer. Sailor. Served as guard and skipper (*skepperen*) on the yacht *Speel* in New Sweden, in 1640-1643, and was "one of the laboring people at Fort Tinicum who was appointed to cut hay for the cattle and also in the meantime to follow the governor [Johan Printz] on the little sloop" in 1643. He arrived in New Sweden on the ship *Kalmar Nyckel* in 1640. [Ref: DJ-699, DJ-706, DJ-710].

ANDERSSON, Sven. Drummer (*trumbeslagaren*). He arrived in New Sweden in 1643, was an officer at Fort Elfsborg in 1643, and served until 1655. He returned to Europe with Director Rising in 1655. [Ref: DH-47, DJ-703, 713, 716, 724].

ANDERTON, Samuel. Private. Born 1727, Kent, Delaware. Laborer. Enlisted in Capt. John Shannon's Company of Foot on July 16, 1746, and served in King George's War against Canada. He was in winter quarters at Albany, New York, 1746-1747, and discharged on October 31, 1747. [Ref: DA-4, DA-6]. (He is not listed in Source DM-40.)

ANDREAS, Peter. Soldier. Planter in Delaware who paid his quit-rent to the governor in 1667. [Ref: DP-27].

ANDREWS, Joseph. Private. Served in Capt. Jonathan Caldwell's Company of the Delaware Regiment of Continental Troops. Enlisted on March 2, 1776, and was on duty (in barracks) at Dover on April 12, 1776. [Ref: DA-41].

ANDRIESE, Andries. Probable militiaman in Delaware who paid his quit-rent to the governor in 1669. [Ref: DP-27, 28].

ANDROS, Edmund. See "James Wells," q.v.

ANGUISH, Martha. See "Joseph Merideth," q.v.

ANSLOW, Richard. Private. Born 1725, Ireland. Enlisted in Capt. John Wright's Company and was on the muster roll of May 11, 1759, during the French and Indian Wars. [Ref: DA-25]. (Name also spelled "Onslow").

ANSTILL, Isaac. Private. Born 1737, Virginia. Laborer. Enlisted on April 21, 1758, during the French and Indian Wars, by Capt. Benjamin Noxon. [Ref: DA-18].

ANTEREY, John. Land patentee and probable militiaman in Delaware in November, 1677. [Ref: DP-167, 168].

ANTHONY, William. Private. Born 1739, Sussex, Delaware. Enlisted in Capt. John Wright's Company and was on the muster roll of May 11, 1759, during the French and Indian Wars. [Ref: DA-25].

ARMSTRONG, Abel. Lieutenant. Served in Capt. James McMeehen's Company in New Castle County, 1747-1748, in King George's War against Canada. [Ref: DA-7].

ARMSTRONG, Alexander. Lieutenant. Served in Capt. David Witherspoon's Company, New Castle County, 1747-1748, in King George's War against Canada. [Ref: DA-7].

ARMSTRONG, Archibald. Captain. Served in New Castle County Company, in 1747-1748, in King George's War against Canada. [Ref: DA-7]. One Archibald Armstrong, gentleman, died testate in Christiana Hundred, in New Castle County, and his will was probated on May 18, 1775, naming his "wife Ann, sons William and John, son-in-law Col. John Armstrong and my daughter Rebecca his wife, son-in-law Rev. George Duffield and Margaret my daughter his wife, and grandsons Archibald and James, sons of my son John." He also mentioned his interest and title to land in Ireland. [Ref: DN-79].

ARMSTRONG, Archibald. Sergeant. Born 1727, Tyrone, Ireland. Laborer. Enlisted on April 26, 1759, in the French and Indian Wars, in Capt. James Armstrong's Company in the Pennsylvania Regiment. [Ref: DA-25].

ARMSTRONG, Hugh. Private. Served in Capt. Charles Pope's Company, Delaware Regiment of Continental Troops. Enlisted January 20, 1776, and was on duty (in quarters) at Lewis Town on April 11, 1776. [Ref: DA-51].

ARMSTRONG, James. Sergeant. Born 1733, Fermanagh, Ireland. Shoemaker. Enlisted on April 20, 1758, in the French and Indian Wars, by Capt. John McClughan "for the campaign in the lower counties." [Ref: DA-17].

ARMSTRONG, James. Captain. Served in a company in the Pennsylvania Regiment on June 1, 1759, during the French and Indian Wars, which was comprised of men from the Delaware area, primarily New Castle. [Ref: DA-25].

ARMSTRONG, John. See "Archibald Armstrong," q.v.

ARMSTRONG, John. Lieutenant. Served in Capt. Thomas Ogle, Jr.'s Company, Christiana Hundred, Upper Regiment, New Castle County, 1756, during the French and Indian Wars. [Ref: DA-11].

ARMSTRONG, John. Private. Served in Capt. Nathan Adams' Company, Delaware Regiment of Continental Troops. Enlisted on January 29, 1776, and was on duty (in barracks) at Dover on April 12, 1776. [Ref: DA-53].

ARMSTRONG, Thomas. Private. Served in Capt. Samuel Smith's Company, Delaware Regiment of Continental Troops. Enlisted January 20, 1776, and on duty (in barracks) at Dover on April 12, 1776. [Ref: DA-54].

ARMSTRONG, William. Corporal. Born 1730, Fermanagh, Ireland. Laborer. Enlisted on April 20, 1758, during the French and Indian Wars, by Capt. John McClughan "for the campaign in the lower counties." [Ref: DA-17].

ARMSTRONG, William. Captain. New Castle County Company, 1747-1748, and served in King George's War against Canada. [Ref: DA-7].

ARMSTRONG, William. Colonel. Served in New Castle County Regiment in 1747-1748, in King George's War against Canada. He was probably the same person who was colonel of the Upper Regiment of New Castle County, 1756, in French and Indian Wars. [Ref: DA-7, DA-11, DM-45].

ARNALL, Samuel. Pilot. Died testate in Lewes, Sussex County, and his will was probated on February 12, 1770, naming his sons John and Samuel Arnall, and his two daughters (unnamed). [Ref: DS-84].

ARNOLD, William. Pilot. Died intestate in Sussex County and the administration of his estate was granted to Isabella Arnold on November 3, 1779. [Ref: DS-130].

ARON, William. Private. Served in Capt. Jonathan Caldwell's Company of the Delaware Regiment of Continental Troops. Enlisted on April 2, 1776, and was on duty (in barracks) at Dover on April 12, 1776. [Ref: DA-41].

ART, Jacob. Pilot. Died in Sussex County and administration of his estate was granted to Hannah Art, widow, circa September, 1770. A later account mentions minors James, Jacob, Hannah, and Baily Art, and also that Hannah Art later married Robert Massey. [Ref: DS-86].

ASHMAN, John. Soldier. Planter in Delaware who paid his quit-rent to the governor in 1669. [Ref: DP-27, 28, DY-89].

ASHMAN, Robert. Soldier. Planter in Delaware who paid his quit-rent to the governor in 1669. [Ref: DP-27, DP-28].

ASKUE, John. Soldier. Planter in Delaware who paid his quit-rent to the governor in 1669. [Ref: DP-27, DP-28]. "Sarjeant John Askue" was granted a certain house and garden in the town of New Castle and also a parcel of marsh ground on Christina Creek on October 1, 1669. [Ref: DY-140, DY-141].

AVERY, John. Captain. Was a lieutenant "on Delaware" by 1675, and president of the court at Whorekill, Sussex County, Delaware on June 25, 1676. [Ref: DP-169, DY-39]. "Capt. John Avery" received a land survey for tract called *Goulden Quartere* [sic] on the west side of Delaware Bay on March 28, 1681. [Ref: DY-69]. He died in 1682, as noted in the county quit-rents in 1705. [Ref: DR-46]. The administration of the estate of "Capt. John Avery" was granted to Robert Clifton in Sussex County on October 6, 1685. [Ref: DS-10]. He served as a Commissioner of Sussex County in 1679. [Ref: DC-27].

BAGGE, Martin. Soldier (*saldater*). Arrived in New Sweden from Roslagen. Along with soldier Martin Thomasson, the Finn, he was "killed by the savages between Christina and Elfsborg" on March 4, 1643. [Ref: DJ-707, 708].

BAGWELL, William and Thomas. See "John Adams," q.v.

BAIL, Robert. Quartermaster. Served in the Delaware Battalion of Continental Troops. Commissioned on January 13, 1776. [Ref: DA-35].

BAILEY, Edward. Private. Born 1738, Kent, Delaware. Enlisted in Capt. John Wright's Company and was on the muster roll of May 11, 1759, during the French and Indian Wars. [Ref: DA-25].

BAILEY, James. Pilot. Died testate in Sussex County and his will was probated on May 8, 1745, naming his sons James and Steward, and daughters Hannah and Ann. [Ref: DS-52].

BAILEY, Jonathan. Captain. He held this rank by 1709 when he was a Court Justice of Sussex County. [Ref: DC-47, DC-48].

BAILEY, Nathaniel and Jean. See "John Shankland," q.v.

BAILEY, Robert. Private. Served in Capt. Henry Darby's Company, Delaware Regiment of Continental Troops. Enlisted on January 24, 1776, and was on duty (in barracks) at Dover on April 12, 1776. [Ref: DA-46].

BAILEY, Thomas. Private. Enlisted on May 19, 1758, in Capt. French Battell's Company of Lower County Provincials, during the French and Indian Wars. [Ref: DA-16].

BAILEY, Zachariah. Private. Served in Capt. Jonathan Caldwell's Company, Delaware Regiment of Continental Troops. Enlisted January 15, 1776, and on duty (in barracks) at Dover on April 12, 1776. [Ref: DA-41].

BALL, Jeremiah. See "Evan Rice," q.v.

BALL, William. Ensign. Served in Capt. Evan Rees' Company, Mill Creek Hundred, Upper Regiment, New Castle County, 1756, during the French and Indian Wars. [Ref: DA-11].

BAMBURY, John. Private. Born 1725, Kent, Delaware. Laborer. Enlisted in Capt. John Shannon's Company of Foot on July 14, 1746, and served in King George's War against Canada. He made his mark when paid for services on June 6, 1747. He was in winter quarters at Albany, New York, during 1746-1747, and was discharged on October 31, 1747. [Ref: DA-4, DA-5, DA-6, DM-40].

BANNING, Charles. Private. Served in Capt. Joseph Vaughan's Company of the Delaware Regiment of Continental Troops. Enlisted on January 22, 1776, and was on duty (in barracks) at Dover on April 12, 1776. [Ref: DA-59].

BARCLAY, Eleanor Porter. See "Alexander Porter," q.v.

BARCLAY, James. Private. Served in Capt. Samuel Smith's Company, Delaware Regiment of Continental Troops. Enlisted on January 20, 1776, and was on duty (in barracks) at Dover on April 12, 1776. [Ref: DA-54].

BARD, Samuel. Private. Born 1734, Ireland. Enlisted in Capt. John Wright's Company and was on the muster roll of May 11, 1759, during the French and Indian Wars. [Ref: DA-25].

BARLOW, Samuel. Private. Born 1725, Lancaster, England. Dyer. Enlisted on May 12, 1758, during the French and Indian Wars, as a private by Capt. John McClughan "for the campaign in the lower counties." [Ref: DA-17].

BARNES, John. Captain. Served in militia company in upper part of Little Creek Hundred, Kent County, upon Delaware, in 1756, during the French and Indian Wars. [Ref: DA-12, DM-46]. One "John Barns" died in Little Creek Hundred and his will was probated on January 10, 1767, naming his sons John, William and Stephen Barns, daughter Percilla Barns, and Robert Brashear, Elizabeth Rowe, and John Vining (no relationships given). [Ref: DK-225].

BARR, David. Lieutenant. Served in Capt. Lewis Thomas' Company in Pencader Hundred, Lower Regiment, New Castle County, 1756, during the French and Indian Wars. [Ref: DA-12].

BARR, George. Ensign. Served in the War of Jenkins' Ear in 1739-1741 in a company which may have included soldiers from Delaware (muster rolls not extant). [Ref: DM-32].

BARRETT, James. Private. Born 1735, Ireland. Laborer. "Formerly with ye Royal Americans," he enlisted on April 24, 1758, during the French and Indian Wars, by Capt. Benjamin Noxon. [Ref: DA-18].

BARRETT, Wallace. Private. Served in Capt. Nathan Adams' Company, Delaware Regiment of Continental Troops. Enlisted on April 1, 1776, and on duty (in barracks) at Dover on April 12, 1776. [Ref: DA-53].

BASSET, John. Private. Born 1732, Wales. Laborer. Enlisted on April 29, 1758, in the French and Indian Wars, by Capt. Benjamin Noxon. [Ref: DA-18].

BASSNET, Mary and Ralph. See "Nathaniel Walker," q.v.

BASTON, John. Private. Born 1730, America. Laborer. Enlisted on May 7, 1758, during the French and Indian Wars, by Capt. Benjamin Noxon. [Ref: DA-18].

BATEMAN, John. Private. Served in Capt. Jonathan Caldwell's Company of the Delaware Regiment of Continental Troops. Enlisted on January 13, 1776, and was on duty (in barracks) at Dover on April 12, 1776. [Ref: DA-41].

BATTELL, French. Captain. Served as ensign in Capt. David Finney's Company, New Castle County, 1747-1748, in King George's War against Canada. He also served in the French and Indian Wars as lieutenant in Capt. John Clayton's Company, Town of Dover, in Kent County, upon Delaware, in 1756, and was first lieutenant in Capt. Richard Wells' Company on April 20, 1758. He was then promoted to quartermaster "of the lower government on Delaware" under Major Richard Wells on June 7, 1758. French Battell was the captain of a company of Lower County Provincials [Delaware] in 1758, and captain of one of the three companies "of the lower counties" in the 3rd Battalion of the Pennsylvania Regiment on May 22, 1759. [Ref: DA-7, DA-12, DA-16, DA-17, DA-20, DA-22, DM-47, DM-48, DM-49]. Administration of the estate of "French Battle, Colonel, Town of Dover" was granted to Elizabeth "Battle" in January, 1782. [Ref: DK-336]. Also, the administration of the estate of "French Battell" was granted to John and Elizabeth "Battell" on November 12, 1792. The administrator *de bonis non* on March 10, 1794, was James Battell, who was also the administrator for Elizabeth and John French Battell, appointed on that same day. An administration account mentioned the heirs of French Battell as John F., French, James, and Cornelius Battell. [Ref: DK-459, 475].

BATTELL, Mary and William. See "John French," q.v.

BATTELL, William. Captain. Served in New Castle County, and was son-in-law of Col. John French who died in 1728. [Ref: DN-27].

BEANE, William. Private. Born 1733, Maryland. Cordwainer. Enlisted on April 29, 1758, during the French and Indian Wars, by Capt. Benjamin Noxon. [Ref: DA-18].

BEATSON, John. Sergeant. Served in Capt. Joseph Stedham's Company, Delaware Battalion of Continental Troops. Enlisted on January 27, 1776, and was in quarters at Dover on April 12, 1776. [Ref: DA-39].

BEATTY, John. Private. Born 1734, Ireland. Weaver. Enlisted May 1, 1758, in the French and Indian War, by Capt. Benjamin Noxon. [Ref: DA-18].

BEAUCHAMP, Mary and John. See "Richard Downham," q.v.

BECKELEY, Thomas. Second Lieutenant. Served in the War of Jenkins' Ear in 1739-1741 who served in a company which may have included soldiers from Delaware (muster rolls not extant). [Ref: DM-32].

BECKET, John. Private. Served in Capt. Charles Pope's Company, Delaware Regiment of Continental Troops. Enlisted on January 15, 1776, and was on duty (in quarters) at Lewis Town on April 11, 1776. [Ref: DA-51]. (Same source spelled his name "John Bicket").

BEDFORD, Gunning. Lieutenant Colonel. Served as lieutenant in the French and Indian Wars in 1756. He married Mary Read, daughter of Col. John Read, but had no issue. Gunning Bedford was commissioned lieutenant colonel in the Delaware Battalion of Continental Troops on January 19, 1776. He was also "D. M. M. General" in the Delaware Regiment of Continental Troops by January 13, 1776. After the Revolutionary War he became Governor of Delaware. [Ref: DA-35, DA-43, DA-47, DA-50, DH-186b]. (It should be noted that Source DA-35 refers to him as "Gunning Bedford, Jr." and Source DH-186b refers to him as "Gunning Bedford, Sr." This is rather strange use of Jr. and Sr. when one considers that he had apparently left no issue.)

BEDWELL, James. Private. Served in Capt. John Caton's Company, April 25, 1757, and served in the French and Indian Wars. [Ref: DA-13]. One James Bedwell died intestate in Kent County and administration of his estate was granted to Robert Bedwell, next-of-kin, on February 15, 1771. [Ref: DK-256].

BEDWELL, Thomas. Private. Served in Capt. John Caton's Company, April 25, 1757, during the French and Indian Wars. [Ref: DA-14]. One Thomas Bedwell died testate in Kent County and his will was probated on April 17, 1794, naming his wife Jemima, sons Thomas, George, James, Preston, and Caleb, and daughters Sarah Bedwell and Elizabeth Stant (and her daughter Easter Stant). [Ref: DK-477].

BELL, Elizabeth, Henry, and John. See "Jonathan Caldwell," q.v.

BELL, James. Private. Served in Capt. Henry Darby's Company of the Delaware Regiment of Continental Troops. Enlisted on January 27, 1776, and was on duty (in barracks) at Dover on April 12, 1776. [Ref: DA-46].

BELL, John. Soldier. Planter in Delaware who paid his quit-rent to the governor in 1671, having been granted some land on the west of Delaware Bay on June 17, 1671. [Ref: DP-29, DY-151].

BELL, Stephen. Private. Served in Capt. David Hall's Company of the Delaware Regiment of Continental Troops. Enlisted January 17, 1776, and was on duty (in barracks) at Lewis Town on April 11, 1776. [Ref: DA-42].

BELL, William. Private. Born 1740, Maryland. Tanner. Enlisted on May 5, 1758, during the French and Indian Wars, by Capt. Benjamin Noxon. [Ref: DA-18].

BELLVILLE, John. Private. Born 1742, Delaware. Tailor. Enlisted on April 26, 1758, during the French and Indian Wars by Capt. Benjamin Noxon. [Ref: DA-18].

BELLVILLE, Nicholas. Private. Born 1723, New York. Weaver. Enlisted on April 29, 1758, during the French and Indian Wars, by Capt. Benjamin Noxon. [Ref: DA-18].

BELLVILLE, Philip. Private. Born 1739, Delaware. Tailor. Enlisted on April 25, 1758, during the French and Indian Wars, by Capt. Benjamin Noxon. [Ref: DA-18].

BENGTSSON, Erick. Soldier. Arrived in New Sweden on the ship *Orn* in 1654. He returned to Europe with Director Rising in 1655. [Ref: DJ-717, 724]. (Name also spelled "Erich Benckson").

BENGTSSON, Israel. Soldier. Arrived in New Sweden on the ship *Orn* in 1654. [Ref: Ref: DJ-717].

BENGTSSON, Mans. Skipper. Served on the ship *Katt* in the ninth expedition to New Sweden in 1649. [Ref: DJ-761].

BENNET, Jacob. Private. Served in Capt. Joseph Stedham's Company, Delaware Battalion of Continental Troops. Enlisted on February 5, 1776, and was in quarters at Dover on April 12, 1776. [Ref: DA-39].

BENNET, James. Private. Served in Capt. Joseph Stedham's Company, Delaware Battalion of Continental Troops. Enlisted on January 17, 1776, and was in quarters at Dover on April 12, 1776. [Ref: DA-39].

BENNETT, Isaac. Private. Born 1716, East Jersey. Laborer. Enlisted in Capt. John Shannon's Company of Foot on July 13, 1746, and he served in King George's War against Canada. He signed his name when paid for his services on June 6, 1747. He was in winter quarters at Albany, New York, during 1746-1747, and was discharged on October 31, 1747. [Ref: DA-4, DA-5, DA-6, DM-40].

BENNETT, Stephen. Private. Born 1728, Ipswich, Massachusetts. Laborer. Enlisted May 12, 1758, during the French and Indian Wars, by Capt. John McClughan "for the campaign in the lower counties." [Ref: DA-17].

BENNETT, Thomas. Ensign. Served in Capt. George Gano's Company, New Castle County, in 1747-1748, in King George's War against Canada. [Ref: DA-7]. A Thomas Bennett was also an ensign in Capt. George Gano's Company, Apoquinamink Hundred, Lower Regiment, New Castle County, 1756, during the French and Indian Wars. [Ref: DA-12]. One "Thomas Bennet, yeoman," died testate in Apoquinamink Hundred, New Castle County, and his will was probated on August 5, 1779, naming his wife Elizabeth, sons Thomas, Ebenezer, Perry, and John, and daughters Elizabeth Hawkins and Mary Taylor. [Ref: DN-92, DN-93].

BENSON, John. Private. Served in Capt. Joseph Vaughan's Company, Delaware Regiment of Continental Troops. Enlisted on January 22, 1776, and was on duty (in barracks) at Dover on April 12, 1776. [Ref: DA-57, 59]. (Same source spelled his name "John Benston").

BENSON, Thomas. Mariner. Died testate in Kent County and his will was probated on September 21, 1748, naming among others his mother (no name given), and apparently no wife or children. [Ref: DK-127].

BERRY, Benjamin. Private. Served in Capt. Nathan Adams' Company, Delaware Regiment of Continental Troops. Enlisted on February 12, 1776, and was on duty (in barracks) at Dover on April 12, 1776. [Ref: DA-53].

BERRY, David. Private. Served in Capt. Samuel Smith's Company, Delaware Regiment of Continental Troops. Enlisted on February 14, 1776, and was on duty (in barracks) at Dover on April 12, 1776. [Ref: DA-54].

BERRY, James. Private. Served in Capt. David Hall's Company of the Delaware Regiment of Continental Troops. Enlisted January 17, 1776,

and was on duty (in barracks) at Lewis Town on April 11, 1776. [Ref: DA-42].
BERRY, John. Captain. He was "on Delaware" by 1667, at which time he paid his quit-rent to the governor. [Ref: DP-29].
BERRY, John. Private. Served in Capt. Nathan Adams' Company, Delaware Regiment of Continental Troops. Enlisted on January 20, 1776, and was on duty (in barracks) at Dover on April 12, 1776. [Ref: DA-52].
BERRY, Mordecai. Private. Served in Capt. Samuel Smith's Company, Delaware Regiment of Continental Troops. Enlisted on January 18, 1776, and was on duty (in barracks) at Dover on April 12, 1776. [Ref: DA-54].
BERRY, Thomas. Sergeant. Served in Capt. Joseph Vaughan's Company, Delaware Regiment of Continental Troops. Enlisted on January 15, 1776, and on duty (in barracks) at Dover on April 12, 1776. [Ref: DA-57, DA-59]. (This same source spelled his name "Thomas Berrey").
BERTILSSON, Olaf Likagod. See "Likagod, Olaf Bertilsson," q.v.
BESSWICIK, Sarah and Robert. See "Matthew Crozier," q.v.
BEST, Abraham. Private. Served in Capt. Charles Pope's Company, Delaware Regiment of Continental Troops. Enlisted on January 17, 1776, and on duty (in quarters) at Lewis Town on April 11, 1776. [Ref: DA-51]. (This same source spelled his name "Abraham Besh").
BETTS, William. Private. Served in Capt. Jonathan Caldwell's Company, Delaware Regiment of Continental Troops. Enlisted on February 1, 1776, and was on duty (in barracks) at Dover on April 12, 1776. [Ref: DA-41]. Also see "John Caton," q.v.
BICE, Peter. Private. Served in Capt. Jonathan Caldwell's Company, Delaware Regiment of Continental Troops. Enlisted on January 15, 1776, and was on duty (in barracks) at Dover on April 12, 1776. [Ref: DA-41].
BICKLEY, Joseph. Private. Born 1737, England. Laborer. Enlisted on May 9, 1758, during the French and Indian Wars, by Capt. Benjamin Noxon. [Ref: DA-18].
BIGGS, James. Private. Served in Capt. Joseph Stedham's Company, Delaware Battalion of Continental Troops. Enlisted on January 26, 1776, and was in quarters at Dover on April 12, 1776. [Ref: DA-39].
BIGNAL, John. Private. Served in Capt. David Hall's Company of the Delaware Regiment of Continental Troops. Enlisted January 23, 1776, and was on duty (in barracks) at Lewis Town on April 11, 1776. [Ref: DA-43].

BILDSTEIN, Francis. Private. Served in Capt. Nathan Adams' Company, Delaware Regiment of Continental Troops. Enlisted March 20, 1776, and on duty (in barracks) at Dover on April 12, 1776. [Ref: DA-53].

BIORNSONN, Lars. Sailor. Laborer. From Gothenburg he arrived in New Sweden as a midshipman in 1641 and was an "officer" at Fort Tinicum in 1643. [Ref: DJ-705, DJ-712, DH-45]. (Also spelled "Bjornsson").

BIRD, Empsena. Lieutenant. Served in Capt. James Latimer's Company, in Christiana Hundred, Upper Regiment, New Castle County, in 1756, during the French and Indian Wars. [Ref: DA-11]. One Thomas Bird, carpenter, died testate in Christiana Hundred, New Castle County, and his will was probated on December 10, 1726, naming his wife Sarah Bird and a son "Empson" Bird (among others). [Ref: DN-26].

BIRMINGHAM, Richard. Lieutenant Colonel. Served with a regiment of volunteers (appointed by Governor of Pennsylvania) in the counties of New Castle, Kent and Sussex in 1724. [Ref: *Governor's Register, State of Delaware, Volume I*, "The Appointments and Other Transactions by Executives of the State from 1674 to 1851," (Wilmington, Delaware: Press of the Star Publishing Co., 1926), page 10]. "John Bermingham (Birmingham)" died testate in Kent County in 1732 and his will mentioned his brother Richard Birmingham. [Ref: DK-75].

BISHOP, Robert. Captain. Served in the War of Jenkins' Ear in 1739-1741 in a company which may have included soldiers from Delaware (muster rolls not extant). [Ref: DM-32].

BLACK, Ann. See "Emanuel Grubb," q.v.

BLACK, George. Private. Born 1734, Armagh, Ireland. Weaver. Enlisted on April 20, 1758, during the French and Indian Wars, by Capt. John McClughan "for the campaign in the lower counties." [Ref: DA-17].

BLACK, James and Mary. See "Samuel Patterson," q.v.

BLACK, Thomas. Private. Born 1726, Ireland. Cooper. Enlisted in Capt. John Shannon's Company of Foot on July 9, 1746, and served in King George's War against Canada. He made his mark when he was paid for services on June 6, 1747. He was in winter quarters at Albany, New York, during 1746-1747, and was discharged on October 31, 1747. [Ref: DA-4, DA-5, DA-6, DM-40].

BLACKBURN, William. Private. Served in Capt. Richard McWilliams' Company, New Castle County. Enlisted on December 28, 1757, during the French and Indian Wars. [Ref: DA-14].

BLACKSHAVE, Miriam. See "Michael Reynolds," q.v.

BLACKSHIRE, Robert. Captain. Kent County Company, 1747-1748, and served in King George's War against Canada. [Ref: DA-8]. "Robert

Blackshare" died intestate and Jean and Morgan Blackshare were named administrators on March 14, 1778. A subsequent account showed that Jean (Jane) Blackshare married Michael Numbers. [Ref: DK-316].

BLADES, Edmond. Private. Born 1732, Maryland. Carpenter. Enlisted on May 2, 1758, in the French and Indian Wars, by Capt. Benjamin Noxon. [Ref: DA-18].

BLAIR, Frances. Private. Served in Capt. Jonathan Caldwell's Company, Delaware Regiment of Continental Troops. Enlisted on January 16, 1776, and was on duty (in barracks) at Dover on April 12, 1776. [Ref: DA-41].

BLANEY, Daniel. Private. Served in Capt. Samuel Smith's Company, Delaware Regiment of Continental Troops. Enlisted on January 16, 1776, and was on duty (in barracks) at Dover on April 12, 1776. [Ref: DA-54].

BLANEY, James. Private. Served in Capt. Samuel Smith's Company, Delaware Regiment of Continental Troops. Enlisted on January 17, 1776, and was on duty (in barracks) at Dover on April 12, 1776. [Ref: DA-54].

BLANEY, John. Private. Served in Capt. Samuel Smith's Company, Delaware Regiment of Continental Troops. Enlisted January 20, 1776, and on duty (in barracks) at Dover on April 12, 1776, at which time he transferred to Capt. Henry Darby's Company. [Ref: DA-54, DA-56].

BLEE, Charles. Private. Served in Capt. Samuel Smith's Company, Delaware Regiment of Continental Troops. Enlisted on February 13, 1776, and was on duty (in barracks) at Dover on April 12, 1776. [Ref: DA-54].

BLEW, Michael. Private. Served in Capt. Richard McWilliams' Company, New Castle County. Enlisted on December 28, 1757, during the French and Indian Wars. [Ref: DA-14].

BLOCK, Hans. Soldier. Planter in Delaware who paid his quit-rent to the governor in 1669. [Ref: DP-27, 28]. He was in the Delaware area by October 1, 1664, at which time he was sworn to the "Oath of Allegiance to his Majesty of Great Britain." [Ref: DY-24].

BOARK, Thomas. Private. Born 1721, Ireland. Miller. Enlisted in Capt. John Shannon's Company of Foot on July 13, 1746, and he served in King George's War against Canada. He made his mark when paid for services on June 6, 1747. He was in winter quarters at Albany, New York, during 1746-1747, and was discharged October 31, 1747. [Ref: DA-4, 5, 6]. Source DM-40 gives the name as "Roark."

BOCK, Nicklas. Soldier. Arrived in New Sweden in 1643 and was a soldier (*saldater*) at Fort Elfsborg, 1643-1644, and later became a corporal. [Ref: DJ-703, DJ-713, DH-47]. Peter Bock, who signed the Indian certificates of July 13 and July 16, 1651, may have been a son of Nicklas. [Ref: DJ-715]. (Also spelled "Nickolaus Borck").

BOCKHORN, Jan Jansson. Sailor. Mate on the ship *Swan* during the eighth expedition to New Sweden between 1647-1648, mate on the ship *Katt* during the ninth expedition in 1649, and captain on the ship *Orn* during the tenth expedition in 1654. [Ref: DJ-761].

BOGGS, James. Private. Served in Capt. Richard McWilliams' Company, New Castle County. Enlisted on December 28, 1757, during the French and Indian Wars. [Ref: DA-14].

BOGGS, John. Private. Served in Capt. John Caton's Company, April 25, 1757, and served in the French and Indian Wars. [Ref: DA-13]. One John Boggs died intestate in Kent County and the administration of his estate was granted to Matthew Boggs, next-of-kin, on October 18, 1765. A later account named a minor son John Jr. [Ref: DK-219].

BOICE, Cathrine. See "Alexander Bryan," q.v.

BOIJE, Christer. Captain. Served in New Sweden in 1643 and returned home to Sweden in 1644. [Ref: DJ-709]. (Name also spelled "Boje").

BOLLEN, James. Soldier. Planter in Delaware who paid his quit-rent to the governor in 1670, having been granted land on west side of Delaware Bay, April 2, 1670. [Ref: DP-29, DY-145].

BOND, John. Private. Enlisted on May 17, 1758, in Capt. French Battell's Company of Lower County Provincials, during the French and Indian Wars. [Ref: DA-16].

BONDE, Anders Svensson. Gunner (*constaple*). Arrived in New Sweden on the ship *Kalmar Nyckel* in 1640. He was "one of the laboring people at Fort Tinicum who was appointed to cut hay for the cattle and also in the meantime follow the governor on the little sloop" in 1643. He served as gunner at New Gothenburg from May 1, 1643 to September 1, 1653, and returned to Sweden with Governor Printz in 1653. He later returned to the colony. [Ref: DJ-706, 710].

BONES, Hanse. Soldier. Planter in Delaware who paid his quit-rent to the governor in 1669. [Ref: DP-27, 28]. "Hans Bones" was granted land on Christine Kill on August 1, 1668, and "Hans Bons" received a house and lot in New Castle on October 1, 1669. [Ref: DY-132, 133, 140].

BONZELL, Rebeccah and Honour. See "Andrew Frauberg [Tranberg]."

BOOGS, Ruth. See "Evan Lewis," q.v.

BOOTH, John. Private. Served in Capt. Richard McWilliams' Company, New Castle County. Enlisted on December 28, 1757, during the French and Indian Wars. [Ref: DA-14].

BOOTH, Joseph. Private. Enlisted on May 10, 1758, in Capt. French Battell's Company of Lower County Provincials, during the French and Indian Wars. [Ref: DA-16].

BOUDEN, James. Private. Enlisted on May 13, 1758, in Capt. French Battell's Company of Lower County Provincials, during the French and Indian Wars. [Ref: DA-16].

BOUNDS, Jacob and William. See "Burton Waples," q.v.

BOWEN, George. Private. Enlisted on May 17, 1759, in the French and Indian Wars, and his name appeared on a return of Capt. Henry Van Bibber's Company of the Lower Counties on Delaware Troops at New Castle on June 4, 1759. [Ref: DA-26].

BOWEN, Nathan. Private. Served in Capt. Jonathan Caldwell's Company of the Delaware Regiment of Continental Troops. Enlisted on January 13, 1776, and was on duty (in barracks) at Dover on April 12, 1776. [Ref: DA-41].

BOWMAN, Nathaniel. Mariner. Lived in Sussex County in Indian River Hundred prior to February 2, 1773, at which time he purchased 350 acres of land "it being the same where he now lives." [Ref: DD-76].

BOYCE, Naomi. See "William Prettyman," q.v.

BOYCE, John. Private. Served in Capt. Samuel Smith's Company of the Delaware Regiment of Continental Troops. Enlisted February 2, 1776, and on duty (in barracks) at Dover on April 12, 1776. [Ref: DA-54].

BOYD, John. Private. Enlisted on May 14, 1759, in the French and Indian Wars, and his name appeared on a return of Capt. Henry Van Bibber's Company of the Lower Counties on Delaware Troops, at New Castle, on June 4, 1759. [Ref: DA-26].

BOYD, John. Private. Served in Capt. Richard McWilliams' Company, New Castle County. Enlisted on December 28, 1757, during the French and Indian Wars. [Ref: DA-15].

BOYERS, John. Soldier. Granted land on Christina Creek in Delaware on October 1, 1669. [Ref: DY-142].

BOYLE, Timothy. Private. Served in Capt. Samuel Smith's Company, Delaware Regiment of Continental Troops. Enlisted on January 17, 1776, and was on duty (in barracks) at Dover on April 12, 1776. [Ref: DA-54].

BOZMAN, Thomas. Private. Served in Capt. Nathan Adams' Company, Delaware Regiment of Continental Troops. Enlisted on January 16,

1776, and was on duty (in barracks) at Dover on April 12, 1776. [Ref: DA-52].

BRADBORNE, John. Soldier. Planter in Delaware who paid his quit-rent to the governor in 1671. "John Bradbourn" received land patents on June 17 and 27, 1671. [Ref: DP-29, DY-35, DY-149].

BRADON, William. Private. Served in Capt. Jonathan Caldwell's Company, Delaware Regiment of Continental Troops. Enlisted on February 8, 1776, and was on duty (in barracks) at Dover on April 12, 1776. [Ref: DA-41].

BRADY, John. Private. Served in Capt. Samuel Smith's Company, Delaware Regiment of Continental Troops. Enlisted on January 19, 1776, and was on duty (in barracks) at Dover on April 12, 1776. [Ref: DA-54].

BRANNEN, Mathew. Private. Served in Capt. Joseph Stedham's Company, Delaware Battalion of Continental Troops. Enlisted on February 16, 1776, and was in quarters at Dover on April 12, 1776. [Ref: DA-40].

BRANT, John. Private. Served in Capt. Joseph Stedham's Company, Delaware Battalion of Continental Troops. Enlisted on February 6, 1776, and was in quarters at Dover on April 12, 1776. [Ref: DA-39].

BRASEY, Richard. Land patentee and probable militiaman in Delaware in November, 1677. [Ref: DP-167, 168].

BRASEY, Robert Sr. Land patentee and probable militiaman in Delaware in November, 1677. [Ref: DP-167, 168].

BRASHEAR, Robert. See "John Barnes," q.v.

BRASIDY, Robert Jr. Land patentee and probable militiaman in Delaware in November, 1677. [Ref: DP-167, 168].

BRATTON, James. Sergeant. Served in Capt. Nathan Adams' Company, Delaware Regiment of Continental Troops. Enlisted on January 26, 1776, and was on duty (in barracks) at Dover on April 12, 1776. [Ref: DA-52].

BREADY, Thomas. Private. Served in Capt. Henry Darby's Company, Delaware Regiment of Continental Troops. Enlisted on February 13, 1776, and reported "deserted" on February 14, 1776. [Ref: DA-46].

BRIGS, John. Captain. He held this rank sometime between 1680 and 1700, during which time he was an attorney in Sussex County. [Ref DC-50].

BRINCKLE, Benjamin. Captain. Served in a company of militia in lower part of Mispillim [Mispillion] Hundred, Kent County, upon Delaware, in 1756, during the French and Indian Wars. [Ref: DA-12, DM-46].

Administration of the estate of one "Benjamin Brinckley" in Kent County was granted to his widow "Bettey Brinckley" on June 8, 1764. An administration account indicates "Betty Brinckle" later married George Monro and mentions heirs Mary, William, Benjamin, and Joseph "Brincklee," and Leah "Brinckley," wife of Joshua Cottman. [Ref: DK-213].

BRINCKLE, Jemima and John. See "John Molleston," q.v.

BRINCKLE, John. Captain. Served in a company of militia in the lower part of Little Creek Hundred, Kent County, upon Delaware, 1756, during the French and Indian Wars. [Ref: DA-12, DM-46]. The unsigned will of one John Brinckle was made on September 25, 1764 in Kent County, naming his wife (no name given), nephew Spencer Cole, and nieces Sarah, Mary, and Emilia Cole (among other people, but no relationships given), but no date of probate was given. On December 19, 1769, a John Brinckle was named administrator (as the next of kin) to John Brinckle. [Ref: DK-214, 246]. See "Lieutenant Colonel John Brinckle," q.v.

BRINCKLE, John. Lieutenant Colonel. Served in a regiment of militia from Kent County, upon Delaware, 1756, during the French and Indian Wars. [Ref: DA-12, DM-46]. See "Captain John Brinckle," q.v.

BRINCKLE, Joseph. Private. Enlisted on May 24 1758, in Capt. French Battell's Company of Lower County Provincials, during the French and Indian Wars. [Ref: DA-16].

BRINCKLEY, Benjamin. See "Benjamin Brinckle," q.v.

BRINCKLEY, Joseph. Private. Served in Capt. Nathan Adams' Company, Delaware Regiment of Continental Troops. Enlisted on January 15, 1776, and was on duty (in barracks) at Dover on April 12, 1776. [Ref: DA-52].

BRINCKLOE, John. Captain. Lived in Dover Hundred, Kent County, as noted in the 1693 tax assessment list. [Ref: DR-22]. He died in Kent County and his will was probated on December 8, 1721, naming his wife Elizabeth, cousin Peter Brinckloe, friend Thomas Crawford, and Evis, Mary, Leititia, and Elizabeth Crawford (daughters of Thomas). [Ref: DK-43].

BRINCKLY, Pheby. See "Joseph Marrat," q.v.

BRIND, Isaac. Private. Born 1724, Wiltshire, England. Shoemaker. Enlisted on May 1, 1758, during the French and Indian Wars, by Capt. John McClughan "for the campaign in the lower counties." An Isaac Brind enlisted on May 7, 1759, and appeared on the return of Capt.

Henry Van Bibber's Company of the Lower Counties on Delaware Troops, at New Castle, on June 4, 1759. [Ref: DA-17, DA-26].

BRISON, Patrick. Private. Served in Capt. Jonathan Caldwell's Company, Delaware Regiment of Continental Troops. Enlisted on February 1, 1776, and was on duty (in barracks) at Dover on April 12, 1776. [Ref: DA-41].

BRITT, William. Private. Served in Capt. Samuel Smith's Company, Delaware Regiment of Continental Troops. Enlisted on January 29, 1776, and was on duty (in barracks) at Dover on April 12, 1776. [Ref: DA-54].

BROCHSON, Joseph. Private. Born 1741, Three Runs, Delaware. Planter. Enlisted on April 19, 1758, during the French and Indian Wars, as a private by Capt. John McClughan "for the campaign in the lower counties." [Ref: DA-17].

BROCK, John. Private. Served in Capt. Richard McWilliams' Company, New Castle County. Enlisted on December 28, 1757, during the French and Indian Wars. [Ref: DA-14].

BROERS, Synick. Soldier. Planter who paid his quit-rent to the governor in 1669, having received a grant on September 1, 1669. [Ref: DP-27, DP-28, DY-139]. (Also spelled "Sinick Broers").

BROOKS, John. Private. Served in Capt. Nathan Adams' Company, Delaware Regiment of Continental Troops. Enlisted on January 20, 1776, and was on duty (in barracks) at Dover on April 12, 1776. [Ref: DA-52].

BROOKS, Samuel. Private. Served in Capt. John Caton's Company, April 25, 1757, in the French and Indian Wars. [Ref: DA-14].

BROOKS, Seth. Private. Served in Capt. Charles Pope's Company, Delaware Regiment of Continental Troops. Enlisted January 15, 1776, and was on duty (in quarters) at Lewis Town on April 11, 1776. [Ref: DA-51].

BROOMFIELD, Francis. Private. Born 1743, Charlestown, Maryland. Tailor. Enlisted on April 29, 1759, during the French and Indian Wars, in Capt. James Armstrong's Company in the Pennsylvania Regiment. [Ref: DA-25].

BROWN, Caleb. Private. Served in Capt. Charles Pope's Company, Delaware Regiment of Continental Troops. Enlisted January 15, 1776, and was on duty (in quarters) at Lewis Town on April 11, 1776. [Ref: DA-51].

BROWN, David. Colonel. He held that rank by 1694 when mentioned in an Action of Debt in Sussex County. [Ref: DC-928].

BROWN, George. Corporal. Born 1732, Derry, Ireland. Tanner. Enlisted on April 25, 1758, during the French and Indian Wars, by Capt. John McClughan "for the campaign in the lower counties." [Ref: DA-17].

BROWN, Gustavus and Elenor. See "Samuel Patterson," q.v.

BROWN, Hannah. See "William Faries," q.v.

BROWN, James. Private. Served in Capt. Joseph Vaughan's Company, Delaware Regiment of Continental Troops. Enlisted on January 21, 1776, and was on duty (in barracks) at Dover on April 12, 1776. [Ref: DA-59].

BROWN, James. Private. Served in Capt. Joseph Stedham's Company, Delaware Battalion of Continental Troops. Enlisted on March 2, 1776, and was in quarters at Dover on April 12, 1776. [Ref: DA-40].

BROWN, John. Private. Served in Capt. Henry Darby's Company of the Delaware Regiment of Continental Troops. Enlisted on February 11, 1776, and was on duty (in barracks) at Dover on April 12, 1776. [Ref: DA-46].

BROWN, Nicholas. Private. Served in Capt. David Hall's Company, Delaware Regiment of Continental Troops. Enlisted January 17, 1776, and was on duty (in barracks) at Lewis Town on April 11, 1776. [Ref: DA-42].

BROWN, Thomas. Private. Born 1735, Ireland. Laborer. Enlisted on May 3, 1759, in the French and Indian Wars, in Capt. James Armstrong's Company in the Pennsylvania Regiment. [Ref: DA-25].

BROWN, Thomas. Private. Served in Capt. Henry Darby's Company, Delaware Regiment of Continental Troops. Enlisted on March 4, 1776, and on duty (in barracks) at Dover on April 12, 1776. [Ref: DA-46].

BROWN, William. See "William Hodgson," q.v.

BROWNE, Thomas. Soldier. Planter in Delaware who paid his quit-rent to the governor in 1667, having received a land grant on Christeen Kill on January 19, 1667. [Ref: DP-27, DY-128].

BRUMWELL, Jacob. Private. Served in Capt. John Caton's Company, April 25, 1757, in the French and Indian Wars. [Ref: DA-14].

BRYAN, Alexander. Ensign. Served in Capt. Adam Peterson's Company, St. George's Hundred, Lower Regiment, New Castle County, 1756, in the French and Indian Wars. [Ref: DA-11]. One Alexander Bryan died testate in St. George's Hundred and his will was probated December 15, 1760, naming his brothers James, John, and Andrew, and sisters Mary ----, Agnes ----, and Cathrine [sic] Boice. [Ref: DN-58].

BRYAN, Charles Sr. Ensign. Served in Capt. Evan Rice's Company, New Castle County, in 1747-1748, in King George's War against Canada. [Ref: DA-7].

BRYAN, John. Private. Born 1738, Ireland. Schoolmaster. 6 ft. 1/2 in. tall. Enlisted at New Castle, Delaware on May 15, 1758, during the French and Indian Wars, by Capt. Paul Jackson, from "the three lower counties" to serve in the Pennsylvania Troops. [Ref: DA-27].

BRYAN, John. Second Lieutenant. Served as ensign in Capt. Alexander Porter's Company, New Castle Hundred, Upper Regiment, in New Castle County, 1756, during the French and Indian Wars. He was promoted to second lieutenant under Capt. John McClughan on April 22, 1758. [Ref: DA-11, DA-16, DM-47].

BRYAN, Jonathan. Private. Served in Capt. Nathan Adams' Company, Delaware Regiment of Continental Troops. Enlisted on January 15, 1776, and was on duty (in barracks) at Dover on April 12, 1776, at which time he was reported to be "sick in quarters." [Ref: DA-52].

BRYAN, William. Private. Born 1724, St, Martin's, Maryland. Planter. Enlisted on May 3, 1758, during the French and Indian Wars, by Capt. John McClughan "for the campaign in the lower counties." [Ref: DA-17].

BUCKANNON, Polly, Betty, and Sally. See "Robert Killen," q.v.

BUCKHANIN, David. Private. Served in Capt. Charles Pope's Company, Delaware Regiment of Continental Troops. Enlisted January 15, 1776, and was on duty (in quarters) at Lewis Town on April 11, 1776. [Ref: DA-51].

BUCKLER, Elizabeth. See "James Rattledge," q.v.

BUCKMASTER, Catherine (and others). See "Richard Wells," q.v.

BUCKMASTER, Wilson. Lieutenant. Served in Capt. John Brinckle's Company, in the lower part of Little Creek Hundred, Kent County, upon Delaware, 1756, in the French and Indian Wars. [Ref: DA-12]. The administration of his estate was granted to his widow, Esther, in Kent County on May 31, 1768. "Ester (Hester) Buckmaster" died and left a will that was probated February 15, 1786, stating she was the widow of Wilson Buckmaster and naming sons John Clifford, George, and Wilson Buckmaster, and heirs of daughters Ann Vanhoy (wife of John Vanhoy) and Elizabeth Owen (wife of William Owen). [Ref: DK-236, DK-380].

BUCKWORTH, Charles. Private. Served in Capt. Joseph Vaughan's Company of the Delaware Regiment of Continental Troops. Enlisted on January 19, 1776, and was on duty (in barracks) at Dover on April 12, 1776. [Ref: DA-59].

BUDD, John. Soldier. Enlisted on May 13, 1759, during the French and Indian Wars, and his name appeared on a return of Capt. Henry Van Bibber's Company of the Lower Counties on Delaware Troops, at New Castle, on June 4, 1759. [Ref: DA-26].

BULLET, Bedy. Private. Born 1738, Maryland. Enlisted in Capt. John Wright's Company and was on the muster roll of May 11, 1759, during the French and Indian Wars. [Ref: DA-25].

BULLOCK, George. Private. Born 1732, Ireland. Weaver. Enlisted on May 15, 1758, during the French and Indian Wars, by Capt. Benjamin Noxon. [Ref: DA-18].

BULLY, Robert. Ensign. He was named as an ensign in the commission issued to Capt. John Shannon on June 25, 1746, in King George's War against Canada. However, Capt. Shannon's account book from August 3, 1746, through June 24, 1747. indicates that Joseph Morgan was his ensign and not Robert Bully. [Ref: DM-40].

BURK, Patrick. Private. Served in Capt. Joseph Vaughan's Company, Delaware Regiment of Continental Troops. Enlisted on January 17, 1776, and was on duty (in barracks) at Dover on April 12, 1776. [Ref: DA-59].

BURK, Peter. Private. Served in Capt. Charles Pope's Company fo the Delaware Regiment of Continental Troops. Enlisted January 17, 1776, and was on duty (in quarters) at Lewis Town on April 11, 1776. [Ref: DA-51].

BURRESS, Thomas. Private. Served in Capt. Nathan Adams' Company, Delaware Regiment of Continental Troops. Enlisted on January 21, 1776, and was on duty (in barracks) at Dover on April 12, 1776. [Ref: DA-53].

BURTON, John. Lieutenant. Served in Capt. Burton Waples' Company, Southern District of Indian River Hundred, in regiment of Sussex County, 1756, and became lieutenant in Capt. Waples' Indian River District Company on March 18, 1758. [Ref: DA-13, DA-15]. One John Burton died testate in Sussex County in 1750 and his will named a son John Burton. [Ref: DS-56].

BURTON, Rachel. See "Cord Hazzard," q.v.

BURTON, William. Boatman. Lived in Indian River Hundred by February 6, 1772, at which time he purchased part of tract called *Long Neck* in Sussex County, Delaware, which was granted to a William Burton, Esq. of Virginia, by patent dated September 27, 1677. [Ref: DD-48].

BURTON, William. Private. Served in Capt. David Hall's Company, Delaware Regiment of Continental Troops. Enlisted January 17, 1776, and was on duty (in barracks) at Lewis Town on April 11, 1776. [Ref: DA-42].

BUSH, Charles. Ensign. Served in Capt. David Bush's Company, New Castle County, in 1747-1748, in King George's War against Canada. [Ref: DA-7].

BUSH, David. Captain. Served in a New Castle County Company during 1747-1748 in King George's War against Canada. [Ref: DA-7].

BUSH, John. Private. Served in Capt. John Caton's Company on April 25, 1757, in the French and Indian Wars. [Ref: DA-13].

BUSH, Paul. Private. Served in Capt. Jonathan Caldwell's Company, Delaware Regiment of Continental Troops. Enlisted on January 30, 1776, and was on duty (in barracks) at Dover on April 12, 1776. [Ref: DA-41].

BUTLER, Thomas. Private. Served in Capt. Henry Darby's Company, Delaware Regiment of Continental Troops. Enlisted on February 23, 1776, and was on duty (in barracks) at Dover on April 12, 1776. [Ref: DA-46].

BUTTLER, John. Private. Served in Capt. Jonathan Caldwell's Company of the Delaware Regiment of Continental Troops. Enlisted on January 13, 1776, and on duty (in barracks) at Dover on April 12, 1776. [Ref: DA-41].

BUYS, Cornelis. Soldier. Planter in Delaware who paid his quit-rent to the governor in 1671. [Ref: DP-29]. "Cornelius Buijs" received a land grant on June 16, 1671. [Ref: DY-151, 152].

BYLES, Daniel. Lieutenant. Served in Capt. William Trent's Company on June 4, 1746, during King George's War against Canada. He was in winter quarters at Albany, New York, 1746-1747, and his company was discharged on October 31, 1747. [Ref: DA-6].

BYRUM, James. Private. Served in Capt. John Caton's Company on April 25, 1757, in the French and Indian Wars. [Ref: DA-14]. One "James Byrem" died intestate in Kent County and administration of his estate was granted to Nancy Harden on November 25, 1786. [Ref: DK-386].

CAGER, Richard. Ensign. Served in the War of Jenkins' Ear in 1739-1741 in a company which may have included soldiers from Delaware (muster rolls not extant). [Ref: DM-32].

CAHOON, James. Sergeant. Served in Capt. Henry Darby's Company, Delaware Regiment of Continental Troops. Enlisted on January 17,

1776, and was on duty (in barracks) at Dover on April 12, 1776. [Ref: DA-45].

CAHOON, John. Ensign. Served in Capt. David Clark's Company, upper part of Duck Creek Hundred, Kent County, upon Delaware, in 1756, during the French and Indian Wars. [Ref: DA-12].

CAHOON, John. Private. Served in Capt. Charles Pope's Company, Delaware Regiment of Continental Troops. Enlisted on January 16, 1776, and on duty (in quarters) at Lewis Town on April 11, 1776. [Ref: DA-51]. (This same source spelled his name "John Cohoon").

CAHOON, Samuel. Private. Served in Capt. John Caton's Company, April 25, 1757, in the French and Indian Wars. [Ref: DA-14].

CAHOON, William. Private. Served in Capt. John Caton's Company, April 25, 1757, in the French and Indian Wars. [Ref: DA-14]. One William Cahoon died testate in Kent County and his will was probated on October 23, 1795, naming his wife Lydia, sons Samuel, William, and John, and daughters Ann Leatherbury, Mary Cahoon and Sary Cahoon. [Ref: DK-496].

CAIN, Daniel. Private. Served in Capt. John Caton's Company, April 25, 1757, in the French and Indian Wars. [Ref: DA-14].

CAIN, Francis. Private. Served in Capt. John Caton's Company, April 25, 1757, in the French and Indian Wars. [Ref: DA-14].

CAIN, Mannassey. Private. Served in Capt. John Caton's Company, April 25, 1757, in the French and Indian Wars. [Ref: DA-13]. Rachel Cain died testate in Kent County and her will was probated on July 26, 1760, naming her sons Manasses, Oen [sic] and James. "Manasses Caine" was named as the administrator. [Ref: DK-188]. "Owen Cain, yeoman," died testate and his will was probated on December 9, 1741, naming his sons Menasses and Owen, and his wife (no name given) was the executrix. [Ref: DK-92].

CAIN, Owen. Private. Served in Capt. John Caton's Company, April 25, 1757, in the French and Indian Wars. [Ref: DA-13]. Rachel Cain died testate in Kent County and her will was probated on July 26, 1760, naming her sons Manasses, Oen [sic] and James. [Ref: DK-188]. "Owen Cain, yeoman," died testate and his will was probated on December 9, 1741, naming his sons Menasses and Owen, and his wife (no name given) was the executrix. [Ref: DK-92].

CAIN, Thomas. Private. Served in Capt. John Caton's Company, April 25, 1757, in the French and Indian Wars. [Ref: DA-14].

CALDWELL, Andrew. Major. Served in a regiment of militia for Kent County, upon Delaware, 1756, in the French and Indian Wars. [Ref:

DA-12, DM-46]. Administration of the estate of an "Andrew Caldwell, Esq.," was granted to James Sykes, Esq., on November 14, 1774, in Kent County. [Ref: DK-293]. The will of another Andrew Caldwell was probated April 8, 1775, naming his wife Mary, daughter Jean Gray, son David Caldwell, grandsons Andrew Gray, Andrew Reynolds (son of daughter Ann Reynolds), William Reynolds, and granddaughter Jean Reynolds. William Gray, Merchant, was the executor. [Ref: DK-297]. Also see "Joseph Hodgson," q.v.

CALDWELL, David. Clerk. Served in Capt. John Caton's Company, April 25, 1757, in the French and Indian Wars. [Ref: DA-13].

CALDWELL, James. Lieutenant. Served as an ensign in Capt. John Caton's Company, Tidberry, Kent County, upon Delaware, 1756-1757, and promoted to lieutenant on March 29, 1758. [Ref: DA-12, 13, 15]. One James Caldwell died testate in Kent County and his will was probated on April 30, 1783, naming his wife Hannah, James Caldwell (son of Joseph and Joannah Caldwell), and Janet Smith (no relationship given). [Ref: DK-350].

CALDWELL, Jonathan. Private. Served in Capt. John Caton's Company, April 25, 1757, during the French and Indian Wars, and ensign in one of the three companies "of the lower counties" [Delaware] in the 3rd Battalion of the Pennsylvania Regiment under Col. Hugh Mercer on May 23, 1759. [Ref: DA-13, DA-20, DM-49]. Jonathan Caldwell was a captain in the 2nd Company of Delaware State Troops in Continental Service, commissioned on January 15, 1776. [Ref: DA-34, 36]. One "Jonathan Caldwell, yeoman," died testate in Murder Kill Hundred, Kent County and his will was probated on September 11, 1781, naming his wife Margaret, his brother Timothy Caldwell, his sister Esther Caldwell, nephews James, Timothy, John, Jabez and Jonathan (sons of brother Joseph Caldwell), niece Mary Caldwell (daughter of Timothy) and the following (no relationships given): Elizabeth Bell, wife of Henry Bell; John Bell, son of Elizabeth Bell; Nathan Stevens, son of Henry and his late wife Ann Stevens. [Ref: DK-332].

CALDWELL, Joseph. Lieutenant. Served in Capt. John Caton's Company from Tidberry, Kent County, upon Delaware, 1756-1757, during the French and Indian Wars, and resigned March 29, 1758. [Ref: DA-12, DA-13, DA-15]. He was commissioner of Kent County in 1759. [Ref: DM-50]. One "Joseph Caldwell, yeoman," died intestate in Kent County and his widow, Mary Caldwell, was named his administratrix on March 10, 1763. [Ref: DK-206].

CALHOON, Jeremiah. See "James Rattledge," q.v.

CALLAGER, John. Soldier. Enlisted on May 9, 1759, during the French and Indian Wars, and his name appeared on a return of Capt. Henry Van Bibber's Company of the Lower Counties on Delaware Troops, at New Castle, on June 4, 1759. [Ref: DA-26].

CALLAHAUN, Edward. Private. Enlisted on May 22, 1758, in Capt. French Battell's Company of Lower County Provincials, during the French and Indian Wars. [Ref: DA-16].

CALLEY, John. Private. Served in Capt. Samuel Smith's Company, Delaware Regiment of Continental Troops. Enlisted on January 15, 1776, and was on duty (in barracks) at Dover on April 12, 1776. [Ref: DA-54, DA-56]. (Same source spelled his name "John Cally").

CALLINAN, John. Private. Served in Capt. Henry Darby's Company, Delaware Regiment of Continental Troops. Enlisted on January 18, 1776, and was on duty (in barracks) at Dover on April 12, 1776. [Ref: DA-46].

CALLY, Joseph. Captain. He held that rank by 1683 when he was mentioned in an Action of Debt in Sussex County. [Ref: DC-241].

CAMBLE, John. Private. Served in Capt. Samuel Smith's Company, Delaware Regiment of Continental Troops. Enlisted on January 18, 1776, and was on duty (in barracks) at Dover on April 12, 1776. [Ref: DA-54].

CAMBLE, Samuel. Private. Served in Capt. Samuel Smith's Company, Delaware Regiment of Continental Troops. Enlisted on January 17, 1776, and was on duty (in barracks) at Dover on April 12, 1776. [Ref: DA-54].

CAMERON, Daniel. Private. Born 1736, Inverness, Scotland. Clerk. Enlisted May 2, 1759, in the French and Indian Wars, in Capt. James Armstrong's Company in the Pennsylvania Regiment. [Ref: DA-25].

CAMPANIUS, Johann. Reverend. Military preacher. Son of Jonas Peter, was born at Stockholm in the congregation of St. Klara on August 15, 1601. He studied theology at the University of Upsala and was ordained on July 19, 1633. On February 3, 1642, he was formally called by the government to go to New Sweden where he remained over five years and served also as a military preacher (*pastoren*) and "officer" at Fort Christina in New Sweden from 1643 to 1648. He returned to Sweden with his family in May, 1648. His services in New Sweden were appreciated by the authorities and he was made first preacher to the Admiralty on the Skeppsholm, an island in Stockholm (the station of the Swedish Navy). He died on September 17, 1683 and was buried in the Church of Frosthult. [Ref: DJ-678, 679, 700, 715, DH-47]. (His name, when written as "Johan Campanius Holm," indicates he was from Stockholm. There was also a military preacher "Anders Campanius" on the ship *Fortuna* in 1653. The name was also spelled "Companius").

CAMPBELL, David. Private. Served in Capt. Richard McWilliams' Company, New Castle County. Enlisted on December 28, 1757, during the French and Indian Wars. [Ref: DA-15].

CAMPBELL, Joseph. Sergeant. Served in Capt. Jonathan Caldwell's Company of the Delaware Regiment of Continental Troops. Enlisted on January 15, 1776, and was on duty (in barracks) at Dover on April 12, 1776. [Ref: DA-41].

CAMPHERT, Valentine. Private. Served in Capt. Joseph Stedham's Company, Delaware Battalion of Continental Troops. Enlisted on March 2, 1776, and was in quarters at Dover on April 12, 1776. [Ref: DA-40].

CAMPWELL, James. Private. Served in Capt. Joseph Stedham's Company, Delaware Battalion of Continental Troops. Enlisted on January 24, 1776, and was in quarters at Dover on April 12, 1776. However, a subsequent entry in the record stated he deserted on April 3, 1776. [Ref: DA-39, 40].

CANN, John. Officer. His name appeared on a nomination list for officers in New Castle circa 1675 (list not dated). [Ref: DP-170].

CANN, William. Private. Served in Capt. Samuel Smith's Company, Delaware Regiment of Continental Troops. Enlisted on January 20, 1776, and was on duty (in barracks) at Dover on April 12, 1776. [Ref: DA-54].

CANNON, Alexander. Private. Served in Capt. Joseph Stedham's Company, Delaware Battalion of Continental Troops. Enlisted on February 2, 1776, and was in quarters at Dover on April 12, 1776. [Ref: DA-39].

CANNON, Jacob. Soldier. Applied in New Castle County in June, 1776, stating he desired to take an active part in the Flying Camp of the Third Pennsylvania Battalion. [Ref: DA-65].

CANNON, John. Private. Served in Capt. Henry Darby's Company, Delaware Regiment of Continental Troops. Enlisted on January 24, 1776, and was on duty (in barracks) at Dover on April 12, 1776. [Ref: DA-46].

CANNON, Matthew. Private. Served in Capt. Richard McWilliams' Company, New Castle County. Enlisted on December 28, 1757, during the French and Indian Wars. [Ref: DA-14].

CANNUN, Alexander. Private. Served in Capt. Samuel Smith's Company, Delaware Regiment of Continental Troops. Enlisted January 23, 1776, and on duty (in barracks) at Dover on April 12, 1776. [Ref: DA-54].

CANTWELL, Edmond. Captain. Held the rank of captain plus surveyor general in the Delaware Bay area in the 1660's and 1670's. [Ref: DP-62, DY-34].

CANTWELL, Mary and Richard. See "William Dyre," q.v.

CANTWELL, Richard and Lydia. See "Adam Peterson," q.v.

CAPSON, Jared. Sergeant. Served in Capt. Charles Pope's Company, Delaware Regiment of Continental Troops. Enlisted January 16, 1776, and was on duty (in quarters) at Lewis Town on April 11, 1776. [Ref: DA-51].

CARLILE, Patrick. Private. Served in Capt. Joseph Stedham's Company, Delaware Battalion of Continental Troops. Enlisted on April 3, 1776, and was in quarters at Dover on April 12, 1776. [Ref: DA-40].

CARLIN, John. Private. Born 1737, Maryland. Laborer. Enlisted on May 3, 1758, during the French and Indian Wars, by Capt. Benjamin Noxon. [Ref: DA-18].

CARLOS, Christina. See "John Andersson Stalcop," q.v.

CARMAN, John. Private. Served in Capt. Samuel Smith's Company, Delaware Regiment of Continental Troops. Enlisted on January 17, 1776, and was on duty (in barracks) at Dover on April 12, 1776, at which time he was reported to be "sick and absent." [Ref: DA-54].

CARNES, John. Private. Born 1742, Maryland. Laborer. Enlisted on May 3, 1758, during the French and Indian Wars, by Capt. Benjamin Noxon. [Ref: DA-18].

CAROLLY, Laurenty. Soldier. Planter in Delaware who paid his quit-rent to the governor in 1668. [Ref: DP-28]. "Laurentius Carolus" was granted the tract *Teckquarasy* on the west side of the Delaware River circa 1670 (date incomplete). [Ref: DY-109, DY-110].

CARR, Andrew. Soldier. Planter in Delaware in 1667 and 1669. [Ref: DP-27, 28]. "Andren [Andrew or Andries] Carr and wife Margarett, heretofore ye widow and relect of Joost de la Grange," were granted land on Matiniconck Island in the Delaware River on October 1, 1669. [Ref: DY-141]. (Name also spelled "Carre").

CARR, James. Private. Served in Capt. Samuel Smith's Company of the Delaware Regiment of Continental Troops. Enlisted on March 4, 1776, and on duty (in barracks) at Dover on April 12, 1776. [Ref: DA-54].

CARR, John. Captain. Was "on Delaware" by June 20, 1665, at which time he received a land patent and paid quit-rent to the governor. He petitioned the governor and council to build a new fort at New Castle since "the town was the strength of the river and was only capable to defend itself against the sudden violence and incursion of Indians..and..the inhabitants should not have some more than ordinary encouragement..[to defend themselves].." [Ref: DP-25, DP-27, DY-25]. (Name also spelled "Carre").

CARR, Patrick. Soldier. Planter in Delaware who paid his quit-rent to the governor in 1671, having received a land grant on Beaver Creek on June 17, 1671. [Ref: DP-29, DY-151]. (Name also spelled "Carre").

CARR, Robert. Sir. Knight. Commissioned by the Duke of York to go to Delaware Bay to generate trade and "endeavor to bring that place and all strangers thereabouts in obedience to his Majesty" on September 3, 1664, and further "commanding all officers at sea and land and all souldyers [soldiers] to obey said Sir Robert Carr." [Ref: DY-22, 23, 24]. Also see "John Ogle" and "James Crawford."

CARR, William. Private. Born 1715, Ireland. Laborer. Enlisted in Capt. John Shannon's Company of Foot on July 21, 1746, and served in King George's War against Canada. He was in winter quarters at Albany, New York, during 1746-1747, and was discharged on October 31, 1747. [Ref: DA-4, DA-6]. However, Source DM-40 stated that a "William Karr" was listed as a deserter in Capt. Shannon's record.

CARR, William. Private. Enlisted May 7, 1759, during the French and Indian Wars, and his name appeared on a return of Capt. Henry Van Bibber's Company of the Lower Counties on Delaware Troops, at New Castle, on June 4, 1759. [Ref: DA-26].

CARSON, Charles. Lieutenant. Served in Capt. Alexander Chance's Company, Apoquinamink Hundred, Lower Regiment, New Castle County, 1756, during the French and Indian Wars. [Ref: DA-11]. (Name also spelled "Casson").

CARSON, James. Private. Served in Capt. Charles Pope's Company of the Delaware Regiment of Continental Troops. Enlisted on January 19, 1776, and was on duty (in quarters) at Lewis Town on April 11, 1776. [Ref: DA-51].

CARSON, William. See "John Scott," q.v.

CARSONS, James. Private. Served in Capt. Jonathan Caldwell's Company, Delaware Regiment of Continental Troops. Enlisted on January 10, 1776, and was on duty (in barracks) at Dover on April 12, 1776. [Ref: DA-41].

CARTER, John. Private. Served in Capt. John Caton's Company, April 25, 1757, in the French and Indian Wars. [Ref: DA-13].

CARTER, Joseph. Private. Born 1735, Maryland. Enlisted in Capt. John Wright's Company and was on the muster roll of May 11, 1759, during the French and Indian Wars. [Ref: DA-25].

CARTWRIGHT, Jacob. Soldier. Enlisted on May 19, 1759, during the French and Indian Wars, and his name appeared on a return of Capt. Henry Van Bibber's Company of the Lower Counties on Delaware Troops at New Castle on June 4, 1759. [Ref: DA-26].

CARTY, Abraham. Ensign. Served in the 7th Company, Delaware State Troops in Continental Service. Commissioned January 20, 1776, and was on duty (in barracks) with Capt. Samuel Smith at Dover on April 12, 1776. [Ref: DA-35, 36, 53]. (Name also spelled "Abram Carty").

CARTY, Thomas. Corporal. Born 1716, Ireland. Tailor. Enlisted in Capt. John Shannon's Company of Foot on July 5, 1746, and served in King George's War against Canada. He was a corporal by June 6, 1747, and signed his name when he was paid for services. He was in winter quarters at Albany, New York, during 1746-1747, and was discharged on October 31, 1747. [Ref: DA-4, DA-5, DA-6, DM-40].

CARVER, Isaac. Private. Served in Capt. Joseph Stedham's Company, Delaware Battalion of Continental Troops. Enlisted on February 29, 1776, and was in quarters at Dover on April 12, 1776. [Ref: DA-40].

CATCHMORE, Thomas. Soldier. Enlisted on May 13, 1759, during the French and Indian Wars, and his name appeared on a return of Capt. Henry Van Bibber's Company of the Lower Counties on Delaware Troops at New Castle on June 4, 1759. [Ref: DA-26].

CATLIN, Mary and Joseph. See "Robert Hodgson," q.v.

CATLIN, Robert. Lieutenant. Served in Capt. John Caton's Company, Kent County, 1747-1748, in King George's War against Canada. [Ref: DA-8]. One "Robert Cattlin" died intestate in Kent County and his widow, Mary Cattlin, was named administratrix on March 9, 1772. [Ref: DK-265].

CATON, Benjamin. Lieutenant. He initially served as a private in Capt. John Caton's Company on April 25, 1757, during the French and Indian Wars. "Benjamin Catin" was an ensign in Capt. Richard Wells' Company on April 26, 1758. "Benjamin Caton" was a lieutenant in one of the companies of "the lower counties" [now Delaware] in the 3rd Battalion of the Pennsylvania Regiment under Col. Hugh Mercer on May 21, 1759. [Ref: DA-13, DA-16, DA-20, DM-48, DM-49]. A "John Caton, Sr." died in Kent County and his will was probated on June 4, 1744, naming his sons Thomas, Benjamin, Robert, and John, Jr., among other heirs. [Ref: DK-101]. The administration of the estate of one Benjamin Caton was granted to Mary Caton in Kent County on November 7, 1797. [Ref: DK-530]. (Name was also spelled "Caten").

CATON, John. Captain. Served in a Kent County Company, 1747-1748, in King George's War against Canada. He was a captain of a company of militia at Tidberry, in Kent County, upon Delaware, in 1756, in the French and Indian Wars. One "Jon Caton," also spelled "John Caten," was a captain of militia on an April 25, 1757 list. "John Caton" was a captain of militia in Upper District of Mother Kill Hundred, Kent County, on March 29, 1758. [Ref: DA-8, 12, 13, 14, 15, DM-46]. One "John Caton" died testate in Kent County and his will was probated on August 19, 1769, naming his wife Elizabeth, brother Benjamin, sisters Esther Pearce and Jenat Chaplin, stepson William Betts, and nephews James Caton (son of brother Benjamin), and John and Sampson Williamson. Elizabeth Caton may have married William Carpenter later. [Ref: DK-243, 244]. One "John Caton, Sr." died testate in Kent County and his will was probated June 4, 1744, naming his wife Agnas, sons Thomas, John Jr., Benjamin, Robert, and daughters Margrett, Sarah, Betty, Ester, Jennett, and granddaughter Susannah "Caten." [Ref: DK-101].

CATON, Robert. Private. Served in Capt. Charles Pope's Company of the Delaware Regiment of Continental Troops. Enlisted January 16, 1776, and was on duty (in quarters) at Lewis Town on April 11, 1776. [Ref: DA-51].

CATTS, William. Corporal. Served in Capt. Nathan Adams' Company, Delaware Regiment of Continental Troops. Enlisted on January 20, 1776, and was on duty (in barracks) at Dover on April 12, 1776. [Ref: DA-52].

CAVENDAR, Thomas and Sarah. See "William Wheeler," q.v.

CAZIER, Levi. Private. Served in Capt. Samuel Smith's Company, Delaware Regiment of Continental Troops. Enlisted on January 17, 1776, and was on duty (in barracks) at Dover on April 12, 1776. [Ref: DA-54, 56]. (Name also spelled "Cozier").

CEARSEY, Archabald. Private. Served in Capt. John Caton's Company, April 25, 1757, in the French and Indian Wars. [Ref: DA-13].

CHAMBERS, Joseph. Private. Born 1738, Maryland. Laborer. Enlisted on April 29, 1758, in the French and Indian Wars, by Capt. Benjamin Noxon. [Ref: DA-18].

CHANCE, Alexander. Captain. Served as a lieutenant in Capt. Edward Fitzrandolph's Company in New Castle County, in 1747-1748, in King George's War against Canada. [Ref: DA-7]. He was also captain of a company in Apoquinamink Hundred, Lower Regiment, New Castle County, 1756, during the French and Indian Wars. [Ref: DA-11, DM-46]. One "Alexander Chance, yeoman," died testate in Apoquinamink Hundred and his will was probated on January 12, 1773, naming his wife Elizabeth, sons Edmund and John Chance, daughter Mary Allfoard, grandsons John Chance and Thomas Allfoard, and his granddaughter Elizabeth Fields. [Ref: DN-71].

CHANCE, Lydia. See "John Rees," q.v.

CHANDLER, David. Private. Born 1737, Greenwich, New Jersey. Weaver. Enlisted on April 24, 1758, in the French and Indian Wars, by Capt. John McClughan "for the campaign in lower counties." [Ref: DA-17].

CHAPLIN, Jenat. See "John Caton," q.v.

CHARLES, James. Private. Served in Capt. Henry Darby's Company, Delaware Regiment of Continental Troops. Enlisted January 29, 1776, and on duty (in barracks) at Dover on April 12, 1776. [Ref: DA-46].

CHEICK, John. Private. Served in Capt. Samuel Smith's Company, Delaware Regiment of Continental Troops. Enlisted on January 16, 1776, and was on duty (in barracks) at Dover on April 12, 1776. [Ref: DA-54].

CHERRY, James. Private. Served in Capt. Nathan Adams' Company, Delaware Regiment of Continental Troops. Enlisted on February 6, 1776, and he reportedly died on February 28, 1776. [Ref: DA-53].

CHILDS, Thomas. Private. Served in Capt. Joseph Vaughan's Company, Delaware Regiment of Continental Troops. Enlisted on January 20, 1776, and on duty (in barracks) at Dover on April 12, 1776. [Ref: DA-57, DA-59]. (Same source spelled his name "Thomas Childes").

CHIPMAN, James. Lieutenant. Served in Capt. John Haveloe's Company, Northern District of Broad Kill Hundred, in the regiment of Sussex County, 1756, in the French and Indian Wars. He was reported "dead" on the muster roll of March 18, 1758. [Ref: DA-13, DA-15].

CHIPMAN, Peris. Private. Served in Capt. John Caton's Company on April 25, 1757, in the French and Indian Wars. [Ref: DA-14]. "Peres Chipman" witnessed the will of Benjamin Chipman in Kent County on April 19, 1772. [Ref: DK-267]. One "Paris Chipman, blacksmith," died in Sussex County and his will was probated September 14, 1781, naming his wife Judah, sons Draper and Paris, and daughters Sarah, Betsey, Kezia, Lovey, Milley, and Memory Chipman. [Ref: DS-139].

CHIPPY, Isaac. Private. Served in Capt. Jonathan Caldwell's Company in the Delaware Regiment of Continental Troops. Enlisted on January 13, 1776, and reported deserted on February 12, 1776. [Ref: DA-41].

CLAESEN, Hendrick. Soldier. Planter in Delaware who paid his quit-rent to the governor in 1668, having received land patent near Christine Kill on March 24, 1668. [Ref: DP-28, DY-136].

CLAESEN, Pieter. Soldier. Planter in Delaware who paid his quit-rent to the governor in 1669, received a patent for land near the Christine Kill on November 5, 1669. [Ref: DP-27, DY-143].

CLAMPIT, Jonathan. See "William Wallace," q.v.

CLARK, David. Captain. Served as a lieutenant in Capt. David Marshall's Company, Kent County, in June, 1748, and captain of a company of militia in the upper part of Duck Creek Hundred, Kent County, upon Delaware, in 1756, during the French and Indian Wars. [Ref: DA-8, DA-12, DM-46].

CLARK, John. Private. Born 1729, Ireland. Laborer. Enlisted April 24, 1758, in the French and Indian Wars, by Capt. Benjamin Noxon. [Ref: DA-18].

CLARK, William. Private. Served in Capt. Charles Pope's Company, Delaware Regiment of Continental Troops. Enlisted January 15, 1776, and was on duty (in quarters) at Lewis Town on April 11, 1776. [Ref: DA-51].

CLARK, William. Private. Served in Capt. Richard McWilliams' Company, New Castle County. Enlisted on December 28, 1757, during the French and Indian Wars. [Ref: DA-14].

CLARKE, Harmon. Private. Served in Capt. Jonathan Caldwell's Company, Delaware Regiment of Continental Troops. Enlisted on January 27, 1776, and was on duty (in barracks) at Dover on April 12, 1776. [Ref: DA-41].

CLARKE, Thomas. Captain. Served in a company of militia in upper part of Mispillim [Mispillion] Hundred, Kent County, upon Delaware, 1756, during the French and Indian Wars. [Ref: DA-12, DM-46]. One "Thomas Clark" died in Kent County and his will was probated on December 13, 1763, naming his wife Sarah [her will in 1772 stated she was the widow of Thomas], sons John and Benjamin, and daughters Ann McKnatt, Priscilla Henderson, Sarah Finchwait, Ruth Tharp, and Elizabeth Herrington. [Ref: DK-210, 263].

CLARKE, Thomas. Captain. Served in the War of Jenkins' Ear in 1739-1741 in a company that may have included soldiers from Delaware (muster rolls not extant). [Ref: DM-32].

CLASEN, Abbe. Skipper. Served on the ship *Orn* arrived in New Sweden in 1654. [Ref: DJ-717].
CLAWSON, Jesper. Private. Served in Capt. Richard McWilliams' Company, New Castle County. Enlisted on December 28, 1757, during the French and Indian Wars. [Ref: DA-15].
CLAYPOOLE, George. Ensign. Served in Capt. John Haverloe's Company, Northern District of Broad Kill Hundred, in the regiment of Sussex County in 1756, during the French and Indian Wars, and served to at least March 18, 1758. [Ref: DA-13, 15]. "George Claypoole, yeoman," died in Sussex County and administration of his estate was granted to George Conwell, Fisher Conwell, and Elias Conwell, administrator *de bonis non*, on September 3, 1763. [Ref: DS-76]. Another "George Claypoole" died in Sussex County and his will was probated on June 12, 1798, naming only a friend, Anthony Ingram. [Ref: DS-299]. (His name was also spelled "George Claypool").
CLAYTON, John. Captain. Served in a company of militia in Town of Dover, Kent County, upon Delaware, 1756, during the French and Indian Wars. [Ref: DA-12, DM-46].
CLEMENT, Abraham. Land patentee and probable militiaman in Delaware in November, 1677, He was dead by 1678. [Ref: DP-167, 168, 170].
CLEMENTSE, Olle. Soldier. Planter in Delaware who paid his quit-rent to the governor in 1669. [Ref: DP-27, DP-28]. "Olle Clementsen" received a land patent on Christeen Kill on November 5, 1669. [Ref: DY-144, DY-145].
CLEMENTSSON, Anders. Soldier. Arrived in New Sweden on the ship *Orn* in 1654. [Ref: DJ-718]. (Name also spelled "Clemetson").
CLERCK, Sander. Sailor. Served on the ship *Kalmar Nyckel* during the first expedition to New Sweden between 1637-1639. He was dead by 1640, leaving a widow in Stockholm. [Ref: DJ-758].
CLIFFORD, John. Second Lieutenant. Served in the War of Jenkins' Ear in 1739-1741 in a company which may have included soldiers from Delaware (muster rolls not extant). [Ref: DM-32].
CLIFTON, Dalaney. Private. Served in Capt. Joseph Vaughan's Company of the Delaware Regiment of Continental Troops. Enlisted on January 24, 1776, and on duty (in barracks) at Dover on April 12, 1776. [Ref: DA-59].
CLIFTON, Elihu. Private. Served in Capt. Joseph Vaughan's Company, Delaware Regiment of Continental Troops. Enlisted on February 15,

1776, and on duty (in barracks) at Dover on April 12, 1776. [Ref: DA-58, DA-59]. (Same source spelled his name "Eliha Clifton").

CLIFTON, John. Private. Served in Capt. David Hall's Company of the Delaware Regiment of Continental Troops. Enlisted January 23, 1776, and was on duty (in barracks) at Lewis Town on April 11, 1776. [Ref: DA-43].

CLIFTON, Pemberton. Private. Served in Capt. David Hall's Company, Delaware Regiment of Continental Troops. Enlisted January 23, 1776, and was on duty (in barracks) at Lewis Town on April 11, 1776. [Ref: DA-44].

CLIFTON, Robert. Private. Served in Capt. Joseph Vaughan's Company, Delaware Regiment of Continental Troops. Enlisted February 15, 1776 and on duty (in barracks) at Dover on April 12, 1776. [Ref: DA-59].

CLIFTON, Robert. Lieutenant. He held this rank by 1695 when he was a Justice in Sussex County. [Ref: DC-40]. See "John Avery," q.v.

CLOW, Cheany. Private. Born 1734, Maryland. Laborer. Enlisted on May 2, 1758, during the French and Indian Wars, by Capt. Benjamin Noxon. [Ref: DA-18].

CLOWES, John. Mariner. Lived in Sussex County in Broadkill Forrest prior to May 8, 1771, at which time he conveyed two parcels of land to Foster Dulaven. John Clowes, as executor of John Clowes, Esq., conveyed a lot in the town of Lewes to John Russel, cordwainer, on December 10, 1771. John Clowes was living in Broadkill Hundred by 1765 and was still living there in 1776. [Ref: DD-40, 45, 120].

CLYMER, Mary and Nancy. See "Thomas Needles," q.v.

COB, Samuel. Private. Served in Capt. David Hall's Company of the Delaware Regiment of Continental Troops. Enlisted January 16, 1776, and was on duty (in barracks) at Lewis Town on April 11, 1776. [Ref: DA-42].

COCK, Pieter. Soldier. Planter in Delaware who paid his quit-rent to the governor in 1669. [Ref: DP-27, 28].

COCKRAN, William. Private. Served in Capt. Nathan Adams' Company, Delaware Regiment of Continental Troops. Enlisted on February 8, 1776, and reportedly deserted on February 19, 1776. [Ref: DA-53].

COHOON, John. See "John Cahoon," q.v.

COHRAN, Daniel. Sergeant. Served in Capt. Joseph Stedham's Company, Delaware Battalion of Continental Troops. Enlisted on January 22, 1776, and was in quarters at Dover on April 12, 1776. [Ref: DA-39].

COLE, Mary. See "William Skinner," q.v.

COLE, Spencer, and others. See "John Brinckle," q.v.

COLEGATE, John. Private. Born 1735, America. Cordwainer. Enlisted on May 1, 1758, in the French and Indian Wars, by Capt. Benjamin Noxon. [Ref: DA-18].

COLEMAN, John. Private. Served in Capt. Charles Pope's Company, Delaware Regiment of Continental Troops. Enlisted January 16, 1776, and was on duty (in quarters) at Lewis Town on April 11, 1776, at which time he was reported "sick in quarters." [Ref: DA-50, DA-51].

COLESBERY, Jacob. Private. Served in Capt. Richard McWilliams' Company, New Castle County. Enlisted on December 28, 1757, during the French and Indian Wars. [Ref: DA-14].

COLESBURY, Henry. Lieutenant. Served in Capt. William Danford's Company, New Castle County, 1747-1748, in King George's War against Canada. [Ref: DA-7].

COLIER, Mary. See "Thomas Lewis," q.v.

COLL, Isaac. Private. Born 1717, London, England. Enlisted in Capt. John Wright's Company and was on the muster roll of May 11, 1759, during the French and Indian Wars. [Ref: DA-25].

COLLINS, Mary and John. See "Bethuel Watson," q.v.

COLLINS, Richard. Private. Served in Capt. David Hall's Company, Delaware Regiment of Continental Troops. Enlisted on January 30, 1776, and was on duty (in barracks) at Lewis Town on April 11, 1776. After his name is written "on guard." [Ref: DA-43].

COLLINS, Salathiel. Private. Served in Capt. Joseph Vaughan's Company, Delaware Regiment of Continental Troops. Enlisted January 23, 1776, and on duty (in barracks) at Dover on April 12, 1776. [Ref: DA-59].

COLLINS, Thomas. See "George Martin," q.v.

COLLINS, William. Private. Served in Capt. Samuel Smith's Company, Delaware Regiment of Continental Troops. Enlisted on January 31, 1776, and was reported "deserted" on March 3, 1776. [Ref: DA-54].

COLTER, Cornelius. Private. Served in Capt. David Hall's Company, Delaware Regiment of Continental Troops. Enlisted on January 20, 1776 and was on duty (in barracks) at Lewis Town on April 11, 1776, at which time he was reported "sick in quarters." [Ref: DA-43].

COLTER, Thomas. Private. Born 1737, Sussex, Delaware. Enlisted in Capt. John Wright's Company and was on the muster roll of May 11, 1759, during the French and Indian Wars. [Ref: DA-25].

COLTER, William. Private. Born 1739, Sussex, Delaware. Enlisted in Capt. John Wright's Company and was on the muster roll of May 11, 1759, during the French and Indian Wars. [Ref: DA-25].

COMBS, William. Private. Born 1734, England. Mariner. Enlisted on May 13, 1758, during the French and Indian Wars, by Capt. Benjamin Noxon. [Ref: DA-18].

COMEGYS, Cornelius. Drummer and fifer. Served in Capt. Jonathan Caldwell's Company, Delaware Regiment of Continental Troops. Enlisted on January 15, 1776, and was on duty (in barracks) at Dover on April 12, 1776. [Ref: DA-41].

CONAWAY, Rolin. Private. Served in Capt. Joseph Vaughan's Company, Delaware Regiment of Continental Troops. Enlisted on February 19, 1776, and on duty (in barracks) at Dover on April 12, 1776. [Ref: DA-58, DA-59]. (Same source spelled his name "Rowland Conniway").

CONAWAY, Samuel. Private. Served in Capt. Joseph Vaughan's Company, Delaware Regiment of Continental Troops. Enlisted on February 7, 1776, and was on duty (in barracks) at Dover on April 12, 1776. [Ref: DA-58, 59]. (Same source spelled his name "Samuel Conneway").

CONGLETON, Benjamin. Soldier. Enlisted on May 21, 1759, during the French and Indian Wars, and appeared on a return of Capt. Henry Van Bibber's Company of the Lower Counties on Delaware Troops, at New Castle, on June 4, 1759. [Ref: DA-26].

CONNELLY, Bryan. Private. Born 1738, Monaghan, Ireland. Laborer. Enlisted on April 20, 1758, during the French and Indian Wars, by Capt. John McClughan "for the campaign in the lower counties." [Ref: DA-17].

CONNER, Edward. Private. Served in Capt. Samuel Smith's Company, Delaware Regiment of Continental Troops. Enlisted on January 21, 1776, and was on duty (in barracks) at Dover on April 12, 1776. [Ref: DA-54].

CONNER, John. Soldier. Enlisted on May 21, 1759, during the French and Indian Wars, and his name appeared on a return of Capt. Henry Van Bibber's Company of the Lower Counties on Delaware Troops, at New Castle, on June 4, 1759. [Ref: DA-26].

CONNER, John. Private. Served in Capt. Joseph Stedham's Company, Delaware Battalion of Continental Troops. Enlisted on February 2, 1776, and was in quarters at Dover on April 12, 1776. [Ref: DA-39].

CONNER, William. Private. Served in Capt. Samuel Smith's Company, Delaware Regiment of Continental Troops. Enlisted on January 21, 1776, and on duty (in barracks) at Dover, April 12, 1776, at which time he transferred to Capt. Henry Darby's Company. [Ref: DA-54].

CONOLY, George. Private. Served in Capt. Samuel Smith's Company, Delaware Regiment of Continental Troops. Enlisted on January 23,

1776, and was on duty (in barracks) at Dover on April 12, 1776. [Ref: DA-54].

CONWELL, George, Fisher, and Elias. See "George Claypoole," q.v.

CONWELL, Elias. Corporal. Born 1739, Sussex, Delaware. Served in Capt. John Wright's Company on May 11, 1759, during the French and Indian Wars. [Ref: DA-25]. One Elias Conwell died in Sussex County and his will was probated on August 14, 1782, naming these heirs: sons George, Fisher, Elias, and David Conwell; daughter Sarah King (wife of William Conwell); grandsons Shepard, Claudius and John (sons of son Jeremiah Conwell, deceased); and, grandson John (son of son George Conwell). [Ref: DS-144]. Also see "Joseph Conwell."

CONWELL, Joseph. Pilot. Lived in Sussex County prior to April 2, 1770, at which time his son and daughter, Jacob and Rachel Conwell, received a bill of sale for a negro girl named "Pheabe" from John Conwell, yeoman, and witnessed by Elias Conwell. [Ref: DD-18].

CONWELL, William. Lieutenant. Served in one of three companies of "the lower counties" in the 3rd Battalion of Pennsylvania Regiment under Col. Hugh Mercer on May 23, 1759. [Ref: DA-20]. This same source spelled his name "William Conwell" and indicate that he was commissioned a lieutenant on May 23, 1759. However, it gave his name as "William Connell" on May 11, 1759, in the French and Indian Wars. [Ref: DA-25]. Source DM-49 gave his name as "Conwell."

COOCH, Thomas. Captain. Served in a company in Pencader Hundred, Lower Regiment, New Castle County, 1756, during the French and Indian Wars. [Ref: DA-12, DM-46]. One "Thomas Cooch, Jr." died testate in New Castle Hundred and his will was probated on February 3, 1785, naming his wife Sarah, sons Thomas, Francis, and William, and daughter Elizabeth Maxwell. [Ref: DN-104].

COOK, Daniel. Private. Born 1725, New Castle, Delaware. Laborer. Enlisted in Capt. John Shannon's Company of Foot on July 8, 1746, and served in King George's War against Canada. He made his mark when paid for services on June 6, 1747. He was in winter quarters at Albany, New York, in 1746-1747, and was discharged October 31, 1747. [Ref: DA-4, DA-5, DA-6, DM-40]. (Name also spelled "Cooke").

COOK, John. Private. Born 1729, Tyrone, Ireland. Laborer. Enlisted on April 28, 1759, in the French and Indian Wars, in Capt. James Armstrong's Company in the Pennsylvania Regiment. [Ref: DA-25].

COOK, John. Private. Served in Capt. Henry Darby's Company of the Delaware Regiment of Continental Troops. Enlisted on January 19,

1776, and was on duty (in barracks) at Dover on April 12, 1776. [Ref: DA-46].

COOK, Timothy. Private. Served in Capt. Charles Pope's Company, Delaware Regiment of Continental Troops. Enlisted on January 17, 1776, and was on duty (in quarters) at Lewis Town on April 11, 1776, at which time he was reported to be "on guard." [Ref: DA-51].

COOKE, Edward. Land patentee and probable militiaman in Delaware in November, 1677. [Ref: DP-167, 168].

COOKE, Jonathan. Private. Served in Capt. Samuel Smith's Company, Delaware Regiment of Continental Troops. Enlisted January 28, 1776, and was on duty (in barracks) at Dover on April 12, 1776, at which time he transferred to Capt. Henry Darby's Company. [Ref: DA-54, DA-56]. (This same source also spelled his name "Jonathan Cook").

COOKE, Nathaniel. Private. Born 1739, Whitly Creek, Delaware. Farmer. Enlisted on May 5, 1758, during the French and Indian Wars, by Capt. John McClughan "for the campaign in the lower counties." [Ref: DA-17].

COOPER, Elizabeth and Absalum. See "Job Merideth," q.v.

COOPER, James. Private. Born 1729, Ireland. Laborer. Enlisted on May 2, 1759, during the French and Indian Wars, in Capt. James Armstrong's Company in the Pennsylvania Regiment. [Ref: DA-25].

COOPER, James. Private. Enlisted on May 12, 1758, in Capt. French Battell's Company of Lower County Provincials, during the French and Indian Wars. [Ref: DA-16].

COPE, Robert. Private. Enlisted on May 15, 1758, in Capt. French Battell's Company of Lower County Provincials, during the French and Indian Wars. [Ref: DA-16].

CORBIT, John. Private. Served in Capt. Samuel Smith's Company, Delaware Regiment of Continental Troops. Enlisted on February 1, 1776, and was on duty (in barracks) at Dover on April 12, 1776. [Ref: DA-54].

CORD, Jane. See "John Miers," q.v.

CORD, Joseph. Captain. Served in a company in regiment of Sussex County, Southern District of Broad Kill Hundred, 1756-1758, during the French and Indian Wars. [Ref: DA-13, DA-15, DM-46]. One "Joseph Cord, planter," died testate in Broadkill Hundred and his will was probated on May 5, 1738, naming his wife Ann, sons John, Hezekiah, and Joseph, and daughters Ann, Esther, and Elizabeth. [Ref:DS-45]. One Hezekiah Cord died testate in Sussex County and his will was probated on June 4, 1767, naming his brother Joseph. [Ref: DS-80].

CORDBIRD, Garrett. Private. Born 1720, England. Laborer. Enlisted in Capt. John Shannon's Company of Foot on July 16, 1746, and he served in King George's War against Canada. He made his mark when paid for his services on June 6, 1747. He was in winter quarters at Albany, New York, during 1746-1747, and was discharged on October 31, 1747. [Ref: DA-4, DA-5, DA-6, DM-40].

CORKERLIN, James. Private. Enlisted on May 20, 1758, in Capt. French Battell's Company of Lower County Provincials, during the French and Indian Wars. [Ref: DA-16].

CORNELISEN, Jacob. Sailor. Mate on the ship *Fama* during the sixth expedition to New Sweden between 1643-1644. [Ref: DJ-760].

CORNELIUS, John. Land patentee and probable militiaman in Delaware in November, 1677. [Ref: DP-167, 168].

CORNWELL, Samuel. Private. Born 1737, Virginia. Enlisted in Capt. John Wright's Company and was on the muster roll of May 11, 1759, during the French and Indian Wars. [Ref: DA-25].

CORRY, Samuel. See "John Elliott," q.v.

CORSE, John. Sergeant. Served in Capt. Jonathan Caldwell's Company, Delaware Regiment of Continental Troops. Enlisted January 15, 1776, and on duty (in barracks) at Dover on April 12, 1776. [Ref: DA-41].

COSGRIFT, John. Private. Born 1730, Ireland. Laborer. Enlisted on April 25, 1758, in the French and Indian Wars, by Capt. Benjamin Noxon. [Ref: DA-18].

COTTMAN, Leah and Joshua. See "Benjamin Brinckley," q.v.

COUDREY, Josias. Land patentee and probable militiaman in Delaware in November, 1677. [Ref: DP-167, 168]. (Name could be "Elias?").

COUPLEDITCH, John. Private. Served in Capt. Samuel Smith's Company, Delaware Regiment of Continental Troops. Enlisted on March 4, 1776, and was reported to have deserted on March 27, 1776. [Ref: DA-54].

COVERDIL, Benjamin. Private. Served in Capt. Joseph Vaughan's Company, Delaware Regiment of Continental Troops. Enlisted January 19, 1776, and was on duty (in barracks) at Dover on April 12, 1776. [Ref: DA-57, 59]. (This same source spelled his name "Coverdell").

COUSINS, John. Soldier who was granted land on Christina Creek in Delaware on October 1, 1669. [Ref: DY-142].

COWARD, Penelope Holt. See "Ryves Holt," q.v.

COWENHOVEN, Pieter. Soldier. Planter in Delaware who paid his quit-rent to the governor in 1669, having been granted "a small hooke or corner of land at New Castle in Delaware River" on October 1, 1669. [Ref: DP-27, DP-28, DY-142, DY-143].

COX, Isaac. Private. Served in Capt. Jonathan Caldwell's Company, Delaware Regiment of Continental Troops. Enlisted on January 18, 1776, and was on duty (in barracks) at Dover on April 12, 1776. [Ref: DA-41].

COX, John Gunr. Private. Served in Capt. Charles Pope's Company, Delaware Regiment of Continental Troops. Enlisted January 16, 1776, and was on duty (in quarters) at Lewis Town on April 11, 1776. [Ref: DA-51].

COYLE, Charles. Private. Born 1714, Ireland. Cordwainer. Enlisted in Capt. John Shannon's Company of Foot, July 14, 1746, and served in King George's War against Canada. He was in winter quarters at Albany, New York, during 1746-1747, and was discharged on October 31, 1747. [Ref: DA-4, DA-6]. (He is not listed in Source DM-40.)

CRAFORD, John. Private. Served in Capt. Joseph Stedham's Company, Delaware Battalion of Continental Troops. Enlisted on February 7, 1776, and was in quarters at Dover on April 12, 1776. [Ref: DA-39].

CRAGE, Robert. Private. Served in Capt. Samuel Smith's Company, Delaware Regiment of Continental Troops. Enlisted on January 19, 1776, and was on duty (in barracks) at Dover on April 12, 1776. [Ref: DA-54].

CRAIG, James. Private. Served in Capt. Richard McWilliams' Company in New Castle County on December 28, 1757, during the French and Indian Wars. [Ref: DA-14]. On October 28, 1759, he petitioned the assembly for payment since he provided quarters for soldiers, and he was allowed 7 pounds, 2 shillings, 6 pence. [Ref: DM-51].

CRAIG, James. See "William Wheeler," q.v.

CRAIG, Thomas. Ensign. Served in Capt. William Rhoades' Company, lower part of Murder Kill Hundred, Kent County, upon Delaware, in 1756, during the French and Indian Wars. [Ref: DA-12]. One "Thomas Craige" died intestate in Kent County and his widow Nancy was named his administratrix on January 20, 1768. However, this account was later administered by Edward and Nanny Stradly. [Ref: DK-232].

CRAIG, William. Lieutenant. Served in Capt. Joseph Cord's Company, Southern District of Broad Kill Hundred, in the regiment of Sussex County, 1756, during the French and Indian Wars. "William Craige" was a lieutenant in Capt. Cord's Company on March 18, 1758. [Ref:

DA-13, 15]. One "William Craig, yeoman," died in Sussex County and his was will was probated on February 5, 1755, naming a son William Craig and daughters Elenor Prettyman (wife of Robert Prettyman) and Jane McIlvaine (wife of James McIlvaine, Jr.). [Ref: DS-64].

CRAIGE, Rachel and Elizabeth. See "Richard White," q.v.

CRAIGH, Sophiah. See "Joseph Smith," q.v.

CRANE, Thomas. Private. Born 1723, Kent, Delaware. Laborer. Enlisted in Capt. John Shannon's Company of Foot on July 16, 1746, and served in King George's War against Canada. He made his mark when paid for services on June 6, 1747. He was in winter quarters at Albany, New York, during 1746-1747, and was discharged October 31, 1747. [Ref: DA-4, DA-5, DA-6]. (Not listed in Source DM-40.)

CRANFIELD, Hezekiah. Private. Enlisted, Capt. John Caton's Company, on April 25, 1757, in the French and Indian Wars. [Ref: DA-14].

CRANSTON, Miriam. See "Evan Lewis," q.v.

CRAPPER, Levin, and others. See "Levin Cropper," q.v.

CRAWFORD, Alexander. Private. Served in Capt. Henry Darby's Company of the Delaware Regiment of Continental Troops. Enlisted on January 20, 1776, and on duty (in barracks) at Dover on April 12, 1776. [Ref: DA-46].

CRAWFORD, Elizabeth. See "Caesar Rodney," q.v.

CRAWFORD, James. Soldier. Served in the military expedition of Col. Richard Nicolls who captured New Amsterdam (New York) in 1664, and he also served under Sir Robert Carr on the Delaware. After his military service James settled in New Castle County, Delaware, near his comrades John Ogle and Thomas Wollaston. He married Judy ---- and their daughter Mary married Thomas Ogle. James was a soldier and planter in Delaware who paid his quit-rent to the governor in 1669; still living in 1675. [Ref: DP-27, DP-28, DF-23]. In consideration of his good service performed by him as a soldier, James was granted "a piece of land in Christine Kill or Creek" and also "a small tenement or cottage house with a back side there unto belonging" in the town of New Castle. [Ref: DY-126].

CRAWFORD, John. Private. Born 1733, Donegal, Ireland. Laborer. Enlisted on April 29, 1758, during the French and Indian Wars, as a private by Capt. John McClughan "for the campaign in the lower counties." [Ref: DA-17].

CRAWFORD, John. Private. Served in Capt. Nathan Adams' Company, Delaware Regiment of Continental Troops. Enlisted on January 15,

1776, and was on duty (in barracks) at Dover on April 12, 1776. [Ref: DA-52].

CRAWFORD, Mary. See "Thomas Ogle," q.v.

CRAWFORD, Thomas, and daughters. See "John Brinckloe," q.v.

CREAGOR, Marton. Captain. He held that rank by 1681 when mentioned in an Attachment in Sussex County. [Ref: DC-135, DC-139, Dc-142].

CREATH, William. Private. Served in Capt. Richard McWilliams' Company, New Castle County. Enlisted on December 28, 1757, during the French and Indian Wars. [Ref: DA-14].

CREMER, Jacob. See "Jacob Kreamer," q.v.

CRISTE, John. Private. Served in Capt. Joseph Stedham's Company, Delaware Battalion of Continental Troops. Enlisted on February 17, 1776, and was in quarters at Dover on April 12, 1776. [Ref: DA-40].

CROCKETT, Jesse. Private. Served in Capt. Nathan Adams' Company, Delaware Regiment of Continental Troops. Enlisted on January 16, 1776, and was on duty (in barracks) at Dover on April 12, 1776. [Ref: DA-52].

CROCKETT, Jonathan. Private. Served in Capt. Nathan Adams' Company, Delaware Regiment of Continental Troops. Enlisted February 7, 1776, and on duty (in barracks) at Dover on April 12, 1776. [Ref: DA-53].

CROOKHAM, William. Soldier. Tailor. Enlisted in Wilmington Township in 1758 by Capt. Samuel Grubb to serve in the Pennsylvania Troops. [Ref: DA-27].

CROPPER, Levin. Ensign. Served in Capt. Benjamin Wyncoop's Company in the Northern District of Cedar Creek Hundred, in the regiment of Sussex County, 1756, and ensign in Capt. Benjamin Wynkoop's [sic] Cedar Creek District Company on March 18, 1758. [Ref: DA-13, 15]. One "Levin Crapper" died testate in Sussex County and his will was probated on April 23, 1775, naming his wife Betty, sons Milton and Levin, and daughters Amelia Crapper, Leah Parker (wife of John), and Sarah Rench (wife of James). A later account showed the estate was settled on February 12, 1791, by Sydenham Thorne and his wife, Betty (late Betty Crapper). [Ref: DS-102].

CROSBY, John. Private. Served in Capt. Samuel Smith's Company, Delaware Regiment of Continental Troops. Enlisted on January 17, 1776, and was on duty (in barracks) at Dover on April 12, 1776. [Ref: DA-54].

CROSS, David. Private. Served in Capt. Henry Darby's Company, Delaware Regiment of Continental Troops. Enlisted on February 13,

1776, and was on duty (in barracks) at Dover on April 12, 1776. [Ref: DA-46].

CROUT, John. Private. Served in Capt. Samuel Smith's Company, Delaware Regiment of Continental Troops. Enlisted on February 5, 1776, and was on duty (in barracks) at Dover on April 12, 1776. [Ref: DA-54].

CROUTCH, John. See "Thomas Pemberton," q.v.

CROWDER, Thomas. Private. Served in Capt. Nathan Adams' Company, Delaware Regiment of Continental Troops. Enlisted on January 20, 1776, and was on duty (in barracks) at Dover on April 12, 1776. [Ref: DA-52].

CROWLEY, Bartholomew. Private. Born 1725, Ireland. Tinner. Enlisted in Capt. John Shannon's Company of Foot on July 2, 1746, and served in King George's War against Canada. He was in winter quarters at Albany, New York, during 1746-1747, and was discharged on October 31, 1747. [Ref: DA-4, DA-6, DM-40].

CROWLEY, James. Private. Born 1718, Ireland. Laborer. Enlisted in Capt. John Shannon's Company of Foot on August 4, 1746, and served in King George's War against Canada. He was in winter quarters at Albany, New York, during 1746-1747, and was discharged on October 31, 1747. [Ref: DA-4, DA-6]. (He is not listed in Source DM-40.)

CROWLEY, Owen. Private. Born 1731 (place not stated). Laborer. Enlisted on May 19, 1759, in the French and Indian Wars, in Capt. James Armstrong's Company in Pennsylvania Regiment. [Ref: DA-25].

CROZIER, Matthew. Ensign. Served in Capt. John Barnes' Company, upper part of Little Creek Hundred, Kent County, upon Delaware, 1756, in the French and Indian Wars. [Ref: DA-12]. Administration of the estate of "Matthew Crozier, yeoman," of Duck Creek Hundred in Kent County was granted to Rachel Crozier, widow, on September 27, 1773. Administration accounts indicate that Rachel Crozier married Thomas Parry, and Matthew Crozier left these heirs: Mary Robinson (*nee* Crozier, wife of Charles Robinson), Sarah Besswicik (*nee* Crozier, wife of Robert Besswicik), Rhoda Crozier, Matthew Crozier, and Robert Crozier. [Ref: DK-282].

CULLEN, William. Private. Served in Capt. John Caton's Company, April 25, 1757, in the French and Indian Wars. [Ref: DA-14]. One William Cullen died intestate in Kent County and the administration of his estate was granted to Sarah Cullen on December 2, 1778. The account showed these heirs: Ruth Tripitt, wife of William Trippett [sic]; John Cullen; William Cullen; Mary Cullen; James Cullen; Thomas Cullen;

David Cullen; Nathan Cullen; and, Nathaniel Cullen. It also showed Sarah Cullen married William Thomson. [Ref: DK-320].

CUMMING, John. Private. Born 1723, Ireland. Smith. 5 ft. 9 in. tall. Enlisted at New Castle, Delaware on May 22, 1758, during the French and Indian Wars, by Capt. Paul Jackson, from "the three lower counties" to serve in the Pennsylvania Troops. [Ref: DA-27].

CUNNIGAN, John. Private. Served in Capt. Jonathan Caldwell's Company, Delaware Regiment of Continental Troops. Enlisted on February 15, 1776, and was on duty (in barracks) at Dover on April 12, 1776. [Ref: DA-41].

CURREY, Thomas. Private. Served in Capt. Samuel Smith's Company, Delaware Regiment of Continental Troops. Enlisted on January 15, 1776, and was on duty (in barracks) at Dover on April 12, 1776. [Ref: DA-54].

CURREY, William. Private. Served in Capt. Joseph Stedham's Company, Delaware Battalion of Continental Troops. Enlisted on March 13, 1776, and reportedly deserted on March 20, 1776. [Ref: DA-40].

CURRY, Benjamin. Private. Served in Capt. Nathan Adams' Company, Delaware Regiment of Continental Troops. Enlisted on February 26, 1776, and was on duty (in barracks) at Dover on April 12, 1776. [Ref: DA-53].

CURRY, John. Corporal. Served in Capt. Charles Pope's Company, Delaware Regiment of Continental Troops. Enlisted January 17, 1776, and was on duty (in quarters) at Lewis Town on April 11, 1776. [Ref: DA-51].

CURRY, Neil. Private. Born 1723, Scotland. Cooper. Enlisted on April 22, 1758, in the French and Indian Wars, by Capt. Benjamin Noxon. [Ref: DA-19].

CURWITHEN, John. Private. Served in Capt. David Hall's Company, Delaware Regiment of Continental Troops. Enlisted January 21, 1776, and on duty (in barracks) at Lewis Town on April 11, 1776. [Ref: DA-43]. "John Cirwithen" died in Sussex County and administration of his estate was granted to Mark Davis as administrator *de bonis non* in right of Isaac Wattson circa June 13, 1798. [Ref: DS-294].

CUSTIS, William. Captain. He held that rank by 1686 when mentioned in an Action of Debt by Attachment in Sussex County. [Ref: DC-373].

D'HINIOSA, Alexander. See "Mattys Eschelson," q.v.

DAGNESS, Patrick. Private. Served in Capt. Samuel Smith's Company, Delaware Regiment of Continental Troops. Enlisted January 21, 1776, and on duty (in barracks) at Dover on April 12, 1776. [Ref: DA-54].

DAINTY, John. Private. Born 1733, Grapner, England. Miller. Enlisted on May 1, 1758, in the French and Indian Wars, by Capt. John McClughan "for the campaign in lower counties." [Ref: DA-17].

DALBO, Anders Larsson. Provost-marshal (*profoss*). Arrived from Dalbo on the island of Gothland or may have come from Dalarna. He arrived in New Sweden in 1640 on the ship *Kalmar Nyckel* and was a tobacco planter in 1644. On November 1, 1647, "he was hired by Governor Printz to serve among the soldiers as provost-marshal at the rate of 6 *riksdalers* per month." He served until November 15, 1648, left, and entered the service again circa December 15, 1650. He was "a freeman" in New Sweden in 1654. [Ref: DJ-711, DJ-718].

DAMATT, Joseph. Private. Served in Capt. Joseph Vaughan's Company, Delaware Regiment of Continental Troops. Enlisted on February 10, 1776, and was on duty (in barracks) at Dover on April 12, 1776. [Ref: DA-59].

DANALDLEY, James. Private. Served in Capt. Joseph Vaughan's Company of the Delaware Regiment of Continental Troops. Enlisted February 16, 1776, and was on duty (in barracks) at Dover on April 12, 1776. [Ref: DA-58, DA-59]. (This same source spelled his name "Danaley").

DANFORD, William. Captain. New Castle County Company, 1747-1748, and served in King George's War against Canada. [Ref: DA-7].

DANIELSSON, Josta. Soldier. Hired in Stockholm in 1653 and arrived in New Sweden on the ship *Orn* in 1654. [Ref: DJ-718].

DANIELSSON, Johan. Gunner (*arklimastare*). Arrived in New Sweden on the ship *Orn* in 1654. [Ref: DJ-718].

DARBY, Henry. Captain. Served in the 4th Company of Delaware State Troops in Continental Service. Commissioned January 17, 1776, and was on duty (in barracks) with the Delaware Regiment of Continental Troops at Dover on April 12, 1776. [Ref: DA-34, DA-36, DA-45].

DARLING, James. See "Robert Gordon," q.v.

DARRACH, John. See "William White," q.v.

DAUGHERTY, Benjamin. Private. Served in Capt. David Hall's Company, Delaware Regiment of Continental Troops. Enlisted on January 20, 1776, and was on duty (in barracks) at Lewis Town on April 11, 1776. [Ref: DA-43].

DAUGHERTY, James. Corporal. Served in Capt. Joseph Stedham's Company, Delaware Battalion of Continental Troops. Enlisted on February 14, 1776, and was in quarters at Dover on April 12, 1776. [Ref: DA-39].

DAVID, Thomas. Private. Born 1724, in Maryland. Laborer. Enlisted in Capt. John Shannon's Company of Foot on July 14, 1746, and he served in King George's War against Canada. "Thomas David" made his mark when paid for services on June 6, 1747, and he was in winter quarters at Albany, New York, during 1746-1747. He was discharged October 31, 1747. [Ref: DA-4, DA-5, DA-6]. (Source DA-4 spelled his name "David" and "Davis." Source DM-40 also spelled it "David").

DAVID, Mary. See "Robert Patton," q.v.

DAVID, Richard. See "Richard Davis," q.v.

DAVID, William. See "William Wallace," q.v.

DAVIDS, John. Private. Born 1723, New Castle, Delaware. Laborer, 5 ft. 9 in. tall. Enlisted at New Castle, Delaware, May 13, 1758, in the French and Indian Wars, by Capt. Paul Jackson, from "the three lower counties" to serve in the Pennsylvania Troops. [Ref: DA-27].

DAVIES, William. Private. Born 1721, England. Laborer. Enlisted in Capt. John Shannon's Company of Foot on July 14, 1746, and served in King George's War against Canada. "William Davies" made his mark when paid for services on June 6, 1747, and was in winter quarters at Albany, New York, in 1746-1747. He was discharged on October 31, 1747. [Ref: DA-4, 5, 6]. (Source DA-4 spelled his name "Davis" and "Davies," while source DM-40 spelled it "Davies").

DAVIS, Ann and Elizabeth. See "Richard Manwaring," q.v.

DAVIS, Elizabeth and Nathan. See "Samuel Johnson," q.v.

DAVIS, Hall. See "Valentine Davis," q.v.

DAVIS, James. Private. Born 1739, Down, Ireland. Farmer. Enlisted on April 22, 1758, in the French and Indian Wars, by Capt. John McClughan "for the campaign in the lower counties." [Ref: DA-17].

DAVIS, James. Sergeant. Born 1725, Philadelphia, Pennsylvania. Peruke maker. Enlisted as a private in Capt. John Shannon's Company of Foot on June 28, 1746, and served in King George's War against Canada. A sergeant by June 6, 1747, he signed his name when paid for his services. He was in winter quarters at Albany, New York, during 1746-1747, and was discharged October 31, 1747. [Ref: DA-4, DA-5, DA-6, DM-40].

DAVIS, John. Private. Served in Capt. Joseph Stedham's Company, Delaware Battalion of Continental Troops. Enlisted on February 5, 1776, and was in quarters at Dover on April 12, 1776. [Ref: DA-39].

DAVIS, John. Private. Served in Capt. John Caton's Company, April 25, 1757, in the French and Indian Wars. [Ref: DA-13].

DAVIS, Mark. See "John Curwithen," q.v.

DAVIS, Nehemiah. Ensign. Served in Capt. Thomas Till's Company, Southern District of Cedar Creek Hundred in the regiment of Sussex County, 1756, and ensign in Capt. Till's Slaughter Neck District Company on March 18, 1758. [Ref: DA-13, 15]. One Nehemiah Davis died testate in Sussex County and his will was probated on March 8, 1787, naming his wife Rachel, son Mark Tilney Davis, and daughters Elizabeth and Ann Davis. Nehemiah's father, Mark Davis, was his executor. [Ref: DS-183]. One "Nehemiah Davis, Sr." died testate in Sussex County and his will was probated on April 13, 1789, naming heirs: wife Susannah; sons Nehemiah, Mark, and William; daughter Elizabeth Draper; grandson Nehemiah Davis (son of Nehemiah); heirs of Eunice Draper (widow of Samuel Draper, deceased); heirs of Sarah Draper (widow of Henry Draper, deceased); and, heirs of Elizabeth Draper (widow of Joseph Draper, deceased). [Ref: DS-201].

DAVIS, Richard. Private. Served in Capt. Charles Pope's Company, Delaware Regiment of Continental Troops. Enlisted on January 17, 1776, and was on duty (in quarters) at Lewis Town on April 11, 1776, at which time he was reported to be "on guard." [Ref: DA-50, DA-51]. (This same source spelled his name "Richard David").

DAVIS, Samuel. Pilot. Lived in Sussex County in the town of Lewes prior to January 16, 1762, at which time he purchased a lot on 2nd Street from John and Ann Jones, and Comfort Poor, heirs of Thomas Marshall who died intestate. [Ref: DD-1].

DAVIS, Samuel. Private. Served in Capt. David Hall's Company of the Delaware Regiment of Continental Troops. Enlisted January 16, 1776, and was on duty (in barracks) at Lewis Town on April 11, 1776. [Ref: DA-42].

DAVIS, Samuel. Sergeant. Served in Capt. Charles Pope's Company, Delaware Regiment of Continental Troops. Enlisted January 19, 1776, and was on duty (in quarters) at Lewis Town on April 11, 1776. [Ref: DA-51].

DAVIS, Thomas. Land patentee and probable militiaman in Delaware in November, 1677. [Ref: DP-167, 168].

DAVIS, Thomas. See "Peter Lowber, Jr.," q.v.

DAVIS, Valentine. Private. Born 1716, Ireland. Cordwainer. Enlisted in Capt. John Shannon's Company of Foot on July 20, 1746 and served in King George's War against Canada. (Note: Source DA-5 states that "Hall Davis" made his mark when paid for services on June 6, 1747. There was no "Hall Davis" on the company rolls, so this must have been "Vall. Davis," i. e., Vallentine or Valentine Davis.) He was in winter quarters at Albany, New York, during 1746-1747, and was discharged October 31, 1747. [Ref: DA-4, DA-5, DA-6]. (Source DM-40 also transcribed the name as "Hall Davis").

DAVISON, James and Mary. See "John Shankland," q.v.

DE LA GRANGE, Joost. See "Andrew Carr," q.v.

DE LA VALLEE, George. Lieutenant. Served as adjutant and first lieutenant in the War of Jenkins' Ear in 1739-1741, in a company which may have included soldiers from Delaware (rolls not extant). [Ref: DM-32].

DE VRIES, David Peterson. Officer. He established the first colony in what is now Delaware on the Hoornekill [Whorekill, now Lewes], May 5, 1631, which settlement was called *Zwaandendael* (Valley of Swans). He and his small group became "soldiers" in the true sense of the word due to their constant fights with the Indians. In the summer of 1633 they abandoned this "colony." [Ref: DH-12, 22, 34].

DEEN, Abraham. See "Abraham Dun," q.v.

DEHAES, Johannes. Officer. His name appeared on a nomination list for New Castle officers circa 1675 (list undated). [Ref: DP-170].

DEHORTY, Sarah. See "Thomas Needles," q.v.

DEIMER, John. Captain. Commissioned on June 4, 1746, during King George's War against Canada. He was in winter quarters at Albany, New York, during 1746-1747, and his company was discharged on October 31, 1747. [Ref: DA-6].

DELANAWAY, Philloman. Private. Served in Capt. John Caton's Company on April 25, 1757, in the French and Indian Wars. [Ref: DA-14].

DELANY, John. Private. Served in Capt. Samuel Smith's Company, Delaware Regiment of Continental Troops. Enlisted on February 18, 1776, and was on duty (in barracks) at Dover on April 12, 1776, at which time he was reported to be "sick." [Ref: DA-54].

DELAVALL, Thomas. Captain. He held that rank by 1681 when mentioned in an Action of Debt in Sussex County. [Ref: DC-109, DC-157].

DEMPSEY, Dennis. Private. Served in Capt. Joseph Stedham's Company, Delaware Battalion of Continental Troops. Enlisted on March 11, 1776, and was in quarters at Dover on April 12, 1776. [Ref: DA-40].

DEMPSEY, Richard. Private. Served in Capt. Joseph Stedham's Company of the Delaware Battalion of Continental Troops. Enlisted February 10, 1776, and in quarters at Dover on April 12, 1776. [Ref: DA-40].

DENNY, William, Esq. Governor and Commander. He was The Honorable Governor of the Province of Pennsylvania, and Commander of the

Pennsylvania Regiment in 1759 (during the French and Indian Wars), which included soldiers from the Delaware area. [Ref: DA-27, 28].

DEPOISTER, John. Sergeant. Served in Capt. Jonathan Caldwell's Company, Delaware Regiment of Continental Troops. Enlisted on January 12, 1776, and was on duty (in barracks) at Dover on April 12, 1776. [Ref: DA-41].

DERHAM, Richard. Private. Served in Capt. Richard McWilliams' Company, New Castle County. Enlisted on December 28, 1757, during the French and Indian Wars. [Ref: DA-14].

DERICK, John. Private. Served in Capt. Charles Pope's Company, Delaware Regiment of Continental Troops. Enlisted January 13, 1776, and was on duty (in quarters) at Lewis Town on April 11, 1776. [Ref: DA-51].

DERIKSON, Gysbert. Officer. His name appeared on a nomination list of officers in New Castle circa 1675 (list undated). [Ref: DP-170].

DERISKSON, Mary. See "Benjamin Ford," q.v.

DERRY, William. Private. Born 1735, Delaware. Cooper. Enlisted on April 24, 1758, in the French and Indian Wars, by Capt. Benjamin Noxon. [Ref: DA-19].

DESERT, Benjamin. Private. Born 1742, Cumberland, Pennsylvania. Cordwainer. Enlisted on May 5, 1759, during the French and Indian Wars, in Capt. James Armstrong's Company in the Pennsylvania Regiment. [Ref: DA-25].

DEVELIN, Lazarus. Private. Served in Capt. Henry Darby's Company, Delaware Regiment of Continental Troops. Enlisted on January 22, 1776, and was on duty (in barracks) at Dover on April 12, 1776. [Ref: DA-46].

DEVELIN, Patrick. Private. Served in Capt. Henry Darby's Company, Delaware Regiment of Continental Troops. Enlisted on January 29, 1776, and was on duty (in barracks) at Dover on April 12, 1776. [Ref: DA-46].

DEVINING, Cornelius. Private. Served in Capt. Richard McWilliams' Company, New Castle County. Enlisted on December 28, 1757, during the French and Indian Wars. [Ref: DA-15].

DEWEES, John. Corporal. Served in Capt. Jonathan Caldwell's Company of the Delaware Regiment of Continental Troops. Enlisted on January 13, 1776, and was on duty (in barracks) at Dover on April 12, 1776. [Ref: DA-41].

DEWISON, Walter. See "John Shannon," q.v.

DEXTER, Enos. Ensign. Served in the War of Jenkins' Ear in 1739-1741 in a company which may have included soldiers from Delaware (muster rolls not extant). [Ref: DM-32].

DICK, Thomas. Private. Served in Capt. Henry Darby's Company, Delaware Regiment of Continental Troops. Enlisted on January 24, 1776, and was reported deserted on January 25, 1776. [Ref: DA-46].

DICKEY, David. Private. Served in Capt. Henry Darby's Company, Delaware Regiment of Continental Troops. Enlisted on February 13, 1776, and was on duty (in barracks) at Dover on April 12, 1776. [Ref: DA-46].

DICKEY, James. Private. Born 1735, Octararo, Pennsylvania. Smith. Enlisted on April 24, 1758, during the French and Indian Wars, as a private by Capt. John McClughan "for the campaign in the lower counties." [Ref: DA-17].

DICKSON, John. First Lieutenant. Served in 7th Company, Delaware State Troops in Continental Service. Commissioned on January 20, 1776, and was on duty (in barracks) with Capt. Samuel Smith at Dover on April 12, 1776. [Ref: DA-34, DA-36, DA-53, DA-55].

DICKSON, William. Private. Served in Capt. Samuel Smith's Company, Delaware Regiment of Continental Troops. Enlisted on January 18, 1776, and was on duty (in barracks) at Dover on April 12, 1776, at which time he was reported "dead" (no date given). [Ref: DA-54].

DICKSON, William. Sergeant. Served in Capt. Joseph Stedham's Company, Delaware Battalion of Continental Troops. Enlisted on January 19, 1776, and was in quarters at Dover on April 12, 1776. [Ref: DA-39].

DIEUS, William. Private. Enlisted on May 15, 1759, during the French and Indian Wars, and his name appeared on a return of Capt. Henry Van Bibber's Company of the Lower Counties of Delaware Troops at New Castle on June 4, 1759. [Ref: DA-26].

DIXSON, William. Private. Born 1733, New Castle, Delaware. Farmer. Enlisted on April 2, 1758, in the French and Indian Wars, by Capt. John McClughan "for the campaign in lower counties." [Ref: DA-17].

DOBSON, Sarah. See "Thomas Prettyman," q.v.

DOD, Rachel. See "Baptist Newcomb," q.v.

DODD, William. Private. Served in Capt. David Hall's Company of the Delaware Regiment of Continental Troops. Enlisted January 19, 1776, and was on duty (in barracks) at Lewis Town on April 11, 1776. [Ref: DA-42].

DOIL, Enos. Private. Served in Capt. Charles Pope's Company of the Delaware Regiment of Continental Troops. Enlisted on January 20, 1776, and on duty (in quarters) at Lewis Town on April 11, 1776, at which time he was reported "sick in quarters." [Ref: DA-50, DA-51].

DONELLY, Abner. Private. Born 1739, Maryland. Enlisted in Capt. John Wright's Company, on the muster roll of May 11, 1759, in the French and Indian Wars. [Ref: DA-25]. (Name also spelled "Danily").

DONNELLY, John. Corporal. Born 1716, Ireland. Laborer. Enlisted in Capt. John Shannon's Company of Foot on July 22, 1746, and served in King George's War against Canada. He was a corporal by June 6, 1747, and signed his name when paid for services. He was in winter quarters at Albany, New York, 1746-1747, and was discharged October 31, 1747. [Ref: DA-4, DA-5, DA-6]. (Not listed in Source DM-40.)

DONOLY, Hugh. Private. Served in Capt. Joseph Stedham's Company, Delaware Battalion of Continental Troops. Enlisted on January 22, 1776, and was in quarters at Dover on April 12, 1776. [Ref: DA-39].

DONOUHY, James. Private. Served in Capt. Henry Darby's Company, Delaware Regiment of Continental Troops. Enlisted on January 27, 1776, and was on duty (in barracks) at Dover on April 12, 1776. [Ref: DA-46].

DONY, John. Private. Served in Capt. Charles Pope's Company of the Delaware Regiment of Continental Troops. Enlisted January 16, 1776, and was on duty (in quarters) at Lewis Town on April 11, 1776. [Ref: DA-51].

DORMAN, Mathew. Sergeant. Served in Capt. David Hall's Company, Delaware Regiment of Continental Troops. Enlisted January 17, 1776, and was on duty (in barracks) at Lewis Town on April 11, 1776. [Ref: DA-42].

DOUGHERTY, Charles. Sergeant. Born 1729, Donegal, Ireland. Farmer. Enlisted on April 22, 1758, in the French and Indian Wars, by Capt. John McClughan "for the campaign in lower counties." [Ref: DA-17].

DOUGHERTY, John. Private. Born 1741, Donegal, Ireland. Farmer. Enlisted May 5, 1758, in the French and Indian Wars, by Capt. John McClughan "for the campaign in the lower counties." [Ref: DA-17].

DOUGHERTY, Owen. Private. Born 1725, Donegal, Ireland. Laborer. Enlisted on April 26, 1758, in the French and Indian Wars, by Capt. John McClughan "for the campaign in lower counties." [Ref: DA-17].

DOUGHERTY, Patrick. Private. Born 1734, Donegal, Ireland. Laborer. Enlisted on April 23, 1758, in the French and Indian Wars, by Capt. John McClughan "for the campaign in lower counties." [Ref: DA-17].

DOUGHTY, Nath. Private. Served in Capt. Charles Pope's Company, Delaware Regiment of Continental Troops. Enlisted January 17, 1776, and was on duty (in quarters) at Lewis Town on April 11, 1776. [Ref: DA-51].

DOUGLASS, Duncan. Private. Born 1725, Scotland. Laborer. Enlisted in Capt. John Shannon's Company of Foot on July 1, 1746, and served in King George's War against Canada. He was in winter quarters at Albany, New York, during 1746-1747, and was discharged on October 31, 1747. [Ref: DA-4, DA-6, DM-40].

DOWAL, John. Private. Served in Capt. Richard McWilliams' Company, New Castle County. Enlisted on December 28, 1757, during the French and Indian Wars. [Ref: DA-14].

DOWDES, William. Private. Served in Capt. Joseph Stedham's Company, Delaware Battalion of Continental Troops. Enlisted on March 15, 1776, and was in quarters at Dover on April 12, 1776. [Ref: DA-40].

DOWNHAM, Mary and Thomas. See "John Rash," q.v.

DOWNHAM, Richard. Private. Served in Capt. John Caton's Company on April 25, 1757, in the French and Indian Wars. [Ref: DA-13]. One Richard Downham died testate in Kent County and his will was probated on June 18, 1773, naming his daughters Ruth Downham, Mary Beauchamp (wife of John), Sarah Downham, Elizabeth Downham, Rachel Downham, and sons Isaac (executor) and Richard. His brother-in-law William Powell was an executor. [Ref: DK-280], Mary, widow of John Beauchamp, died testate and her will was probated on November 12, 1788, Mentioning her father Richard Downham, dec'd. [Ref: DK-405].

DOWNS, Joseph. Private. Born 1729, London, England. Laborer. Enlisted May 1, 1759, in the French and Indian Wars, in Capt. James Armstrong's Company in the Pennsylvania Regiment. [Ref: DA-25].

DOWNS, Thomas. Private. Born 1738, England. Glass blower. Enlisted on April 29, 1758, in the French and Indian Wars, by Capt. Benjamin Noxon. [Ref: DA-19].

DOWNY, Thomas. Private. Served in Capt. Jonathan Caldwell's Company of the Delaware Regiment of Continental Troops. Enlisted February 1, 1776, and was on duty (in barracks) at Dover on April 12, 1776. [Ref: DA-41].

DOWNS, Thomas. Private. Born 1738, Maryland. Laborer. Enlisted on April 29, 1758, in the French and Indian Wars, by Capt. Benjamin Noxon. [Ref: DA-19].

DRAPER, Elizabeth. See "Isaac Watson," q.v.

DRAPER, Eunice, Sarah, Elizabeth, and others. See "Nehemiah Davis."
DRUM, James Heroit. Private. Born 1740, New Castle, Delaware. Laborer. Enlisted on May 3, 1759, during the French and Indian Wars, in Capt. James Armstrong's Company, in the Pennsylvania Regiment. [Ref: DA-26].
DUFF, Thomas. Ensign. Served in Capt. James Latimer's Company, Christiana Hundred, Upper Regiment, New Castle County, 1756, during the French and Indian Wars. [Ref: DA-11].
DUFFIELD, George. See "Archibald Armstrong," q.v.
DULAVAN, Foster. See "John Clowes," q.v.
DUN, Abraham. Private. Served in Capt. Joseph Vaughan's Company, Delaware Regiment of Continental Troops. Enlisted on February 1, 1776, and was on duty (in barracks) at Dover on April 12, 1776. [Ref: DA-58, DA-59]. (Same source spelled his name "Abraham Deen").
DUNBAR, John. Private. Born 1733, Ireland. Laborer. Enlisted May 8, 1759, during the French and Indian Wars, in Capt. James Armstrong's Company in the Pennsylvania Regiment. [Ref: DA-26].
DUNBAR, John. Private. Born 1734, Tryone, Ireland. Weaver. Enlisted on April 25, 1758, during the French and Indian Wars, by Capt. John McClughan "for the campaign in the lower counties." [Ref: DA-17].
DUNFEE, Michael. Private. Born 1736, Wexford, England. Laborer. Enlisted May 2, 1758, during the French and Indian Wars, by Capt. John McClughan "for the campaign in lower counties." [Ref: DA-17].
DUNLAP, Allen. Private. Served in Capt. John Caton's Company, April 25, 1757, during the French and Indian Wars. [Ref: DA-14]. The administration of the estate of one Allen Dunlap was granted to Peter Dunlap in Kent County on July 30, 1756 (the same day he was granted administration of Matthew Dunlap's estate). Perhaps Allen Dunlap, the soldier, was a son of this Allen Dunlap. [Ref: DK-165].
DUNLAP, John. Private. Born 1730, Ireland. Laborer. Enlisted May 6, 1758, in the French and Indian Wars, by Capt. John McClughan "for the campaign in the lower counties." [Ref: DA-17].
DUNLAP, John. Private. Served in Capt. John Caton's Company, April 25, 1757, during the French and Indian Wars. [Ref: DA-14]. Peter Dunlap was named administrator of the estate of John Dunlap in Kent County on May 24, 1758. [Ref: DK-176].
DUNLAP, Peter. Private. Served in Capt. John Caton's Company, April 25, 1757, in the French and Indian Wars. [Ref: DA-14]. One "Peter Dunlap, yeoman" was administrator of the estates of Allen Dunlap and Matthew Dunlap in Kent County on July 30, 1756. One "Peter Dunlap,

planter" was administrator of the estate of John Dunlap in Kent County on May 24, 1758. [Ref: DK-165, DK-176].

DUNN, John. Private. Served in Capt. Charles Pope's Company of the Delaware Regiment of Continental Troops. Enlisted January 15, 1776, and was on duty (in quarters) at Lewis Town on April 11, 1776. [Ref: DA-51].

DUNN, Patrick. Private. Served in Capt. Joseph Stedham's Company, Delaware Battalion of Continental Troops. Enlisted on February 2, 1776, and was in quarters at Dover on April 12, 1776. [Ref: DA-39].

DUNN, Thomas. Lieutenant. Served in Capt. Samuel Patterson's Company, White Clay Creek Hundred, Upper Regiment, in New Castle County, 1756, during the French and Indian Wars. [Ref: DA-11].

DUPRE, John. Land patentee and probable militiaman in Delaware in November, 1677. [Ref: DP-167, 168].

DURAGHAN, John and Martha. See "Samuel Platt," q.v.

DURBORROW, Hugh and Susanna. See "Matthew Lowber," q.v.

DURBORROW, Isaac. Private. Enlisted on May 28, 1758, in Capt. French Battell's Company of Lower County Provincials, during the French and Indian Wars. [Ref: DA-16].

DURGAN, Martha. See "Samuel Platt," q.v.

DUSHANE, Benjamin. Private. Served in Capt. Samuel Smith's Company, Delaware Regiment of Continental Troops. Enlisted on March 4, 1776, and was on duty (in barracks) at Dover on April 12, 1776. [Ref: DA-54, DA-56]. (This source also spelled his name "Benjamin Deshane").

DUSHANE, Isaac. Ensign. Served in Capt. David Steward's Company, New Castle County, 1747-1748, in King George's War against Canada. [Ref: DA-7]. (Also spelled "Dusheene").

DUSHANE, Jerome. Lieutenant. Served in Capt. David Steward's Company, New Castle County, 1747-1748, in King George's War against Canada. He was also a lieutenant in Capt. John Jones' Company, St. George's Hundred, Lower Regiment, New Castle County, 1756, in the French and Indian Wars. [Ref: DA-7, 11]. "Jerome Dushane, yeoman," died in Red Lion Hundred and his will was probated March 29, 1775, naming wife Hannah, sons Jesse, Anthony, and Thomas, and daughters Hannah, Mary, Katharine, Elizabeth, Margaret, Jaminia, and Francina Martin (wife of Jacob). [Ref: DN-79]. (Also spelled "Dusheene").

DUTTON, Henry. Private. Served in Capt. Joseph Stedham's Company, Delaware Battalion of Continental Troops. Enlisted on January 20, 1776, and was in quarters at Dover on April 12, 1776. [Ref: DA-39].

DUTZ, Samuel. Private. Served in Capt. Richard McWilliams' Company, New Castle County. Enlisted on December 28, 1757, during the French and Indian Wars. [Ref: DA-15].

DUX, Paulus. Soldier. Planter in Delaware who paid his quit-rent to the governor in 1668. [Ref: DP-28]. "Paul Dux and his wife Alice" received a land patent "upon the second hook or neck of land above ye fort at Delaware" on August 1, 1668. (The record also spelled the names as "Paul Duxon" and wife Alice.). [Ref: DY-134].

DYER, Henry. Captain. Served in a New Castle County Company, 1747-1748, in King George's War against Canada. [Ref: DA-7]. One Henry Dyer died testate in New Castle County circa 1748-1749, naming his wife Mary, but the date of probate was not indicated. [Ref: DN-40].

DYER, James. Private. Served in Capt. Richard McWilliams' Company, New Castle County. Enlisted on December 28, 1757, during the French and Indian Wars. [Ref: DA-15].

DYER, Joseph. Drummer and fifer. Served in Capt. Nathan Adams' Company, Delaware Regiment of Continental Troops. Enlisted on February 16, 1776, and was on duty (in barracks) at Dover on April 12, 1776. [Ref: DA-52].

DYRE, William. Major. In Rehoboth Hundred, Sussex County, he held that rank by 1687 as noted in the quit-rents between 1701 and 1713. His daughter Mary married Richard Cantwell prior to 1699. [Ref: DR-50]. Actually, Major William Dyre died testate in Sussex County and his will was probated on June 5, 1688, naming his wife Mary, eldest son William Dyre (of Boston), youngest son Edmund Dyre, son James Dyre, eldest daughter Sarah Dyre and youngest daughter Mary Dyre. A later account mentioned [his] deceased father William Dyre. [Ref: DS-12]. Major William Dyre also served in the General Assembly of Pennsylvania in 1687. [Ref: DC-52]. See "Nathaniel Walker," q.v.

EADES, Jonathan. Private. Served in Capt. Charles Pope's Company, Delaware Regiment of Continental Troops. Enlisted January 18, 1776, and was on duty (in quarters) at Lewis Town on April 11, 1776, at which time he was reported "sick in quarters." [Ref: DA-50, DA-51].

ECCLES, Robert. Private. Served in Capt. Joseph Stedham's Company, Delaware Battalion of Continental Troops. Enlisted on January 19, 1776, and was in quarters at Dover on April 12, 1776. [Ref: DA-39].

ECCLES, William. Private. Served in Capt. Joseph Stedham's Company, Delaware Battalion of Continental Troops. Enlisted on January 17, 1776, and was in quarters at Dover on April 12, 1776. [Ref: DA-39].

EDG, Peter. Private. Served in Capt. Nathan Adams' Company of the Delaware Regiment of Continental Troops. Enlisted on February 4, 1776, and was on duty (in barracks) at Dover on April 12, 1776. [Ref: DA-53].

EDGIN, Benjamin. Private. Born 1735, Maryland. Enlisted in Capt. John Wright's Company and was on the muster roll of May 11, 1759, during the French and Indian Wars. [Ref: DA-25].

EDINGFIELD, John. Private. Served in Capt. Jonathan Caldwell's Company, Delaware Regiment of Continental Troops. Enlisted January 18, 1776, and on duty (in barracks) at Dover on April 12, 1776. [Ref: DA-41].

EDINGFIELD, William. Private. Served in Capt. Jonathan Caldwell's Company, Delaware Regiment of Continental Troops. Enlisted January 16, 1776, and on duty (in barracks) at Dover on April 12, 1776. [Ref: DA-41].

EDSALL, Samuell. Soldier. Planter in Delaware who paid his quit-rent to the governor in 1669. [Ref: DP-27, 28].

EDWARDS, James. Captain. Served in a Kent County Company, August, 1748, in King George's War against Canada. [Ref: DA-8]. One James Edwards died in Duck Creek Hundred and his will was probated on August 11, 1774, naming his sons John and Joshua. [Ref: DK-291].

EDWARDS, John. Captain. Served in a New Castle County Company in August, 1748, during King George's War against Canada. [Ref: DA-7]. One John Edwards, yeoman, died testate in Pencader Hundred, New Castle County, and his nuncupative will was probated on April 25, 1780, naming wife Hannah, daughter Hannah and her husband (no name given), and two youngest daughters (no names given). [Ref: DN-94].

EDWARDS, Josiah. Private. Born 1737, Wales. Tailor. Enlisted on April 22, 1758, in the French and Indian Wars, by Capt. Benjamin Noxon. [Ref: DA-19].

EDWARDS, Samuel. Pilot. Lived in Sussex County near Lewes Creek by February 1, 1773, at which time he and his wife Mary, and William Maull, shipwright, conveyed land to John Maull. [Ref: DD-89, 90].

EGBERTSON, James. Lieutenant. Served in Capt. George Gano's Company in New Castle County during 1747-1748, in King George's War against Canada. [Ref: DA-7].

EGLIN, Richard. Private. Served in Capt. Charles Pope's Company, Delaware Regiment of Continental Troops. Enlisted January 10, 1776, and was on duty (in quarters) at Lewis Town on April 11, 1776. [Ref: DA-51].

EKEN, Bernard. Soldier. Planter who paid his quit-rent to the governor in 1669, having received a patent "at Delaware" on May 28, 1669. [Ref: DP-27, DY-159]. (Name also spelled "Ekon").

ELIAS TOOBAKZPLANTERE. Officer. Served at the Upland Plantation in the Swedish settlement on the Delaware, 1643-1644. [Ref: DJ-704]. (No last name was given. He was simply listed as "Elias the Tobacco Planter," or *toobakzplantere*, an unusual name for an "officer").

ELLIOTT, John. Ensign. Served in Capt. William Empson's Company, Brandywine Hundred, Upper Regiment, New Castle County, 1756, during the French and Indian War. [Ref: DA-11]. "John Elliott, innholder," died in Brandywine Hundred and his will was probated on June 16, 1776, naming his wife Chloe, son Edward, daughters Margaret and Susannah, and brother Thomas. [Ref: DN-79]. A "John Elliot, Esq., Captain of Marines in the Continental Navy," died testate and his will was probated in New Castle County on May 8, 1779, naming his wife (no name given), mother Christian Elliot, brother James Elliot (of New Jersey), sisters Jean Johnston (otherways Elliot) and Sarah Elliott, (of Ireland), cousin Capt. Samuel Corry (of Philadelphia), and Mrs. Elizabeth Hatch (otherways Lehr) of Boston. [Ref: DN-92].

ELMS, Christopher. Drummer. Born 1743, Conococheague, Pennsylvania. Laborer. Enlisted on May 6, 1758, during the French and Indian Wars by Capt. John McClughan "for the campaign in the lower counties." [Ref: DA-17].

ELSWICK, Hendrick. See "Hendrick von Elswick," q.v.

ELVES, Henry. See "Andrew Frauberg [Tranberg]," q.v.

EMORY, Margaret. See "Richard Manwaring," q.v.

EMPSON, William. Captain. Served in a company in Brandywine Hundred in Upper Regiment, New Castle County, 1756, during the French and Indian Wars. [Ref: DA-11, DM-45].

ENDLESS, John. Private. Born 1724, Gregory Strohe, England. Enlisted on April 24, 1758, in the French and Indian Wars, by Capt. John McClughan "for the campaign in lower counties." [Ref: DA-17].

ENLOE, Thomas. Mariner. Died intestate in Kent County and Richbell Mott was named his administrator on March 17, 1758. [Ref: DK-174].

ENNIS, Robert. Private. Born 1736, Scotland. Weaver. Enlisted on May 3, 1758, during the French and Indian Wars, by Capt. Benjamin Noxon. [Ref: DA-19].

ENOS, Joseph. Private. Served in Capt. Richard McWilliams' Company, New Castle County. Enlisted on December 28, 1757, during the French and Indian Wars. [Ref: DA-14].

ENOS, Richard. Private. Served in Capt. Richard McWilliams' Company, New Castle County. Enlisted on December 28, 1757, during the French and Indian Wars. [Ref: DA-14].

ENOS, Stephen. Private. Served in Capt. Richard McWilliams' Company, New Castle County. Enlisted on December 28, 1757, during the French and Indian Wars. [Ref: DA-14].

ENSLEY, John. Private. Born 1725, Ireland. Cooper. Enlisted in Capt. John Shannon's Company of Foot on July 10, 1746, and served in King George's War against Canada. He signed his name when paid for his services on June 6, 1747. He was in winter quarters at Albany, New York, during 1746-1747, and was discharged on October 31, 1747. [Ref: DA-4, DA-5, DA-6, DM-40].

ERICKSE, Jan. Soldier. Planter who paid his quit-rent to the governor in 1668. [Ref: DP-28]. "Jan Erickson" received a land patent on Christine Kill on March 24, 1668/9. [Ref: DY-136].

ERICKSSON, Johan. Soldier. From Angermanland in northeastern Sweden (bordering on the Gulf of Bothnia), he was hired by Mans Kling as a laborer in 1641 and arrived in New Sweden in 1641. "Jan Ericsson" became a soldier on October 1, 1646, and deserted in 1651, leaving a debt of 1,071 *florins* behind. [Ref: DJ-711, DH-45].

ERICKSSON, Olof. Sailor. He was "one of the laboring people at Fort Tinicum who was appointed to cut hay for the cattle and also in the meantime to follow the governor [Johan Printz] on the little sloop" (i. e., the governor's yacht) in 1643. [Ref: DJ-706, DH-45].

ERSKIN, John. Soldier. Planter in Delaware who paid his quit-rent to the governor in 1667, having received a land patent on Christine Kill on January 19, 1667. [Ref: DP-27, DY-128]. He was referred to as "Sergeant Erskin" in 1670. [Ref: DY-146].

ESBJORNSSON, Lars. Soldier. Hired in Stockholm in 1653 and arrived in New Sweden on the ship *Orn* in 1654. One "Lars Essbiornsson, the tailor" was on a list of the soldiers who returned to Europe with Director Rising in 1655. [Ref: DJ-718, 724].

ESCHELSON, Mattys. Soldier. Planter in Delaware who paid his quit-rent to the governor in 1668, having been granted land by Alexander D'Hiniosa, late governor at Delaware, on August 3, 1668. [Ref: DP-28, DY-135].

ESHON, John. Corporal. Served in Capt. Joseph Vaughan's Company, Delaware Regiment of Continental Troops. Enlisted January 20, 1776, and on duty (in barracks) at Dover on April 12, 1776. [Ref: DA-59].

ESKELSSON, Abraham. Soldier. Arrived in New Sweden on the ship *Orn* in 1654. [Ref: DJ-718].

ESKILSONN, Bertil. Officer. Son of Eskil Larsson. Served at Fort Tinicum in 1643. One "Bertill (Bartill) Eskilsson, the Finn" lived at the Schuylkill Plantation in 1654. [Ref: DJ-706, DJ-718, DH-45].

ESSARY, James. Private. Born 1715, England. Laborer. Enlisted in Capt. John Shannon's Company of Foot on August 2, 1746, and served in King George's War against Canada. He was in winter quarters at Albany, New York, during 1746-1747, and was discharged on October 31, 1747. [Ref: DA-4, DA-6]. However, Source DM-40 stated that a "James Issely" [same person?] was listed as a deserter.

EUSTACE, John. Soldier. Planter in Delaware who paid his quit-rent to the governor in 1669. [Ref: DP-27, 28]. "John Eustas" was granted a land patent on May 16, 1669. [Ref: DY-144].

EVANS, Daniel. Private. Enlisted on May 28, 1758, in Capt. French Battell's Company of Lower County Provincials, during the French and Indian Wars. [Ref: DA-16].

EVANS, Elizabeth. See "Samuel Platt," q.v.

EVANS, John. Private. Born 1740, Maryland. Enlisted in Capt. John Wright's Company and was on the muster roll of May 11, 1759, during the French and Indian Wars. [Ref: DA-25].

EVANS, John. Private. Served in Capt. Henry Darby's Company of the Delaware Regiment of Continental Troops. Enlisted January 29, 1776, and on duty (in barracks) at Dover on April 12, 1776. [Ref: DA-46].

EVANS, Solomon. Private. Born 1710, New Castle, Delaware. Whitesmith. Enlisted in Capt. John Shannon's Company of Foot on July 2, 1746, and served in King George's War against Canada. He signed his name when he was paid for his services on June 6, 1747. He was in winter quarters at Albany, New York, 1746-1747, and was discharged on October 31, 1747. [Ref: DA-4, DA-6, DM-40].

EVES, James. Private. Served in Capt. Richard McWilliams' Company, New Castle County. Enlisted on December 28, 1757, during the French and Indian Wars. [Ref: DA-14].

EVES, John. Private. Served in Capt. Richard McWilliams' Company, New Castle County. Enlisted on December 28, 1757, during the French and Indian Wars. [Ref: DA-15].

EVES, William. Soldier. Planter in Delaware who paid his quit-rent to the governor in 1671, having been granted land on west side of Delaware Bay, June 16, 1671. [Ref: DP-29, DY-152].

EWART, Robert. Sergeant. Served in Capt. Joseph Vaughan's Company, Delaware Regiment of Continental Troops. Enlisted January 16, 1776, and on duty (in barracks) at Dover on April 12, 1776. [Ref: DA-59].

FAGAN, Garratt. Private. Served in Capt. Jonathan Caldwell's Company, Delaware Regiment of Continental Troops. Enlisted January 27, 1776, and was on duty (in barracks) at Dover on April 12, 1776, at which time he was reported to be sick. [Ref: DA-41].

FARIES, William. Lieutenant. Served in Capt. Timothy Griffith's Company, New Castle County, 1747-1748, in King George's War against Canada. [Ref: DA-7]. One "William Faries, farmer," died in Pencader Hundred, New Castle County, and his will was probated on January 5, 1787, naming his sons William, John, and James, daughters Mary Ann Murphey, Mary Scott, Jane Adair, Hannah Brown, and Agness Faries, and wife (no name given). [Ref: DN-111]. (Also spelled "Ferris").

FARON, Margaret and William. See "Thomas Montgomery," q.v.

FARRELL, James. Private. Born 1727, Maryland. Laborer. Enlisted on April 15, 1758, during the French and Indian Wars, by Capt. John McClughan (or Capt. Benjamin Noxon) "for the campaign in the lower counties." [Ref: DA-18, 19].

FERREL, Robert. Private. Served in Capt. Jonathan Caldwell's Company, Delaware Regiment of Continental Troops. Enlisted January 16, 1776, and on duty (in barracks) at Dover on April 12, 1776. [Ref: DA-41].

FIELD, Nehemiah. Pilot. Lived in Sussex County in the town of Lewes by January 1, 1769, at which time he purchased a lot on 2nd Street from Henry Fisher and Abraham Wiltbank (both pilots). He purchased additional lots on November 4, 1772, in Lewes Town. [Ref: DD-1].

FIELDS, Elizabeth. See "Alexander Chance," q.v.

FINCHWAIT, Sarah. See "Thomas Clarke," q.v.

FINNEY, Archibald. Second Lieutenant. Served as ensign under Capt. Benjamin Noxon on April 24, 1758, during the French and Indian Wars, and promoted to second lieutenant under Capt. Jacob Gooding, Jr. on June 16, 1758. [Ref: DA-16]. This source spelled his name as "Arch. Finig" and stated he was a lieutenant in one of the three companies "of the lower counties" [Delaware] in the 3rd Battalion of the Pennsylvania Regiment under Col. Hugh Mercer, May 22, 1759.

[Ref: DA-20, DM-47, DM-49]. See comments under "Archibald Towney."
FINNEY, David, Esq. Private. Served in Capt. Richard McWilliams' Company, New Castle. Enlisted on December 28, 1757, during the French and Indian Wars. [Ref: DA-15]. (Attorney by profession).
FINNEY, David. Captain. New Castle County Company, 1747-1748, and served in King George's War against Canada. [Ref: DA-7].
FINNEY, John. Lieutenant Colonel. Served in the Upper Regiment, New Castle County, 1756, in French and Indian Wars. He was commissioner for New Castle County in 1759. [Ref: DA-11, DM-45, DM-50].
FISHER, Finwick. See "Caesar Rodney," q.v.
FISHER, Henry. Pilot. Lived in Sussex County in the town of Lewes by January 1, 1769, at which time he and Abraham Wiltbank, pilot, sold a lot on 2nd Street to Nehemiah Field, pilot. [Ref: DD-1].
FISHER, Nicy and Polly. See "Samuel Bevens Turner," q.v.
FISHER, Thomas. Private. Served in Capt. David Hall's Company of the Delaware Regiment of Continental Troops. Enlisted on March 25, 1776, and was on duty (in barracks) at Lewis Town on April 11, 1776. After his name is written "in gaol." [Ref: DA-43].
FITZGERALD, Isaac. Private. Served in Capt. Nathan Adams' Company, Delaware Regiment of Continental Troops. Enlisted January 27, 1776, and on duty (in barracks) at Dover on April 12, 1776. [Ref: DA-53].
FITZGERALD, John. Drummer. Born 1743, Queen Anne's, Maryland. Smith. Enlisted on May 2, 1758, during the French and Indian Wars, by Capt. John McClughan "for the campaign in the lower counties." [Ref: DA-17].
FITZGERALD, Timothy. Private. Served in Capt. Charles Pope's Company, Delaware Regiment of Continental Troops. Enlisted January 15, 1776, and was on duty (in quarters) at Lewis Town on April 11, 1776. [Ref: DA-51].
FITZIMMONS, John. Private. Born 1730, Ireland. Laborer. 5 ft. 4 in. tall. Enlisted at New Castle, Delaware on May 11, 1758, during the French and Indian Wars in "the three lower counties" by Capt. Paul Jackson to serve in the Pennsylvania Troops. [Ref: DA-27]. (It is possible "John Fitzimmons" and "John Fitzsimmons" were the same).
FITZRANDOLPH, Edward. Captain. New Castle County Company, 1747-1748, and served in King George's War against Canada. [Ref: DA-7].
FITZSIMMONS, John. Private. Born 1731, Dublin, Ireland. Laborer. Enlisted on May 11, 1758, during the French and Indian Wars, as a private by Capt. John McClughan "for the campaign in the lower counties." [Ref: DA-17].

FLECHER, John. Private. Served in Capt. Joseph Stedham's Company, Delaware Battalion of Continental Troops. Enlisted on January 28, 1776, and in quarters at Dover on April 12, 1776. [Ref: DA-39].

FLEETWOOD, Johnson. Private. Served in Capt. David Hall's Company, Delaware Regiment of Continental Troops. Enlisted January 17, 1776, and was on duty (in barracks) at Lewis Town on April 11, 1776. [Ref: DA-42].

FLEETWOOD, Purnal. Private. Served in Capt. David Hall's Company, Delaware Regiment of Continental Troops. Enlisted February 3, 1776, and was on duty (in barracks) at Lewis Town on April 11, 1776. [Ref: DA-43].

FLEETWOOD, Thomas. Private. Served in Capt. David Hall's Company, Delaware Regiment of Continental Troops. Enlisted on February 19, 1776, and was on duty (in barracks) at Lewis Town on April 11, 1776. [Ref: DA-43].

FLEMING, John. Private. Served in Capt. David Hall's Company of the Delaware Regiment of Continental Troops. Enlisted January 23, 1776, and was on duty (in barracks) at Lewis Town on April 11, 1776. [Ref: DA-43].

FLEMING, Klas Larsson. Officer. One of the great names in Swedish history, he was born in 1592 and during his life occupied various responsible positions in the kingdom, including the reorganization of the Swedish Navy. "From the first he took charge of the affairs of the New Sweden Company, and had he lived, it is likely that New Sweden would not have been so greatly neglected. He was killed by a stray bullet from a Danish battery on July 26, 1644." [Ref: DJ-680]. See "Matts Hansson," q.v.

FLEMMING, Archibald. Lieutenant. Served in Capt. Robert Killen's Company, in middle part of Mispillim [Mispillion] Hundred, Kent County, upon Delaware, 1756, during the French and Indian Wars. [Ref: DA-12]. One "Archibald Fleming" died testate in Kent County and his will was probated April 26, 1783, naming his wife Easther, his sons Samuel, George, Andrew, and Alexander, daughters Sarah, Barbary, and Isabel, and his granddaughters Elizabeth and Amilia Fleming (the daughters of son Joseph). [Ref: DK-349]. The will of Isabel Fleming was probated on the same day (April 26, 1783) and she named her sons James, Matthew, Robert, Joseph, and Archibald Fleming, and daughter Cathran Mittan. One of the witnesses was Archibald Fleming, Jr. [Ref: DK-349].

FLEMMING, Archibald. Private. Served in Capt. Nathan Adams' Company of the Delaware Regiment of Continental Troops. Enlisted on January 20, 1776, and on duty (in barracks) at Dover on April 12, 1776. [Ref: DA-52].
FLEMMING, George. Private. Served in Capt. Nathan Adams' Company, Delaware Regiment of Continental Troops. Enlisted January 20, 1776, and on duty (in barracks) at Dover on April 12, 1776. [Ref: DA-52].
FLEMMING, Robert. Private. Served in Capt. Nathan Adams' Company, Delaware Regiment of Continental Troops. Enlisted January 20, 1776, and on duty (in barracks) at Dover on April 12, 1776. [Ref: DA-52].
FLINN, Patrick. Private. Served in Capt. Joseph Stedham's Company, Delaware Battalion of Continental Troops. Enlisted on January 22, 1776, and was in quarters at Dover on April 12, 1776. [Ref: DA-39].
FLINN, Thomas. Private. Served in Capt. Jonathan Caldwell's Company of the Delaware Regiment of Continental Troops. Enlisted on January 17, 1776, and was on duty (in barracks) at Dover on April 12, 1776. [Ref: DA-41].
FLOOD, John. Private. Born 1725, Ireland. Tailor. Enlisted in Capt. John Shannon's Company of Foot on July 15, 1746, and served in King George's War against Canada. He was in winter quarters at Albany, New York, during 1746-1747, and was discharged on October 31, 1747. [Ref: DA-4, DA-6]. (He is not listed in Source DM-40.)
FLOYD, Charles. Soldier. Planter who paid his quit-rent to the governor in 1667. [Ref: DP-27]. He received a land patent in Delaware "lying behind ye town of New Castle" on September 1, 1669, in return for having been a "soldier who came over into these parts in his Majesty's service." [Ref: DY-160].
FLOYD, Gertrude. See "John Gooding," q.v.
FLUVIANDER, Israel Holg. Reverend. Military preacher (*predikanten*). An "officer" at Fort Elfsborg, he "was the son of Governor Printz's sister." He came to America in 1643 and remained here until March, 1647, when he returned home to Sweden. [Ref: DJ-681, 703, 709].
FORBES, John. See "John Furbush," q.v.
FORCUM, John. Private. Served in Capt. Nathan Adams' Company of the Delaware Regiment of Continental Troops. Enlisted January 26, 1776, and on duty (in barracks) at Dover on April 12, 1776. [Ref: DA-53].
FORD, Benjamin Jr. Lieutenant. Served in Capt. Emanuel Grubb's Company, Brandywine Hundred, Upper Regiment, New Castle County, 1756, during the French and Indian War. [Ref: DA-11]. A "Benjamin

Ford, yeoman," died in Brandywine Hundred and his will was probated on February 9, 1774, naming the following: "widow and six children, Benjamin, and David, and Elizabeth Howell, Mary Deriskson, Hannah Perkins, and Jane Golden; three youngest sons, William, Philip and Joseph Ford; four youngest daughters Prudence, Jemima, Ann, and Sarah." His son-in-law Thomas Perkins was executor. [Ref: DN-74].

FORD, Elizabeth. See "Joseph Merideth," q.v.

FORD, Isaac. Private. Served in Capt. Charles Pope's Company of the Delaware Regiment of Continental Troops. Enlisted January 20, 1776, and was on duty (in quarters) at Lewis Town on April 11, 1776. [Ref: DA-51].

FORD, Jacob. Private. Served in Capt. John Caton's Company, April 25, 1757, in the French and Indian Wars. [Ref: DA-14].

FORD, Jehosephat. Private. Served in Capt. John Caton's Company on April 25, 1757, in the French and Indian Wars. [Ref: DA-14].

FORD, John. Private. Served in Capt. John Caton's Company, April 25, 1757, in the French and Indian Wars. [Ref: DA-14]. One John Ford died testate in Kent County and his will was probated on January 16, 1773, naming his wife Mary, sons James, John, Isaac, Thomas, Jessy, William, Robart, Edward, Richard, and daughters Elizabeth, Haziel, Rachel, Ann, Mary, and Barshby. [Ref: DK-272].

FORD, Ruben. Private. Served in Capt. Joseph Stedham's Company of the Delaware Battalion of Continental Troops. Enlisted January 25, 1776, and was in quarters at Dover on April 12, 1776. [Ref: DA-39].

FORD, Thomas. Private. Served in Capt. Charles Pope's Company of the Delaware Regiment of Continental Troops. Enlisted January 18, 1776, and was on duty (in quarters) at Lewis Town on April 11, 1776. [Ref: DA-51].

FORD, William. Private. Served in Capt. Nathan Adams' Company of the Delaware Regiment of Continental Troops. Enlisted on March 29, 1776, and was on duty (in barracks) at Dover on April 12, 1776, at which time he was reported to be "sick in quarters." [Ref: DA-53].

FORKCUM, John. Private. Served in Capt. John Caton's Company on April 25, 1757, in the French and Indian Wars. [Ref: DA-13]. The administration of the estate of one "John Forcum" was granted to Joshua Forcum in Kent County on October 29, 1791. [Ref: DK-449]. Also see "John Forcum," q.v.

FORKCUM, Renn. Private. Served in Capt. John Caton's Company, April 25, 1757, in the French and Indian Wars. [Ref: DA-13]. John Rash died testate in Kent County and his will was probated on January 3, 1761.

Among his heirs was daughter "Hannah Forkham, wife of Renn Forkham." Also, "Wren Forkham" witnessed the will of Joseph Howell in Murderkill Hundred, August 13, 1756. [Ref: DK-166, 192].

FORKHAM, Renn and Hannah. See "John Rash," q.v.

FORREST, Samuel. Private. Born 1723, England. Laborer. Enlisted in Capt. John Shannon's Company of Foot on July 21, 1746, and served in King George's War against Canada. He was in winter quarters at Albany, New York, during 1746-1747, and was discharged on October 31, 1747. [Ref: DA-4, DA-6]. (He is not listed in Source DM-40.)

FORSMAN, Gabriel Samuelson. Soldier. Arrived in New Sweden on the ship *Orn* in 1654. [Ref: DJ-718].

FORSTER, James. Second Lieutenant. Served in the War of Jenkins' Ear in 1739-1741 in a company which may have included soldiers from Delaware (muster rolls not extant). [Ref: DM-32].

FORTESCUE, Aaron. Private. Served in Capt. David Hall's Company, Delaware Regiment of Continental Troops. Enlisted January 17, 1776, and was on duty (in barracks) at Lewis Town on April 11, 1776. [Ref: DA-42].

FOSTER, Fucher. Private. Born 1730, Rehoboth, Delaware. Planter. Enlisted on April 20, 1758, in the French and Indian Wars, by Capt. John McClughan "for the campaign in lower counties." [Ref: DA-17].

FOSTER, William. Private. Born 1731, Maryland. Enlisted in Capt. John Wright's Company and was on the muster roll of May 11, 1759, during the French and Indian Wars. [Ref: DA-25].

FOSTER, William. Private. Served in Capt. David Hall's Company, Delaware Regiment of Continental Troops. Enlisted January 22, 1776, and was on duty (in barracks) at Lewis Town on April 11, 1776. [Ref: DA-43].

FOSTER, William. Private. Served in Capt. Jonathan Caldwell's Company, Delaware Regiment of Continental Troops. Enlisted March 31, 1776, and on duty (in barracks) at Dover on April 12, 1776. [Ref: DA-41].

FOURLOUNG, Edward. Land patentee and probable militiaman in Delaware in November, 1677. [Ref: DP-167, 168].

FOWLER, Rebecca. See "John Gooding," q.v.

FOWLER, Rhoda. See "Cord Hazzard," q.v.

FRANCES, Hubertos. Land patentee and probable militiaman in Delaware in November, 1677. [Ref: DP-167, 168].

FRANKLIN, William. Ensign. Commissioned in Capt. John Deimer's Company on June 4, 1746, during King George's War against Canada.

He was in winter quarters at Albany, New York, during 1746-1747, and his company was discharged on October 31, 1747. [Ref: DA-6].

FRAUBERG [TRANBERG?], Andrew. Captain. Served in a militia company in Christiana Hundred, Upper Regiment, New Castle County, in 1756, during the French and Indian Wars. [Ref: DA-11, DM-45]. Although the latter source states his name was "Frauberg," the wills in New Castle County give the name as "Tranberg." One "Peter Tranberg" died testate and his will was probated December 27, 1748, naming his wife Ann Catharine, eldest son, Andrew, son Peter, daughters Rebecca and Elizabeth, and his sister Annika Tranberg in Sweden. Also, "Ann Catherin Tranberg, widow," died testate and her will was probated on October 11, 1764, naming her sister Magdalen Robinson, and daughters Rebeccah Bonzell and Elizabeth Springer (wife of Gabriel), granddaughters Honour Bonzell and Cathrine Parlen, and Mr. Henry Elves. [Ref: DN-43, 61].

FREAME, Thomas. Captain. Served in the War of Jenkins' Ear in 1739-1741 in a company that may have included soldiers from Delaware (muster rolls not extant). [Ref: DM-32].

FREELAND, John. Private. Enlisted on May 13, 1758, in Capt. French Battell's Company of Lower County Provincials, during the French and Indian Wars. [Ref: DA-16].

FRENCH, James. Private. Served in Capt. Charles Pope's Company, Delaware Regiment of Continental Troops. Enlisted January 16, 1776, and was on duty (in quarters) at Lewis Town on April 11, 1776. [Ref: DA-51].

FRENCH, John. Colonel. Died testate in New Castle County and his will was probated on December 12, 1728, naming his wife Eves, daughter Mary ----, son-in-law Capt. William Battell, daughter Sybilla ----, grandson (no name given), son-in-law Robert Robertson, granddaughter Mary Battell, granddaughter Eves ----, granddaughter Mary Robertson, and "daughter Mary French." [Ref: DN-27].

FRIDAY, John Augustus. Private. Born 1739, Hanover, Germany. Laborer. Enlisted on April 23, 1758, during the French and Indian Wars, by Capt. John McClughan "for the campaign in the lower counties." [Ref: DA-17].

FROM, Hindrick Larsson. Soldier. Arrived in New Sweden on the ship *Orn* in 1654. (Footnote: *From* meant *good, pious*). [Ref: DJ-718].

FRUMP, John. See "John Trump," q.v.

FRY, John. Private. Born 1720, England. Laborer. Enlisted in Capt. John Shannon's Company of Foot on July 13, 1746, and served in King

George's War against Canada. He was in winter quarters at Albany, New York, during 1746-1747, and was discharged on October 31, 1747. [Ref: DA-4, DA-6]. (He is not listed in Source DM-40.)

FURBE, Caleb. Ensign. Served in Capt. Daniel James' Company, Lower District of Mother Kill Hundred, Kent County, March 29, 1758. [Ref: DA-15]. One "Caleb Furbee" died intestate in Kent County and "Sarah Furbee" was named his administratrix on May 9, 1796. A subsequent administration account mentioned a "Jacob Furby." [Ref: DK-507].

FURBUSH, John. Private. Served in Capt. Joseph Vaughan's Company, Delaware Regiment of Continental Troops. Enlisted January 19, 1776, and was on duty (in barracks) at Dover on April 12, 1776. [Ref: DA-57, 59]. (This same source also spelled his name "John Forbes").

FURGUSON, Robert. Private. Served in Capt. Joseph Stedham's Company of the Delaware Battalion of Continental Troops. Enlisted January 23, 1776, and in quarters at Dover on April 12, 1776. [Ref: DA-39].

FURNANTZ, Anthony. Private. Born 1727, Maderia, Portugal. Laborer. Enlisted on May 1, 1758, during the French and Indian Wars, as a private by Capt. John McClughan "for the campaign in the lower counties." [Ref: DA-17].

FURNISS, Robert. Private. Served in Capt. Richard McWilliams' Company, New Castle County. Enlisted on December 28, 1757, during the French and Indian Wars. [Ref: DA-15].

FUTCHER, John and William. See "Thomas Prettyman," q.v.

FUTHEY, Henry. Private. Born 1725, England. Laborer. Enlisted in Capt. John Shannon's Company of Foot on July 22, 1746, and served in King George's War against Canada. He signed his name when paid for services on June 6, 1747. He was in winter quarters at Albany, New York, during 1746-1747, and was discharged October 31, 1747. [Ref: DA-4, DA-5, DA-6, DM-40].

GALE, Thomas. Private. Served in Capt. David Hall's Company of the Delaware Regiment of Continental Troops. Enlisted January 17, 1776, and was on duty (in barracks) at Lewis Town on April 11, 1776. [Ref: DA-42].

GALLAGHER, Felix. Private. Born 1724, Ireland. Laborer. Enlisted in Capt. John Shannon's Company of Foot on July 19, 1746, and served in King George's War against Canada. He was in winter quarters at Albany, New York, during 1746-1747, and was discharged on October 31, 1747. [Ref: DA-4, 6]. Source DM-40 spelled his name "Gallaher" and also listed him as a deserter in Capt. Shannon's record book.

GALLAWAY, Richard. Private. Served in Capt. John Caton's Company, April 25, 1757, in the French and Indian Wars. [Ref: DA-13]. One "Richard Galloway" died intestate in Kent County and his widow, Lydia Galloway, was named administratrix on June 6, 1761. A later account showed Lydia married Peter Goforth, and it also mentioned Henrietta Smith, Elizabeth Galloway, Samuel Galloway, and Joseph Galloway as heirs of Richard Galloway. [Ref: DK-195].

GALOON, Roger. Private. Served in Capt. Charles Pope's Company, Delaware Regiment of Continental Troops. Enlisted January 18, 1776, and was on duty (in quarters) at Lewis Town on April 11, 1776. [Ref: DA-51].

GANDY, William. Private. Served in Capt. Henry Darby's Company, Delaware Regiment of Continental Troops. Enlisted on March 25, 1776, and was on duty (in barracks) at Dover on April 12, 1776. [Ref: DA-46].

GANO, Daniel. Private. Born 1737, Delaware. Laborer. Enlisted on April 29, 1758, in the French and Indian Wars, by Capt. Benjamin Noxon. [Ref: DA-19].

GANO, George. Captain. New Castle County Company, 1747-1748, and served in King George's War against Canada. He was also captain of a company in Apoquinamink Hundred, Lower Regiment, in New Castle County, 1756, in French and Indian Wars. [Ref: DA-7, DA-12, DM-46].

GANTHONY, Peter. Sailor. Served on the brigantine *Bleakney* under the command of Mr. Moses Minshall. He died testate in Christiana Hundred in New Castle County by November, 1758, leaving a daughter Ann Ganthony and "cousin" Margaret Smith. [Ref: DN-56].

GARDINER, James M. See "William Rees," q.v.

GARDNER, Mary, and children. See "Samuel Patterson," q.v.

GAREY, John. Private. Born 1721, Sussex, Delaware. Laborer. Enlisted in Capt. John Shannon's Company of Foot on July 15, 1746, and served in King George's War against Canada. He made his mark when paid for services on June 6, 1747. He was in winter quarters at Albany, New York, 1746-1747, and was discharged on October 31, 1747. [Ref: DA-4, DA-5, DA-6, DM-40]. (Name also spelled "Geary").

GARLAND, William. Private. Served in Capt. Charles Pope's Company, Delaware Regiment of Continental Troops. Enlisted January 16, 1776, and was on duty (in quarters) at Lewis Town on April 11, 1776. [Ref: DA-51].

GARRATSON, Cornus [Cornelius]. Private. Served in Capt. Richard McWilliams' Company, New Castle. Enlisted on December 28, 1757, during the French and Indian Wars. [Ref: DA-14].

GARRAWAY, William. Ensign. Served in Capt. John Vance's Company, New Castle County, 1747-1748, in King George's War against Canada. [Ref: DA-7].

GARRETSON, Eliakim. See "Samuel Vanleuvenigh," q.v.

GARRETSON, John. Private. Served in Capt. Joseph Stedham's Company, Delaware Battalion of Continental Troops. Enlisted on January 26, 1776, and was in quarters at Dover on April 12, 1776. [Ref: DA-39].

GARRETT, John. Private. Born 1735, Maryland. Laborer. Enlisted on April 24, 1758, in the French and Indian Wars, by Capt. Benjamin Noxon. [Ref: DA-19]. A John Garrett (February 19, 1737 - March 23, 1806), New Castle County, Delaware, served as a militia captain in the Revolutionary War. [Ref: DF-2].

GARRETT, Richard. Private. Born 1738, Maryland. Laborer. Enlisted on May 1, 1758, in the French and Indian Wars, by Capt. Benjamin Noxon. [Ref: DA-19].

GARRETT, Robert. Private. Served in Capt. Jonathan Caldwell's Company, Delaware Regiment of Continental Troops. Enlisted February 1, 1776, and on duty (in barracks) at Dover on April 12, 1776. [Ref: DA-41].

GARRISON, Alpheus. Private. Served in Capt. Nathan Adams' Company, Delaware Regiment of Continental Troops. Enlisted January 16, 1776, and on duty (in barracks) at Dover on April 12, 1776. [Ref: DA-52].

GARRISON, Benjamin. Private. Born 1737, New Castle, Delaware. Laborer. Enlisted on April 25, 1759, in the French and Indian Wars, in Capt. James Armstrong's Company in the Pennsylvania Regiment. [Ref: DA-26].

GARRISON, John. Private. Born 1740, New Castle, Delaware. Laborer. Enlisted on May 20, 1759, in the French and Indian Wars, in Capt. James Armstrong's Company in Pennsylvania Regiment. [Ref: DA-26].

GAUF, Nathan. Private. Served in Capt. Jonathan Caldwell's Company, Delaware Regiment of Continental Troops. Enlisted January 18, 1776, and on duty (in barracks) at Dover on April 12, 1776. [Ref: DA-41].

GEORGE, Richard. First Lieutenant. Served in the War of Jenkins' Ear in 1739-1741 in a company which may have included soldiers from Delaware (muster rolls not extant). [Ref: DM-32].

GERRARD, William. See "William Rhoades," q.v.

GERRITS, Martin. Soldier. Planter in Delaware who paid his quit-rent to the governor in 1667, having received a land grant on Christeen Creek on January 19, 1667. [Ref: DP-27, DY-128].

GERTSE, Evert. Soldier. Planter in Delaware who paid his quit-rent to the governor in 1669. [Ref: DP-27, 28]. "Evert Gertsen" received a patent to a piece of land in New Castle town between Otter and Calves Street on March 26, 1669. [Ref: DY-139].

GETTEGEN, Patrick. Private. Served in Capt. Joseph Stedham's Company, Delaware Battalion of Continental Troops. Enlisted January 27, 1776, and in quarters at Dover on April 12, 1776. [Ref: DA-39].

GIBBENS, Samuel. Private. Served in Capt. Joseph Vaughan's Company, Delaware Regiment of Continental Troops. Enlisted February 9, 1776, and on duty (in barracks) at Dover on April 12, 1776. [Ref: DA-59].

GIBBIN, Daniel. Private. Born 1737, Ireland. Laborer. Enlisted on May 3, 1758, during the French and Indian Wars, by Capt. Benjamin Noxon. [Ref: DA-19].

GIBBONS, John. Private. Born 1730, Devon, England. Labor. Enlisted on April 26, 1758, during the French and Indian Wars, by Capt. John McClughan "for the campaign in the lower counties." [Ref: DA-17].

GIBBONS, John. Private. Served in Capt. Samuel Smith's Company, Delaware Regiment of Continental Troops. Enlisted January 29, 1776, and on duty (in barracks) at Dover on April 12, 1776. [Ref: DA-54].

GIBBONS, Steven. Private. Served in Capt. Samuel Smith's Company, Delaware Regiment of Continental Troops. Enlisted February 4, 1776, and on duty (in barracks) at Dover on April 12, 1776. [Ref: DA-54].

GIBSON, William. Private. Born 1729, Ireland. Laborer. Enlisted on April 27, 1759, in the French and Indian Wars, in Capt. James Armstrong's Company in the Pennsylvania Regiment. [Ref: DA-26].

GILLESPIE, John. Private. Served in Capt. Henry Darby's Company, Delaware Regiment of Continental Troops. Enlisted January 25, 1776, and on duty (in barracks) at Dover on April 12, 1776. [Ref: DA-46].

GILMOR, William. Private. Born 1741, Kent, Delaware. Tailor. Enlisted by Capt. John Hasslet on May 10, 1758, during the French and Indian Wars, from "the three lower counties" to serve in the Pennsylvania Troops. [Ref: DA-27].

GLEGHORN, Matthew. Private. Born 1724, Ireland. Laborer. Enlisted on May 8, 1758, in the French and Indian Wars, by Capt. Benjamin Noxon. [Ref: DA-19].

GLOVER, William. Private. Served in Capt. Samuel Smith's Company, Delaware Regiment of Continental Troops. Enlisted January 21, 1776, and on duty (in barracks) at Dover on April 12, 1776. [Ref: DA-54].

GOFORTH, Peter. See "Richard Gallaway," q.v.

GOGGIN, John. Private. Served in Capt. Joseph Stedham's Company, Delaware Battalion of Continental Troops. Enlisted on January 24, 1776, and was in quarters at Dover on April 12, 1776. [Ref: DA-39].

GOLDEN, Anthony. Ensign. Served in Capt. David Witherspoon's Company, New Castle County, 1747-1748, in King George's War against Canada. [Ref: DA-7]. "Abraham Golden, Sr., yeoman" died testate in St. George's Hundred and his will was probated on July 7, 1749, naming wife Ann and a son Anthony (among others). [Ref: DN-45].

GOLDEN, Eleazer. Private. Born 1724, Cape May, New Jersey. Sailor (by occupation). Enlisted on April 25, 1758, during the French and Indian Wars, as a private by Capt. John McClughan "for the campaign in the lower counties." [Ref: DA-17].

GOLDEN, Jane. See "Benjamin Ford," q.v.

GOLDEN, Maria and John. See "Francis Janvier," q.v.

GOODFELLOW, Daniel. Private. Born 1726, Ireland. Laborer. Enlisted in Capt. John Shannon's Company of Foot on July 21, 1746, and he served in King George's War against Canada. He made his mark when paid for services on June 6, 1747. He was in winter quarters at Albany, New York, during 1746-1747, and was discharged on October 31, 1747. [Ref: DA-4, DA-5, DA-6, DM-40].

GOODING, Isaac. Ensign. Served in Capt. John Jones' Company, St. George's Hundred, Lower Regiment, New Castle County, 1756, during the French and Indian Wars. [Ref: DA-11].

GOODING, Jacob. Captain. Served in a company in Red Lyon [Lion] Hundred, Lower Regiment, New Castle County, 1756, during the French and Indian Wars. [Ref: DA-12, DM-46].

GOODING, Jacob Jr. First Lieutenant. Commissioned on April 18, 1758, during the French and Indian Wars, and promoted to captain under Major Richard Wells on June 13, 1758, when Capt. Benjamin Noxon resigned. [Ref: DA-16, DM-47].

GOODING, John. Captain. New Castle County Company, 1747-1748, and served in King George's War against Canada. [Ref: DA-7]. One "John Gooding, Esq." died testate in Duck Creek Hundred in Kent County and his will was probated on October 24, 1760, naming his wife Sarah, son John, daughters Rebecca Fowler and Gertrude Floyd, and grandchildren William and Susannah Gooding. [Ref: DK-190]. (See "John Gooding, Sr.," q.v. This information might pertain to him.)

GOODING, John. Private. Served in Capt. John Caton's Company, April 25, 1757, in the French and Indian Wars. [Ref: DA-14].

GOODING, John Sr. Colonel. New Castle County Regiment, 1747-1748, and served in King George's War against Canada. [Ref: DA-7]. (See "Capt. John Gooding" for possible information on this John, Sr.)

GOODRICH, John. Corporal. Served in Capt. Charles Pope's Company, Delaware Regiment of Continental Troops. Enlisted January 19, 1776, and was on duty (in quarters) at Lewis Town on April 11, 1776. [Ref: DA-51].

GORDON, Archibald. Captain. Served in the War of Jenkins' Ear in 1739-1741. His company may have included soldiers from Delaware (muster rolls not extant). [Ref: DM-32].

GORDON, James. Private. Served in Capt. Henry Darby's Company, Delaware Regiment of Continental Troops. Enlisted January 25, 1776, and on duty (in barracks) at Dover on April 12, 1776. [Ref: DA-46].

GORDON, James. Second Lieutenant. Served in 6th Company, Delaware State Troops in Continental Service. Commissioned on January 19, 1776, and was on duty (in barracks) with Capt. Nathan Adams and the Delaware Regiment of Continental Troops at Dover on April 12, 1776. [Ref: DA-34, 36, 52].

GORDON, Mary and Elizabeth. See "Caesar Rodney," q.v.

GORDON, Patrick. Private. Served in Capt. Jonathan Caldwell's Company, Delaware Regiment of Continental Troops. Enlisted February 18, 1776 and on duty (in barracks) at Dover on April 12, 1776. [Ref: DA-41].

GORDON, Robert. Private. Served in Capt. John Caton's Company on April 25, 1757, in the French and Indian Wars. [Ref: DA-13]. One Robert Gordon died testate in Kent County and his will was probated on February 15, 1759, naming his wife Filles [Philis], sons John and Robert, brothers James and Seath, and nephew James Darling. A later account shows Philis married William Merydith. [Ref: DK-179].

GOSLIN, John. Private. Served in Capt. Joseph Vaughan's Company, Delaware Regiment of Continental Troops. Enlisted on February 19, 1776, and was on duty (in barracks) at Dover on April 12, 1776. [Ref: DA-58, 59]. (Same source spelled his name "John Gauslin").

GOULD, James. Private. Served in Capt. Joseph Vaughan's Company, Delaware Regiment of Continental Troops. Enlisted on February 16,

1776, and was on duty (in barracks) at Dover on April 12, 1776. [Ref: DA-59].

GRACE, John. See "John Griss," q.v.

GRAHAM, Archibald. First Lieutenant. Served in the War of Jenkins' Ear in 1739-1741 in a company which may have included soldiers from Delaware (muster rolls not extant). [Ref: DM-32].

GRAHAM, Francis. Ensign. Served in Capt. William McCrea's Company, New Castle County, 1747-1748, in King George's War against Canada. [Ref: DA-7]. One "Francis Graham, yeoman," died testate in Mill Creek Hundred in New Castle County, and his will was probated on February 19, 1772, naming wife Jeane, sons William, Robert, Francis and John, and daughters Elizabeth, Mary, and Agnes. [Ref: DN-69].

GRAHAM, Francis. Private. Born 1723, Ireland. Laborer. "Formerly with Sir William Pepperal," enlisted on April 26, 1758, during the French and Indian Wars, by Capt. Benjamin Noxon. [Ref: DA-19].

GRAHAM, John. Private. Born 1737, Slator Neck, Delaware. Laborer. Enlisted on April 24, 1758, in the French and Indian Wars, by Capt. John McClughan "for the campaign in lower counties." [Ref: DA-17].

GRAHAM, Robert. Private. Served in Capt. Jonathan Caldwell's Company, Delaware Regiment of Continental Troops. Enlisted January 16, 1776, and on duty (in barracks) at Dover on April 12, 1776. [Ref: DA-41].

GRANNON, Thomas. Private. Served in Capt. Samuel Smith's Company, Delaware Regiment of Continental Troops. Enlisted on March 28, 1776, and was on duty (in barracks) at Dover on April 12, 1776. [Ref: DA-54].

GRANTLET, John. Private. Born 1735, Maryland. Laborer. Enlisted on April 29, 1758, in the French and Indian Wars, by Capt. Benjamin Noxon. [Ref: DA-19].

GRAY, Benjamin. Private. Born 1741, New Castle, Delaware. Miller. Enlisted May 7, 1759, in the French and Indian Wars, in Capt. James Armstrong's Company in the Pennsylvania Regiment. [Ref: DA-26].

GRAY, James. Private. Served in Capt. Joseph Stedham's Company of the Delaware Battalion of Continental Troops. Enlisted February 2, 1776, and was in quarters at Dover on April 12, 1776. [Ref: DA-39].

GRAY, Thomas. Captain. Served in a company in Mill Creek Hundred, Upper Regiment, New Castle County, 1756, during the French and Indian Wars. [Ref: DA-11, DM-45].

GRAY, William, Jean, and Andrew. See "Andrew Caldwell," q.v.

GREEN, Alice and John. See "Jacob Kollock, Jr.," q.v.

GREEN, Stephen. Mariner. Died testate in Lewes and Rehoboth Hundred and his will was probated August 28, 1780, in Sussex County, naming his brothers Ambrose and Richard and father Stephen. [Ref: DS-135].

GREEN, William. Sergeant. Born 1737, Sussex, Delaware. Carpenter. Served in Capt. John Wright's Company on May 11, 1759, during the French and Indian Wars. [Ref: DA-25]. The administration of the estate of one William Green was granted to Nehemiah Green in Sussex County on June 9, 1790. A later account mentions Patty, Nelly and John Green, deceased. [Ref: DS-217].

GREEN, William. Ensign. Served in Capt. David Marshall's Company, Kent County, June, 1748, during King George's War against Canada. [Ref: DA-8].

GREENWOOD, Joseph. Private. Enlisted on May 18, 1758, in Capt. French Battell's Company of Lower County Provincials, during the French and Indian Wars. [Ref: DA-16]. One Joseph Greenwood died intestate and the administration of his estate was granted to his widow, Sarah, in Kent County on February 3, 1773. [Ref: DK-275].

GREENWOOD, Joseph. Private. Served in Capt. Charles Pope's Company, Delaware Regiment of Continental Troops. Enlisted January 15, 1776, and was on duty (in quarters) at Lewis Town on April 11, 1776. [Ref: DA-51].

GREENWOOD, Joseph. Private. Served in Capt. Nathan Adams' Company, Delaware Regiment of Continental Troops. Enlisted January 15, 1776, and on duty (in barracks) at Dover on April 12, 1776. [Ref: DA-52].

GREGG, John and Alice. See "William Wheeler," q.v.

GREWELL, John. Private. Served in Capt. John Caton's Company, April 25, 1757, in the French and Indian Wars. [Ref: DA-13]. The administration of the estate of one John Grewell was granted to Jonathan Grewell in Kent County on May 11, 1764. [Ref: DK-213].

GRIBBIN, James. Private. Born 1731, Maryland. Laborer. Enlisted on April 29, 1758, in the French and Indian Wars, by Capt. Benjamin Noxon. [Ref: DA-19].

GRIER, Andrew. Private. Served in Capt. Henry Darby's Company, Delaware Regiment of Continental Troops. Enlisted January 27, 1776, and was reported as "deserted" on February 8, 1776. [Ref: DA-46].

GRIFFIN, George. Private. Served in Capt. Charles Pope's Company, Delaware Regiment of Continental Troops. Enlisted January 16, 1776, and was on duty (in quarters) at Lewis Town on April 11, 1776. [Ref: DA-51].

GRIFFITH, John. Private. Served in Capt. Nathan Adams' Company, Delaware Regiment of Continental Troops. Enlisted February 5, 1776, and on duty (in barracks) at Dover on April 12, 1776. [Ref: DA-53].
GRIFFITH, Mary. See "John Rees," q.v.
GRIFFITH, Timothy. Captain. New Castle County Company, 1747-1748, and served in King George's War against Canada. [Ref: DA-7].
GRIMES, Hugh. Private. Served in Capt. Henry Darby's Company of the Delaware Regiment of Continental Troops. Enlisted February 1, 1776, and on duty (in barracks) at Dover on April 12, 1776. [Ref: DA-46].
GRIMES, James. Private. Served in Capt. Samuel Smith's Company, Delaware Regiment of Continental Troops. Enlisted January 21, 1776, and on duty (in barracks) at Dover on April 12, 1776. [Ref: DA-54].
GRIMES, Richard. Private. Served in Capt. Henry Darby's Company, Delaware Regiment of Continental Troops. Enlisted January 31, 1776, and on duty (in barracks) at Dover on April 12, 1776. [Ref: DA-46].
GRISS, John. Private. Served in Capt. Joseph Vaughan's Company, Delaware Regiment of Continental Troops. Enlisted on March 12, 1776, and on duty (in barracks) at Dover when reported "deserted" on April 8, 1776. [Ref: DA-58, 60]. (Name also spelled "Grace").
GRISSAL, William. Private. Born 1726, Stroud, England. Scribler [sic]. Enlisted on May 12, 1758, during the French and Indian Wars, by Capt. John McClughan "for the campaign in the lower counties." [Ref: DA-17].
GRONEBERGH, Constantinos. Soldier. From Mark Brandeborg, he arrived in New Sweden in 1643, and was a common soldier (*saldater*) at Fort Elfsborg, and a freeman by 1654. [Ref: DJ-703, DJ-713, DJ-718, DH-47]. (Name also spelled "Constantinus or Konstantin Grunenborgh").
GROVES, Robert. Drummer and fifer. Served in Capt. David Hall's Company of Delaware Regiment of Continental Troops. Enlisted on February 27, 1776, and was on duty (in barracks) at Lewis Town on April 11, 1776. [Ref: DA-42].
GRUBB, Emanuel. Captain. Served in a company in Brandywine Hundred, Upper Regiment, New Castle County, 1756, during the French and Indian Wars. [Ref: DA-11, DM-45]. An "Emanuel Grubb, yeoman," died testate in Brandywine Hundred and his will was probated on August 19, 1767, naming his wife Ann, sons Emanuel, Thomas, and Benjamin, daughters Edith Thatcher and Ann Black, and the heirs of son Joseph, the heirs of son Nicholas, the heirs of son Peter, and the heirs of son John. [Ref: DN-65]. Another "Emanuel Grubb, yeoman,"

died testate in Brandywine Hundred and his will was probated August 17, 1799, naming wife Anne, sons Benjamin, Peter, James, Nathaniel, and William Ford Grubb, and nephew Amer Grubb. [Ref: DN-148].

GRUBB, John. Private. Born 1732, Brandywine Hundred, Delaware. Tanner. Enlisted on May 11, 1758, during the French and Indian War, by Capt. John McClughan "for the campaign in the lower counties." [Ref: DA-17].

GRUBB, Samuel. Captain. Recruited soldiers from "the three lower counties" [Delaware] to serve in Pennsylvania Troops. [Ref: DA-27].

GRUNDY, Thomas. Private. Born 1725, Liverpool, England. Bricklayer. Enlisted on April 27, 1758, in the French and Indian Wars, by Capt. John McClughan "for the campaign in lower counties." [Ref: DA-17].

GRUNG, Peter. Ensign. Served in the War of Jenkins' Ear in 1739-1741 in a company which may have included soldiers from Delaware (muster rolls not extant). [Ref: DM-32].

GRUNNET, Christopher. Private. Born 1729, Germany. Saddler. Enlisted May 1, 1759, in the French and Indian Wars, in Capt. James Armstrong's Company in the Pennsylvania Regiment. [Ref: DA-26].

GRUWELL, Peter. Private. Served in Capt. Jonathan Caldwell's Company, Delaware Regiment of Continental Troops. Enlisted January 17, 1776, and on duty (in barracks) at Dover on April 12, 1776. [Ref: DA-41].

GUESSFORD, Sarah. See "Richard Manwaring," q.v.

GUMRY, Samuel. Private. Born 1738, England. Weaver. Enlisted on May 2, 1758, in the French and Indian Wars, by Capt. Benjamin Noxon. [Ref: DA-19].

GUSTAFSSON, Johan. Soldier. From Kinekulle, Sweden, he arrived in New Sweden on the ship *Swan* in 1643, and served as a common soldier (*saldater*) at Fort Elfsborg to 1653. [Ref: DJ-703, DJ-714, DJ-718, DH-47]. (Name also spelled "Gustafzonn or Gostasson").

GUTHRIE, William. Private. Served in Capt. Henry Darby's Company, Delaware Regiment of Continental Troops. Enlisted on February 13, 1776, and was on duty (in barracks) at Dover on April 12, 1776. [Ref: DA-46].

GUY, Nicholas. Private. Born 1738, Virginia. Enlisted in Capt. John Wright's Company and was on the muster roll of May 11, 1759, during the French and Indian Wars. [Ref: DA-25].

GYLLENGREN, Elias. Gunner (*constaple*). From Fort Korsholm, he arrived in New Sweden in 1643. He was a also a soldier (*saldater*), "who daily followed and served the governor" [Johan Printz] at Fort

Tinicum in 1643 until March 1, 1648, when he served again as gunner from that date until July 31, 1651, and then he returned to Sweden. He came here again on the ship *Orn* in 1654, by which time he was a lieutenant. [Ref: DJ-705, DJ-706, DJ-713, DJ-716]. In May, 1654, he held the post of lieutenant and took part in the capture of Fort Casimir, by Governor Rising. "He forced his way into the fort by order of Commander Sven Schute, took possession of the guns, and striking down the Dutch flag, raised the Swedish in its stead." [Ref: DH-47]. (His name was also spelled "Elias Gyllenngrenn").

HADEN, Peter. Private. Served in Capt. Charles Pope's Company of the Delaware Regiment of Continental Troops. Enlisted January 16, 1776, and was on duty (in quarters) at Lewis Town on April 11, 1776. [Ref: DA-51].

HADLY, George. Private. Served in Capt. Jonathan Caldwell's Company of the Delaware Regiment of Continental Troops. Enlisted on January 29, 1776, and on duty (in barracks) at Dover on April 12, 1776. [Ref: DA-41].

HAGAN, John. Private. Served in Capt. Jonathan Caldwell's Company, Delaware Regiment of Continental Troops. Enlisted March 29, 1776, and on duty (in barracks) at Dover on April 12, 1776. [Ref: DA-41].

HAGARD, William. Private. Born 1739, Ulster, Ireland. Cordwainer. Enlisted on April 29, 1759, in the French and Indian Wars, in Capt. James Armstrong's Company in Pennsylvania Regiment. [Ref: DA-26].

HAHAN, Lawrance. See "John Shannon," q.v.

HAINES, Juobus Jr. Private. Served in Capt. Richard McWilliams' Company, New Castle County. Enlisted on December 28, 1757, during the French and Indian Wars. [Ref: DA-14].

HAINS, John. Fifer and drummer. Served in Capt. Joseph Stedham's Company in the Delaware Battalion of Continental Troops. Enlisted January 17, 1776, and was in quarters at Dover on April 12, 1776. [Ref: DA-39].

HAKANSSON, Karl. Corporal. An "officer" in New Sweden who died at Fort Elfsborg on July 18, 1643. [Ref: DJ-707]. (Name also spelled "Carll Hackensonn").

HALL, Anne. See "Burton Waples," q.v.

HALL, David. Captain. Served in a company in the regiment of Sussex County, Northern District of Lewes and Rehoboth Hundred, 1756, and captain of the Lewes District Company in 1758. [Ref: DA-13, DA-15, DM-46]. He was Commissioner of Sussex County in 1759. [Ref: DM-50].

HALL, David. Captain. Served in 3rd Company of the Delaware State Troops in Continental Service. Commissioned January 16, 1776, and was on duty (in barracks) at Lewis Town on April 11, 1776. [Ref: DA-34, 36, 42].

HALL, George. Private. Born 1736, Milford Hundred, Delaware. Cooper. Enlisted May 10, 1758, during the French and Indian Wars, by Capt. John McClughan "for the campaign in the lower counties." [Ref: DA-17].

HALL, Isaac. Ensign. Served in Capt. Benjamin Brinckle's Company, in lower part of Mispillim [Mispilion] Hundred, Kent County, upon Delaware, 1756, in the French and Indian Wars. [Ref: DA-12]. One John Hall died testate in Kent County and his will was probated on October 2, 1760, naming a son Isaac (among others). [Ref: DK-189].

HALL, James. Private. Served in Capt. John Caton's Company, April 25, 1757, in the French and Indian Wars. [Ref: DA-13].

HALL, James. Private. Served in Capt. Joseph Stedham's Company, Delaware Battalion of Continental Troops. Enlisted January 26, 1776, and was in quarters at Dover on April 12, 1776. [Ref: DA-39].

HALL, James. Private. Served in Capt. David Hall's Company of the Delaware Regiment of Continental Troops. Enlisted January 19, 1776, and was on duty (in barracks) at Lewis Town on April 11, 1776. [Ref: DA-42].

HALL, Jesse. Private. Served in Capt. David Hall's Company of the Delaware Regiment of Continental Troops. Enlisted January 20, 1776, and was on duty (in barracks) at Lewis Town on April 11, 1776. [Ref: DA-42].

HALL, John. Ensign. Served in Capt. David Hall's Company, Northern District of Lewes and Rehoboth Hundred, in the regiment of Sussex County, 1756, during the French and Indian Wars. He was reported "dead" by March 18, 1758. [Ref: DA-13, 15].

HALL, Jonas. Private. Born 1721, Ireland. Blacksmith. Enlisted in Capt. John Shannon's Company of Foot on July 14, 1746, and served in King George's War against Canada. He was in winter quarters at Albany, New York, during 1746-1747, and was discharged on October 31, 1747. [Ref: DA-4, DA-6]. (He is not listed in Source DM-40.)

HALL, Moses. Private. Born 1731, Maryland. Enlisted in Capt. John Wright's Company and was on the muster roll of May 11, 1759, during the French and Indian Wars. [Ref: DA-25].

HALL, Nathaniel. Mariner. Died testate in Lewes, Sussex County, and his will was probated on February 7, 1734/5, naming his wife Jane, sons

David and Peter Hall, daughters Bersheba and Lydia Hall, and the children of daughter Mary (no last name given, but two of the witnesses to the will were Mary and Ralph Bassnet). [Ref: DS-42].

HALL, Thomas. Private. Enlisted on May 20, 1758, in Capt. French Battell's Company of Lower County Provincials, during the French and Indian Wars. [Ref: DA-16]. One John Hall died testate in Kent County and his will was probated on October 2, 1760, naming his children, including son Thomas Hall. [Ref: DK-189]. One Thomas Hall died testate in Kent County and his will was probated on June 26, 1772, naming his wife Rebecca, sons Asa, Nathan, Allen, Rynear, and Jordan Hall, and daughters Perthena and Rebecca. [Ref: DK-268].

HALL, William. Corporal. Served in Capt. David Hall's Company, Delaware Regiment of Continental Troops. Enlisted January 17, 1776, and was on duty (in barracks) at Lewis Town on April 11, 1776. After his name is written "Tayr." [Ref: DA-42].

HALL, William. Private. Enlisted on May 21, 1759, during the French and Indian Wars, and his name appeared on a return of Capt. Henry Van Bibber's Company of the Lower Counties on Delaware Troops, at New Castle, on June 4, 1759. [Ref: DA-26].

HALL, William. Private. Served in Capt. Jonathan Caldwell's Company of the Delaware Regiment of Continental Troops. Enlisted on January 18, 1776, and was on duty (in barracks) at Dover on April 12, 1776. [Ref: DA-41].

HALL, William. Private. Served in Capt. David Hall's Company, Delaware Regiment of Continental Troops. Enlisted January 19, 1776, and was on duty (in barracks) at Lewis Town on April 11, 1776. After his name is written "bird." [Ref: DA-42].

HALL, William. Private. Served in Capt. John Caton's Company on April 25, 1757, in the French and Indian Wars. [Ref: DA-13]. One John Hall died testate in Kent County and his will was probated October 2, 1760, naming son William (among others). [Ref: DK-189].

HALL, William. Sergeant. Served in Capt. David Hall's Company, Delaware Regiment of Continental Troops. Enlisted January 16, 1776, and was on duty (in barracks) at Lewis Town on April 11, 1776. [Ref: DA-42].

HAMILTON, George. Corporal. Served in Capt. Nathan Adams' Company, Delaware Regiment of Continental Troops. Enlisted February 2, 1776, and on duty (in barracks) at Dover on April 12, 1776. [Ref: DA-52].

HAMILTON, James. Private. Born 1737, Pennsylvania. Hunter. Enlisted on May 2, 1758, in the French and Indian Wars, by Capt. Benjamin Noxon. [Ref: DA-19].

HAMILTON, Matthew. Corporal. Served in Capt. Henry Darby's Company, Delaware Regiment of Continental Troops. Enlisted January 27, 1776, and on duty (in barracks) at Dover on April 12, 1776. [Ref: DA-45].

HAMILTON, William. Private. Served in Capt. Charles Pope's Company, Delaware Regiment of Continental Troops. Enlisted January 18, 1776, and was on duty (in quarters) at Lewis Town on April 11, 1776. [Ref: DA-51].

HAMMON, John. Private. Born 1716, Ireland. Laborer. Enlisted in Capt. John Shannon's Company of Foot on July 22, 1746, and served in King George's War against Canada. "John Hamon" made his mark when he was paid for his services on June 6, 1747. He was in winter quarters at Albany, New York, during 1746-1747, and was discharged on October 31, 1747. [Ref: DA-4, DA-6, DM-40].

HAMMOND, Lawrence. Private. Enlisted on May 19, 1758, in Capt. French Battell's Company of Lower County Provincials, during the French and Indian Wars. [Ref: DA-16].

HANEY, Patrick. Private. Served in Capt. Samuel Smith's Company, Delaware Regiment of Continental Troops. Enlisted February 6, 1776, and on duty (in barracks) at Dover on April 12, 1776. [Ref: DA-54].

HANLY, Joseph. Private. Served in Capt. Joseph Stedham's Company, Delaware Battalion of Continental Troops. Enlisted on February 22, 1776, and was in quarters at Dover on April 12, 1776. [Ref: DA-40].

HANNA, Robert. Private. Served in Capt. Henry Darby's Company, Delaware Regiment of Continental Troops. Enlisted February 6, 1776, and was reported as "deserted" on February 14, 1776. [Ref: DA-46].

HANSON, Charles. Soldier. Applied from New Castle County in June, 1776, stating he desired to take an active part in the Flying Camp of the Third Pennsylvania Battalion. [Ref: DA-65].

HANSON, Mary and Peter. See "Thomas Ogle," q.v.

HANSSON, Anders. Gunner. He was probably the Anders Hansson who was paid by the Admiralty in 1641. He was on the ship *Orn* in 1654 to New Sweden and may have died on the journey. [Ref: DJ-723]. Anders Hansson, or Jansson, was the brother of Mats Hansson, the gunner, and he cultivated tobacco and was a freeman by 1648. [Ref: DH-44].

HANSSON, Martin. Soldier (*saldater*.) Served at Fort Christina in New Sweden, 1643-1644. [Ref: DJ-701]. (Also spelled "Marthen").

HANSSON, Mats. Gunner. Arrived in New Sweden on the ship *Kalmar Nyckel* in 1641 and was appointed a gunner (*constaple*). An "officer" at Fort Christina, in 1643-1644, he served in that capacity until December 1, 1646, when he was made a freeman. [Ref: DJ-701, 711]. He was probably the Matts Hansson, from Borga (Finland), who was "the servant of the late Mr. Klas Fleming [who] was sent here [New Sweden] in 1641 to serve the company and was later made a freeman." [Ref: DJ-712]. He was probably the same Mats Hansson who was hired in 1641 at Gothenburg, Sweden, to serve as a gunner at Christina in New Sweden. [Ref: DJ-718], Mats Hansson, or Jansson, accompanied by his wife, worked in agriculture and also served as a gunner at Fort Christina in 1644. He was a freeman by 1648. [Ref: DH-44].

HANZER, Samuel. Private. Born 1735, Sussex, Delaware. Enlisted in Capt. John Wright's Company and appeared on the muster roll of May 11, 1759, during the French and Indian Wars. [Ref: DA-25]. One "Aminadab Handzer," son of Aminadab and Rose Handzer, died testate in Sussex County [no date of probate], having written his will on October 26, 1777, and naming his parents, his brother Samuel, and his sisters Ann and Mary Handzer. [Ref: DS-119].

HANZER, Thomas. Private. Born 1740, Sussex, Delaware. Enlisted in Capt. John Wright's Company and was on the muster roll of May 11, 1759, during the French and Indian Wars. [Ref: DA-25].

HARBADGE, Edward. Private. Born 1734, London, England. Brush maker. Enlisted on April 26, 1758, during the French and Indian Wars, as a private by Capt. John McClughan "for the campaign in the lower counties." [Ref: DA-17].

HARDEN, Nancy. See "James Byrum," q.v.

HARIGAN [HARAGON], Cornelius. Private. Born 1730, Ireland. Laborer. Enlisted on April 25, 1758, during the French and Indian Wars, by Capt. Benjamin Noxon. [Ref: DA-19].

HARKINS, James. Private. Born 1712, Ireland. Laborer. Enlisted in Capt. John Shannon's Company of Foot on July 22, 1746, and served in King George's War against Canada. He was in winter quarters at Albany, New York, during 1746-1747, and was discharged on October 31, 1747. [Ref: DA-4, DA-6]. (He is not listed in Source DM-40.)

HARKINS, Samuel. Private. Served in Capt. Henry Darby's Company, Delaware Regiment of Continental Troops. Enlisted on February 15, 1776, and was on duty (in barracks) at Dover on April 12, 1776. [Ref: DA-46].

HARMAN, Job. Private. Born 1725, Sussex, Delaware. Laborer. Enlisted in Capt. John Shannon's Company of Foot on July 14, 1746, and served in King George's War against Canada. "Joab Harmon" made his mark when paid for his services on June 6, 1747, and he was in winter quarters at Albany, New York, during 1746-1747. He was discharged on October 31, 1747. [Ref: DA-4, DA-5, DA-6, DM-40].

HARMER, Gottfried. See "Gottfriedt Hermansson," q.v.

HARNEY, Jonathan. First Lieutenant. Served in 3rd Company, Delaware State Troops in Continental Service. Commissioned on January 16, 1776. "Genethan Harney" was on duty (in barracks) at Lewis Town on April 11, 1776. [Ref: DA-34, 36, 42].

HARNEY, Joshua. Private. Served in Capt. David Hall's Company, Delaware Regiment of Continental Troops. Enlisted January 17, 1776, and was on duty (in barracks) at Lewis Town on April 11, 1776. [Ref: DA-42].

HARPER, Allen. Corporal. Served in Capt. Joseph Vaughan's Company, Delaware Regiment of Continental Troops. Enlisted on February 10, 1776, and was on duty (in barracks) at Dover on April 12, 1776. [Ref: DA-59].

HARPER, David. Private. Served in Capt. Joseph Vaughan's Company, Delaware Regiment of Continental Troops. Enlisted on February 10, 1776, and was on duty (in barracks) at Dover on April 12, 1776. [Ref: DA-59].

HARPER, John. Corporal. Served in Capt. Joseph Vaughan's Company, Delaware Regiment of Continental Troops. Enlisted on February 10, 1776, and was on duty (in barracks) at Dover on April 12, 1776. [Ref: DA-59].

HARPER, John. Private. Served in Capt. Nathan Adams' Company, Delaware Regiment of Continental Troops. Enlisted on March 25, 1776, and was on duty (in barracks) at Dover on April 12, 1776. [Ref: DA-53].

HARPER, Joseph. Corporal. Served in Capt. Joseph Vaughan's Company, Delaware Regiment of Continental Troops. Enlisted February 9, 1776, and on duty (in barracks) at Dover on April 12, 1776. [Ref: DA-59].

HARPER, Mark. Private. Served in Capt. John Caton's Company, April 25, 1757 in the French and Indian Wars. [Ref: DA-14]. One John Harper died testate in Kent County and his will probated on October 18, 1749, named his children, including a son Mark. [Ref: DK-135].

HARRAGAN, Cornelius. Private. Enlisted on May 9, 1759, during the French and Indian Wars, and his name appeared on a return of Capt.

Henry Van Bibber's Company of the Lower Counties on Delaware Troops at New Castle on June 4, 1759. [Ref: DA-26].
HARRINGTON, Jacob. See "Joseph Marrat," q.v.
HARRIS, George. Private. Served in Capt. David Hall's Company, Delaware Regiment of Continental Troops. Enlisted January 21, 1776, and was on duty (in barracks) at Lewis Town on April 11, 1776. After his name is written "on guard." [Ref: DA-43].
HARRIS, Henry. Private. Born 1716, Wales. Laborer. Enlisted in Capt. John Shannon's Company of Foot on July 24, 1746, and served in King George's War against Canada. He was in winter quarters at Albany, New York, during 1746-1747, and was discharged on October 31, 1747. [Ref: DA-4, DA-6]. (He is not listed in Source DM-40.)
HARRIS, Jacob. Private. Served in Capt. Samuel Smith's Company, Delaware Regiment of Continental Troops. Enlisted January 20, 1776, and was on duty (in barracks) at Dover on April 12, 1776, at which time he transferred to Capt. Henry Darby's Company. [Ref: DA-54].
HARRIS, John. Private. Served in Capt. Richard McWilliams' Company, New Castle County. Enlisted on December 28, 1757, during the French and Indian Wars. [Ref: DA-15].
HARRIS, Judah. See "Thomas Ogle," q.v.
HARRIS, Patrick. Fifer. Served in Capt. Henry Darby's Company, Delaware Regiment of Continental Troops. Enlisted January 31, 1776, and on duty (in barracks) at Dover on April 12, 1776. [Ref: DA-45].
HARRIS, William. Private. Served in Capt. John Caton's Company, April 25, 1757, in the French and Indian Wars. [Ref: DA-14]. One William Harris died in Kent County and his will was probated on June 29, 1771, naming wife Hannah and son Abraham. [Ref: DK-259].
HARRISON, Edward. Ensign. Served in the War of Jenkins' Ear in 1739-1741 in a company which may have included soldiers from Delaware (muster rolls not extant). [Ref: DM-32].
HART, John. Private. Served in Capt. Jonathan Caldwell's Company, Delaware Regiment of Continental Troops. Enlisted January 16, 1776, and on duty (in barracks) at Dover on April 12, 1776. [Ref: DA-41].
HART, Robert Jr. Land patentee and probable militiaman in Delaware in November, 1677. [Ref: DP-167, 168].
HARTMAN, Johan. Soldier (*saldater*). From Hamburg, he served in New Sweden and died in November, 1643, at Fort Tinicum. [Ref: DJ-708].
HARTSHORN, Ann. See "Joseph Merideth," q.v.

HARVEY, Thomas. Soldier. He was listed as a deserter from the company of Capt. John Shannon in 1747 in King George's War against Canada. [Ref: DM-40].

HASLET, John. Colonel. Served as captain of a militia company in New Castle, 1758-1759, in the French and Indian Wars, and recruited soldiers from "the three lower counties" [Delaware] to serve in the Pennsylvania Troops. [Ref: DA-23, 27]. He was commissioned colonel of the Delaware Battalion of Continental Troops, January 19, 1776. [Ref: DA-35]. He died testate in Mispillion Hundred in Kent County and his will was probated March 6, 1777, naming wife Jemima, sons Joseph and John, and daughters Mary (married ---- McGarment), Ann (married Major John Patten), and Jemima Haslet. [Ref: DK-309]. (Name also spelled "Hasslet").

HASLETT, Kinler. Private. Served in Capt. Jonathan Caldwell's Company, Delaware Regiment of Continental Troops. Enlisted January 24, 1776, and on duty (in barracks) at Dover on April 12, 1776. [Ref: DA-41].

HASSETT, Gillis. Commissary. Served on the expedition that created the small colony on the Hoornkill [Whorekill, now Lewes], Delaware, called *Zwaanendael* (Valley of Swans) on May 5, 1631. This "whaling colony" was abandoned in the summer of 1633. [Ref: DH-32, DH-34].

HASTINGS, Robert. Private. Served in Capt. Joseph Vaughan's Company of the Delaware Regiment of Continental Troops. Enlisted on January 26, 1776, and on duty (in barracks) at Dover on April 12, 1776. [Ref: DA-59].

HATCH, Elizabeth. See "John Elliott," q.v.

HATFIELD, John Jr. Private. Served in Capt. John Caton's Company, April 25, 1757, in the French and Indian Wars. [Ref: DA-13].

HATFIELD, Sarah and Mary. See "Richard White," q.v.

HATFIELD, Thomas. Private. Served in Capt. John Caton's Company, April 25, 1757, in the French and Indian Wars. [Ref: DA-13]. The administration of the estate of one "John Hatfield, soldier in the Delaware Regiment," was granted to a Thomas Hatfield in Murderkill Hundred in Kent County on November 12, 1788. [Ref: DK-405].

HATFIELD, Whitly. Private. Born 1741, Maryland. Enlisted in Capt. John Wright's Company and was on the muster roll of May 11, 1759, during the French and Indian Wars. [Ref: DA-25]. "William Hatfield, yeoman," died testate in Kent County and his was will was probated on June 5, 1797, naming his wife Mary and a son "Wheatly" Hatfield (among others). [Ref: DK-526].

HATFIELD, William. Private. Served in Capt. John Caton's Company, April 25, 1757, during the French and Indian Wars. [Ref: DA-13]. One "William Hatfield, yeoman," died testate in Kent County and his will was probated on June 5, 1797, naming wife Mary and son William Hatfield (among others). [Ref: DK-526].

HATTABUCK, Jacob. Private. Served in Capt. Nathan Adams' Company, Delaware Regiment of Continental Troops. Enlisted January 15, 1776, and on duty (in barracks) at Dover on April 12, 1776. [Ref: DA-52].

HAVELOE, John. Captain. Served in a militia company in regiment of Sussex County, Northern District of Broad Kill Hundred, in 1756, in the French and Indian Wars. [Ref: DA-13, DM-46]. A "John Heaveloe" died in Sussex County and administration of his estate was granted to Hannah Heaveloe on February 5, 1784. [Ref: DS-154]. One "John Heavelo" died testate in Broadkill Hundred in Sussex County and his will was probated February 3, 1798, naming son John Heavelo [sic], and daughters Sally Heavelo, Elizabeth Heavelo, Hannah Heavelo, and Polly Johnson. [Ref: DS-290]. (Name also spelled "John Haverloe").

HAWKINS, Elizabeth. See "Thomas Bennett," q.v.

HAY, William. Lieutenant. Served in Capt. Andrew Frauberg's [or Tranberg's?] Company, Christiana Hundred, Upper Regiment, in New Castle County, 1756, in the French and Indian Wars. [Ref: DA-11]. "William Hay, innholder," died testate in Wilmington, Delaware, and his will was probated on March 1, 1763, naming sons Jehu and David, daughter Elizabeth, and brother-in-law Isaac Weaver. [Ref: DN-60].

HAZZARD, Cord. Captain. Served in a company in regiment of Sussex County, Northern District of Indian River Hundred, in 1756. He was commissioned captain of the Angola District in Sussex County on March 18, 1758, during the French and Indian Wars, "but would not take the qualifications." [Ref: DA-13, DA-15, DM-46]. One "Cord Hazzard, yeoman," died testate in Sussex County and his will was probated on January 11, 1771, naming wife Rachel, sons Joseph and David, daughters Hannah Robinson, Arcada Robinson, Rhoda Fowler, Rachel Burton, and Mary King, and his granddaughters Mary Hazzard (daughter of son William Hazzard, deceased), and Elizabeth Hazzard (daughter of son Cord Hazzard, deceased). [Ref: DS-87]. The will of Rev. William Becket (Missionary), written in Sussex County, August 17, 1743, named among his heirs "Capt. Cord Hazzard." [Ref: DS-49].

HAZZARD, Cord. Ensign. Served in 3rd Company, Delaware State Troops in Continental Service. Commissioned on January 16, 1776, and was on duty (in barracks) with Capt. David Hall's Delaware Regiment of Troops at Lewis Town on April 11, 1776. [Ref: DA-34, DA-36, DA-42].

HAZZARD, Joseph. Private. Served in Capt. David Hall's Company, Delaware Regiment of Continental Troops. Enlisted February 22, 1776, and was on duty (in barracks) at Lewis Town on April 11, 1776. [Ref: DA-43].

HEARN, John. Private. Served in Capt. Joseph Vaughan's Company, Delaware Regiment of Continental Troops. Enlisted January 20, 1776, and was on duty (in barracks) at Dover on April 12, 1776. [Ref: DA-57, DA-59]. (This same source also spelled his name "John Hern").

HEATHCOTE, George. Land patentee and probable militiaman "on an island in Delaware" in January, 1677. [Ref: DP-169].

HEBBITS, William. Private. Served in Capt. John Caton's Company, April 25, 1757, in the French and Indian Wars. [Ref: DA-13].

HEINES, Cornelius. Private. Served in Capt. Richard McWilliams' Company, New Castle County. Enlisted on December 28, 1757, during the French and Indian Wars. [Ref: DA-15].

HELME, Israel. Soldier. Planter in Delaware who paid his quit-rent to the governor in 1668, having received a grant to land above New Castle, June 18, 1668. [Ref: DP-27, DP-28, DY-131].

HEMMINS, James. Private. Born 1742, Sussex, Delaware. Enlisted in Capt. John Wright's Company and was on the muster roll of May 11, 1759, during the French and Indian Wars. [Ref: DA-25].

HEMMINS, John. Private. Born 1737, Sussex, Delaware. Enlisted in Capt. John Wright's Company and was on the muster roll of May 11, 1759, during the French and Indian Wars. [Ref: DA-25]. One "John Hemmons" died testate in Sussex County and his will was probated on December 8, 1789, naming his wife Elizabeth, sons Thomas Hemmons and Wiliam Leather Hemmons, daughters Mary Hemmons and Elizabeth Jacobs, and granddaughter Mary Jacobs. [Ref: DS-207].

HENDERSON, James. Private. Born 1722, Scotland. Tailor. Enlisted in Capt. John Shannon's Company of Foot on July 11, 1746, and served in King George's War against Canada. He was in winter quarters at Albany, New York, during 1746-1747, and was discharged October 31, 1747. [Ref: DA-4, DA-6]. However, Source DM-40 stated that James Henderson was listed as a deserter in Capt. Shannon's record book.

HENDERSON, James. Private. Born 1728, Antrim, Ireland. Laborer. Enlisted on May 8, 1758, in the French and Indian Wars, by Capt. John McClughan "for the campaign in lower counties." [Ref: DA-17].

HENDERSON, Priscilla. See "Thomas Clarke," q.v.

HENDRICKS, Johannes. Soldier. Planter in Delaware who paid his quit-rent to the governor in 1671, having received a land patent on January 8, 1667. [Ref: DP-29, DY-123, DY-124].

HENDRICKSEN, Barent. Soldier. Planter in Delaware who paid his quit-rent to the governor in 1671, having been granted land on Appoqueminy Creek on August 14, 1667. [Ref: DP-29, DY-146].

HENDRICKSON, Cornelis. Captain. "Explored part of the Delaware in 1615-1616, met and traded with the Minquas (probably at the mouth or upon the Christina), and redeemed from them 3 Dutch prisoners. His intercourse with them was the beginning of the Delaware for trade." [Ref: DH-12, DH-27]. ("Minquas" were also "Susquehannas").

HENDRICKSON, John. Ensign. Served in Capt. Thomas Ogle, Jr.'s Company in Christiana Hundred, Upper Regiment, New Castle County, 1756, during the French and Indian Wars. [Ref: DA-11]. One "John Hendrickson, mariner," died testate in Wilmington and his will was probated on May 18, 1768, naming his sisters Mary Hendrickson and Rachel Peterson, and his stepfather Peter Peterson. [Ref: DN-65].

HENDRICKSON, John. Private. Served in Capt. Joseph Stedham's Company, Delaware Battalion of Continental Troops. Enlisted on February 21, 1776, and was in quarters at Dover on April 12, 1776. [Ref: DA-40].

HENEY, James. Private. Served in Capt. Henry Darby's Company, Delaware Regiment of Continental Troops. Enlisted February 13, 1776, and was on duty (in barracks) at Dover on April 12, 1776. [Ref: DA-46].

HENRY, Henry. Private. Born 1727, Ireland. Laborer. Enlisted in Capt. John Shannon's Company of Foot on July 20, 1746, and served in King George's War against Canada. He was in winter quarters at Albany, New York, during 1746-1747, and was discharged on October 31, 1747. [Ref: DA-4, DA-6]. (He is not listed in Source DM-40.)

HENRY, John. Soldier. Planter who paid his quit-rent to the governor in 1667. [Ref: DP-27]. He received patent in Delaware for land "lying behind ye town of New Castle" on September 1, 1669, since he had been "a soldier who came over into these parts in His Majesty's service." [Ref: DY-160].

HENRY, Matthew. Private. Served in Capt. John Caton's Company on April 25, 1757, in the French and Indian Wars. [Ref: DA-13]. The administration of the estate of one Matthew Henry was granted to Archibald McSparron in Kent County, March 28, 1786. [Ref: DK-381].

HERBERT, John. Private. Served in Capt. Nathan Adams' Company, Delaware Regiment of Continental Troops. Enlisted January 30, 1776, and on duty (in barracks) at Dover on April 12, 1776. [Ref: DA-53].

HEREFORD, James. Private. Served in Capt. Henry Darby's Company, Delaware Regiment of Continental Troops. Enlisted February 3, 1776, and on duty (in barracks) at Dover on April 12, 1776. [Ref: DA-46].

HERLOCK, Isaac. Private. Born 1727, Kent, Delaware. Laborer. Enlisted in Capt. John Shannon's Company of Foot on July 17, 1746 and served in King George's War against Canada. He was in winter quarters at Albany, New York, during 1746-1747, and was discharged October 31, 1747. [Ref: DA-4, DA-6]. However, Source DM-40 stated that he was listed as a deserter in Capt. Shannon's record book.

HERMANSSON, Gottfriedt. Guard. Arrived in New Sweden on the ship *Charitas* in 1641 as a cabin guard, and he became an assistant to commissary Hendrick Huygen by 1648. [Ref: DJ-71]. Source DH-45 states he was a steward on the ship *Charitas* in 1644]. (His name has also been spelled "Gottfried Harmer" or "Gottfried Hermer").

HERRINGTON, Elizabeth. See "Thomas Clarke," q.v.

HERRINGTON, Naomi. See "Bethuel Watson," q.v.

HERVILL, John. Private. Enlisted on May 16, 1758, in Capt. French Battell's Company of Lower County Provincials, during the French and Indian Wars. [Ref: DA-16].

HETHERINGTON, John. Private. Served in Capt. Henry Darby's Company, Delaware Regiment of Continental Troops. Enlisted February 23, 1776 and on duty (in barracks) at Dover on April 12, 1776. [Ref: DA-46].

HEYES, Pieter. Captain. Served on the expedition that established the small colony on the Hoornkill [now Lewes] in Delaware on May 5, 1631, which he had "purchased" from the Indians. This "whaling colony" was abandoned in the summer of 1633. [Ref: DH-22, DH-34].

HICKMAN, Spencer. Private. Served in Capt. David Hall's Company, Delaware Regiment of Continental Troops. Enlisted January 16, 1776, and was on duty (in barracks) at Lewis Town on April 11, 1776. [Ref: DA-42].

HICKS, John. Private. Served in Capt. Joseph Vaughan's Company, Delaware Regiment of Continental Troops. Enlisted February 9, 1776, and on duty (in barracks) at Dover on April 12, 1776. [Ref: DA-59].

HICKS, William. Sergeant. Served in Capt. Joseph Vaughan's Company, Delaware Regiment of Continental Troops. Enlisted February 9, 1776, and on duty (in barracks) at Dover on April 12, 1776. [Ref: DA-59].

93

HIGGINS, Andrew. Private. Served in Capt. Joseph Stedham's Company, Delaware Battalion of Continental Troops. Enlisted February 1, 1776, and was in quarters at Dover on April 12, 1776. [Ref: DA-39].

HIGGINS, James. Private. Served in Capt. Samuel Smith's Company, Delaware Regiment of Continental Troops. Enlisted January 23, 1776, and on duty (in barracks) at Dover on April 12, 1776. [Ref: DA-54].

HILL, Arthur. Private. Enlisted on May 17, 1758, in Capt. French Battell's Company of Lower County Provincials, during the French and Indian Wars. [Ref: DA-16].

HILL, John. Captain. He held this rank by 1705 when he was a Court Justice in Sussex County. [Ref: DC-45]. He was one of the executors of the will of Isaac Wiltbank that was probated on April 20, 1708, in Sussex County. [Ref: DS-22]. Also see "Harmanes Wildbank," q.v.

HILL, John. Private. Served in Capt. John Caton's Company, April 25, 1757, in the French and Indian Wars. [Ref: DA-14]. One "John Hill, yeoman," died intestate in Duck Creek Hundred, Kent County, and administration of his estate was granted to Thomas Hill and Joseph Hill, next-of-kin, on June 2, 1772. [Ref: DK-267].

HILL, Jonathan. Private. Born 1741, Sussex, Delaware. Enlisted in Capt. John Wright's Company, and was on the muster roll of May 11, 1759, during the French and Indian Wars. [Ref: DA-25].

HILL, Richard. Land patentee and probable militiaman in Delaware in November, 1677. [Ref: DP-167, 168].

HILLYARD, Charles. Captain. Served in a company of militia in lower part of Duck Creek Hundred, Kent County, upon Delaware, in 1756, in the French and Indian Wars. [Ref: DA-12, DM-46]. Administration of the estate of one "Charles Hilyard" was granted to Charles Hilyard, the younger on August 14, 1789. [Ref: DK-414]. See "George Martin."

HILLYARD, Charles. Lieutenant. Served in Capt. Daniel Robinson's Company, Murder Kill Hundred, Kent County, upon Delaware, 1756, during the French and Indian Wars. He resigned on March 29, 1758. [Ref: DA-12, DA-15]. See notes under "Charles Hillyard, Captain."

HINDERSSON, Erick. Soldier (*saldater*). From Soderteljie, he served in New Sweden and died on July 5, 1643, at Fort Christina. [Ref: DJ-707]. (This source also spelled his name "Erich Hindersonn").

HINDRICKSEN, Jan van de Waeter. Skipper. Served on *Kalmar Nyckel* in the first expedition to New Sweden during 1637-1639. [Ref: DJ-758].

HINDRICKSEN, Thering. Skipper. Served on the ship *Fama* during the fifth expedition to New Sweden during 1642-1643. [Ref: DJ-760].

HINDRICKSSON, Bengt. Soldier. He was a common soldier (*saldater*) at Fort Elfsborg in 1643 and returned to Sweden in 1648. [Ref: DJ-703, DJ-716]. (Name also spelled "Hindrichsonn" and "Hinderson").

HINDRICKSSON, Hindrick. Soldier. Arrived in New Sweden on the ship *Orn* in 1654. [Ref: DJ-719].

HINDRICKSSON, Johan. Gunner (*constaple*). Served in New Sweden from 1640 to 1643, and returned to Europe in 1643. [Ref: DJ-700].

HINDRICKSSON, Enert. Captain. A laborer and soldier in 1648, he was banished from Upland in 1663 (reason not stated) and later settled at Crane Hook below the Christiana. He became captain of a company there and was a participant in the insurrection of the "Long Finn," for which he was fined 300 *guilders*. [Ref: DH-45]. He has also been referred to as "Enert Hindricsson, the Finn").

HINDSLEY, Amos. Private. Served in Capt. John Caton's Company on April 25, 1757, in the French and Indian Wars. [Ref: DA-14]. One "Amos Hinsley, Sr., yeoman," died testate in Murderkill Hundred, Kent County, and his will was probated on February 4, 1796, naming his wife Pations, sons James, John, Amos, and Daniel, and daughters Meriam Scotton, Hannah Hinsley, and Pations Hinsley. [Ref: DK-502].

HIORT, Peder Larsson. Reverend. Military preacher. An officer in New Sweden, he arrived on the ship *Orn* in 1654 and returned to Europe with Director Rising in 1655. [Ref: DJ-716, DJ-724]. (Name also spelled "Peter Larsson Hjort" or "Petrus Larsson Hjort").

HIRONS, Mark. Ensign. Served in Capt. John Hume's Company in Kent County, 1747-1748, in King George's War against Canada. [Ref: DA-8]. One Mark Hirons died intestate in Kent County and his widow Sarah was named his administratrix on April 3, 1769. [Ref: DK-241].

HIRONS, William. Lieutenant. Served in Capt. John Hume's Company, Kent County, 1747-1748, in King George's War against Canada. [Ref: DA-8]. One William Hirons died testate in Duck Creek Hundred and his will was probated September 12, 1757, naming his son John and hias daughter Grace. [Ref: DK-171]. William Leatherbury, yeoman, was named administrator of "William Hirons, yeoman" on February 27, 1760. [Ref: DK-185].

HODGE, Henry. Second Lieutenant. Served in the War of Jenkins' Ear in 1739-1741 in a company which may have included soldiers from Delaware (muster rolls not extant). [Ref: DM-32].

HODGKINSON, Hester and Peter. See "Jacob Kollock, Jr.," q.v.

HODGSON, Joseph. Ensign. Served in Capt. John Caton's Company, Kent County, 1747-1748, and served in King George's War against

Canada. [Ref: DA-8]. One "Joseph Hodgson (Hudgson)," died testate and his will was probated on November 2, 1759, naming his sons Jonathan and John, daughters Sarah and Mary, and uncle Andrew Caldwell. Also mentioned were his brother Robert Hodgson, Jr. (executor) and his mother Train Hodgson (trustee). [Ref: DK-183].

HODGSON, Robert. Private. Served in Capt. John Caton's Company on April 25, 1757, in the French and Indian Wars. [Ref: DA-14]. He may have been the Robert Hodgson who served as second lieutenant in a militia company from the lower counties of Delaware in April, 1758, during the French and Indian Wars. [Ref: DM-48]. One Robert Hodgson died intestate in Kent County and administration of his estate was granted to Joseph Hodgson and George Truitt, Esq., on May 10, 1791. A later account showed heirs as follows: Margaret Pritchett, Robert Pritchard, Mary Catlen (the wife of Joseph Catlen), Joseph Hodgson, Jonathan Hodgson, William Hodgson and Caleb Jackson. [Ref: DK-444].

HODGSON, William. Private. Served in Capt. John Caton's Company on April 25, 1757, in the French and Indian Wars. [Ref: DA-13]. One William Hodgson died in Kent County and his will was probated May 11, 1770, naming wife Nancy, son Joseph, daughters Esther and Train and brother David. [Ref: DK-250, 251]. (Same source states that a later administration account showed Nancy Hodgson married Andrew Saxton, while another account showed she married William Brown.)

HOLDING, Benjamin. Private. Served in Capt. Nathan Adams' Company, Delaware Regiment of Continental Troops. Enlisted on March 26, 1776, and was on duty (in barracks) at Dover on April 12, 1776. [Ref: DA-53].

HOLLAND, Thomas. Adjutant. Served in the Delaware Battalion of Continental Troops. Commissioned on January 13, 1776. [Ref: DA-35].

HOLLAND, Thomas. Ensign. Served in the 1st Company, Delaware State Troops, Continental Army. Commissioned on January 13, 1776. [Ref: DA-34, 36].

HOLLAND, Thomas. Private. Served in Capt. Charles Pope's Company, Delaware Regiment of Continental Troops. Enlisted January 15, 1776, and was on duty (in quarters) at Lewis Town on April 11, 1776. [Ref: DA-51].

HOLLANDSWORTH, John. Private. Served in Capt. Nathan Adams' Company, Delaware Regiment of Continental Troops. Enlisted March 16, 1776, and on duty (in barracks) at Dover on April 12, 1776. [Ref: DA-53].

HOLME, Thomas. Captain. He held that rank by 1683 when he served in the General Assembly of Pennsylvania, possibly from Philadelphia, and mentioned in the Sussex County court records. [Ref: DC-54].

HOLSTON, William. Private. Born 1736, Pocomock, Maryland. Shoemaker who enlisted May 10, 1758, in the French and Indian Wars, by Capt. John McClughan "for the campaign in lower counties." [Ref: DA-17].

HOLSTON, William. Private. Served in Capt. David Hall's Company, Delaware Regiment of Continental Troops. Enlisted February 3, 1776, and was on duty (in barracks) at Lewis Town on April 11, 1776. [Ref: DA-43].

HOLT, Ryves Jr. Ensign. Served in one of the three companies "of the lower counties" in 3rd Battalion of the Pennsylvania Regiment under Col. Hugh Mercer, May, 1759, during the French and Indian Wars, in Capt. John Wright's Company. [Ref: DA-20, DA-25, DM-49].

HOLT, Ryves. Lieutenant Colonel. Served in the regiment of Sussex County, 1756-1758, during the French and Indian Wars. [Ref: DA-13, DA-15, DM-46]. One "Rives Holt, Esqr.," was deceased by August 8, 1771, at which time administratices Catharine Holt and Penelope Holt Coward had sold his land on Mispillion Creek. [Ref: DD-41]. Catherine Holt, widow, died in Sussex County, having written her will on November 9, 1774. It was probated in 1779 (exact date not given) naming her granddaughter Penelope Holt Jones. [Ref: DS-126].

HOMMAN, Anders Anderson. Soldier. From Saltuna Stockholm, arrived in New Sweden on the ship *Swan* in 1643, served as a soldier until March 1, 1648, "from which time until 1653 he served as trumpeter." [Ref: DJ-713]. "Anders Andersson Homan was born in December, 1620, in Sweden, and was a soldier in the governor's guard at Tinicum in 1644 and 1648. He lived at Carkoons Hook in 1677 and at Trumpeters Creek in 1697. He left several children." [Ref: DH-47].

HOMSTEAD, John. Private. Served in Capt. John Caton's Company on April 25, 1757, in the French and Indian Wars. [Ref: DA-13]. One "John Homestead" was mentioned in the will of William Rodney when it was probated in Kent County, September 13, 1787. [Ref: DK-395].

HOOK, Sven. Lieutenant. Arrived in New Sweden on the ship *Orn* in 1648. This or another Sven Hook was lieutenant on the ship *Gyllene Haj* during the eleventh expedition to New Sweden in 1654, but "did not reach New Sweden" [sic]. He returned to Europe with Director Rising in 1655. [Ref: DJ-681, 716, 724, 761].

HOPKINS, John. Private. Served in Capt. Joseph Vaughan's Company, Delaware Regiment of Continental Troops. Enlisted on February 17, 1776, and was on duty (in barracks) at Dover on April 12, 1776. [Ref: DA-59].

HOPKINS, Nathaniel. Private. Served in Capt. David Hall's Company, Delaware Regiment of Continental Troops. Enlisted January 23, 1776, and was on duty (in barracks) at Lewis Town on April 11, 1776. [Ref: DA-43].

HORAN, Henry. Private. Served in Capt. Richard McWilliams' Company, New Castle County. Enlisted on December 28, 1757, during the French and Indian Wars. [Ref: DA-15].

HOSKINS, Jane. See "Harmanes Wildbank," q.v.

HOSMAN, Joseph. Sergeant. Served in Capt. David Hall's Company, Delaware Regiment of Continental Troops. Enlisted January 16, 1776, and was on duty (in barracks) at Lewis Town on April 11, 1776. [Ref: DA-42].

HOTHAM, Joseph. Ensign. Served in Capt. Edward Fitzrandolph's Company, New Castle County, 1747-1748, in King George's War against Canada. [Ref: DA-7].

HOUSTON, Alexander. Private. Born 1733, Toboyne, Ireland. Laborer. Enlisted on May 1, 1758, in the French and Indian Wars, by Capt. John McClughan "for the campaign in lower counties." [Ref: DA-17].

HOUSTON, Margaret. See "William Prettyman," q.v.

HOWARD, Catherine. See "Thomas Ogle," q.v.

HOWARD, William. Private. Served in Capt. Joseph Stedham's Company, Delaware Battalion of Continental Troops. Enlisted on March 17, 1776, and was in quarters at Dover on April 12, 1776. [Ref: DA-40].

HOWELL, David. Ensign. Served in Capt. John Gooding's Company, New Castle County, 1747-1748, in King George's War against Canada. He was ensign in Capt. Jacob Gooding's Company, in Red Lion Hundred, Lower Regiment, New Castle, 1756, in the French and Indian Wars. [Ref: DA-7, 12]. One David Howell died in Pencader Hundred and his will, probated June 5, 1792, named wife Sarah, sons David, Thomas, Oliver, and Samuel, and daughters Dinah and Nancy. [Ref: DN-126].

HOWELL, Elias. Private. Served in Capt. John Caton's Company, April 25, 1757, in the French and Indian Wars. [Ref: DA-14].

HOWELL, Elizabeth. See "Benjamin Ford," q.v.

HOWELL, James. See "John Webb," q.v.

HOWELL, Joseph. See "Renn Forkcum," q.v.

HOWELL, Joseph Jr. Private. Served in Capt. John Caton's Company, April 25, 1757, in the French and Indian Wars. [Ref: DA-14].

HOWELL, Lewis. First Lieutenant. Served in 1st Company, Delaware State Troops in Continental Service. Commissioned on January 13, 1776, and on was duty (in barracks) with Capt. Henry Darby at Dover on April 12, 1776. [Ref: DA-34, 36, 45].

HOWELL, Samuel. Private. Served in Capt. John Caton's Company on April 25, 1757, in the French and Indian Wars. [Ref: DA-14].

HOWELL, William. Private. Born 1711, Wales. Cooper. Enlisted in Capt. John Shannon's Company of Foot on July 2, 1746, and he served in King George's War against Canada. He was in winter quarters at Albany, New York, during 1746-1747, and was discharged on October 31, 1747. [Ref: DA-4, 6].

HUDSON, Henry. Captain. He was the first European explorer (perhaps with the possible exception of a Spanish "ride by" in the 1500's) to enter the Delaware Bay (called *Lenape Wihitituck* by the Indians, meaning "the river of the Lenape") on August 28, 1609, after which he sailed up the coast in his ship the *Half Moon* and discovered the great river in New York that bears his name. [Ref: DH-9, 10, 24].

HUDSON, John. Shallopman. Private. Served in Capt. John Caton's Company, April 25, 1757, in the French and Indian Wars. [Ref: DA-13]. One John Hudson died testate in Kent County and his will was probated January 13, 1796, naming sons John, William, and Ebenezer, and daughters Lydia, Mary, Margret, and Senty [sic]. [Ref: DK-501].

HUES, Mathew. Private. Served in Capt. Samuel Smith's Company, Delaware Regiment of Continental Troops. Enlisted January 17, 1776, and on duty (in barracks) at Dover on April 12, 1776. [Ref: DA-54].

HUGG, John. Sergeant. Born 1711, West Jersey. Cooper. Enlisted in Capt. John Shannon's Company of Foot on July 11, 1746, and served in King George's War against Canada. He was a sergeant by June 6, 1747, and signed his name when paid for services. He was in winter quarters at Albany, New York, during 1746-1747, and was discharged on October 31, 1747. [Ref: DA-4, DA-5, DA-6, DM-40].

HUGHES, Patrick. Private. Served in Capt. Richard McWilliams' Company, New Castle County. Enlisted on December 28, 1757, during the French and Indian Wars. [Ref: DA-14].

HUME, John. Captain. Served in a Kent County Company, 1747-1748, in King George's War against Canada. [Ref: DA-8].

HUMES, John. Private. Served in Capt. Richard McWilliams' Company, New Castle County. Enlisted on December 28, 1757, during the French and Indian Wars. [Ref: DA-14].

HUMES, William. Private. Served in Capt. Richard McWilliams' Company, New Castle County. Enlisted on December 28, 1757, during the French and Indian Wars. [Ref: DA-14].

HUMPHREYS, Lewis. Private. Served in Capt. Jonathan Caldwell's Company, Delaware Regiment of Continental Troops. Enlisted January 23, 1776, and on duty (in barracks) at Dover on April 12, 1776. [Ref: DA-41].

HUMPHREYS, William. Private. Born 1733, Maryland. Laborer. Enlisted on May 2, 1758, in the French and Indian Wars, by Capt. Benjamin Noxon. [Ref: DA-19].

HUNN, Mary and John. See "Nathaniel Silsbee," q.v.

HUNT, William. Private. Served in Capt. Richard McWilliams' Company, New Castle County. Enlisted on December 28, 1757, during the French and Indian Wars. [Ref: DA-14].

HUNTER, William. Private. Born 1736, England. Laborer. Enlisted on May 8, 1758, during the French and Indian Wars, by Capt. Benjamin Noxon. [Ref: DA-19].

HURLEY, Joanor. Private. Served in Capt. Joseph Vaughan's Company, Delaware Regiment of Continental Troops. Enlisted January 16, 1776, and was on duty (in barracks) at Dover on April 12, 1776. [Ref: DA-57, DA-59]. (This same source spelled his name "Joannah Hurley").

HURT, Beachamp. Private. Served in Capt. Joseph Vaughan's Company, Delaware Regiment of Continental Troops. Enlisted January 20, 1776, and on duty (in barracks) at Dover on April 12, 1776. [Ref: DA-59].

HUSTON, Robert. Private. Born 1728, Ireland. Cordwainer. Enlisted on April 22, 1758, during the French and Indian Wars, by Capt. Benjamin Noxon. [Ref: DA-19].

HUTCHINS, Charles. Soldier. Planter who paid his quit-rent to the governor in 1671, having been granted a land patent on northeast St. Jones Creek on June 19, 1671. [Ref: DP-29, DY-152].

HUTCHINSON, Joseph. Lieutenant. Served in Capt. William Rhoades' Company, lower part of Murder Kill Hundred, Kent County, upon Delaware, 1756, during the French and Indian Wars. [Ref: DA-12].

HUTCHISON, James. Private. Served in Capt. David Hall's Company, Delaware Regiment of Continental Troops. Enlisted January 27, 1776, and was on duty (in barracks) at Lewis Town on April 11, 1776. [Ref: DA-43].

HUTCHISON, John. Private. Served in Capt. David Hall's Company, Delaware Regiment of Continental Troops. Enlisted January 17, 1776, and was on duty (in barracks) at Lewis Town on April 11, 1776. After his name is written "on duty." [Ref: DA-42].

HUYGEN, Hendrick. Commander. Served as commissary at Fort Christina in New Sweden in 1638 and he was second commander or captain of the ship *Mercurius* during the twelfth expedition to New Sweden between 1655 and 1656. [Ref: DJ-699, DJ-700, DJ-761, DJ-762]. (His name has also been spelled "Hindrich Hugenn" or "Hindrick Hugens").

HYATT, John. Soldier. Son of Capt. Peter Hyatt. He applied from New Castle County, June, 1776, stating he wanted to take an active part in the Flying Camp, of Third Pennsylvania Battalion. [Ref: DA-65].

HYATT, Peter. See "John Hyatt," q.v.

IIKORN, Hans. Soldier. Served in New Sweden and returned to Europe with Director Rising in 1655. [Ref: DJ-724, 726]. (A note in this record stated that the name "*Iikorn*" also "*Ekor*" meant "*squirrel*").

INGRAM, Anthony. See "George Claypoole," q.v.

INGRAM, Mary. See "Thomas Prettyman," q.v.

INGRUM, Daniel. Private. Served in Capt. John Caton's Company, April 25, 1757, in the French and Indian Wars. [Ref: DA-14].

INNEPHAR, ----. Colonel. He held that rank by 1688 when mentioned in the deposition of John Barker in Sussex County. [Ref: DC-605].

INNIS, Timothy. Private. Born 1728, Kildare, Ireland. Tailor. Enlisted on May 9, 1758, during the French and Indian Wars, as a private by Capt. John McClughan "for the campaign in the lower counties." [Ref: DA-17].

IONSSON, Lars. Soldier. Served in New Sweden and returned to Europe with Director Rising in 1655. [Ref: DJ-724]. (His name has also been spelled "Lars Jonsson").

IRONS, Mark. Private. Served in Capt. Jonathan Caldwell's Company, Delaware Regiment of Continental Troops. Enlisted January 18, 1776, and was on duty (in barracks) at Dover on April 12, 1776. [Ref: DA-41]. Also see "Mark Hirons," q.v.

IRONS, Owen. Private. Served in Capt. John Caton's Company, April 25, 1757, in the French and Indian Wars. [Ref: DA-14]. When Thomas Irons wrote his will in Kent County on December 25, 1784, he named his brother Owen Irons (and other family members). [Ref: DK-366].

ISGATE, John. Private. Born 1726, Maryland. Laborer. Enlisted in Capt. John Shannon's Company of Foot on July 20, 1746, and served in King

George's War against Canada. He was in winter quarters at Albany, New York, during 1746-1747, and was discharged on October 31, 1747. [Ref: DA-4, DA-6]. (He is not listed in Source DM-40.)

ISGRA, Olof. Soldier. Arrived in New Sweden on the ship *Orn* in 1654. [Ref: DJ-719]. (His name has also been spelled "Icegrey").

ISTGATE, Henry. Private. Served in Capt. Nathan Adams' Company, Delaware Regiment of Continental Troops. Enlisted January 22, 1776, and on duty (in barracks) at Dover on April 12, 1776. [Ref: DA-53].

ISTGATE, William. Private. Served in Capt. Nathan Adams' Company, Delaware Regiment of Continental Troops. Enlisted January 22, 1776, and on duty (in barracks) at Dover on April 12, 1776. [Ref: DA-53].

JACKSON, Benjamin. Private. Enlisted on May 23, 1758, in Capt. French Battell's Company of Lower County Provincials, during the French and Indian Wars. [Ref: DA-16].

JACKSON, Caleb. See "Robert Hodgson," q.v.

JACKSON, Charles. Private. Born 1701, England. Laborer. Enlisted in Capt. John Shannon's Company of Foot on July 21, 1746, and served in King George's War against Canada. He was in winter quarters at Albany, New York, during 1746-1747, and was discharged on October 31, 1747. [Ref: DA-4, DA-6]. (He is not listed in Source DM-40.)

JACKSON, Christopher. Land patentee and probable militiaman in Delaware in November, 1677. [Ref: DP-167, 168].

JACKSON, George. Private. Born 1731, Maryland. Enlisted in Capt. John Wright's Company and was on the muster roll of May 11, 1759, during the French and Indian Wars. [Ref: DA-25].

JACKSON, Joseph. Private. Served in Capt. John Caton's Company, April 25, 1757, in the French and Indian Wars. [Ref: DA-14]. One "Joseph Jackson, farmer," died testate in Kent County and his will was probated on June 19, 1789, naming his wife Elizabeth, sons Noah and John, and daughters Nancy and Elizabeth. [Ref: DK-412, 413]. It should be noted that Daniel Virdin died in Kent County and his wife Elizabeth was named administratrix on May 15, 1776. A later account shows that Elizabeth Virdin married Joseph Jackson. [Ref: DK-304].

JACKSON, Moses. Private. Served in Capt. Nathan Adams' Company, Delaware Regiment of Continental Troops. Enlisted February 7, 1776, and on duty (in barracks) at Dover on April 12, 1776. [Ref: DA-53].

JACKSON, Paul. Captain. Recruited soldiers from "the three lower counties" [Delaware] to serve with the Pennsylvania Troops in 1758, during the French and Indian Wars. [Ref: DA-27].

JACKSON, Samuel. Private. Served in Capt. Samuel Smith's Company, Delaware Regiment of Continental Troops. Enlisted January 19, 1776, and on duty (in barracks) at Dover on April 12, 1776. [Ref: DA-54].

JACKSON, Southey. Private. Born 1738, Indian River, Maryland. Shoemaker. Enlisted on April 19, 1758, during the French and Indian Wars, as a private by Capt. John McClughan "for the campaign in the lower counties." [Ref: DA-17].

JACKSON, Thomas. Private. Served in Capt. John Caton's Company, April 25, 1757, in the French and Indian Wars. [Ref: DA-14]. One Thomas Jackson died in Kent County and the administration of his estate was granted to Ann Jackson on August 1, 1799. A subsequent account mentioned heirs as Marriah Jackson, Samuel Jackson, George Jackson, William Jackson, and Polly Manning. [Ref: DK-554].

JACKSON, Thomas. Soldier. Planter in Delaware who paid his quit-rent to the governor in 1668, having been granted a land patent to one-third of Bread and Cheese Island in Christeen Kill in the Delaware River on August 3, 1668. [Ref: DP-27, DP-28, DY-134].

JACKSON, William. Private. Served in Capt. John Caton's Company, April 25, 1757, in the French and Indian Wars. [Ref: DA-14]. One William Jackson died in Kent County and the administration of his estate was granted to widow Ruth Jackson on August 9, 1775. Heirs were mentioned in a later account as Thomas, Joseph, William, Ruth, Caleb, Jonathan, Mary, Susannah, and James Jackson, and Elizabeth Warran. Also, Ruth Jackson married Samuel Wheelor. [Ref: DK-299].

JACOB, Thomas. Soldier. Planter in Delaware who paid his quit-rent to the governor in 1669. [Ref: DP-27, DP-28].

JACOBS, Elizabeth and Mary. See "John Hemmins," q.v.

JACOBS, Hendrick. Soldier. Planter in Delaware who paid his quit-rent to the governor in 1669. [Ref: DP-27, 28].

JACOBSSON, Lars. Soldier. Arrived in New Sweden in 1643 and was a common soldier (*saldater*) at Fort Christina in 1644 and 1648. [Ref: DJ-701, DJ-713, DH-47]. (Name has also been spelled "Jacobsonn").

JACOBSSON, Dirck. Sailor. Arrived in New Sweden in 1644 and was "skipper on the sloop in the river," [i. e. the governor's yacht], having been taken into the service of the company in New Sweden on August 10, 1646. He died between 1650 and 1652. [Ref: DJ-715]. (His name has also been spelled "Diedrick Jacobsonn").

JACOBSSON, Hindrick. Soldier. Arrived in New Sweden on the ship *Orn* in 1654. This name appeared on a list of colonists from Frijsdalen, in

Varmland, Sweden, indicating he was about to go to New Sweden on October 17, 1655 "with four almost grown sons." [Ref: DJ-719, 725].

JACQUET, Peter. Ensign. Served in Capt. William Danford's Company, New Castle County, 1747-1748, in King George's War against Canada. [Ref: DA-7]. "Peter Jacquett, Jr." was an ensign in Capt. Henry Darby's Company, Delaware Regiment of Continental Troops, commissioned on January 17, 1776, and was on duty (in barracks) at Dover on April 12, 1776. [Ref: DA-45]. See "Peter Jaquet," q.v.

JAKE, Robert. Private. Enlisted on May 23, 1759, during the French and Indian Wars, and his name appeared on a return of Capt. Henry Van Bibber's Company of the Lower Counties on Delaware Troops, at New Castle, on June 4, 1759. [Ref: DA-26].

JAMES, Daniel. Captain. Served in a militia company in the Lower District of Mother Kill Hundred, Kent County, on March 29, 1758, during the French and Indian Wars. [Ref: DA-15]. One "Daniel James, gentleman" died testate, but without issue, in 1799. [Ref: DK-555].

JAMES, George. Private. Served in Capt. Richard McWilliams' Company, New Castle County. Enlisted on December 28, 1757, during the French and Indian Wars. [Ref: DA-15].

JAMES, James. Ensign. Served in Capt. James Edwards' Company, Kent County, in August, 1748, during King George's War against Canada. [Ref: DA-8]. One "James James, yeoman," was named administrator of Nathaniel James, mariner, on January 12, 1756. James James died intestate in Kent County and James Edwards, yeoman, was named his administrator on March 3, 1756 (and was also the administrator of Nathaniel James). [Ref: DK-162, DK-163].

JAMES, Nathaniel. See "James James," q.v.

JAMES, Thomas. Lieutenant Colonel. New Castle County Regiment, 1747-1748, in King George's War against Canada. [Ref: DA-7].

JAMES, Thomas. Major. Served in the Lower Regiment of New Castle County, 1756, in the French and Indian Wars. [Ref: DA-11, DM-46].

JANEKE, Hans. Barber-surgeon (*balberenn*). From Konigsbergh, he was an "officer" at Fort Christina, arriving in New Sweden on the ship *Fama* in 1643, and settled there in 1644 "in service of the Crown." [Ref: DJ-701, DJ-710, DH-50]. (Name also spelled "Hans Janche").

JANSE, Jurian. Soldier. Planter who paid his quit-rent to the governor in 1669. [Ref: DP-27, 28]. "Juryen Jans" received a land patent above the town of New Castle on March 24, ---- (year not stated). [Ref: DY-156].

JANSEN, Andrian. Skipper. Served on the ship *Kalmar Nyckel* during the fourth expedition to New Sweden, 1641-1642. [Ref: DJ-759].

JANSEN, Hendrick. Soldier. Planter in Delaware who paid his quit-rent to the governor in 1671, having received a land patent on January 8, 1667. [Ref: DP-29, DY-123].

JANSEN, Juriaen. Soldier. Planter in Delaware who paid his quit-rent to the governor in 1668. [Ref: DP-28]. "Juryaen Jansen" received a land patent on March 24, 1668/9. [Ref: DY-138].

JANSEN, Mattys. Soldier. Planter in Delaware who paid his quit-rent to the governor in 1668. [Ref: DP-28]. "Mattijs Jansen" received a land patent on March 24, 1668/9/ [Ref: DY-137].

JANSEN, Pauwel. Commander. Served on the ship *Kalmar Nyckel* during the second expedition to New Sweden in 1638-1640. [Ref: DJ-759].

JANSSON, Clas. Soldier (*saldater*). Served at Fort Christina in New Sweden, 1638-1640. [Ref: DJ-699]. (First name also spelled "Klas").

JANSSON, Jacob. Sailor. Mate on the ship *Mercurius* during the twelfth expedition to New Sweden in 1655-1656. [Ref: DJ-761, 762].

JANUARY, Benjamin. Private. Born 1715, New Castle, Delaware. Shoemaker. Enlisted April 23, 1758, in the French and Indian Wars, and was serving in Capt. Johnston's Company of the Pennsylvania Troops on May 12, 1759. [Ref: DA-27].

JANVIER, Francis. Lieutenant. Served in Capt. David Finney's Company, New Castle County, 1747-1748, in King George's War against Canada. [Ref: DA-7]. One Francis Janvier died testate in New Castle Hundred and his will was probated on November 14, 1798, naming his wife Sarah, brothers John and Philip Janvier, sister Sarah, and Maria Golden, daughter of John Golden, of Baltimore. [Ref: DN-145].

JANVIER, Isaac. Private. Served in Capt. Richard McWilliams' Company, New Castle County. Enlisted on December 28, 1757, during the French and Indian Wars. [Ref: DA-14]. (It appears there were two men by this name serving in this company.) One Isaac Janvier died testate in New Castle and his will was probated on February 5, 1772, naming his mother Mary, brothers Samuel and Philip, and sisters Mary and Sarah. [Ref: DN-69].

JANVIER, Jacob. Private. Served in Capt. Richard McWilliams' Company, New Castle County. Enlisted on December 28, 1757, during the French and Indian Wars. [Ref: DA-14].

JANVIER, Philip. Private. Served in Capt. Richard McWilliams' Company, New Castle County. Enlisted on December 28, 1757, during the French and Indian Wars. [Ref: DA-14].

JANVIER, Richard. Private. Served in Capt. Richard McWilliams' Company, New Castle County. Enlisted on December 28, 1757, during the French and Indian Wars. [Ref: DA-15].
JANVIER, Samuel. Private. Served in Capt. Richard McWilliams' Company, New Castle County. Enlisted on December 28, 1757, during the French and Indian Wars. [Ref: DA-14].
JAQUET, Paul. Soldier. Land patentee and planter who paid his quit-rent to the governor in 1669 and whose name appeared on a nomination list of officers in New Castle circa 1675 (list not dated). [Ref: DP-170]. "Jean Paul Jacques" received a land patent on March 26, 1669. [Ref: DY-158]. (Also spelled "Paulus Jaques").
JAQUET, John. Private. Served in Capt. Richard McWilliams' Company, New Castle County. Enlisted on December 28, 1757, during the French and Indian Wars. [Ref: DA-14].
JAQUET, Joseph. Private. Served in Capt. Richard McWilliams' Company, New Castle County. Enlisted on December 28, 1757, during the French and Indian Wars. [Ref: DA-14].
JAQUET, Peter. See "Nathaniel Silsbee" and "Peter Jacquet," q.v.
JAQUET, Peter. Private. Served in Capt. Richard McWilliams' Company, New Castle County. Enlisted on December 28, 1757, during the French and Indian Wars. [Ref: DA-14]. (It appears there were two men by this name serving in this company.) See "Peter Jacquet," q.v.
JAQUET, Peter Jr. Ensign. Served in the 4th Company, Delaware State Troops in Continental Service. Commissioned on January 17, 1776. [Ref: DA-34, DA-36]. (Name also spelled "Jaquett" and "Jacquet").
JAQUET, Thomas. Private. Served in Capt. Richard McWilliams' Company, New Castle County. Enlisted on December 28, 1757, during the French and Indian Wars. [Ref: DA-15].
JARRARD, William. See "John Rhodes," q.v.
JEFFRES, John. Private. Served in Capt. Joseph Stedham's Company, Delaware Battalion of Continental Troops. Enlisted on January 29, 1776, and was in quarters at Dover on April 12, 1776. [Ref: DA-39].
JEFFS, James. Private. Served in Capt. Henry Darby's Company, Delaware Regiment of Continental Troops. Enlisted January 22, 1776, and on duty (in barracks) at Dover on April 12, 1776. [Ref: DA-46].
JEGO, Pieter. Soldier. Planter who paid his quit-rent to the governor in 1670, having received a patent on Champone Kill on April 2, 1670. [Ref: DP-29, DY-146]. (First name spelled "Peter").
JESTER, Ebenezer. Private. Served in Capt. Joseph Vaughan's Company, Delaware Regiment of Continental Troops. Enlisted January 17, 1776,

and was on duty (in barracks) at Dover on April 12, 1776. [Ref: DA-57, 59]. (Same source spelled his name "Ebenezar Jestar").

JESTER, John. Private. Enlisted on May 16, 1758, in Capt. French Battell's Company of Lower County Provincials, during the French and Indian Wars. [Ref: DA-16].

JINKINS, John. Private. Served in Capt. Joseph Vaughan's Company, Delaware Regiment of Continental Troops. Enlisted February 8, 1776, and was on duty (in barracks) at Dover on April 12, 1776, at which time he was reported to be "sick in quarters." [Ref: DA-58, 59].

JOCHIMSEN, Jan. Gunner and Captain. "Johan Joachimss" was a gunner on the ship *Kalmar Nyckel* during the first expedition to New Sweden between 1637-1639. [Ref: DJ-758]. From Cappel, "Jan Jochimsen" was the captain on the ship *Gyllene Haj* during the seventh expedition to New Sweden between 1646-1647. [Ref: DJ-760]. (Name also spelled "Johan Jochimsson").

JOCHIMSON, Peter. Soldier. From Slesvik-Holstein, he arrived in New Sweden in 1643 and was a common soldier (*saldater*) at Fort Elfsborg in 1643-1644. [Ref: DH-47, DJ-703, DJ-714]. (His name has also been spelled "Petter Jochim" or "Peter Joachim").

JOENSSON, Anders. Soldier. Engaged by the nobleman Johan Papegoja on December 1, 1643 and living in New Sweden in 1648. [Ref: DH-50].

JOHANNSON, Simon. Soldier. Arrived in New Sweden on the ship *Orn* in 1654. [Ref: DJ-719].

JOHANSS, Peter. Boatswain. "From the Bemster who succeeded Andres Lucassen" [sic] he was an upper boatswain on the ship *Kalmar Nyckel* on the first expedition to New Sweden in 1637-1639. [Ref: DJ-758].

JOHANSSON, Karl. Commissary. An "officer placed over the provisions and accounts" at Fort Tinicum in 1643. [Ref: DJ-705].

JOHN, Daniel. Private. Born 1731, Pencader, Delaware. Laborer. Enlisted on May 8, 1758, during the French and Indian Wars, as a private by Capt. John McClughan "for the campaign in the lower counties." [Ref: DA-17].

JOHN, David. Lieutenant. Served in Capt. John Edwards' Company, New Castle County, August, 1748, in King George's War against Canada. [Ref: DA-7]. One "David John, yeoman," died testate in Pencader Hundred, New Castle County,, and his will was probated on February 7, 1780, naming his wife Mary, son Jehu, and niece Susanna Wattson (wife of Thomas Wattson). [Ref: DN-93].

JOHNSON, Henrik. Officer. His name appeared on a nomination list of officers in New Castle circa 1675 (list not dated). [Ref: DP-170].

JOHNSON, John. Soldier. Planter in Delaware who paid his quit-rent to the governor in 1671, having received a patent to land on St. Jones Creek on June 19, 1671. [Ref: DP-29, DY-153].
JOHNSON, Joshua. Private. Served in Capt. Joseph Vaughan's Company, Delaware Regiment of Continental Troops. Enlisted January 20, 1776, and was reported as deserted on March 20, 1776. [Ref: DA-59].
JOHNSON, Martin Gill. Soldier. Enlisted on May 15, 1759, during the French and Indian Wars, and appeared on a return of Capt. Henry Van Bibber's Company of the Lower Counties on Delaware Troops, at New Castle, on June 4, 1759. [Ref: DA-26].
JOHNSON, Polly. See "John Haveloe," q.v.
JOHNSON, Samuel. Private. Served in Capt. John Caton's Company, April 25, 1757, during the French and Indian Wars. [Ref: DA-14]. One Samuel Johnson died in Kent County and his will was probated on October 29, 1792, naming his wife Mary Ann, sons William, Nathan, Purnal, and James, and daughters Elizabeth Davis (wife of Nathan Davis), Sarah, Mary, Priscilla, Nancy, and Phebe. [Ref: DK-459].
JOHNSTON, Jean. See "John Elliott," q.v.
JOHNSTON, John. Private. Born 1736, Ulster, Ireland. Laborer. Enlisted on May 2, 1759, in the French and Indian Wars, in Capt. James Armstrong's Company in Pennsylvania Regiment. [Ref: DA-26].
JOHNSTON, John. Private. Served in Capt. Joseph Stedham's Company, Delaware Battalion of Continental Troops. Enlisted on March 12, 1776, and was in quarters at Dover on April 12, 1776. [Ref: DA-40].
JONES, Abel. Private. Born 1730 (place not stated). Joiner. Enlisted on May 1, 1759, in the French and Indian Wars, in Capt. James Armstrong's Company, Pennsylvania Regiment. [Ref: DA-26].
JONES, Ann and John. See "Samuel Davis," q.v.
JONES, Benjamin. Private, Capt. Joseph Vaughan's Company, Delaware Regiment of Continental Troops. Enlisted February 16, 1776, and was on duty (in barracks) at Dover on April 12, 1776. [Ref: DA-58, 59]. (This same source also spelled his name "Benjamin Joanes").
JONES, Christopher. Private. Born 1733, West Meath, Ireland. Miller. Enlisted on April 26, 1758, during the French and Indian Wars, as a private by Capt. John McClughan "for the campaign in the lower counties." [Ref: DA-17].
JONES, Ebenezer. Private. Served in Capt. Nathan Adams' Company, Delaware Regiment of Continental Troops. Enlisted January 20, 1776, and on duty (in barracks) at Dover on April 12, 1776. [Ref: DA-52].

JONES, Edmond. Private. Served in Capt. Joseph Vaughan's Company, Delaware Regiment of Continental Troops. Enlisted February 1, 1776, and was on duty (in barracks) at Dover on April 12, 1776. [Ref: DA-58, DA-59]. (This same source spelled his name "Edmond Joans").

JONES, Evan. Private. Served in Capt. Charles Pope's Company, Delaware Regiment of Continental Troops. Enlisted January 15, 1776, and was on duty (in quarters) at Lewis Town on April 11, 1776. [Ref: DA-51].

JONES, Francis. Private. Served in Capt. Joseph Vaughan's Company, Delaware Regiment of Continental Troops. Enlisted on February 16, 1776, and was on duty (in barracks) at Dover on April 12, 1776. [Ref: DA-58, 59]. (Same source spelled his name "Francis Joanes").

JONES, James. Private. Served in Capt. Joseph Vaughan's Company, Delaware Regiment of Continental Troops. Enlisted February 3, 1776, and was on duty (in barracks) at Dover on April 12, 1776. [Ref: DA-58, DA-59]. (THis same source spelled his name "James Joanes").

JONES, James. See "William Wheeler," q.v.

JONES, John. Sergeant. Born 1738, Philadelphia, Pennsylvania. Barber. Enlisted on April 19, 1758, during the French and Indian Wars, by Capt. John McClughan "for the campaign in the lower counties." [Ref: DA-17].

JONES, John. Private. Born 1733, Wales. Laborer. Enlisted on April 15, 1758, during the French and Indian Wars, by Capt. Benjamin Noxon. [Ref: DA-19].

JONES, John. Private. Born 1724, New England. Cordwainer. Enlisted in Capt. John Shannon's Company of Foot on June 26, 1746, and he served in King George's War against Canada. He signed his name when paid for services on June 6, 1747. He was in winter quarters at Albany, New York, during 1746-1747, and was discharged on October 31, 1747. [Ref: DA-4, DA-5, DA-6, DM-40].

JONES, John. Captain. Served in a company in St. George's Hundred, Lower Regiment, New Castle County, 1756, during the French and Indian Wars. [Ref: DA-11, DM-46].

JONES, Joseph. Private. Born 1738, Wales. Joiner. Enlisted on April 24, 1758, during the French and Indian Wars, by Capt. Benjamin Noxon. [Ref: DA-19].

JONES, Layton and Mary. See "William Wallace," q.v.

JONES, Martha and Selathial. See "Joseph Marrat," q.v.

JONES, Matthias. Private. Served in Capt. Nathan Adams' Company, Delaware Regiment of Continental Troops. Enlisted January 27, 1776, and on duty (in barracks) at Dover on April 12, 1776. [Ref: DA-53].

JONES, Moses. Private. Served in Capt. Nathan Adams' Company, Delaware Regiment of Continental Troops. Enlisted January 16, 1776, and on duty (in barracks) at Dover on April 12, 1776. [Ref: DA-52].

JONES, Nicholas Thomas. Captain. He held that rank by 1706 when mentioned in an Action of Debt in Sussex County. [Ref: DC-1220].

JONES, Rees. Captain. Served with a company in White Clay Creek Hundred, Upper Regiment, New Castle County, 1756, during the French and Indian Wars. [Ref: DA-11, DM-45].

JONES, Penelope Holt. See "Ryves Holt," q.v.

JONES, Reese. See "John Shannon," q.v.

JONES, Richard Mariot. Private. Born 1724, Kent County. Laborer. 5 ft. 11 in. tall, long visaged, with brown hair, brown complexion, slender limbed. He enlisted on May 12, 1759, during the French and Indian Wars, in Philadelphia, Pennsylvania, by Capt. Samuel Neilson for the Pennsylvania Regiment. [Ref: DA-28].

JONES, Robert. Private. Born 1712, Ireland. Bricklayer. Enlisted in Capt. John Shannon's Company of Foot on June 30, 1746, and served in King George's War against Canada. He was in winter quarters at Albany, New York, during 1746-1747, and was discharged on October 31, 1747. [Ref: DA-4, DA-6]. (He is not listed in Source DM-40.)

JONES, Robert. Soldier. Planter in Delaware who paid his quit-rent to the governor in 1669, having been granted "a small parcel of land convenient to keep a ferry in Christeen Kill at Delaware" on October 1, 1669. [Ref: DP-27, DP-28, DY-143].

JONES, Thomas. Private. Born 1736, Wales. Laborer. Enlisted on April 24, 1758, in the French and Indian Wars, by Capt. Benjamin Noxon. [Ref: DA-19].

JONES, Thomas. Private. Served in Capt. Nathan Adams' Company, Delaware Regiment of Continental Troops. Enlisted January 16, 1776, and on duty (in barracks) at Dover on April 12, 1776. [Ref: DA-52].

JONES, Vincent. Private. Served in Capt. Nathan Adams' Company, Delaware Regiment of Continental Troops. Enlisted January 19, 1776, and on duty (in barracks) at Dover on April 12, 1776. [Ref: DA-52].

JONES, William. Drummer. Served in Capt. Samuel Smith's Company, Delaware Regiment of Continental Troops. Enlisted January 15, 1776, and on duty (in barracks) at Dover on April 12, 1776. [Ref: DA-54].

JONES, William. Private. Served in Capt. Joseph Vaughan's Company, Delaware Regiment of Continental Troops. Enlisted January 21, 1776, and was on duty (in barracks) at Dover on April 12, 1776. [Ref: DA-57, DA-59]. (This same source spelled his name "William Joans").

JONSSON, Hans. Soldier. Arrived in New Sweden on the *Orn* in 1654. Maybe the same as "Hans Jansson, the Finn." [Ref: DJ-719]. (This same source also spelled his name "Hans Janssen").

JONSSON, Anders. Soldier. He was a common soldier (*saldater*) at Fort Elfsborg, 1643, and was "probably the same as Anders Jonsson, from Nykoping, who was here [in New Sweden] in 1642. In that case he returned to Sweden in 1643 and came here a second time in 1644 on the ship *Fama*. He was engaged as a soldier on December 1, 1643, by the nobleman Johan Papegoja, and served until his execution on August 1, 1643" (no reason stated in source). [Ref: DJ-703, 714]. (Name also spelled "Anders Joensonn").

JONSSON, Powell. Soldier. From Jamtland he was hired by Mans Kling as a farm hand in 1641 and arrived in New Sweden that year. "On October 1, 1646, Governor [Johan] Printz hired him as a soldier for 4 *riksdalers* a month. He returned to Sweden." [Ref: DJ-711]. "Pal Joransson, or Jonsson" was a soldier in 1648. [Ref: DH-45]. (Name also spelled Pafvel Joensonn").

JONSSON, Anders. Officer. Served as a lieutenant on the ship *Swan* in the eighth expedition to New Sweden, 1647-1648. [Ref: DJ-761]. (His name also been spelled "Andreas Joranson").

JONSSON, Anders. Soldier. Arrived in New Sweden on the ship *Orn* in 1654. [Ref: DJ-719].

JONSTON, John. Private. Served in Capt. Henry Darby's Company, Delaware Regiment of Continental Troops. Enlisted February 23, 1776, and was on duty (in barracks) at Dover on April 12, 1776. [Ref: DA-46].

JORANSEN, Andrian. Skipper. Served on the ship *Kalmar Nyckel* during the first expedition to New Sweden, 1637-1639. [Ref: DJ-758].

JORANSSON, Anders. Gunner (*constaple*). Served in New Sweden, 1640-1643. [Ref: DJ-700].

JORANSSON, Nils. Soldier. Arrived in New Sweden on the ship *Orn* in 1654. [Ref: DJ-719].

JORANSSON, Pal. See "Powell Jonsson," q.v.

JORENSON, Clemet. Soldier. Served as an "officer" at Fort Tinicum in 1643. [Ref: DJ-705]. "Clement Joransson" was a courier and one of the "forest destroying Finns" of the parish of Lund, Vermland. He "enlisted for punishment in the soldiery" and was permitted by a local governor to go to New Sweden. He was a freeman by 1648. [Ref: DH-45].

JEWETT, Robert. First Officer. Served with Capt. Henry Hudson on the ship *Half Moon* and was the first Englishman to site the [now] Delaware Bay on August 28, 1609. With this discovery the Dutch founded their claim to the lands adjacent to the North and South Rivers, now known as the Hudson and Delaware Rivers. [Ref: DH-24].

JULIUS, Carl. Secretary (*schreiber*). An "officer" in New Sweden, he arrived on the ship *Orn* in 1654 and returned with Director Rising to Europe in 1655. [Ref: DJ-716, DJ-724].

JUMP, Benjamin. Private. Served in Capt. Nathan Adams' Company, Delaware Regiment of Continental Troops. Enlisted February 6, 1776, and was on duty (in barracks) at Dover on April 12, 1776, at which time he was reported to be "sick in quarters." [Ref: DA-53].

JUNGE, Jacob. Clerk (*packhauschreiber*). An "officer" in New Sweden, he arrived on the ship *Orn* in 1654. [Ref: DJ-716].

JURIANSEN, Juriaen. Soldier. Planter in Delaware who paid his quitrent to the governor in 1669, having been granted land on Christeen Kill, November 5, 1669. [Ref: DP-27, 28, DY-143].

KABELIAW, Peter Pawelsson. Skipper. Served on the ship *Fama* in sixth expedition to New Sweden, 1643-1644. [Ref: DJ-760]. (Name also spelled "Cabeliau").

KAGHEY, Robert. Fifer. Served in Capt. Samuel Smith's Company, Delaware Regiment of Continental Troops. Enlisted January 17, 1776, and on duty (in barracks) at Dover on April 12, 1776. [Ref: DA-54].

KAIN, Daniel. Private. Born 1729, Antrim, Ireland. Shoemaker. Enlisted on April 20, 1758, during the French and Indian Wars, as a private by Capt. John McClughan "for the campaign in the lower counties." [Ref: DA-17].

KAIN, Thomas. Private. Served in Capt. Joseph Stedham's Company, Delaware Battalion of Continental Troops. Enlisted on January 24, 1776, and was in quarters at Dover on April 12, 1776. [Ref: DA-39].

KAMPE, Anders. Armorer (*rustmastaren*). An "officer" in New Sweden, he arrived on the ship *Orn* in 1654 and he returned to Europe with Director Rising in 1655. [Ref: DJ-716]. See "Andhers Kiampe," q.v.

KAYLE, Thomas. Private. Born 1728 (no place given). Carpenter. Enlisted on May 12, 1758, in the French and Indian Wars, by Capt. John McClughan "for the campaign in lower counties." [Ref: DA-17].

KEARNS, James. Private. Served in Capt. Jonathan Caldwell's Company of Delaware Regiment of Continental Troops. Enlisted February 11,

1776, and was on duty (in barracks) at Dover on April 12, 1776. [Ref: DA-41].

KEEN, Juriaen. Soldier. Planter in Delaware who paid his quit-rent to the governor in 1668. [Ref: DP-28].

KEITH, Charles. Soldier. Enlisted May 28, 1759, during the French and Indian Wars, and his name appeared on a return of Capt. Henry Van Bibber's Company of the Lower Counties on Delaware Troops, at New Castle, on June 4, 1759. [Ref: DA-26].

KELLAM, Benjamin. Ensign. Served in Capt. Emanuel Grubb's Company, Brandywine Hundred, Upper Regiment, New Castle County, 1756, during the French and Indian Wars. [Ref: DA-11]. A Benjamin Kellam died in Brandywine Hundred and his will was probated on February 3, 1775, naming his wife Mary, brother Moses, and nephew John. [Ref: DN-78].

KELLY, John. Private. Born 1730, Down, Ireland. Laborer. Enlisted on April 20, 1758, in the French and Indian Wars, by Capt. John McClughan "for the campaign in the lower counties." [Ref: DA-17].

KELLY, John. Private. Served in Capt. Jonathan Caldwell's Company, Delaware Regiment of Continental Troops. Enlisted January 16, 1776, and on duty (in barracks) at Dover on April 12, 1776. [Ref: DA-41].

KELLY, Matthew. Private. Born 1733, Ireland. Laborer. Enlisted on April 24, 1758, in the French and Indian Wars, by Capt. Benjamin Noxon. [Ref: DA-19].

KELLY, Peter. Private. Born 1710, Ireland. Tanner. Enlisted in Capt. John Shannon's Company of Foot on July 2, 1746, and served in King George's War against Canada. He was in winter quarters at Albany, New York, during 1746-1747, and was discharged on October 31, 1747. [Ref: DA-4, DA-6]. (He is not listed in Source DM-40.)

KELLY, Thomas. Sergeant. Served in Capt. Nathan Adams' Company, Delaware Regiment of Continental Troops. Enlisted January 23, 1776, and on duty (in barracks) at Dover on April 12, 1776. [Ref: DA-52].

KELLY, William. Private. Served in Capt. Joseph Stedham's Company, Delaware Battalion of Continental Troops. Enlisted February 9, 1776, and was in quarters at Dover on April 12, 1776. [Ref: DA-40].

KELSE, Richard. Soldier. Enlisted May 21, 1759, during the French and Indian Wars, and his name appeared on a return of Capt. Henry Van Bibber's Company of the Lower Counties on Delaware Troops, at New Castle, on June 4, 1759. [Ref: DA-26].

KEMMEY, Job. Private. Enlisted on May 19, 1758, in Capt. French Battell's Company of Lower County Provincials, during the French and Indian Wars. [Ref: DA-16].

KENEDY, David. Corporal. Served in Capt. Samuel Smith's Company, Delaware Regiment of Continental Troops. Enlisted January 17, 1776, and on duty (in barracks) at Dover on April 12, 1776. [Ref: DA-54].

KENNEDY, James. Private. Born 1735 (place not stated). Laborer. Enlisted May 6, 1759, in the French and Indian Wars, Capt. James Armstrong's Company in the Pennsylvania Regiment. [Ref: DA-26].

KENT, John. Private. Born 1724, Kent, Delaware. Laborer. Enlisted in Capt. John Shannon's Company of Foot on July 14, 1746, serving in King George's War against Canada. He was in winter quarters at Albany, New York, during 1746-1747, and was discharged on October 31, 1747. [Ref: DA-4, DA-6]. (He is not listed in Source DM-40.)

KERREL, William. Private. Served in Capt. Joseph Stedham's Company, Delaware Battalion of Continental Troops. Enlisted January 27, 1776, and was in quarters at Dover on April 12, 1776. [Ref: DA-39].

KERSEY, Archibald. Private. Served in Capt. Nathan Adams' Company, Delaware Regiment of Continental Troops. Enlisted January 22, 1776, and on duty (in barracks) at Dover on April 12, 1776. [Ref: DA-53].

KERSEY, William. Private. Served in Capt. Nathan Adams' Company, Delaware Regiment of Continental Troops. Enlisted February 5, 1776, and on duty (in barracks) at Dover on April 12, 1776. [Ref: DA-53].

KERSHAW, Mitchell. Private. Served in Capt. Joseph Vaughan's Company, Delaware Regiment, Continental Troops. Enlisted January 20, 1776, and on duty (in barracks) at Dover on April 12, 1776. [Ref: DA-57, 59]. (This same source spelled his name "Kirshaw").

KETCHMORE, Thomas. Private. Born 1736, England. Blacksmith. Enlisted on April 19, 1758, during the French and Indian Wars, by Capt. Benjamin Noxon. [Ref: DA-19].

KEYS, Rachel and John. See "Job Merideth," q.v.

KEYS, William. Private. Enlisted on May 17, 1758, in Capt. French Battell's Company of Lower County Provincials, during the French and Indian Wars. [Ref: DA-16].

KIAMPE. Andhers. Soldier. His name appeared on the list of soldiers who returned to Europe with Director Rising in 1655. [Ref: DJ-724].

KIDD, Charles. Sergeant. Served in Capt. Joseph Vaughan's Company, Delaware Regiment of Continental Troops. Enlisted January 15, 1776, and on duty (in barracks) at Dover on April 12, 1776. [Ref: DA-59].

KILLEN, James. Private. Served in Capt. Joseph Stedham's Company, Delaware Battalion of Continental Troops. Enlisted January 24, 1776, and was in quarters at Dover on April 12, 1776. [Ref: DA-39].

KILLEN, Robert. Captain. Served in a company of militia in middle part of Mispillim [Mispillion] Hundred, Kent County, upon Delaware, 1756, in the French and Indian Wars. One "Robert Killen, Esq." died testate in Kent County and his will was probated January 18, 1771, naming his wife Mary, sons Robert, William, Adam, Henry, John, and Mark, and his grandchildren Polly, Betty, and Sally Buckannon. His widow, Mary, died in Mispillion Hundred in November, 1783, and son Henry was named administrator. [Ref: DA-12, DM-46, DK-256, DK-354].

KILLEN, William and Rebecca (and family). See "Jacob Allee," q.v.

KILPATRICK, John. Private. Served in Capt. Nathan Adams' Company, Delaware Regiment of Continental Troops. Enlisted January 15, 1776, and on duty (in barracks) at Dover on April 12, 1776. [Ref: DA-52].

KILPATRICK, Patrick. Private. Born 1734, Faughboyne, Ireland. Weaver. Enlisted on April 24, 1758, during the French and Indian Wars, as a private by Capt. John McClughan "for the campaign in the lower counties." [Ref: DA-18].

KILTY, William. Private. Served in Capt. Henry Darby's Company, Delaware Regiment of Continental Troops. Enlisted January 22, 1776, and on duty (in barracks) at Dover on April 12, 1776. [Ref: DA-46].

KIMMEY, John. Private. Served in Capt. John Caton's Company, April 25, 1757, in the French and Indian Wars. [Ref: DA-14].

KING, Alexander. Private. Served in Capt. Henry Darby's Company, Delaware Regiment of Continental Troops. Enlisted January 27, 1776, and on duty (in barracks) at Dover on April 12, 1776. [Ref: DA-46].

KING, Comfort. See "Burton Waples," q.v.

KING, James. Lieutenant. Served in Capt. Alexander Porter's Company in New Castle County, 1747-1748, during King George's War against Canada. [Ref: DA-7].

KING, John. Officer. His name appeared on a nomination list for officers for the Whorekill in Sussex County, Delaware circa 1675 (list not dated). [Ref: DP-170].

KING, Mary. See "Cord Hazzard," q.v.

KING, Sarah and William. See "Elias Conwell," q.v.

KINK, John. Private. Served in Capt. Richard McWilliams' Company, New Castle County. Enlisted on December 28, 1757, during the French and Indian Wars. [Ref: DA-15].

KINNAMON, John. Private. Served in Capt. Jonathan Caldwell's Company, Delaware Regiment of Continental Troops. Enlisted January 12, 1776, and on duty (in barracks) at Dover on April 12, 1776. [Ref: DA-41].

KINNEY, Daniel. Private. Served in Capt. John Caton's Company on April 25, 1757, in the French and Indian Wars. [Ref: DA-13].

KINSEY, Gilbert. Private. Born 1702, England. Cordwainer. Enlisted in Capt. John Shannon's Company of Foot on July 16, 1746, serving in King George's War against Canada. He was in winter quarters at Albany, New York, during 1746-1747, and was discharged on October 31, 1747. [Ref: DA-4, DA-6]. (He is not listed in Source DM-40.)

KINSEY, John. See "John Shannon," q.v.

KIRKE, John. Land patentee and probable militiaman in Delaware in November, 1677. [Ref: DP-167, 168].

KIRKPATRICK, David. Second Lieutenant. Served in Capt. John McClughan's Company on April 25, 1758, during the French and Indian Wars, and was later reported "dead" (no date given). [Ref: DA-16].

KIRKPATRICK, John. Private. Born 1733, Ireland. Laborer. Enlisted on May 23, 1758, in the French and Indian Wars, by Capt. Benjamin Noxon. [Ref: DA-19].

KIRKWOOD, Robert Jr. First lieutenant. Served in the 4th Company, Delaware State Troops in Continental Service. Commissioned on January 17, 1776. [Ref: DA-34, 36].

KIRKWOOD, Thomas. Private. Served in Capt. Henry Darby's Company, Delaware Regiment of Continental Troops. Enlisted January 19, 1776, and was reported as "deserted" on February 4, 1776. [Ref: DA-46].

KITSON, Thomas. Private. Born 1724, Worcester, England. Laborer. Enlisted on April 24, 1758, during the French and Indian Wars, as a private by Capt. John McClughan "for the campaign in the lower counties." [Ref: DA-18].

KITTLE, Magnus. Private. Served in Capt. Richard McWilliams' Company, New Castle County. Enlisted on December 28, 1757, during the French and Indian Wars. [Ref: DA-14].

KLING, Mans Nilsson. Commander. Officer at Fort Christina in New Sweden, 1638-1640, and was lieutenant (*leutenampten*) in New Sweden from 1640 to 1643, at the Schuylkill Plantation. He returned to Sweden in 1648. [Ref: DJ-699, DJ-704, DJ-715, DH-44].

KNIGHTS, Haward. See "Thomas Pemberton," q.v.

KNOCK, Thomas. Corporal. Served in Capt. Samuel Smith's Company, Delaware Regiment of Continental Troops. Enlisted January 17, 1776, and on duty (in barracks) at Dover on April 12, 1776. [Ref: DA-54].

KNOCK, William. Private. Served in Capt. Charles Pope's Company, Delaware Regiment of Continental Troops. Enlisted January 13, 1776, and was on duty (in quarters) at Lewis Town on April 11, 1776. [Ref: DA-51].

KNOTTS, John. Sergeant. Served in Capt. Nathan Adams' Company, Delaware Regiment of Continental Troops. Enlisted January 20, 1776, and on duty (in barracks) at Dover on April 12, 1776. [Ref: DA-52].

KOCH, Friedrich Hans. Barber-surgeon. An "officer" in New Sweden, he returned to Sweden in 1648. [Ref: DJ-716].

KOLLOCK, Cornelius. Captain. Pre-deceased his wife Hannah who had died on October 14, 1774, as noted in the records of the Lewes and Coolspring Presbyterian Church in Lewes, Delaware. [Ref: DV-115].

KOLLOCK, Jacob. Lieutenant. Served in Capt. John Shannon's Company on June 25, 1746, during King George's War against Canada. He was in winter quarters at Albany, New York, during 1746-1747, and his company was discharged October 31, 1747. He was probably the same Jacob Kollock who was colonel of the militia regiment of Sussex County, 1756-1758, during the French and Indian Wars. [Ref: DA-6, DA-13, DM-46]. One "Jacob Kollock, Esq.," of Lewes, Delaware, died testate and his will was probated February 21, 1772, naming wife Margaret, sons Philip and Jacob, Jr., daughters Hester Kollock, Mary Kollock, Catherine Wiltbank (wife of Abraham), Hannah Nunez (wife of Daniel) and Magdelan Swift, plus granddaughter Mary Swift, and children of deceased daughter Jane Lewis. [Ref: DS-90, DS-100].

KOLLOCK, Jacob Jr. Lieutenant. Served in Capt. David Hall's Company in the Northern District of Lewes and Rehoboth Hundred, and in the regiment of Sussex County in 1756, during the French and Indian Wars. He was a lieutenant in the Lewes District Company on March 19, 1758. [Ref: DA-13, DA-15]. He served as Commissioner of Sussex County in 1759. [Ref: DM-50]. One "Jacob Kollock, gentleman," died in Sussex County and his will was probated on November 4, 1790, naming his wife Mary, his sons Cornelius, John Leech, Phillip, and Jacob, and daughters Rebecca Kollock, Mary Train, Alice Green (wife of John) and Hester Hodgkinson (wife of Peter). [Ref: DS-220, 221].

KOLLOCK, Jacob, Esq. See "Richard Wells," q.v.

KOLLOCK, Phillip and Jacob. See "Jacob Phillips," q.v.

KREAMER, Jacob. Private. Born 1739, Thorlowitz, Germany. Laborer. Enlisted on May 11, 1758, during the French and Indian Wars, by Capt. John McClughan "for the campaign in the lower counties." [Ref: DA-17]. (Name also spelled "Cremer").

KRUM, Martin. Soldier. Arrived in New Sweden on the ship *Orn* in 1654 and he returned to Europe with Director Rising in 1655. [Ref: DJ-720, 724]. (Name also spelled "Marten Crum").

KRYSNER, Mickel. Soldier (*saldater*). Served in New Sweden and died on June 10, 1643 at Fort Christina. [Ref: DJ-707].

LACKLAND, Joseph. Private. Served in Capt. Henry Darby's Company, Delaware Regiment of Continental Troops. Enlisted January 25, 1776, and on duty (in barracks) at Dover on April 12, 1776. [Ref: DA-46].

LAERSEN, Olle. Soldier. Planter in Delaware who paid his quit-rent to the governor in 1668, having received a patent to land on Christine Kill on March 24, 1668. [Ref: DP-28, DY-138]. Source DY-136 also spelled his name "Olle Laerten" in the patents.

LAERSEN, Paul. Soldier. Planter in Delaware who paid his quit-rent to the governor in 1668, having received a patent for land on Christeen Kill on March 24, 1668. [Ref: DP-28, DY-137].

LAKE, John. Private. Born 1728, Great Hornet, England. Butcher. Enlisted on May 6, 1758, during the French and Indian Wars, as a private by Capt. John McClughan "for the campaign in the lower counties." [Ref: DA-18].

LAMB, Abner. Captain. He married Sally White on February 4, 1767, as noted in the records of the Lewes and Coolspring Presbyterian Church in Lewes, Delaware. [Ref: DV-124].

LAMBERT, John. See "Whelor Merideth," q.v.

LANCASTER, Henry. Private. Born 1735, Maryland. Laborer. Enlisted on April 29, 1758, during the French and Indian Wars, by Capt. Benjamin Noxon. [Ref: DA-19].

LANCASTER, Samuel. Private. Served in Capt. Samuel Smith's Company, Delaware Regiment of Continental Troops. Enlisted February 2, 1776, and on duty (in barracks) at Dover on April 12, 1776. [Ref: DA-54].

LANCASTER, Sinclair. Private. Born 1737, Maryland. Cordwainer. Enlisted on April 25, 1758, during the French and Indian Wars, by Capt. Benjamin Noxon. [Ref: DA-19].

LAND, Dorcas. See "Samuel Alricks," q.v.

LAND, Samuell. Officer. His name appeared on a nomination list for officers in New Castle circa 1675 (list not dated). [Ref: DP-170].

LANGREL, Sally. See "Samuel Bevens Turner," q.v.

LAPPIN, Paul. Private. Born 1727, Ireland. Laborer. Enlisted in Capt. John Shannon's Company of Foot on July 21, 1746, and served in King George's War against Canada. He made his mark when he was paid for his services on June 6, 1747. He was in winter quarters at Albany, New York, during 1746-1747, and was discharged on October 31, 1747. [Ref: DA-4, DA-5, DA-6, DM-40].

LAREY, Dennis. See "Dennis Learea," q.v.

LARIMORE, Hugh. Private. Born 1723, Ireland. Weaver. Enlisted May 3, 1758, in the French and Indian Wars, by Capt. Benjamin Noxon. [Ref: DA-19].

LARKIN, Henry. Private. Served in Capt. Henry Darby's Company, Delaware Regiment of Continental Troops. Enlisted on February 15, 1776, and was on duty (in barracks) at Dover on April 12, 1776. [Ref: DA-46].

LARKINS, John. Private. Enlisted on May 22, 1758, in Capt. French Battell's Company of Lower County Provincials, during the French and Indian Wars. [Ref: DA-16].

LARSSON, Alexander. Soldier. Served in New Sweden in 1654, and was paid various sums by Director Rising for his services. [Ref: DJ-726]. (He was also referred to as "Sander Larson").

LARSSON, Anders. Sergeant. An "officer" in New Sweden, he arrived there on the ship *Orn* in 1654. He may be the same person as "Anders Larsson, freeman," who was ill on June 9, 1654, and was on the ship *Orn* in New Sweden. There was also an Anders Larsson on a list of colonists from Frijsdalen, in Varmland, Sweden, indicating he was about to go to New Sweden on October 17, 1655, "with wife and five children." [Ref: DJ-716, 719, 724].

LARSSON, Eskell. Laborer. He was sent to New Sweden in 1641 by the "College of War to serve as a punishment because he deserted from the Army." Later, he was made a free laborer. "Eskill Larsonn" was an "officer" at Fort Tinicum in 1643. He was the father of "Bertil Eskilsonn," q.v. [Ref: DJ-705, DJ-712, DH-45].

LARSSON, Hindrick. Soldier. Arrived in New Sweden on the ship *Orn* in 1654. [Ref: DJ-720]. (Also referred to as "Hindrick Larsson, the Finn." See "From, Hindrick Larsson," q.v.)

LARSSON, Mans. Soldier (*saldater*). Served in New Sweden and died on July 3, 1643, at Fort Elfsborg. [Ref: DJ-707].

LARSSON, Nils. Constable and prisonkeeper (*gewaldiger, gevalier*). He arrived in New Sweden on the ship *Orn* in 1654. [Ref: DJ-716].

LARSSON, Olof. Soldier. Served in New Sweden in 1654 and was paid various sums by Director Rising for his services. [Ref: DJ-726].

LARSSON, Peder. Soldier. Arrived in New Sweden on the ship *Orn* in 1654. [Ref: DJ-720]. (Also referred to as "Per Larson").

LASHANY, John. Private. Served in Capt. Charles Pope's Company, Delaware Regiment of Continental Troops. Enlisted January 15, 1776, and was on duty (in quarters) at Lewis Town on April 11, 1776. [Ref: DA-51].

LASTLEY, William. Private. Served in Capt. Samuel Smith's Company, Delaware Regiment of Continental Troops. Enlisted January 29, 1776, and on duty (in barracks) at Dover on April 12, 1776. [Ref: DA-54].

LASTLY, Barnabas. Private. Born 1722, Ireland. Laborer. Enlisted in Capt. John Shannon's Company of Foot on July 23, 1746, and served in King George's War against Canada. He was in winter quarters at Albany, New York, during 1746-1747, and was discharged on October 31, 1747. [Ref: DA-4, DA-6]. (He is not listed in Source DM-40.)

LATHBURRY, George. Private. Served in Capt. David Hall's Company, Delaware Regiment of Continental Troops. Enlisted on February 16, 1776, and was on duty (in barracks) at Lewis Town on April 11, 1776. After his name is written "on guard." [Ref: DA-43].

LATIMER, James. Captain. Served in a company in Christiana Hundred, Upper Regiment, New Castle County, in 1756, during the French and Indian Wars. [Ref: DA-11, DM-45].

LAUGHLIN, Robert. Corporal. Served in Capt. Samuel Smith's Company, Delaware Regiment of Continental Troops. Enlisted January 17, 1776, and was on duty (in barracks) at Dover on April 12, 1776. [Ref: DA-54, DA-55]. (This same source spelled his name "Robert Laughlen").

LAURY, William. Provost-marshal. Served at Fort Christina in New Sweden, 1638-1640. He was "probably an Englishman, and returned to Sweden in 1642." [Ref: DJ-699].

LAVEL, David. Private. Born 1744, New Castle, Delaware. Laborer. Enlisted by Capt. John Haslet on May 7, 1759, during the French and Indian Wars, from "the three lower counties" to serve with the Pennsylvania Troops. [Ref: DA-27].

LAWLY, Daniel. Private. Served in Capt. Jonathan Caldwell's Company of the Delaware Regiment of Continental Troops. Enlisted on January 27, 1776, and on duty (in barracks) at Dover on April 12, 1776. [Ref: DA-41].

LAWRIE, Thomas. Captain. Served in the War of Jenkins' Ear in 1739-1741. His company may have included soldiers from Delaware (muster rolls not extant). [Ref: DM-32].

LAWSA, Nealse. Soldier. Planter in Delaware who paid his quit-rent to the governor in 1669. [Ref: DP-27, DP-28].

LAY, Ann. See "Baptist Newcomb," q.v.

LAYTON, Lilliston. Private. Served in Capt. David Hall's Company, Delaware Regiment of Continental Troops. Enlisted on March 10, 1776 and was on duty (in barracks) at Lewis Town on April 11, 1776. [Ref: DA-45].

LEADER, St. John. First Lieutenant. Served in the War of Jenkins' Ear in 1739-1741 in a company which may have included soldiers from Delaware (muster rolls not extant). [Ref: DM-32].

LEAHEA, Timothy. Private. Served in Capt. Joseph Vaughan's Company, Delaware Regiment of Continental Troops. Enlisted on February 18, 1776, and was on duty (in barracks) at Dover on April 12, 1776. [Ref: DA-58, 59]. (Same source spelled his name "Timothy Lahee").

LEAR, Benjamin. Private. Served in Capt. David Hall's Company, Delaware Regiment of Continental Troops. Enlisted February 3, 1776, and was on duty (in barracks) at Lewis Town on April 11, 1776. [Ref: DA-43].

LEAREA, Dennis. Private. Served in Capt. Joseph Vaughan's Company, Delaware Regiment of Continental Troops. Enlisted on March 3, 1776, and was on duty (in barracks) at Dover on April 12, 1776. [Ref: DA-58, DA-60]. (This same source spelled his name "Dennis Larey").

LEARMOUTH, John. Second Lieutenant. Served in the 3rd Company of the Delaware State Troops in Continental Service. Commissioned on January 16, 1776, and was on duty (in barracks) at Lewis Town on April 11, 1776. [Ref: DA-34, 36, 42]. (Name may be "Learmonth").

LEATHERBURY, Ann. See "William Cahoon," q.v.

LEATHERBURY, William. See "William Hirons," q.v.

LECOMPT, Peter. Private. Enlisted on May 24, 1758, in Capt. French Battell's Company of Lower County Provincials, during the French and Indian Wars. [Ref: DA-16].

LEE, James. Private. Born 1716, Ireland. Laborer. Enlisted in Capt. John Shannon's Company of Foot on July 7, 1746, and served in King George's War against Canada. He was in winter quarters at Albany, New York, during 1746-1747, and was discharged on October 31, 1747. [Ref: DA-4, DA-6]. (He is not listed in Source DM-40.)

LEECH, James. Private. Born 1740, Maryland. Laborer. Enlisted on May 9, 1758, during the French and Indian Wars, by Capt. Benjamin Noxon. [Ref: DA-19].

LEECH, James. Private. Enlisted on May 28, 1758, in Capt. French Battell's Company of Lower County Provincials, during the French and Indian Wars. [Ref: DA-16].

LEFEVER, James. Private. Served in Capt. Richard McWilliams' Company, New Castle County. Enlisted on December 28, 1757, during the French and Indian Wars. [Ref: DA-14].

LEGGE, William. Private. Served in Capt. Charles Pope's Company, Delaware Regiment of Continental Troops. Enlisted January 15, 1776, and was on duty (in quarters) at Lewis Town on April 11, 1776. [Ref: DA-51].

LESTON, Ebenezer. Private. Born 1733, Delaware. Laborer. Enlisted on May 3, 1758, in the French and Indian Wars, by Capt. Benjamin Noxon. [Ref: DA-19].

LEWES, Walter. Land patentee and probable militiaman in Delaware in November, 1677. [Ref: DP-167, 168].

LEWIS, David and Sarah. See "Caleb Sipple," q.v.

LEWIS, Evan. Private. Served in Capt. John Caton's Company on April 25, 1757, in the French and Indian Wars. He was promoted to ensign on March 29, 1758. [Ref: DA-14, DA-15]. One "Evan Lewis, Sr." died testate in Murderkill Hundred, in Kent County, and his will was probated on March 13, 1786, named wife Sarah Lewis, sons Robert and Evan, daughters Ruth Boogs, Miriam Cranston, and Elizabeth Newton, grandson David Lewis (son of Evan and Elizabeth), and granddaughter Lydia Lewis (daughter of Abraham and Lydia Lewis). [Ref: DK-381].

LEWIS, James. Lieutenant. Capt. James Edwards Company, Kent County, in August, 1748, in King George's War against Canada. [Ref: DA-8]. One James Lewis died intestate in Kent County and his widow, Jean Lewis was named administratrix on December 16, 1799. [Ref: DK-324].

LEWIS, Jane. See "Jacob Kollock," q.v.

LEWIS, Noble. See "John Shankland," q.v.

LEWIS, Thomas. Private. Served in Capt. John Caton's Company, April 25, 1757, in the French and Indian Wars. [Ref: DA-14]. One Thomas Lewis died in Kent County and the administration of his estate was granted to Mary Lewis on April 7, 1796. A later account showed an only child David Lewis and stated Mary Lewis married ---- Colier. [Ref: DK-505].

LEWIS, William. Private. Born 1719, Chester, Pennsylvania. Laborer. Enlisted on May 10, 1759, in the French and Indian Wars, in Capt. James Armstrong's Company in Pennsylvania Regiment. [Ref: DA-26].

LEWIS, William. Private. Served in Capt. Joseph Stedham's Company, Delaware Battalion of Continental Troops. Enlisted January 17, 1776, and was in quarters at Dover on April 12, 1776. [Ref: DA-39].

LEWKINS, Nathaniel. Mariner. Died testate in Kent County and his will was probated on February 15, 1700. No wife or children were mentioned, but an Elizabeth Wilson (widow of Richard Wilson) was his executrix. [Ref: DK-23].

LIKAGOD, Olof Bertilsson. Soldier. Arrived in New Sweden on the ship *Orn* in 1654. [Ref: DJ-717].

LILJEHOK, Knut. Soldier (*saldater*). He served at Fort Elfsborg in 1643, and returned to Sweden in 1648. [Ref: DJ-703, DJ-715]. (His name has also been spelled "Knute Liliehock").

LILJEHOK, Per. Officer. Served at the Upland Plantation in the Swedish settlement on the Delaware in 1643-1644. [Ref: DJ-704]. (His name has also been spelled "Pader Liliehock").

LILLE, James. Land patentee and probable militiaman in Delaware in November, 1677. [Ref: DP-167, 168].

LIMING, John. Land patentee and probable militiaman in Delaware in November, 1677. [Ref: DP-167, 168].

LINDESTROM, Peter. Military Engineer. Son of Marten Mansson who was knighted and assumed the name of "Lindestrom." He studied at the University of Upsala and specialized in mathematics and the art of fortification. In 1653 he was appointed an engineer and "officer" to go to New Sweden, arriving there on the ship *Orn* in 1654. He returned to Europe with Director Rising in 1655 and continued his work as a fortification engineer with the government. He married and settled at Brosater. About 1679 he "became afflicted with a painful suffering in all his limbs" and suffered until he died in 1691. His widow, Margreta Roos, was age about 60 in 1691, and was paid 200 *riksdalers* in 1693. [Ref: DJ-682, DJ-683, DJ-716, DJ-724].

LINDSEY, George. Private. Enlisted on May 24, 1758, in Capt. French Battell's Company of Lower County Provincials, during the French and Indian Wars. [Ref: DA-16].

LINEGAR, William. Private. Born 1736 (place not stated). Enlisted in Capt. John Wright's Company and was on the muster roll of May 11, 1759, during the French and Indian Wars. [Ref: DA-25].

LINGS, Archibald. Private. Born 1742, Virginia. Enlisted in Capt. John Wright's Company and was on the muster roll of May 11, 1759, during the French and Indian Wars. [Ref: DA-25].

LISLE, James. Private. Served in Capt. Samuel Smith's Company, Delaware Regiment of Continental Troops. Enlisted February 5, 1776, and on duty (in barracks) at Dover on April 12, 1776. [Ref: DA-54].

LITTLE, Absalom. Ensign. Served in Capt. Joseph Cord's Company, Southern District of Broad Kill Hundred, in the regiment of Sussex County, 1756, during the French and Indian Wars. "Absalom Littell" was an ensign in Capt. Joseph Cord's Company on March 18, 1758. [Ref: DA-13, 15].

LITTLE, Adam. Private. Served in Capt. Charles Pope's Company, Delaware Regiment of Continental Troops. Enlisted January 17, 1776, and was on duty (in quarters) at Lewis Town on April 11, 1776. [Ref: DA-51].

LITTLE, Richard. Private. Born 1732, Ireland. Schoolmaster. Enlisted on April 21, 1758, in the French and Indian Wars, by Capt. John McClughan "for the campaign in lower counties." [Ref: DA-18].

LIVINGSTON, Mary. See "Thomas Ogle," q.v.

LOCK, Lars Carlsson. Military preacher. He went to New Sweden on the ship *Swan* from Gothenburg on September 25, 1647, and was still living there in 1654. [Ref: DJ-710, DJ-716]. (His name has also been spelled "Lars Karlsson Loock").

LOCKHART, John. Private. Served in Capt. Charles Pope's Company, Delaware Regiment of Continental Troops. Enlisted January 20, 1776, and was on duty (in quarters) at Lewis Town on April 11, 1776. [Ref: DA-51].

LOCKWOOD, Armwell. Ensign. Born on April 28, 1738, in Kent County, Delaware, and married Gertrude Muncy (January 4, 1743 - February 4, 1818) on January 8, 1761. Their children were as follows: Thomas (born April 12, 1762), Isaac (born February 4, 1764), Richard (born March 6, 1766), Armwell (born August 22, 1768), Mary (born November 26, 1770), Levi (born January 13, 1773), John (born May 30, 1775), Eunity (born November 15, 1777), James (born April 19, 1780), Gertrude (born December 27, 1781), and Margaret (born February 8, 1785). Armwell served in Capt. John Caton's Company on April 25,

1757, and subsequently became an ensign during the French and Indian Wars. He died on January 30, 1806. [Ref: DA-14, DB-96].

LOFLAND, Dorman. See "John Woods," q.v.

LONG, Solomon. Private. Born 1728, Ireland. Laborer. Formerly with ye Royal Americans," enlisted on April 15, 1758, during the French and Indian Wars, by Capt. Benjamin Noxon. [Ref: DA-19].

LONGWILL, James. Private. Born 1736, St. Johnson, Ireland. Farmer. Enlisted on April 27, 1758, during the French and Indian Wars, as a private by Capt. John McClughan "for the campaign in the lower counties." [Ref: DA-18].

LONGWILL, Robert. Private. Served in Capt. Henry Darby's Company, Delaware Regiment of Continental Troops. Enlisted on February 13, 1776, and was on duty (in barracks) at Dover on April 12, 1776. [Ref: DA-46].

LOO, Walle. Soldier. Engaged by the nobleman Johan Papegoja on December 1, 1643, he arrived in New Sweden in 1644 and served as a common soldier (*saldater*) at Fort Elfsborg from 1644. He "seems to have left the service in 1653 and returned to Sweden." [Ref: DJ-703, DJ-714, DH-50]. (Also spelled "Wolle Looer" or "Wolle Lohe").

LOOM, Mans Swensson. Lieutenant. Tailor. Arrived in New Sweden on the ship *Charitas* in 1641 with his wife, two daughters, and little son (no names given). He "had been a lieutenant before." He was a freeman by 1648. The widow of "Mans Lum" was living in New Sweden in 1654. [Ref: DJ-712, DJ-720, DH-44]. (His name has also been spelled "Mans Svensson Lom" and "Mans Svensson Lum").

LORD, Thomas. Private. Served in Capt. Joseph Vaughan's Company, Delaware Regiment of Continental Troops. Enlisted January 21, 1776, and was reported as "deserted" on February 16, 1776. [Ref: DA-59].

LOVE, Robert. Private. Born 1738 (place not stated), but residence in New Castle, Delaware, "a bold looking Scotch man." Enlisted by Capt. John Singleton in May, 1758, from the "three lower counties," and served with the Pennsylvania Troops. [Ref: DA-27].

LOVELACE, Francis. General. In Sussex County he was mentioned in the quit-rents in 1705 concerning a July 2, 1672 patent. [Ref: DR-45]. In a 1671 petition of survey he was referred to as "The Right Honorable Francis Lovelace Esquire Governor General of his Royall Highness Dominions in Ameryca." [Ref: DY-47, DY-138 through 160].

LOWBER, Grace. See "Michael Reynolds," q.v.

LOWBER, Matthew. Private. Served in Capt. John Caton's Company on April 25, 1757, during the French and Indian Wars. [Ref: DA-13]. One

Michael Lowber died testate in Kent County and his will was probated on April 7, 1746, naming his wife Rachel and son Matthew (among others). [Ref: DK-110]. "Matthew Lowber, Sr." died in Kent County and his will was probated on July 29, 1772, naming his wife Hannah, sons Matthew Jr., Peter, and Jonathan, daughters Susanna, Elizabeth, and Meriam, son-in-law William Virdin, granddaughter Elizabeth Virdin (daughter of William) and grandson Hugh Durborrow. A later account mentions daughter "Susanah Durbrow." [Ref: DK-268].

LOWBER, Michiel. Private. Served in Capt. John Caton's Company on April 25, 1757, in the French and Indian Wars. [Ref: DA-14]. One "Michael Lowber" died in Kent County and his will was probated on April 7, 1746, naming a son Michael (among others). [Ref: DK-110].

LOWBER, Peter Jr. Private. Served in Capt. John Caton's Company, April 25, 1757, in the French and Indian Wars. [Ref: DA-14]. One "Peter Lober (Lowber), Jr." died intestate in Kent County and his estate was administered by his widow, Mary, on March 30, 1770. A later administration account showed "Mary Lober" married Thomas Davis. [Ref: DK-249]. It should also be noted that one "Michael Lowber" died testate and his will was probated on April 7, 1746, naming his wife Rachel and son Peter (among others). [Ref: DK-110]. One "Matthew Lowber, Sr." died testate in Kent County and his will was probated on July 29, 1772, naming his wife Hannah and a son Peter (among others). [Ref: DK-268]. See "Matthew Lowber," q.v.

LOWRIE, James. Lieutenant. Served in Capt. Samuel Perry's Company on June 4, 1746, during King George's War against Canada. He was in winter quarters at Albany, New York, 1746-1747, and his company was discharged on October 31, 1747. [Ref: DA-6].

LOWTHER, George. Captain. He held that rank by 1706 when mentioned in a session of the court in Sussex County. [Ref: DC-1245].

LUCASSEN, Andries. Skipper. He was "appointed to be on the sloop continually" (i. e., the governor's yacht) at Fort Christina in New Sweden in 1643. He returned to Holland in 1646. [Ref: DJ-701].

LUCIFER, Cornelius. Captain. Served on the ship *Katt* during the ninth expedition to New Sweden in 1649. [Ref: DJ-761].

LUFF, Caleb. Ensign. Served in Capt. Caesar Rodney's Company in Dover Hundred, Kent County, upon Delaware, 1756, during the French and Indian Wars. [Ref: DA-12]. The administration of the estate of a Caleb Luff was granted in Kent County to Ruben Wallace on March 19, 1783, and a later account mentioned heirs John and Nathaniel Luff. [Ref: DK-348]. One "Nathaniel Luff, Sr., gentleman," died testate in Kent County and his will probated on February 27, 1760, named wife Deborah and a son Caleb (among others). [Ref: DK-186].

LUM, Mans. See "Mans Swennson Loom," q.v.

LUNEBURGER, Hans. Soldier (*saldater*). From Stralsund, he arrived in New Sweden on the ship *Fama* in 1643, and he was one of the men who "daily followed and served the governor" [Printz] at Fort Tinicum in 1643. He died in New Sweden "about the middle of June, 1650." [Ref: DH-47, DJ-705, 713]. (Name also spelled "Hanns Lynberger").

LYMAN, James. Private. Served in Capt. Henry Darby's Company, Delaware Regiment of Continental Troops. Enlisted February 28, 1776, and was on duty (in barracks) at Dover on April 12, 1776. [Ref: DA-46].

LYNCH, John. Sergeant. Served in Capt. Henry Darby's Company, Delaware Regiment of Continental Troops. Enlisted January 20, 1776, and on duty (in barracks) at Dover on April 12, 1776. [Ref: DA-45].

LYON, John. Private. Served in Capt. Joseph Stedham's Company, Delaware Battalion of Continental Troops. Enlisted on January 19, 1776, and was in quarters at Dover on April 12, 1776. [Ref: DA-39].

MACKANING, William. Private. Born 1738, Maryland. Enlisted in Capt. John Wright's Company and was on the muster roll of May 11, 1759, during the French and Indian Wars. [Ref: DA-25].

MAGAHAGAN, William. Private. Served in Capt. Samuel Smith's Company of the Delaware Regiment of Continental Troops. Enlisted February 3, 1776, and was on duty (in barracks) at Dover on April 12, 1776. [Ref: DA-54].

MAGHEE, Thomas. Private. Served in Capt. Joseph Vaughan's Company of the Delaware Regiment of Continental Troops. Enlisted on January 20, 1776, and was on duty (in barracks) at Dover on April 12, 1776, at which time he was reported to be "sick in hospitle" (sic). [Ref: DA-57, DA-59]. (This same source spelled his name "Thomas Megee").

MAGUIRE, Thomas. Private. Served in Capt. Samuel Smith's Company, Delaware Regiment of Continental Troops. Enlisted January 17, 1776, and on duty (in barracks) at Dover on April 12, 1776. [Ref: DA-54].

MAHAN, Thomas. Private. Born 1731, Ireland. Chair maker. Enlisted on May 2, 1758, in the French and Indian Wars, by Capt. Benjamin Noxon. [Ref: DA-19].

MAHOOD, John. Private. Born 1737, Delaware). Carpenter. Enlisted on May 20, 1758, during the French and Indian Wars, by Capt. Benjamin Noxon. [Ref: DA-19].

MAKEL, John. Private. Served in Capt. Richard McWilliams' Company, New Castle County. Enlisted on December 28, 1757, during the French and Indian Wars. [Ref: DA-14].

MALONE, Richard. See "John Shannon," q.v.

MAN, William. Private. Born 1742, Sussex, Delaware. Enlisted in Capt. John Wright's Company and was on the muster roll of May 11, 1759, during the French and Indian Wars. [Ref: DA-25].

MANES, Michael. Private. Served in Capt. Joseph Stedham's Company, Delaware Battalion of Continental Troops. Enlisted on January 17, 1776, and was in quarters at Dover on April 12, 1776. [Ref: DA-39].

MANLOVE, William. Private. Served in Capt. John Caton's Company, April 25, 1757, during the French and Indian Wars. [Ref: DA-14]. One William Manlove died in Kent County and his will was probated on March 24, 1761, naming wife Alse, daughters Mary Mason (wife of Joseph) and Sarah Masten (wife of William), granddaughters Sarah Mason, Mary Manlove, Elizabeth Manlove, and grandson William Masten Jr. [Ref: DK-194].

MANLOVE, William. Private. Served in Capt. Nathan Adams' Company, Delaware Regiment of Continental Troops. Enlisted January 16, 1776, and was on duty (in barracks) at Dover on April 12, 1776, at which time he was reported to be "sick in quarters." [Ref: DA-52].

MANLOVE, William. See "Jacob Williamson," q.v.

MANN, William. Private. Born 1741, Angola Hundred, Delaware. Farmer. Enlisted on April 22, 1758, in the French and Indian Wars, by Capt. John McClughan "for the campaign in the lower counties." [Ref: DA-18].

MANNERLY, William. Private. Enlisted on May 17, 1758, in Capt. French Battell's Company of Lower County Provincials, during the French and Indian Wars. [Ref: DA-16].

MANNING, Benjamin. Private. Served in Capt. Jonathan Caldwell's Company, Delaware Regiment of Continental Troops. Enlisted on March 31, 1776, and was on duty (in barracks) at Dover on April 12, 1776. [Ref: DA-41].

MANNING, John. Private. Served in Capt. Jonathan Caldwell's Company of the Delaware Regiment of Continental Troops. Enlisted on January 12, 1776, and was on duty (in barracks) at Dover on April 12, 1776. [Ref: DA-41].

MANNING, Polly. See "Thomas Jackson," q.v.

MANSSON, Hans. Trooper in New Sweden. He became a freeman in 1648. [Ref: DH-45].

MANSSON, Johan. Soldier. Served in New Sweden in 1654 and was paid various sums by Director Rising for his services. [Ref: DJ-726].

MANWARING, Richard. Private. Served in Capt. John Caton's Company, April 25, 1757, in the French and Indian Wars. [Ref: DA-13]. One Richard Manwaring died testate in Kent County and his will was probated on December 5, 1794, naming his wife Susannah, his sons Charles, Thomas, and Richard, and daughters Hannah Street, Sarah Guessford, Margaret Emory, Ann Davis, and Elizabeth Davis. [Ref: DK-482]. (His name has also been spelled "Richard Mainwaring").

MARFORD, John. Corporal. Served in Capt. Henry Darby's Company, Delaware Regiment of Continental Troops. Enlisted January 29, 1776, and on duty (in barracks) at Dover on April 12, 1776. [Ref: DA-45].

MARKER, Frederick. Private. Served in Capt. John Caton's Company, April 25, 1757, in the French and Indian Wars. [Ref: DA-14].

MARKHAM, William. Captain. Served in that rank by 1683 in Sussex County, at which time he was Deputy Governor. [Ref: DC-30].

MARRAT, Joseph. Ensign. Served in Capt. Thomas Clarke's Company, upper part of Mispillim [Mispillion] Hundred, Kent County, upon Delaware, in 1756, during the French and Indian Wars. [Ref: DA-12]. One "Joseph Marratt" died testate in Kent County and his will was probated on October 21, 1795, naming sons John and Samuel Marratt, daughters Martha Jones and Easter Ann Molonix, and grandchildren (children of Jacob Harrington, Pheby Brinckly, and Rachel Ryan), no names given, plus housekeeper Elinor Russel, and Tamer Welch and Selathial Jones (with no relationships given). The executors were Samuel Marrat and Selathial Jones. [Ref: DK-496].

MARRINAR, Henry. Private. Served in Capt. Joseph Vaughan's Company, Delaware Regiment of Continental Troops. Enlisted January 19, 1776, and was on duty (in barracks) at Dover on April 12, 1776. [Ref: DA-57, DA-59]. (This same source spelled his name "Henry Merrenor").

MARRINER, Sarah. See "Rees Wolf," q.v.

MARSH, Paull. Captain. He was "on Delaware" by 1675, and president of the court at Whorekill in Sussex County, Delaware in November, 1674. [Ref: DP-169]. "Pawell Mash" appeared on a nomination list for officers for the Whorekill in Sussex County, Delaware, circa 1675 (list not dated). [Ref: DP-170]. "Capt. Paull Marsh" received a land survey for tract *Good Hope* on the west side of Delaware Bay on March 8, 1680/1. [Ref: DY-66]. "Capt. Paul Marsh" was a Justice in Sussex County in 1677. [Ref: DC-27]. (Also spelled "Paul Mash").

MARSH, Peter. Ensign. Served in Capt. John Newbold's Company in the Southern District of Lewes and Rehoboth Hundred, in the regiment of Sussex County, in 1756, during the French and Indian Wars, and also ensign in Capt. John Newbold's Rehoboth District Company on March 18, 1758. [Ref: DA-13, DA-15]. Peter Marsh was born in England in 1712 and married first to Esther Purnell and had these children: Peter (born February 26, 1740), Joseph (born September 10, 17--), Mary (born December 17, 1752), Thomas Purnell (born December 21, 1753), and twins John and Philip (born May 6 or May 9, 1757). His second wife was Agnes ----, and they had daughters, Hester (born November 26, 1761), and Sarah (born February 4, 1766). Peter died July 13, 1769. His first wife, Esther, died on September 13, 1757 (but this source mistakenly stated "1797"). [Ref: DB-108, 109]. His will was probated in Sussex County on August 19, 1769, naming his wife Agnes, sons Peter, John, Philip, Thomas, and Purnal [Purnell], and daughters Hester Marsh, Sarah Marsh, and Mary Maull. A later account mentions "Peter Marsh, deceased, grandfather of son Peter." [Ref: DS-84].

MARSHALL, David. Captain. Served in Kent County Company in June, 1748, during King George's War against Canada. [Ref: DA-8].

MARSHALL, Edward. Private. Served in Capt. Joseph Stedham's Company of the Delaware Battalion of Continental Troops. Enlisted on April 3, 1776, and in quarters at Dover on April 12, 1776. [Ref: DA-40].

MARSHALL, John. Soldier. Planter in Delaware who paid his quit-rent to the governor in 1669, having been granted land on Christina Creek on October 1, 1669. [Ref: DP-27, DP-28, DY-142].

MARSHALL, Thomas. See "Samuel Davis," q.v.

MARSHALL, Vincent. Ensign. Served in the War of Jenkins' Ear in 1739-1741 in a company which may have included soldiers from Delaware (muster rolls not extant). [Ref: DM-32].

MARTENSON, Esbjorn. Soldier (*saldater*). From Stockholm, he served in New Sweden in 1643 and returned home to Sweden in 1644. [Ref: DJ-709]. (His name has also been spelled "Esbiornn Marthensonn").

MARTENSON, Knut. See "Knut Martensson Wasa," q.v.

MARTIN, George. Captain. Served with a Kent County Company, 1747-1748, in King George's War against Canada. [Ref: DA-8]. One George Martin died intstate in Kent County and his widow Elizabeth Martin and Thomas Collins were named administrators on January 12, 1756. An subsequent account showed that "Mary Raymond, administratrix of Charles Hillyard, who with his wife Elizabeth and Thomas Collins was administrator of the estate of George Martin." [Ref: DK-162].

MARTIN, George. Captain. Lived in Duck Creek Hundred, Kent County, and was deceased by 1693 as noted in the 1693 tax assessment list when his estate was valued. [Ref: DR-20].

MARTIN, Francina and Jacob. See "Jerome Dushane," q.v.

MARTIN, Hugh. Private. Born 1728, Tyrone, Ireland. Weaver. Enlisted on April 29, 1758, during the French and Indian Wars, by Capt. John McClughan "for the campaign in the lower counties." [Ref: DA-18].

MARTIN, John. Private. Served in Capt. Charles Pope's Company, Delaware Regiment of Continental Troops. Enlisted January 16, 1776, and was on duty (in quarters) at Lewis Town on April 11, 1776. [Ref: DA-51].

MARVEL, Sarah. See "Thomas Prettyman," q.v.

MASON, Elias. Private. Born 1740, Kent, Delaware. Enlisted in Capt. John Wright's Company and was on the muster roll of May 11, 1759, in the French and Indian Wars. [Ref: DA-25]. Administration of the estate of Elias Mason was granted in Kent County to Joseph Mason on February 21, 1794. A later account showed heirs as Sarah, Joseph, Elias, and Elizabeth Mason. [Ref: DK-475].

MASON, Mary and Joseph. See "William Manlove," q.v.

MASON, Peter. Private. Served in Capt. Nathan Adams' Company of the Delaware Regiment of Continental Troops. Enlisted January 28, 1776, and on duty (in barracks) at Dover on April 12, 1776. [Ref: DA-53].

MASSEY, Hannah and Robert. See "Jacob Art," q.v.

MASSEY, Robert. Private. Served in Capt. Nathan Adams' Company, Delaware Regiment of Continental Troops. Enlisted January 15, 1776, and on duty (in barracks) at Dover on April 12, 1776. [Ref: DA-52].

MASTEN, Sarah and William. See "William Manlove," q.v.

MATESEN, Andries. Soldier. Planter in Delaware who paid his quit-rent to the governor in 1668. [Ref: DP-28]. One "Andries Maetsen" received a patent to land on "ye Indians or ye Wild Hook at Delaware" on November 14, 1668. [Ref: DY-135, 136].

MATHEUS, Anders. Sailor. Mate (from Amsterdam) who served on the ship *Gyllene Haj* during the eleventh expedition to New Sweden in 1654, but "did not reach New Sweden." [Ref: DJ-761].

MATHEW, Charles. Ensign. Served in the War of Jenkins' Ear in 1739-1741 in a company which may have included soldiers from Delaware (muster rolls not extant). [Ref: DM-32].

MATHEWS, Thomas. Private. Served in Capt. David Hall's Company, Delaware Regiment of Continental Troops. Enlisted on March 13, 1776, and was on duty (in barracks) at Lewis Town on April 11, 1776. [Ref: DA-43].

MATSSON, Hindrick. Soldier. Hired by Mans Kling as a farm hand in 1641, he arrived in New Sweden that same year. "Hinrich Matzon, the Finn" was hired as a soldier by Johan Printz on October 1, 1646 and served until March 1, 1648 when he was made a freeman. He was still living in New Sweden in 1654. [Ref: DJ-712, DJ-713, DJ-720, DH-45].

MATSSON, Johan. Gunner (*constaple*). Arrived in New Sweden in 1640, and was a gunner at Fort Elfsborg in 1643. He returned to Europe in 1643, and apparently returned to New Sweden by April 1, 1644, on the ship *Fama*, when he was engaged as a gunner at 6 *riksdalers* a month (which was raised to 8 *riksdalers* on December 1, 1646). He served as a gunner until September 1, 1650, when he was engaged as "skipper on the sloop" (i. e., the governor's yacht) at 25 *florins* a month. From August 15, 1651, until September 1, 1653, he served again as a gunner, and returned to Sweden with Governor Printz. One "Johan Matson Shrika, soldier" arrived in New Sweden on the ship *Orn* in 1654. [Ref: DJ-700, DJ-703, DJ-714, DJ-720]. Also see "John Mattson Shrika," q.v. (Name also spelled "Jahaan or Jan Matzonn").

MATSSON, Anders. Soldier. Served in New Sweden in 1654 and was paid various sums by Director Rising for his services. [Ref: DJ-726].

MATTESON, Samuel. Private. Served in Capt. John Caton's Company, April 25, 1757, in the French and Indian Wars. [Ref: DA-14].

MATTHEWS, Isaac. Corporal. Served in Capt. Jonathan Caldwell's Company, Delaware Regiment of Continental Troops. Enlisted January 18, 1776, and was on duty (in barracks) at Dover on April 12, 1776. [Ref: DA-41].

MATTHEWS, John. Private. Served in Capt. Jonathan Caldwell's Company, Delaware Regiment of Continental Troops. Enlisted January 18, 1776, and on duty (in barracks) at Dover on April 12, 1776. [Ref: DA-41].

MATTHEWS, John. See "Joseph Smith," q.v.

MATTHEWS, Owen. Private. Served in Capt. Charles Pope's Company, Delaware Regiment of Continental Troops. Enlisted January 18, 1776, and was on duty (in quarters) at Lewis Town on April 11, 1776. [Ref: DA-51].

MATTHEWS, Townsend. Private. Served in Capt. Richard McWilliams' Company, New Castle County. Enlisted on December 28, 1757, during the French and Indian Wars. [Ref: DA-15].

MATTINGLEY, Thomas. Private. Served in Capt. Joseph Vaughan's Company, Delaware Regiment of Continental Troops. Enlisted January 23, 1776, and on duty (in barracks) at Dover on April 12, 1776. [Ref: DA-59].

MAUGHAR, Thomas. Private. Served in Capt. David Hall's Company, Delaware Regiment of Continental Troops. Enlisted January 27, 1776, and was on duty (in barracks) at Lewis Town on April 11, 1776. [Ref: DA-43].

MAULL, Christopher. See "Samuel Edwards," q.v.

MAULL, John. See "Samuel Edwards" and "Daniel Murphey," q.v.

MAULL, Mary. See "Peter Marsh," q.v.

MAXWELL, Elizabeth. See "Thomas Cooch," q.v.

MAXWELL, Thomas. Private. Served in Capt. John Caton's Company on April 25, 1757, in the French and Indian Wars. [Ref: DA-14]. A Robert Maxwell died in Kent County and his will, probated October 24, 1744, named his heirs, including a son Thomas. [Ref: DK-102].

MAXWELL, William. Private. Served in Capt. Joseph Stedham's Company of the Delaware Battalion of Continental Troops. Enlisted on April 7, 1776, and in quarters at Dover on April 12, 1776. [Ref: DA-40].

MAY, John. Private. Served in Capt. Jonathan Caldwell's Company, Delaware Regiment of Continental Troops. Enlisted January 16, 1776, and on duty (in barracks) at Dover on April 12, 1776. [Ref: DA-41].

MAY, Thomas. See "William Spencer," q.v.

McAFEE, John. Private. Born 1734, Long Island. Enlisted in Capt. John Wright's Company and was on the muster roll of May 11, 1759, in the French and Indian Wars. [Ref: DA-25].

McAFEE, Robert. Private. Born 1724, Ireland. Cooper. Enlisted in Capt. John Shannon's Company of Foot on July 5, 1746, and served in King George's War against Canada. He made his mark when paid for services on June 6, 1747. He was in winter quarters at Albany, New York, during 1746-1747, and was discharged October 31, 1747. [Ref: DA-4, DA-5, DA-6]. (Source DM-40 spelled his name "Robin McAfee").

McANULTY, John. Private. Born 1730, Derry, Ireland. Farmer. Enlisted on April 22, 1758, in the French and Indian Wars, by Capt. John McClughan "for the campaign in lower counties." [Ref: DA-18].

133

McARTHUR, James. Sergeant. Served in Capt. Joseph Stedham's Company of the Delaware Battalion of Continental Troops. Enlisted on March 1, 1776, and in quarters at Dover on April 12, 1776. [Ref: DA-39].

McBRIDE, Archibald. Private. Served in Capt. Henry Darby's Company, Delaware Regiment of Continental Troops. Enlisted January 24, 1776, and on duty (in barracks) at Dover on April 12, 1776. [Ref: DA-46].

McCABE, Alexander. Private. Born 1718, Ireland. Laborer. Enlisted in Capt. John Shannon's Company of Foot on July 3, 1746, and served in King George's War against Canada. He made his mark when paid for services on June 6, 1747. He was in winter quarters at Albany, New York, during 1746-1747, and was discharged on October 31, 1747. [Ref: DA-4, DA-5, DA-6, DM-40].

McCABE, Samuel. Private. Served in Capt. Samuel Smith's Company, Delaware Regiment of Continental Troops. Enlisted January 17, 1776, and on duty (in barracks) at Dover on April 12, 1776. [Ref: DA-54].

McCALL, George. Second Lieutenant. Served in the 2nd Company of the Delaware State Troops in Continental Service. Commissioned January 15, 1776. [Ref: DA-34, DA-36].

McCALLA, Charles. Private. Born 1715, Ireland. Laborer. Enlisted in Capt. John Shannon's Company of Foot on July 22, 1746, and served in King George's War against Canada. He was in winter quarters at Albany, New York, during 1746-1747, and was discharged on October 31, 1747. [Ref: DA-4, DA-6]. (He is not listed in Source DM-40.)

McCANN, Thomas. Private. Served in Capt. Samuel Smith's Company, Delaware Regiment of Continental Troops. Enlisted January 17, 1776, and on duty (in barracks) at Dover on April 12, 1776. [Ref: DA-54].

McCANNON, John. Corporal. Served in Capt. Jonathan Caldwell's Company, Delaware Regiment of Continental Troops. Enlisted January 12, 1776, and was on duty (in barracks) at Dover on April 12, 1776. [Ref: DA-41].

McCASTLE, William. Private. Born 1733, Antrim, Ireland). Laborer. Enlisted on April 30, 1759, in the French and Indian Wars, in Capt. James Armstrong's Company in Pennsylvania Regiment. [Ref: DA-26].

McCASTLETON, Samuel. Private. Served in Capt. Joseph Stedham's Company, Delaware Battalion of Continental Troops. Enlisted on March 2, 1776, and was in quarters at Dover on April 12, 1776. [Ref: DA-40].

McCLAN, William. Private. Served in Capt. Charles Pope's Company, Delaware Regiment of Continental Troops. Enlisted January 15, 1776, and was on duty (in quarters) at Lewis Town on April 11, 1776. [Ref: DA-51].

McCLEAN, Hector. Private. Served in Capt. Henry Darby's Company, Delaware Regiment of Continental Troops. Enlisted on February 16, 1776, and was on duty (in barracks) at Dover on April 12, 1776. [Ref: DA-46].

McCLEAN, John. Private. Born 1711, Ireland. Weaver. Enlisted in Capt. John Shannon's Company of Foot on July 15, 1746, and served in King George's War against Canada. He was in winter quarters at Albany, New York, during 1746-1747, and was discharged on October 31, 1747. [Ref: DA-4, DA-6]. (He is not listed in Source DM-40.)

McCLEARN, James. Private. Born 1731, Londonderry, Ireland. Laborer. Enlisted on May 1, 1758, in the French and Indian Wars, by Capt. John McClughan "for the campaign in lower counties." [Ref: DA-18].

McCLELLAN, James. Private. Born 1729, Antrim, Ireland. Laborer. Enlisted on April 29, 1758, in the French and Indian Wars, by Capt. John McClughan "for the campaign in lower counties." [Ref: DA-18].

McCLOUD, John. Private. Enlisted on May 18, 1758, in Capt. French Battell's Company of Lower County Provincials, during the French and Indian Wars. [Ref: DA-16].

McCLUGHAN, John. Captain. Served in a militia company "of the lower government on Delaware" on April 16, 1758. He was in service until May 21, 1759, during the French and Indian Wars, at which time he was again commissioned, but it was revoked (no reason given). [Ref: DA-14, DA-16, DA-17, DA-20, DA-21, DA-22, DA-23, DM-46, DM-49].

McCLUGHAN, John. Private. Served in Capt. Richard McWilliams' Company, New Castle County. Enlisted on December 28, 1757, during the French and Indian Wars. [Ref: DA-15].

McCLURE, Samuel. Private. Born 1733, Ulster, Ireland. Laborer. Enlisted on April 30, 1759, in the French and Indian Wars, in Capt. James Armstrong's Company in Pennsylvania Regiment. [Ref: DA-26].

McCOLGAN, John. Private. Served in Capt. Henry Darby's Company, Delaware Regiment of Continental Troops. Enlisted February 15, 1776, and was on duty (in barracks) at Dover on April 12, 1776. [Ref: DA-46].

McCOLGAN, Richard. Private. Served in Capt. Henry Darby's Company, Delaware Regiment of Continental Troops. Enlisted January 22, 1776, and on duty (in barracks) at Dover on April 12, 1776. [Ref: DA-46].

McCOLISTER, Patrick. Private. Served in Capt. Nathan Adams' Company of the Delaware Regiment of Continental Troops. Enlisted on January 21, 1776, and was on duty (in barracks) at Dover on April 12, 1776. [Ref: DA-53].

McCOLLISTER, James. Private. Served in Capt. Joseph Vaughan's Company, Delaware Regiment of Continental Troops. Enlisted January 29, 1776, and was on duty (in barracks) at Dover on April 12, 1776. [Ref: DA-58]. (Same source spelled his name "James McCollistar").

McCOLLISTER, John. Private. Served in Capt. Jonathan Caldwell's Company, Delaware Regiment of Continental Troops. Enlisted on March 2, 1776, and on duty (in barracks) at Dover on April 12, 1776. [Ref: DA-41].

McCONOUHY, John. Private. Served in Capt. Henry Darby's Company, Delaware Regiment of Continental Troops. Enlisted January 24, 1776, and on duty (in barracks) at Dover on April 12, 1776. [Ref: DA-46].

McCORMICK, David. Soldier. Enlisted May 28, 1759, during the French and Indian Wars, and his name appeared on a return of Capt. Henry Van Bibber's Company of the Lower Counties on Delaware Troops at New Castle on June 4, 1759. [Ref: DA-26].

McCREA, Margaret. See "Samuel Platt," q.v.

McCREA, William. Major. Served as captain in a New Castle County Company in 1747, and then a major of a New Castle County Regiment, 1747-1748, during King George's War against Canada. [Ref: DA-7].

McCRODEN, Morris. Private. Served in Capt. Samuel Smith's Company, Delaware Regiment of Continental Troops. Enlisted on January 15, 1776, and was on duty (in barracks) at Dover on April 12, 1776. [Ref: DA-54, 55]. (Same source spelled his name "Morris McCrodin").

McCULLOUGH, Authur. Private. Served in Capt. Samuel Smith's Company of the Delaware Regiment of Continental Troops. Enlisted on January 28, 1776, and was on duty (in barracks) at Dover on April 12, 1776, at which time he was reportedly "sick and absent." [Ref: DA-54].

McCULLOUGH, Thomas. Lieutenant. Served in the company of Capt. Archibald Armstrong, New Castle County, 1747-1748, in King George's War against Canada. [Ref: DA-7].

McCULLY, Hugh. Private. Born 1733, Monaghan, Ireland. Cordwainer. Enlisted on April 25, 1759, in the French and Indian Wars, in Capt. James Armstrong's Company in Pennsylvania Regiment. [Ref: DA-26].

McCULLY, Samuel. Private. Born 1737, Ireland. Laborer. Enlisted on May 23, 1758, during the French and Indian Wars, by Capt. Benjamin Noxon. [Ref: DA-19].

McCULPIN, James. Private. Served in Capt. Samuel Smith's Company, Delaware Regiment of Continental Troops. Enlisted January 19, 1776, and on duty (in barracks) at Dover on April 12, 1776. [Ref: DA-54].

McCUND, Joseph. Private. Served in Capt. Henry Darby's Company, Delaware Regiment of Continental Troops. Enlisted February 6, 1776, and on duty (in barracks) at Dover on April 12, 1776. [Ref: DA-46].

McCURDY, William. Sergeant. Served in Capt. Charles Pope's Company, Delaware Regiment of Continental Troops. Enlisted January 16, 1776, and was on duty (in quarters) at Lewis Town on April 11, 1776. [Ref: DA-51].

McDANIEL, Dennis. Private. Born 1721, Ireland. Laborer. Enlisted in Capt. John Shannon's Company of Foot on July 14, 1746, and served in King George's War against Canada. He was in winter quarters at Albany, New York, during 1746-1747, and was discharged on October 31, 1747. [Ref: DA-4, DA-6]. (He is not listed in Source DM-40.)

McDAVID, Neill. Private. Born 1729, Ireland. Shoemaker. Enlisted on May 1, 1759, during the French and Indian Wars, in Capt. James Armstrong's Company in the Pennsylvania Regiment. [Ref: DA-26].

McDONALD, John. Private. Served in Capt. Charles Pope's Company, Delaware Regiment of Continental Troops. Enlisted January 17, 1776, and was on duty (in quarters) at Lewis Town on April 11, 1776, at which time he was reported "sick in quarters." [Ref: DA-50, DA-51].

McDONAUGH, John. Private. Served in Capt. Samuel Smith's Company, Delaware Regiment of Continental Troops. Enlisted on February 19, 1776, and was on duty (in barracks) at Dover on April 12, 1776. [Ref: DA-54].

McDONNALD, Barnard. Private. Served in Capt. Henry Darby's Company, Delaware Regiment of Continental Troops. Enlisted February 13, 1776 and on duty (in barracks) at Dover on April 12, 1776. [Ref: DA-48].

McDONNALD, John. Private. Served in Capt. Henry Darby's Company, Delaware Regiment of Continental Troops. Enlisted January 24, 1776, and on duty (in barracks) at Dover on April 12, 1776. [Ref: DA-46].

McDONNALD, Philip. Private. Served in Capt. Henry Darby's Company, Delaware Regiment of Continental Troops. Enlisted on March 1, 1776, and on duty (in barracks) at Dover on April 12, 1776. [Ref: DA-46].

McDONNELL, John. Private. Born 1719, Ulster, Ireland. Laborer. Enlisted on April 26, 1759, in the French and Indian Wars, in Capt. James Armstrong's Company in Pennsylvania Regiment. [Ref: DA-26].

McDONOUGH, James Jr. Second Lieutenant. Commissioned on January 20, 1776, in the 7th Company, Delaware State Troops in the Continental Service, and was on duty (in barracks) with Capt. Samuel Smith at Dover in April, 1776. A "Lt. James McDonaugh" was reported to have died on April 9, 1776. [Ref: DA-34, DA-36, DA-53, DA-55]. (His name has also been spelled "MacDonough").

McDONOUGH, Thomas. Major. Commissioned on March 22, 1776, in the Delaware Battalion of Continental Troops. [Ref: DA-35]. (His name has also been spelled "Thomas MacDonough" in this same source).

McDONOUGH, Michal. Private. Served in Capt. Samuel Smith's Company, Delaware Regiment of Continental Troops. Enlisted January 25, 1776, and on duty (in barracks) at Dover on April 12, 1776. [Ref: DA-54].

McDOWELL, Alexander. Private. Served in Capt. Jonathan Caldwell's Company, Delaware Regiment of Continental Troops. Enlisted January 27, 1776, and on duty (in barracks) at Dover on April 12, 1776. [Ref: DA-41].

McDOWELL, Isaac. Private. Served in Capt. Richard McWilliams' Company, New Castle County. Enlisted on December 28, 1757, during the French and Indian Wars. [Ref: DA-14].

McELRAY, Abiah. See "Samuel Patterson," q.v.

McFARLAND, John. Private. Served in Capt. Richard McWilliams' Company, New Castle County. Enlisted on December 28, 1757, during the French and Indian Wars. [Ref: DA-15].

McFARLANE, Robert. Private. Served in Capt. Joseph Stedham's Company, Delaware Battalion of Continental Troops. Enlisted on March 9, 1776, and was in quarters at Dover on April 12, 1776. [Ref: DA-40].

McGARMENT, Mary. See "John Haslet," q.v.

McGARVEY, James. Private. Born 1723, Ireland. Laborer. Enlisted in Capt. John Shannon's Company of Foot on July 10, 1746, and served in King George's War against Canada. He was in winter quarters at Albany, New York, during 1746-1747, and was discharged on October 31, 1747. [Ref: DA-4, DA-6]. (He is not listed in Source DM-40.)

McGARVIN, James. Private. Born 1724, Ireland. Laborer. Enlisted on May 23, 1758, during the French and Indian Wars, by Capt. Benjamin Noxon. [Ref: DA-19].

McGEE, Patrick. Private. Served in Capt. Henry Darby's Company of the Delaware Regiment of Continental Troops. Enlisted February 15, 1776, and was on duty (in barracks) at Dover on April 12, 1776. [Ref: DA-46].

McGENNIS, Daniel. Private. Served in Capt. Richard McWilliams' Company, New Castle County. Enlisted on December 28, 1757, during the French and Indian Wars. [Ref: DA-14].

McGERIE, Daniel. Private. Served in Capt. Henry Darby's Company, Delaware Regiment of Continental Troops. Enlisted on February 15, 1776, and was on duty (in barracks) at Dover on April 12, 1776. [Ref: DA-46].

McGILL, Andrew. Private. Born 1735, Maryland. "Indian." Enlisted in Capt. John Wright's Company and was on the muster roll of May 11, 1759, during the French and Indian Wars. [Ref: DA-25].

McGILL, James. Private. Served in Capt. Henry Darby's Company of the Delaware Regiment of Continental Troops. Enlisted February 13, 1776, and was on duty (in barracks) at Dover on April 12, 1776. [Ref: DA-46].

McGILL, John Jr. Private. Served in Capt. Samuel Smith's Company, Delaware Regiment of Continental Troops. Enlisted January 19, 1776, and on duty (in barracks) at Dover on April 12, 1776. [Ref: DA-54].

McGILL, John. Private. Served in Capt. Samuel Smith's Company, Delaware Regiment of Continental Troops. Enlisted January 16, 1776, and on duty (in barracks) at Dover on April 12, 1776. [Ref: DA-54].

McGILL, Patrick. Private. Born 1729, Armagh, Ireland. Laborer. Enlisted on April 25, 1759, in the French and Indian Wars, in Capt. James Armstrong's Company in Pennsylvania Regiment. [Ref: DA-26].

McGILL, Patrick. Private. Born 1732, Kilmore, Ireland. Weaver. Enlisted on April 30, 1758, in the French and Indian Wars, by Capt. John McClughan "for the campaign in lower counties." [Ref: DA-18].

McGINNIS, Arthur. Private. Served in Capt. Joseph Stedham's Company of the Delaware Battalion, Continental Troops. Enlisted February 4, 1776, and reportedly "deserted" on February 23, 1776. [Ref: DA-40].

McGINNIS, John. Private. Served in Capt. Samuel Smith's Company, Delaware Regiment of Continental Troops. Enlisted on January 21, 1776, and on duty (in barracks) at Dover on April 12, 1776. [Ref: DA-54, DA-56]. (This same source spelled his name "John Maginnis").

McGINNIS, Michael. Private. Served in Capt. Jonathan Caldwell's Company, Delaware Regiment of Continental Troops. Enlisted January 12, 1776, and on duty (in barracks) at Dover on April 12, 1776. [Ref: DA-41].

McGLACHLAN, James. Private. Served in Capt. Samuel Smith's Company, Delaware Regiment of Continental Troops. Enlisted February 1, 1776, and on duty (in barracks) at Dover on April 12, 1776. [Ref: DA-54].

McGLOUGHLIN, Cornelius. Private. Served in Capt. Charles Pope's Company, Delaware Regiment of Continental Troops. Enlisted January 18, 1776, and was on duty (in quarters) at Lewis Town on April 11, 1776, at which time he was reported "on guard." [Ref: DA-50, 51].

McGONNEGLE, John. Private. Served in Capt. Joseph Stedham's Company of the Delaware Battalion of Continental Troops. Enlisted on March 14, 1776, and in quarters at Dover on April 12, 1776. [Ref: DA-40].

McGRADY, Cornelius. Private. Served in Capt. Joseph Stedham's Company, Delaware Battalion of Continental Troops. Enlisted March 6, 1776, and in quarters at Dover on April 12, 1776. [Ref: DA-40].

McGRAW, James. Private. Born 1738, Maryland. Tailor. Enlisted in Capt. John Wright's Company and was on the muster roll of May 11, 1759, during the French and Indian Wars. [Ref: DA-25].

McGRAY, George. Private. Born 1737, Sussex, Delaware. Enlisted in Capt. John Wright's Company and was on the muster roll of May 11, 1759, during the French and Indian Wars. [Ref: DA-25].

McGUFFIN, Robert. Sergeant. Served in Capt. Samuel Smith's Company, Delaware Regiment of Continental Troops. Enlisted January 17, 1776, and on duty (in barracks) at Dover on April 12, 1776. [Ref: DA-53].

McGUFFIN, Thomas. Private. Served in Capt. Samuel Smith's Company, Delaware Regiment of Continental Troops. Enlisted January 19, 1776, and on duty (in barracks) at Dover on April 12, 1776. [Ref: DA-54].

McGUIRE, Bartholomew. Private. Born 1728, Ireland. Laborer, 5 ft. 8 in. tall. Enlisted at New Castle, Delaware on May 15, 1758, in the French and Indian Wars, by Capt. Paul Jackson, from "the three lower counties," to serve with Pennsylvania Troops. [Ref: DA-27].

McGUIRE, Nicholas. Private. Born 1701, Ireland. Laborer. Enlisted in Capt. John Shannon's Company of Foot on July 5, 1746, and served in King George's War against Canada. He was in winter quarters at Albany, New York, during 1746-1747, and was discharged on October 31, 1747. [Ref: DA-4, DA-6]. (He is not listed in Source DM-40.)

McGUIRE, Peter. Private. Served in Capt. Henry Darby's Company of the Delaware Regiment of Continental Troops. Enlisted February 11, 1776, and was on duty (in barracks) at Dover on April 12, 1776. [Ref: DA-46].

McILVAINE, David. Private. Served in Capt. David Hall's Company, Delaware Regiment of Continental Troops. Enlisted January 24, 1776, and was on duty (in barracks) at Lewis Town on April 11, 1776. [Ref: DA-45].

McILVAINE, Jane and James, Jr. See "William Craig," q.v.

McILVAINE, John. Private. Served in Capt. David Hall's Company, Delaware Regiment of Continental Troops. Enlisted January 20, 1776, and was on duty (in barracks) at Lewis Town on April 11, 1776. [Ref: DA-43].

McINTIRE, Archibald. Private. Served in Capt. Henry Darby's Company in the Delaware Regiment of Continental Troops. Enlisted February 13, 1776, and was on duty (in barracks) at Dover on April 12, 1776. [Ref: DA-46].

McINTOSH, Hugh. Private. Born 1733, Perth, Scotland. Laborer. Enlisted on May 8, 1758, in the French and Indian Wars, by Capt. John McClughan "for campaign in the lower counties." [Ref: DA-18].

McKEAN, Daniel. Private. Born 1729, Antrim, Ireland. Laborer. Enlisted on April 24, 1759, in the French and Indian Wars, in Capt. James Armstrong's Company in Pennsylvania Regiment. [Ref: DA-26].

McKEAN, Thomas. Attorney. Private. Served in Capt. Richard McWilliams' Company, New Castle. Enlisted on December 28, 1757, during the French and Indian Wars. [Ref: DA-14].

McKEE, Andrew. Private. Born 1721, Ireland. Laborer. Enlisted in Capt. John Shannon's Company of Foot on July 14, 1746, and served in King George's War against Canada. He was in winter quarters at Albany, New York, during 1746-1747, and was discharged on October 31, 1747. [Ref: DA-4, DA-6]. (He is not listed in Source DM-40.)

McKENNEY, Amos. Private. Enlisted on May 20, 1758, in Capt. French Battell's Company of Lower County Provincials, during the French and Indian Wars. [Ref: DA-16].

McKENNY, Charles. Private. Born 1738, Ireland. Cooper. Enlisted on May 1, 1758, during the French and Indian Wars, by Capt. Benjamin Noxon. [Ref: DA-19].

McKIM, Thomas. Lieutenant. Served in Capt. William Empson's Company in Brandywine Hundred, Upper Regiment, New Castle County, in 1756, during the French and Indian Wars. [Ref: DA-11]. One Thomas McKim died in Brandywine Hundred and his will was probated on September 22, 1784, naming his wife Agnes and children Jean, John, Robert, Alexander, and Elizabeth. [Ref: DN-103, 104].

McKINLEY, John. Lieutenant. Served in Capt. David Bush's Company, New Castle County, 1747-1748, in King George's War against Canada. He was major of the Upper Regiment, New Castle County, 1756, in the French and Indian Wars. [Ref: DA-7, DA-11, DM-45].

McKINNEY, James. Private. Served in Capt. Samuel Smith's Company, Delaware Regiment of Continental Troops. Enlisted January 17, 1776, and on duty (in barracks) at Dover on April 12, 1776. [Ref: DA-54, DA-56]. (This same source also spelled his name "James McKindey").

McKNATT, Ann. See "Thomas Clarke," q.v.

McKNIGHT, John. Soldier. Served in Capt. John Shannon's Company of Foot and he made his mark when he was paid for his services on June 6, 1747. He was in winter quarters at Albany, New York, 1746-1747, and discharged on October 31, 1747. [Ref: DA-5, DA-6, DM-40]. (His name was also spelled "McNight").

McKNIGHT, William. Captain. Served in the War of Jenkins' Ear in 1739-1741. His company may have included soldiers from Delaware (muster rolls not extant). [Ref: DM-32].

McLANE, Allen. Lieutenant. Born August 8, 1746, Philadelphia. Died May 22, 1829, Kent County, Delaware. Moved to Kent County in 1774 and enlisted as a lieutenant in Caesar Rodney's Delaware Regiment in 1775, serving with distinction throughout the revolution. He was the grandfather of the Honorable Robert M. McLane, Governor of Maryland. [Ref: DH-208].

McLOY, John. Private. Born 1732, Ireland. Weaver. Enlisted May 8, 1758, in the French and Indian Wars, by Capt. Benjamin Noxon. [Ref: DA-19].

McMANN, Robert. Private. Served in Capt. Richard McWilliams' Company, New Castle County. Enlisted on December 28, 1757, during the French and Indian Wars. [Ref: DA-14].

McMANUS, John. Private. Served in Capt. Joseph Stedham's Company, Delaware Battalion of Continental Troops. Enlisted on January 19, 1776, and reportedly "deserted" on January 23, 1776. [Ref: DA-40].

McMECHEN, Benjamin. Private. Served in Capt. Henry Darby's Company, Delaware Regiment of Continental Troops. Enlisted January 25, 1776, and was reported as having died March 25, 1776. [Ref: DA-46].

McMECHEN, James. Captain. New Castle County Company, in 1747-1748, during King George's War against Canada. [Ref: DA-7]. (Name also spelled "McMeehen").

McMECHEN, William. Lieutenant and Surgeon. Served in Capt. Thomas Gray's Company, in Mill Creek Hundred, Upper Regiment, New Castle County, 1756, in the French and Indian Wars. "William McMeehan" was a surgeon of the lower government on Delaware under Major Richard Wells on April 20, 1758. This man (or perhaps another by the same name) was a second lieutenant in Capt. John McClughan's Company on October 3, 1758. [Ref: DA-11, DA-16]. This same source spelled his name "William McMachon" and stated he was a surgeon on May 7, 1759, in one of the three companies "of the lower counties" [Delaware] in the 3rd Battalion of Pennsylvania Regiment under Col. Hugh Mercer. [Ref: DA-20, DM-45]. "William McMechan" was an ensign and "William McMechen" was a surgeon in 1758, during the French and Indian Wars. There appears to have been two men by this name. [Ref: DM-47, 49].

McMULLEN, James. Private. Served in Capt. Charles Pope's Company, Delaware Regiment of Continental Troops. Enlisted January 17, 1776, and on duty (in quarters) at Lewis Town on April 11, 1776. [Ref: DA-51]. (This same source spelled his name "James McMullin").

McMULLEN, Robert. Private. Served in Capt. Joseph Stedham's Company of the Delaware Battalion of Continental Troops. Enlisted January 24, 1776, and in quarters at Dover on April 12, 1776. [Ref: DA-39].

McMUNNIGAN, Dominick. Private. Served in Capt. Jonathan Caldwell's Company, Delaware Regiment of Continental Troops. Enlisted on March 25, 1776, and was on duty (in barracks) at Dover on April 12, 1776. [Ref: DA-41].

McMURPHY, Archibald. Private. Born 1731, Scotland. Laborer. Enlisted on April 22, 1758, during the French and Indian Wars, by Capt. Benjamin Noxon. [Ref: DA-19].

McNABB, John. Private. Served in Capt. Charles Pope's Company, Delaware Regiment of Continental Troops. Enlisted January 15, 1776, and was on duty (in quarters) at Lewis Town on April 11, 1776. [Ref: DA-51].

McNAMARA, Peter. Enlisted on May 9, 1758, during the French and Indian Wars, as a private by Capt. John McClughan "for the campaign in the lower counties." [Ref: DA-18].

McNAMIE, John. Private. Served in Capt. Richard McWilliams' Company in New Castle County. Enlisted on December 28, 1757, during the French and Indian Wars. [Ref: DA-14].

McNATON, Daniel. Private. Served in Capt. Joseph Stedham's Company, Delaware Battalion of Continental Troops. Enlisted on February 1, 1776, and was in quarters at Dover on April 12, 1776. [Ref: DA-39].

McNATT, John. Private. Served in Capt. Nathan Adams' Company of the Delaware Regiment of Continental Troops. Enlisted January 27, 1776, and on duty (in barracks) at Dover on April 12, 1776. [Ref: DA-53].

McNEIL, Hector. Private. Served in Capt. Richard McWilliams' Company in New Castle County. Enlisted on December 28, 1757, during the French and Indian Wars. [Ref: DA-15].

McNELOS, Connolly. Private. Served in Capt. Henry Darby's Company, Delaware Regiment of Continental Troops. Enlisted January 25, 1776, and on duty (in barracks) at Dover on April 12, 1776. [Ref: DA-46].

McNIGHT, John. Private. Served in Capt. Nathan Adams' Company of the Delaware Regiment of Continental Troops. Enlisted February 17, 1776, and was on duty (in barracks) at Dover on April 12, 1776. [Ref: DA-53].

McNULLAN, James. Private. Served in Capt. Richard McWilliams' Company, New Castle County. Enlisted on December 28, 1757, during the French and Indian Wars. [Ref: DA-15].

McSPARRON, Archibald. See "Matthew Henry," q.v.

McWILLIAMS, Rebecca and Ann. See "Zachariah Vanleuvenigh," q.v.

McWILLIAMS, Richard. Captain. Served in a company in New Castle Hundred, Upper Regiment, New Castle County, 1756-1758, during the French and Indian Wars. [Ref: DA-11, DA-14, DM-45]. One Richard McWilliams died testate in the Town of New Castle and his will was probated on May 19, 1786, naming his wife Rebecca, daughters Ann, Sarah Lewes, Rebecca, Louisa, and Hester McWilliams, and Richard and Elizabeth Spencer (children of William), and brother Stephen. [Ref: DN-110]. (This last source misspelled his name "McWilliam").

MEARS, Robert. Private. Served in Capt. Nathan Adams' Company, Delaware Regiment of Continental Troops. Enlisted January 20, 1776, and was on duty (in barracks) at Dover on April 12, 1776, at which time he was reported to be "sick in quarters." [Ref: DA-52].

MEIRS, Abraham. Private. Served in Capt. Joseph Stedham's Company, Delaware Battalion of Continental Troops. Enlisted on March 9, 1776, and reportedly "deserted" on March 29, 1776. [Ref: DA-40].

MELLAR, Ann and Andrew. See "Nathaniel Silsbee," q.v.

MERCER, Hugh. Colonel. He was the "colonel commandant" of the 3rd Battalion of the Pennsylvania Regiment in 1759, during the French and Indian Wars, which included the three companies of the lower counties [now Delaware] under Captains French Battle [Battell], Henry Vanbeber [Van Bibber], and John Wright. They were in service to at least June 13, 1759. [Ref: DA-20].

MERCHANT, William. Private. Born 1710, Ireland. Laborer. Enlisted in Capt. John Shannon's Company of Foot on July 14, 1746, and he served in King George's War against Canada. He was also in winter quarters at Albany, New York, during 1746-1747, and was discharged on October 31, 1747. [Ref: DA-4, 6]. (Not listed in Source DM-40.)

MEREDITH, Luke. Private. Served in Capt. Nathan Adams' Company, Delaware Regiment of Continental Troops. Enlisted January 20, 1776, and on duty (in barracks) at Dover on April 12, 1776. [Ref: DA-52].

MEREDITH, Philip. Private. Born 1718, Ireland. Laborer. Enlisted in Capt. John Shannon's Company of Foot on July 19, 1746, and served in King George's War against Canada. He was in winter quarters at Albany, New York, during 1746-1747, and was discharged on October 31, 1747. [Ref: DA-5, DA-6]. (He is not listed in Source DM-40.)

MERIDETH, Jobe. Private. Served in Capt. John Caton's Company on April 25, 1757, in the French and Indian Wars. [Ref: DA-13, 14]. (It appears that two men with this name served in this company.) One "Job Merydith" died in Kent County and the administration of his estate was granted to Jonathan Hunn, yeoman, on March 17, 1762. [Ref: DK-199]. Another "Job Meredith" died in Kent County and the administration of his estate was granted to one Lydia Meredith on October 17, 1793. A later account mentioned these heirs: Lydia, David, Peter, Job, Obedi, Henry, Stephen, James, David, Abner, and Benjamin Meredith, Rachel Keys (wife of John Keys), and Elizabeth Cooper (wife of Absolum Cooper). [Ref: DK-469]. A "Robert Merydith" died in Kent County and his will was probated on October 7, 1767, naming his wife Rachel and son "Job Merydith." [Ref: DK-231].

MERIDETH, John. Private. Served in Capt. John Caton's Company on April 25, 1757, in the French and Indian Wars. [Ref: DA-13]. One "John Meridith" died intestate in Kent County and administration of his estate was granted to his widow Sophia Merideth on November 11, 1767. [Ref: DK-231].

MERIDETH, Joseph. Private. Served in Capt. John Caton's Company, April 25, 1757, in the French and Indian Wars. [Ref: DA-13]. One "Joseph Meredith" died in Kent County and administration of his estate was granted to William Meredith, next-of-kin, on April 14, 1795. [Ref: DK-490]. Another "Joseph Meridith" died in Kent County and the administration of his estate was granted to Samuel Meridith on

January 4, 1796. A subsequent account named these heirs: Samuel Meridith, Jacob Meridith, Martha Anguish, Elizabeth Ford, and Ann Hartshorn. [Ref: DK-500].

MERIDETH, Joshua. Private. Served in Capt. John Caton's Company, April 25, 1757, in the French and Indian Wars. [Ref: DA-13]. One "Joshua Meridith, yeoman," died in Murderkill Hundred, Kent County, and the administration of his estate was granted to Ruth Meridith and Luff Meridith on December 28, 1775. [Ref: DK-302].

MERIDETH, Robert Jr. Private. Served in Capt. John Caton's Company, April 25, 1757, in the French and Indian Wars. [Ref: DA-14]. One "Robert Merydith" died testate in Kent County and his will was probated on October 7, 1767, naming his wife Rachel and son Job. [Ref: DK-231].

MERIDETH, Whelor. Private. Served in Capt. John Caton's Company on April 25, 1757, in the French and Indian Wars. [Ref: DA-13]. One "Wheelor Merydith" witnessed the will of Robert Merydith in Kent County on April 1, 1767. [Ref: DK-231]. One "Wheelor Meredith" died in Kent County and administration of his estate was granted to his widow Susannah Meredith on November 15, 1773. A later account showed that she married John Lambert. [Ref: DK-283].

MERIDETH, William. Private. Served in Capt. John Caton's Company, April 25, 1757, in the French and Indian Wars. [Ref: DA-13]. When Joseph Meredith died in Kent County in 1795, one William Meredith, next-of-kin, was named the administrator of his estate on April 14, 1795. [Ref: DK-490]. One "William Meredith" died in Kent County and the administration of his estate was granted to Margaret Meredith on December 28, 1797. [Ref: DK-533].

MERONY, William. Private. Served in Capt. Nathan Adams' Company, Delaware Regiment of Continental Troops. Enlisted January 24, 1776, and was on duty (in barracks) at Dover on April 12, 1776, at which time he was reported to be "sick in quarters." [Ref: DA-53].

MERRITT, Thomas. Soldier. Planter in Delaware who paid his quit-rent to the governor in 1671, and was mentioned in a land record dated July 5, 1679, as "Thomas Merrett, now deceased. [Ref: DP-29, DY-40].

MERYDITH, William. See "Robert Gordon," q.v.

METCALF, Hester. See "Bethuel Watson," q.v.

MEYER, Peter. Soldier. From Gothenburg, he arrived in New Sweden in 1643 and was at Fort Elfsborg in 1648. [Ref: DJ-713, DH-47].

MICHALL, Isaac. Private. Served in Capt. Joseph Vaughan's Company, Delaware Regiment of Continental Troops. Enlisted on February 14,

1776, and was on duty (in barracks) at Dover on April 12, 1776. [Ref: DA-58, 59]. (Same source spelled his name "Isaac Michell").

MICKELSSON, Erick. Soldier. Arrived in New Sweden on the ship *Orn* in 1654. [Ref: DJ-721].

MIDDLETON, James. Private. Served in Capt. Nathan Adams' Company, Delaware Regiment of Continental Troops. Enlisted February 3, 1776, and on duty (in barracks) at Dover on April 12, 1776. [Ref: DA-53].

MIDDLETON, John. Private. Served in Capt. Charles Pope's Company, Delaware Regiment of Continental Troops. Enlisted January 16, 1776, and was on duty (in quarters) at Lewis Town on April 11, 1776. [Ref: DA-51].

MIERS, John. Mariner. Died testate in Sussex County and his will was probated on Februry 28, 1749/50, naming his wife Ann Miers, his daughter Jane Cord, and also Jane Rowland (daughter of Samuel and Tabitha Rowland), Samuel Rowland (son of Thomas and Sarah Rowland), Mary Palmer (daughter of Joseph and Mary Palmer), and Joseph Palmer (son of Daniel and Mary Palmer). [Ref: DS-56].

MILBY, Levin. Mariner. Lived in Indian River Hundred by August 7, 1771, at which time he bought land. He also conveyed some land in Sussex County to Nathaniel Milby, house joiner on February 8, 1775. They were sons of Nathaniel Milby, deceased. [Ref: DD-42, DD-105].

MILLER, David. Drummer and fifer. Served in Capt. Charles Pope's Company, Delaware Regiment of Continental Troops. Enlisted January 16, 1776, and was on duty (in quarters) at Lewis Town on April 11, 1776. [Ref: DA-51].

MILLER, George. Private. Born 1704, England. Tanner. Enlisted in Capt. John Shannon's Company of Foot on June 25, 1746, in King George's War against Canada. He made his mark when he was paid for services on June 6, 1747. He was in winter quarters at Albany, New York, during 1746-1747, and was discharged on October 31, 1747. [Ref: DA-5, DA-6, DM-40].

MILLER, Henry. Private. Born 1712, Ireland. Laborer. Enlisted in Capt. John Shannon's Company of Foot on July 25, 1746, and served in King George's War against Canada. He was in winter quarters at Albany, New York, during 1746-1747, and was discharged on October 31, 1747. [Ref: DA-5, DA-6, DM-40].

MILLER, John. Private. Born 1740, Ulster, Ireland. Laborer. Enlisted on May 1, 1759, in the French and Indian Wars, in Capt. James Armstrong's Company in Pennsylvania Regiment. [Ref: DA-26].

MILLER, John. Private. Served in Capt. Joseph Stedham's Company of the Delaware Battalion of Continental Troops. Enlisted on March 5, 1776, and was in quarters at Dover on April 12, 1776. [Ref: DA-40].

MILLER, William. Private. Served in Capt. Samuel Smith's Company of the Delaware Regiment of Continental Troops. Enlisted February 13, 1776, and was on duty (in barracks) at Dover on April 12, 1776. [Ref: DA-54].

MILLINER, Thomas. Private. Born 1716, England. Surgeon. Enlisted in Capt. John Shannon's Company of Foot on July 7, 1746, and served in King George's War against Canada. He was also in winter quarters at Albany, New York, during 1746-1747, and was discharged on October 31, 1747. [Ref: DA-5, DA-6]. (He is not listed in Source DM-40.)

MILLINGTON, James. Private. Served in Capt. Jonathan Caldwell's Company, Delaware Regiment of Continental Troops. Enlisted January 12, 1776, and on duty (in barracks) at Dover on April 12, 1776. [Ref: DA-41].

MILLIS, Wright. Private. Served in Capt. Jonathan Caldwell's Company, Delaware Regiment of Continental Troops. Enlisted on April 7, 1776, and on duty (in barracks) at Dover on April 12, 1776. [Ref: DA-41].

MILLOWAY, Joseph. Private. Served in Capt. Nathan Adams' Company, Delaware Regiment of Continental Troops. Enlisted January 15, 1776, and on duty (in barracks) at Dover on April 12, 1776. [Ref: DA-52].

MILLS, William. First Lieutenant. Served in the War of Jenkins' Ear in 1739-1741 in a company which may have included soldiers from Delaware (muster rolls not extant). [Ref: DM-32].

MINK, Anders Classon. Probable soldier in New Sweden. He returned to Sweden in 1648. [Ref: DJ-715].

MINSHALL, Moses. Commander. Served on brigantine *Bleakney* in 1757, and mentioned in the will of Peter Ganthony in 1758. [Ref: DN-56].

MINUIT, Peter. First Governor of New Sweden (and the third of New Netherlands). He was born at Wessel on the Rhine circa 1580-1585, the son of Jan and Sara Minuit. He married a relative of Hendrick Huygen, which afforded him much wealth and influence. In the early 1630's he suggested the first practical plan to the chancellor for the colonizing of the Delaware and proposed the name "New Sweden." He was the commander on the ship *Kalmar Nyckel* during the first expedition to New Sweden, arriving in the Delaware in March, 1638. He bought land from the Indians, built a fort at Minquas Kill, and left the colony in June, 1638. On his way home at the island of St.

Christopher, he was invited as a guest on the ship *Flying Deer*. A storm suddenly arose and the ship was blown out to sea, Minuit and the others were never heard of again. [Ref: DJ-684, DJ-758].

MIRERIP, John. Private. Born 1734, New Castle, Delaware. Laborer. Enlisted on April 30, 1759, in the French and Indian Wars, in Capt. James Armstrong's Company in Pennsylvania Regiment. [Ref: DA-26].

MITCHEL, John. Private. Served in Capt. Joseph Stedham's Company, Delaware Battalion of Continental Troops. Enlisted on January 23, 1776, and was in quarters at Dover on April 12, 1776. [Ref: DA-39].

MITCHEL, William. Ensign. Served in Capt. Lewis Thomas' Company, Pencader Hundred, Lower Regiment, New Castle County, 1756, during the French and Indian Wars. [Ref: DA-12].

MITCHELL, Joseph. Private. Born 1738, Down, Ireland. Cooper. Enlisted on May 12, 1758, in the French and Indian Wars, by Capt. John McClughan "for the campaign in lower counties." [Ref: DA-18].

MITTAN, Cathran. See "Archibald Flemming," q.v.

MOFFET, Robert. Private. Born 1737, New Castle, Delaware. Laborer. Enlisted on April 26, 1759, in the French and Indian Wars, in Capt. James Armstrong's Company in Pennsylvania Regiment. [Ref: DA-26].

MOLL, John. Officer. His name appeared on a nomination list for officers in New Castle circa 1675 (list not dated). [Ref: DP-170].

MOLLESTON, Alexander. Officer. He arrived in America in 1663 from Delmhorst, Holland, and by 1671 was in the Delaware area with his wife [name not given], sons Alexander, Hendrik, and Abraham, and he may also have had a daughter Rebecca. He was a land patentee whose name appeared on a nomination list for officers for the Whorekill (now Lewes) in Sussex County circa 1675 (list not dated). He served as a Justice and was very active in Delaware governmental affairs. His date of death is not known. [Ref: DP-168, DP-170, DF-12, DF-13]. (Name also spelled "Sander Molestine" or "Sander Mallesten").

MOLLESTON, John. Lieutenant. Served in Capt. Benjamin Brinckle's Company, in the lower part of Mispillim [Mispillion] Hundred, Kent County, upon Delaware, in 1756, during the French and Indian Wars. [Ref: DA-12]. One Jemima Molleston, wife of Henry Molletson, died testate in Kent County and her will was probated on November 11, 1760, naming sons John, Jonathan, Henry, and William, and daughter Jemima Brinckle (wife of John Brinckle). [Ref: DK-190]. (Name also spelled "John Molliston").

MOLONIX, Easter Ann. See "Joseph Marrat," q.v.

MONEY, Robert. Private. Born 1724, Maryland. Carpenter. Enlisted on April 28, 1758, in the French and Indian Wars, by Capt. Benjamin Noxon. [Ref: DA-19].

MONSEN, Hanse. Soldier. Planter in Delaware who paid his quit-rent to the governor in 1669, having received a land patent on Swar Kill on May 14, 1669. [Ref: DP-27, DP-28, DY-144].

MONTGOMERY, Alexander. Ensign. Served in Capt. Thomas Gray's Company, in Mill Creek Hundred, Upper Regiment, New Castle County, in 1756, during the French and Indian Wars. [Ref: DA-11].

MONTGOMERY, James. Private. Served in Capt. Henry Darby's Company, Delaware Regiment of Continental Troops. Enlisted February 1, 1776, and on duty (in barracks) at Dover on April 12, 1776. [Ref: DA-46].

MONTGOMERY, Joseph. Reverend. Military preacher. Served as Chaplain in the Delaware Battalion of Continental Troops. Commissioned on January 13, 1776. [Ref: DA-35].

MONTGOMERY, Thomas. Ensign. Served in Capt. William Patterson's Company in New Castle County during 1747-1748 in King George's War against Canada. [Ref: DA-7]. One Thomas Montgomery died testate in St. George's Hundred, New Castle County, and his will was probated on December 26, 1794, naming his wife Mary and his brothers and sisters (no names were given). A "Thomas Montgomery, yeoman," died in Mill Creek Hundred, New Castle County, and his will was probated on December 10, 1799, naming his wife Mary, sons Benjamin, William, Alexander, Thomas, James, Robert, Daniel, Samuel, David, and Moses, daughters Margaret (who married William Faron) and Mary, and son John's three children, Minta, Mele, and James. [Ref: DN-134, 148].

MOODEY, John. Private. Served in Capt. Richard McWilliams' Company, New Castle County. Enlisted on December 28, 1757, during the French and Indian Wars. [Ref: DA-14].

MOODY, Alexander. Lieutenant. Served in Capt. William McCrea's Company, New Castle County, 1747-1748, in King George's War against Canada. [Ref: DA-7].

MOODY, George. Private. Served in Capt. Samuel Smith's Company, Delaware Regiment of Continental Troops. Enlisted January 16, 1776, and on duty (in barracks) at Dover on April 12, 1776. [Ref: DA-54].

MOODY, James. Private. Born 1731, Ireland. Tailor. Enlisted April 22, 1758, in the French and Indian Wars, by Capt. Benjamin Noxon. [Ref: DA-19].

MOONES, James. Private. Served in Capt. Joseph Stedham's Company, Delaware Battalion of Continental Troops. Enlisted on March 9, 1776, and was in quarters at Dover on April 12, 1776. [Ref: DA-40].

MOOR, James. Private. Served in Capt. Henry Darby's Company of the Delaware Regiment of Continental Troops. Enlisted February 3, 1776, and on duty (in barracks) at Dover on April 12, 1776. [Ref: DA-46].

MOOR, John. Private. Enlisted on May 22, 1758, in Capt. French Battell's Company of Lower County Provincials, during the French and Indian Wars. [Ref: DA-16].

MOORE, Charles. Private. Served in Capt. John Caton's Company, April 25, 1757, in the French and Indian Wars. [Ref: DA-14].

MOORE, Edward. Private. Served in Capt. Samuel Smith's Company, Delaware Regiment of Continental Troops. Enlisted January 18, 1776, and on duty (in barracks) at Dover on April 12, 1776. [Ref: DA-54].

MOORE, George. Soldier. Planter in Delaware who paid his quit-rent to the governor in 1667, having received a grant for land "called by the name of the old Minquas plantation at Delaware" on January 19, 1667. [Ref: DP-27, DY-128, DY-129].

MOORE, James. First Lieutenant. Served in 6th Company, Delaware State Troops in Continental Service. Commissioned on January 19, 1776, and was on duty (in barracks) with Capt. Nathan Adams and the Delaware Regiment of Continental Troops at Dover on April 12, 1776. [Ref: DA-34, 36, 52].

MOORE, James. Mariner. Died intestate in Sussex County and the administration of his estate was granted to William Smith and wife Nancy Smith (lately Nancy Moore) in January, 1783. [Ref: DS-147].

MOORE, John. Private. Born 1734, Wales. Cordwainer. Enlisted on April 15, 1758, during the French and Indian Wars, by Capt. John McClughan "for the campaign in the lower counties." [Ref: DA-18].

MOORE, John. Private. Born 1734, Maryland. Laborer. Enlisted April 15, 1758, in the French and Indian Wars, by Capt. Benjamin Noxon. [Ref: DA-19].

MOORE, Joshua. Private. Served in Capt. John Caton's Company, April 25, 1757, in the French and Indian Wars. [Ref: DA-13].

MOORE, Rebecca and William. See "Robert Robinson," q.v.

MOORE, Thomas. Private. Served in Capt. John Caton's Company, April 25, 1757, in the French and Indian Wars. [Ref: DA-13]. One Thomas Moore died in Kent County and the administration of his estate was granted to Sarah Moore on June 17, 1796. [Ref: DK-509].

MOORE, William. Private. Born 1742, Chester, Pennsylvania. Hatter. Enlisted on May 9, 1759, in the French and Indian Wars, in Capt. James Armstrong's Company in Pennsylvania Regiment. [Ref: DA-26].

MOORE, William. Private. Served in Capt. John Caton's Company on April 25, 1757, during the French and Indian Wars. [Ref: DA-14].

MORAN, Jane. See "Samuel Patterson," q.v.

MORAN, John. Soldier. Enlisted on May 15, 1759, during the French and Indian Wars, and his name appeared on a return of Capt. Henry Van Bibber's Company of the Lower Counties on Delaware Troops at New Castle on June 4, 1759. [Ref: DA-26]. See "John Moren," q.v.

MORE, John. Private. Served in Capt. Charles Pope's Company of the Delaware Regiment of Continental Troops. Enlisted January 15, 1776, and was on duty (in quarters) at Lewis Town on April 11, 1776. [Ref: DA-51].

MOREHEAD, Matthew. Private. Born 1730, Ireland. Weaver. Enlisted on May 29, 1758, during the French and Indian Wars, by Capt. Benjamin Noxon. [Ref: DA-19].

MOREN, John. Private. Born 1737, Delaware. Laborer. Enlisted on April 26, 1758, during the French and Indian Wars, by Capt. Benjamin Noxon. [Ref: DA-19]. (Name also spelled "John Moran").

MORGAN, Catharine. See "Samuel Patterson," q.v.

MORGAN, John. Private. Served in Capt. David Hall's Company of the Delaware Regiment of Continental Troops. Enlisted January 23, 1776, and was on duty (in barracks) at Lewis Town on April 11, 1776. [Ref: DA-43].

MORGAN, Joseph. See "William Morgan," q.v.

MORGAN, Manlove. Sergeant. Served in Capt. David Hall's Company, Delaware Regiment of Continental Troops. Enlisted January 16, 1776, and was on duty (in barracks) at Lewis Town on April 11, 1776. [Ref: DA-42].

MORGAN, William. Ensign. Served in Capt. John Shannon's Company on June 25, 1746, during King George's War against Canada. He was in winter quarters at Albany, New York, during 1746-1747, and his company was discharged October 31, 1747. [Ref: DA-6]. (Source DM-40 stated that a Joseph Morgan, not William Morgan, was the ensign.)

MORINSON, Hans. Captain. He held the rank of captain by 1679 when he was granted a land certificate in the area of the Whorekill in Delaware. However, he was reported May 13, 1679, as "being out of this pairts [sic] and unacquainted with it." [Ref: DY-54].

MORRIS, Ann and Tabitha. See "Thomas Prettyman," q.v.

MORRIS, Elijah. Lieutenant. Served in Capt. Thomas Clarke's Company in the upper part of Mispillim [Mispillion] Hundred, Kent County, upon Delaware, 1756, in the French and Indian Wars. [Ref: DA-12].

MORRIS, James. Lieutenant. Served in Capt. William Armstrong's Company, New Castle County, 1747-1748, in King George's War against Canada. [Ref: DA-7]. One James Morris died testate in Newport, New Castle County, and his will was probated on March 31, 1750, naming his wife Hannah. [Ref: DN-47].

MORRIS, Michael. Private. Served in Capt. Nathan Adams' Company, Delaware Regiment of Continental Troops. Enlisted January 24, 1776, and on duty (in barracks) at Dover on April 12, 1776. [Ref: DA-53].

MORRIS, Richard. Private. Served in Capt. Charles Pope's Company, Delaware Regiment of Continental Troops. Enlisted January 17, 1776, and was on duty (in quarters) at Lewis Town on April 11, 1776, at which time he was reported to be "on guard." [Ref: DA-51].

MORRIS, Thomas. Private. Served in Capt. John Caton's Company, April 25, 1757, in the French and Indian Wars. [Ref: DA-14].

MORRISON, Pierce. Private. Served in Capt. Joseph Stedham's Company of the Delaware Battalion of Continental Troops. Enlisted February 23, 1776, and in quarters at Dover on April 12, 1776. [Ref: DA-40].

MORT, Petter. Commissary of Stores. Served at New Sweden and he returned to Europe with Director Rising in 1655. [Ref: DJ-724].

MORTON, Peter. Private. Served in Capt. Richard McWilliams' Company in New Castle County. Enlisted on December 28, 1757, during the French and Indian Wars. [Ref: DA-15].

MOTT, Richbell. See "Thomas Enloe," q.v.

MOTT, William. Private. Served in Capt. Jonathan Caldwell's Company of the Delaware Regiment of Continental Troops. Enlisted on January 27, 1776, and was on duty (in barracks) at Dover on April 12, 1776. [Ref: DA-41].

MOUNCE, Luke. Ensign. Served in Capt. John Almond's Company, New Castle County, 1747-1748, during King George's War against Canada. [Ref: DA-7].

MOUNSEY, Nathaniel. Private. Served in Capt. John Caton's Company, April 25, 1757, in the French and Indian Wars. [Ref: DA-14].

MOUNSEY, Thomas. Private. Served in Capt. John Caton's Company on April 25, 1757, during the French and Indian Wars. [Ref: DA-13]. "Thomas Muncey" was one of the heirs named in the administration of the estate of "Levey Muncey" after April 20, 1776, in Kent County. [Ref: DK-304].

MOUNSON, Hans. Captain. Received a certified survey for land at the Schuykill from Capt. Cantwell on September 20, 1675. [Ref: DY-55].

MOUNTEGUE, James. Private. Served in Capt. Nathan Adams' Company, Delaware Regiment of Continental Troops. Enlisted January 15, 1776, and was on duty (in barracks) at Dover on April 12, 1776, at which time he was reported to be "sick in quarters." [Ref: DA-52].

MULLAN, Daniel. Private. Born 1740, Dunluce, Ireland. Miller. Enlisted on April 29, 1758, during the French and Indian Wars, as a private by Capt. John McClughan "for the campaign in the lower counties." [Ref: DA-18].

MULLEN, Edward. Corporal. Served in Capt. Henry Darby's Company, Delaware Regiment of Continental Troops. Enlisted January 16, 1776, and on duty (in barracks) at Dover on April 12, 1776. [Ref: DA-45].

MUNCEY, Levey. See "Thomas Mounsey," q.v.

MUNCY, Gertrude. See "Armwell Lockwood," q.v.

MUNCY, Margaret. See "Robert Patton," q.v.

MUNDT, Heindrich. Barber-surgeon. "Officer" on the ship *Mercurius* on the twelfth expedition to New Sweden, 1655-1656. [Ref: DJ-762].

MURPHEY, Ann. See "William Faries," q.v.

MURPHEY, Daniel. Pilot. Married in Sussex County to Hannah Jacobs, a daughter of John Jacobs who died intestate, leaving land to his two daughters, Hannah Murphey (wife of Daniel Murphey, mariner), and Mary Ranken (wife of David Ranken, cordwainer), who sold the land on Lewes Creek to John Maull on August 9, 1770. [Ref: DD-26].

MURPHEY, James. Soldier. Served in Capt. Jacob Gooding's Company during the French and Indian Wars, and he petitioned the assembly on October 28, 1759, for payment since he had been captured by the Indians. He asked for 64 pounds, 11 shillings, and 6 pence, but was not allowed anything (no reason was given in record). [Ref: DM-51].

MURPHEY, James. Sergeant. Served in Capt. Samuel Smith's Company, Delaware Regiment of Continental Troops. Enlisted January 19, 1776, and on duty (in barracks) at Dover on April 12, 1776. [Ref: DA-53].

MURPHEY, Taylor. Private. Served in Capt. David Hall's Company, Delaware Regiment of Continental Troops. Enlisted February 1, 1776, and was on duty (in barracks) at Lewis Town on April 11, 1776. [Ref: DA-45].

MURPHEY, Thomas. Private. Served in Capt. John Caton's Company, April 25, 1757, during the French and Indian Wars. [Ref: DA-13]. One Thomas Murphey died in Kent County and the administration of his estate was granted to his widow, Margrett Murphey, on September 30, 1771. [Ref: DK-260].

MURPHEY, William Jr. Private. Served in Capt. Joseph Vaughan's Company, Delaware Regiment of Continental Troops. Enlisted January 17, 1776, and on duty (in barracks) at Dover on April 12, 1776. [Ref: DA-59].

MURPHEY, William Taylor. Private. Served in Capt. Joseph Vaughan's Company, Delaware Regiment of Continental Troops. Enlisted January 27, 1776, and on duty (in barracks) at Dover on April 12, 1776. [Ref: DA-59].

MURPHY, Bryan. Private. Born 1743, Tyrone, Ireland. Laborer. Enlisted on May 1, 1759, in the French and Indian Wars in Capt. James Armstrong's Company, Pennsylvania Regiment. [Ref: DA-26].

MURPHY, James. Private. Born 1737, Ireland. Schoolmaster. Enlisted on May 2, 1758, in the French and Indian Wars, by Capt. Benjamin Noxon. [Ref: DA-19].

MURRAIN, John. Private. Born 1730, Dublin, Ireland. Laborer. Enlisted on May 7, 1758, during the French and Indian Wars, by Capt. John McClughan "for the campaign in the lower counties." [Ref: DA-18].

MURRAY, Philip. Private. Served in Capt. Samuel Smith's Company, Delaware Regiment of Continental Troops. Enlisted January 19, 1776, and on duty (in barracks) at Dover on April 12, 1776. [Ref: DA-54].

MURRAY, Richard. Drummer. Served in Capt. Henry Darby's Company, Delaware Regiment of Continental Troops. Enlisted January 19, 1776, and on duty (in barracks) at Dover on April 12, 1776. [Ref: DA-45].

MURRAY, Samuel. Private. Served in Capt. Joseph Vaughan's Company, Delaware Regiment of Continental Troops. Enlisted January 23, 1776, and was on duty (in barracks) at Dover on April 12, 1776. [Ref: DA-58, DA-59]. (This same source spelled his name "Samuel Murrey").

MURREY, John. Private. Served in Capt. Joseph Vaughan's Company, Delaware Regiment of Continental Troops. Enlisted January 19, 1776, and on duty (in barracks) at Dover on April 12, 1776. [Ref: DA-59].

NARRIER, Daniel. Private. Born 1741, Tyrone, Ireland. Laborer. Enlisted on May 3, 1759, in the French and Indian Wars, in Capt. James Armstrong's Company in Pennsylvania Regiment. [Ref: DA-26].

NAWOOD, Daniel. Private. Born 1739, Angola Hundred, Delaware. Farmer. Enlisted on April 19, 1758, during the French and Indian Wars, as a private by Capt. John McClughan "for the campaign in the lower counties." [Ref: DA-18].

NAWOOD, Nathan. Private. Born 1735, Indian River, Delaware. Planter who enlisted April 19, 1758 in the French and Indian Wars, by Capt. John McClughan, "for the campaign in lower counties." [Ref: DA-18].

NEAL, John. Private. Born 1738 (place not stated, but residence was in New Castle, Delaware). Enlisted by Capt. John Singleton in May, 1758, during the French and Indian Wars, from "the three lower counties" to serve with the Pennsylvania Troops. [Ref: DA-27].

NEAL, John. Private. Born 1718, Ireland. Laborer. Enlisted in Capt. John Shannon's Company of Foot on July 23, 1746, and served in King George's War against Canada. "John Neale" made his mark when paid for services on June 6, 1747. He was in winter quarters at Albany, New York, during 1746-1747, and was discharged on October 31, 1747. [Ref: DA-5, DA-6, DM-40]. Source DM-40 spelled his name "Neale."

NEEDLES, Thomas. Private. Served in Capt. John Caton's Company on April 25, 1757, in the French and Indian Wars. [Ref: DA-14]. One "Thomas Needles, farmer," died in Kent County and his will was probated on December 10, 1791, naming wife Sarah, son William, and daughters Mary and Nancy Clymer, and Sarah Dehorty. [Ref: DK-451].

NEILSON, Samuel. See "Richard Mariot Jones," q.v.

NERTUNIUS, Matthias Nicolaus. Reverend. Military preacher. Engaged to go to American in 1649 on the ship *Katt*, but he was shipwrecked near Porto Rico. After suffering through several years of privation and want, Matthias again tried his luck in New Sweden and this time reached his destination safely. He served as preacher and "officer" in New Sweden after arriving on the ship *Orn* in 1654, and returned to Europe with Director Rising in 1655. [Ref: DJ-685, 716, 724].

NESBIT, William. Private. Served in Capt. Richard McWilliams' Company, New Castle County. Enlisted on December 28, 1757, during the French and Indian Wars. [Ref: DA-15].

NEWBOLD, John. Sergeant. Born 1737, Maryland. Carpenter. Served in Capt. John Wright's Company on May 11, 1759, during the French and Indian Wars. [Ref: DA-25].

NEWBOLD, John. Private. Born 1736, Somerset, Maryland. Farmer. Enlisted on May 5, 1758, in the French and Indian Wars, by Capt. John McClughan "for the campaign in lower counties." [Ref: DA-18].

NEWBOLD, John. Captain. Commanded a company in regiment of Sussex County, Southern District of Lewis [Lewes] and Rehoboth Hundred in 1756, and was captain of the Rehoboth District Company in March, 1758, during the French and Indian War. [Ref: DA-13, DA-15, DM-46]. One "John Newbold, yeoman," died intestate in Sussex County and the administration of his estate was granted to Charles Rickards and wife Ann (lately Ann Newbold) on November 9, 1792. [Ref: DS-238].

NEWCOMB, Baptist. Private. Born 1736, Sussex, Delaware. Enlisted in Capt. John Wright's Company and was on the muster roll of May 11, 1759, during the French and Indian Wars. [Ref: DA-25]. One "Baptis Newcomb" died testate in Sussex County and his will was probated on May 10, 1739, naming wife Rachel Newcomb, sons Baptis Newcomb and Thomas Newcomb, daughter Rachel Dod, and the children of Ann Lay, and the children of Thomas Newcomb. [Ref: DS-45].

NEWCOMB, Thomas. Private. Born 1740, Sussex, Delaware. Enlisted in Capt. John Wright's Company and was on the muster roll of May 11, 1759, during the French and Indian Wars. [Ref: DA-25]. See "Baptist Newcomb," q.v.

NEWIL, William. Private. Served in Capt. Samuel Smith's Company, Delaware Regiment of Continental Troops. Enlisted January 25, 1776, and on duty (in barracks) at Dover on April 12, 1776. [Ref: DA-54].

NEWMAN, Michael. Private. Served in Capt. Samuel Smith's Company, Delaware Regiment of Continental Troops. Enlisted January 16, 1776, and on duty (in barracks) at Dover on April 12, 1776. [Ref: DA-54].

NEWMAN, Nathaniel. Private. Enlisted on May 28, 1758, in Capt. French Battell's Company of Lower County Provincials, during the French and Indian Wars. [Ref: DA-16].

NEWTON, Elizabeth. See "Evan Lewis," q.v.

NEWTON, John. Private. Born 1741, Maryland. Enlisted in Capt. John Wright's Company and was on the muster roll of May 11, 1759, during the French and Indian Wars. [Ref: DA-25].

NICHOLAS, David. Private. Born 1725, Ireland. Weaver. Enlisted in Capt. John Shannon's Company of Foot on July 13, 1746, and served in King George's War against Canada. He made his mark when paid for services on June 6, 1747. He was in winter quarters at Albany, New York, during 1746-1747, and was discharged October 31, 1747. [Ref: DA-5, DA-6, DM-40]. Source DM-40 spelled his name "David Nocholas."

NICHOLLS, Mathias. Captain. He held that rank by 1699 when he was mentioned in the court records in Sussex County. [Ref: DC-1086].

NICHOLSON, Parker. Private. Served in Capt. David Hall's Company, Delaware Regiment of Continental Troops. Enlisted January 17, 1776, and was on duty (in barracks) at Lewis Town on April 11, 1776. [Ref: DA-42].

NICKELL, John. Private. Born 1728, Bedony, Ireland. Laborer. Enlisted on April 26, 1758, in the French and Indian Wars, by Capt. John McClughan "for the campaign in lower counties." [Ref: DA-18].

NICKERSON, John. Private. Served in Capt. Jonathan Caldwell's Company, Delaware Regiment of Continental Troops. Enlisted January 15, 1776, and on duty (in barracks) at Dover on April 12, 1776. [Ref: DA-41].

NICKLAS, Master. Gunsmith (*bosse smedenn*). Served as an "officer" at Fort Tinicum in 1643. [Ref: DJ-705, DA-706]. (His name was also spelled "Mester Niklaus").

NICOLLS, Richard. Colonel. Officer in Delaware during the 1660's, and noted in a land patent dated May 16, 1670, as "my predecessor Coll. Richard Nicolls." [Ref: DY-24, 25]. His military expedition had defeated the Dutch and established English rule in New York and Delaware in 1664. See "John Ogle," q.v. and "James Crawford," q.v.

NIELS, Niel. Soldier. Planter in Delaware who paid his quit-rent to the governor in 1671. [Ref: DP-29]. "Niels Nielsen" received a grant to land on May 16, 1670. [Ref: DY-24, DY-25].

NILSSON, Mickel. Blacksmith (*smedenn*). Arrived in New Sweden in 1643 and he was an "officer" at Upland Plantation in the Swedish settlement on Delaware. [Ref: DJ-704, DJ-714, DH-47]. (Name also spelled "Michell Nielsson").

NILSSON, Jon. Soldier. Soldier. Tailor (*skreddere*). Served as a common soldier (*saldater*) at Fort Elfsborg in 1644 and 1648. [Ref: DJ-703, DH-47]. "Joen Nielsson" was a soldier "from Skaningsharad" who arrived in New Sweden in 1643. [Ref: DJ-713].

NILSSON, Mans. Soldier. "From Trannegiald," he was one of those men "who daily followed and served the governor" [Johan Printz] at Fort Tinicum in 1643. He returned to Sweden in 1648. [Ref: DJ-706, 715].

NILSSON, Peder. Soldier. Arrived in New Sweden on the ship *Orn* in 1654. [Ref: DJ-721]. (Name also spelled "Per Nilsson").

NISBIT, Henry. Private. Served in Capt. Charles Pope's Company, Delaware Regiment of Continental Troops. Enlisted January 16, 1776, and was on duty (in quarters) at Lewis Town on April 11, 1776. [Ref: DA-51]. (This same source spelled his name "Henry Nesbit").

NIXON, Thomas Jr. Ensign. Served in the 6th Company, Delaware State Troops in Continental Service. Commissioned on January 19, 1776. "Thomas Nixon, ensign," was on duty (in barracks) with Capt. Nathan Adams and the Delaware Regiment of Continental Troops at Dover on April 12, 1776. [Ref: DA-35, 36, 52].

NOBLE, William. Private. Born 1727, England. Laborer. Enlisted on April 19, 1758, in the French and Indian Wars, by Capt. Benjamin Noxon. [Ref: DA-19].

NOBLEMAN, Richard. Private. Born 1738, Maryland. Carpenter. Enlisted on April 29, 1758, during the French and Indian Wars, by Capt. Benjamin Noxon. [Ref: DA-19].

NOLES, Patience. See "Thomas Prettyman," q.v.

NORMAN, Edward. Private. Born 1718, England. Laborer. Enlisted in Capt. John Shannon's Company of Foot on July 13, 1746, and served in King George's War against Canada. He was in winter quarters at Albany, New York, during 1746-1747, and was discharged on October 31, 1747. [Ref: DA-5, DA-6]. (He is not listed in Source DM-40.)

NORTH, Richard. Private. Served in Capt. John Caton's Company, April 25, 1757, in the French and Indian Wars. [Ref: DA-14]. One Richard North died testate in Kent County and his will was probated on March 16, 1781, naming his wife Rachel, sons Thomas, John, and Daniel, and daughters Ann Wiat (wife of Thomas Wiat), Mary North, and Rachel North. [Ref: DK-329].

NORTON, Edward. Soldier. Enlisted May 21, 1759, during the French and Indian Wars, and his name appeared on a return of Capt. Henry Van Bibber's Company of the Lower Counties on Delaware Troops, at New Castle, on June 4, 1759. [Ref: DA-26].

NORTON, William. Land patentee and probable militiaman in Delaware in November, 1677. [Ref: DP-167, 168].

NOTTINGHAM, Abel. Private. Served in Capt. David Hall's Company, Delaware Regiment of Continental Troops. Enlisted January 30, 1776, and was on duty (in barracks) at Lewis Town on April 11, 1776. [Ref: DA-43].

NOWLAND, Matthias and Louisa. See "David Sheahorn," q.v.

NOXON, Benjamin. Captain. Served in the French and Indian Wars and was under Major Richard Wells on April 15, 1758. He resigned on June 13, 1758. [Ref: DA-16].

NUMBERS, Michael. See "Robert Blackshire," q.v.

NUNEZ, Hannah. See "Jacob Kollock" and "Jacob Phillips," q.v.

O'DONOLLY, Michael. Private. Born 1724, Ireland. Laborer. Enlisted in Capt. John Shannon's Company of Foot on July 22, 1746, in King George's War against Canada. "Michael O'Donaly" made his mark when paid for his services on June 6, 1747. He was in winter quarters at Albany, New York, during 1746-1747, and was discharged October 31, 1747. [Ref: DA-5, DA-6, DM-40]. (Name also spelled "O'Donnell").

O'NEAL, Hugh. Private. Served in Capt. Joseph Vaughan's Company, Delaware Regiment of Continental Troops. Enlisted January 20, 1776, and on duty (in barracks) at Dover on April 12, 1776. [Ref: DA-59].

O'NEAL, Nehemiah. Private. Served in Capt. Joseph Vaughan's Company of the Delaware Regiment of Continental Troops. Enlisted on January 20, 1776, and was on duty (in barracks) at Dover on April 12, 1776. [Ref: DA-59].

OGLE, John. Soldier. Born 1648/9, County Northumberland, England. Son of Capt. John Ogle (Ogall) and Eleanor Pringle. At the age of 14 he immigrated to America as a soldier in the military expedition of Colonel Richard Nicolls who defeated the Dutch and established English rule in New York and Delaware. After serving under Richard Nicolls and Robert Carr, John Ogle settled in New Castle County at White Clay Kill on the Delaware as a planter in 1664, and paid his quit-rent to the governor in 1668. He married Elizabeth [possibly Wollaston] and had two sons, Thomas and John, Jr. John, Sr. died intestate in 1683. [Ref: DP-28, DF-14 to DF-27, DY-133, DY-161].

OGLE, Thomas. Captain. Born 1705, New Castle County, Delaware. Son of Thomas Ogle and Mary Crawford. He was also known as "Thomas Ogle of Ogletown." He also owned land in both Delaware and Cecil County, Maryland, as well as several mills. He married first circa 1733 to Mary Livingston and had five children: Thomas, George, Joseph, Mary and James. His second marriage was to Catherine Howard of Maryland, and had three more children: Anne, Benjamin, and Catherine. Thomas served as an ensign in Capt. James McMeehen's Company, New Castle County, 1747-1748, during King George's War against Canada. "Thomas Ogle, Jr." was a captain of a company in Christiana Hundred, Upper Regiment of New Castle County in 1756, during the French and Indian Wars. He died on December 23, 1771. Two of his brothers, Joseph and Benjamin, had removed to Frederick County, Maryland prior to 1745. [Ref: DA-7, DA-11, DM-45, DF-21, DF-22, DF-23, DF-24, DF-25]. The will of Thomas Ogle, of White Clay Creek Hundred, was probated on December 31, 1771, naming his wife Catherine, sons Thomas, George, Joseph, James, and Benjamin, daughters Catherine Ogle and Mary Hanson (wife of Peter), and sister Judah Harris. [Ref: DN-68].

OGLESBY, Thomas. Private. Served in Capt. Joseph Vaughan's Company, Delaware Regiment of Continental Troops. Enlisted January 20, 1776, and was on duty (in barracks) at Dover on April 12, 1776. [Ref:

DA-57, DA-59]. (This same source spelled his name "Thomas Ogalsbey").

OHARO, Peter. Private. Served in Capt. Samuel Smith's Company, Delaware Regiment of Continental Troops. Enlisted February 2, 1776, and on duty (in barracks) at Dover on April 12, 1776. [Ref: DA-54].

OLIVER, Daniel. Corporal. Born 1729, New England. Served in Capt. John Wright's Company on May 11, 1759, during the French and Indian Wars. [Ref: DA-25].

OLIVER, George. Private. Served in Capt. David Hall's Company, Delaware Regiment of Continental Troops. Enlisted January 23, 1776, and was on duty (in barracks) at Lewis Town on April 11, 1776. [Ref: DA-43].

OLIVER, Samuel. Private. Served in Capt. Nathan Adams' Company, Delaware Regiment of Continental Troops. Enlisted February 12, 1776, and was on duty (in barracks) at Dover on April 12, 1776. [Ref: DA-53].

OLLESON, Pieter. Soldier. Planter in Delaware who paid his quit-rent to the governor in 1668, having been granted a land patent on Christine Kill on March 24, 1668/9. [Ref: DP-28, DY-137].

OLOFSSON, Johan. Provost-marshal (*proposenn*). He served at Fort Christina in 1643-1644. [Ref: DJ-701]. "He was hired to serve as provost-marshal in 1642, came here [to New Sweden] on the ship *Fama* [in 1643], and he returned [to Sweden] with [Governor] Printz in 1653." It also appears that he returned to New Sweden on the ship *Orn* in 1654. [Ref: DJ-713, DJ-721]. "Johan Ofsson" was provost at Fort Christina in 1644 and a soldier in 1648. [Ref: DH-47]. (Name also spelled "Jahan Oluffzonn").

OLOFSSON, Anders. Corporal. An "officer" in New Sweden, having arrived there on the ship *Orn* in 1654. He returned to Europe with Director Rising in 1655. [Ref: DJ-716, DJ-724]. (Name also spelled "Olufsson" or "Olsson").

OLOFSSON, Biorn. Soldier. Freeman in New Sweden. His name appeared on a list of officers and soldiers who had returned to Europe with Director Rising in 1655. [Ref: DJ-724]. (Name spelled "Olufsson").

OLOFSSON, Hindrick. Soldier. Arrived in New Sweden in 1644, entered the government's service as a soldier on September (or December) 1, 1646, and was still living in September, 1653, when he owed the company 28.32 *riksdalers*. [Ref: DJ-715]. (He was also referred to as "Hindrick Olufsson, the Finn").

OLOFSSON, Matz. Sailor. Arrived in New Sweden as a sailor on the ship *Kalmar Nyckel* in 1641 and became a wood sawyer by 1648. [Ref: DJ-712, DH-45]. "Mats Olofsson" was a soldier in New Sweden in 1654, and lived at the Schuylkill. [Ref: DJ-721]. (Name was also spelled "Matz Olufsson").

OLSSON, Bengt. Sailor. Second Mate on the ship *Gyllene Haj* during the eleventh expedition to New Sweden in 1654, but "did not reach New Sweden." [Ref: DJ-761].

OLSSON, Joran. Provost-marshal. From Stockholm, he was serving in New Sweden in 1640 and returned to Europe in 1643. [Ref: DJ-699, DJ-700]. (Name also spelled "Goran Olsson" or "Jurgen Olsson").

ORAM, Robert. Corporal. Served in Capt. Jonathan Caldwell's Company in Delaware Regiment, Continental Troops. Enlisted January 14, 1776 and on duty (in barracks) at Dover on April 12, 1776. [Ref: DA-41].

ORR, Comfort. See "Rees Wolf," q.v.

OSBORNE, John. Captain. He held this rank by 1682 when mentioned in Sussex County as being "of Sumersett County." [Ref: DC-170, 190].

OSBOURN, James. Private. Served in Capt. Jonathan Caldwell's Company, Delaware Regiment of Continental Troops. Enlisted on March 19, 1776, and was on duty (in barracks) at Dover on April 12, 1776. [Ref: DA-41].

OTTEN, John. Land patentee and probable soldier in Delaware in November, 1677. [Ref: DP-167, 168].

OTTO, Gerard. Soldier. Planter who paid his quit-rent to the governor in 1669, having received a patent to one-fourth of Swarten Nutten Island in the Delaware River on August 7, 1668. [Ref: DP-27, DP-28, DY-129, DY-130]. The name of one "Gerett Otto" appeared on a nomination list for officers in New Castle, Delaware circa 1675 (list was not dated). [Ref: DP-170].

OTTO, Herman. Soldier. Planter in Delaware who paid his quit-rent to the governor in 1669, having received a patent to one-fourth of Swarten Nutten Island in the Delaware River on August 7, 1668. [Ref: DP-27, DP-28, DY-129, DY-130].

OUTHOUT, Pop. Officer. His name appeared on a nomination list for officers in New Castle circa 1675 (list not dated). [Ref: DP-170].

OWEN, Elizabeth and William. See "Wilson Buckmaster," q.v.

OWENS, David. Private. Served in Capt. Joseph Vaughan's Company, Delaware Regiment of Continental Troops. Enlisted January 17, 1776, and was on duty (in barracks) at Dover on April 12, 1776. [Ref: DA-57, DA-59]. (This same source spelled his name "David Owings").

OWENS, Joseph. Private. Served in Capt. Joseph Stedham's Company, Delaware Battalion of Continental Troops. Enlisted January 24, 1776, and was in quarters at Dover on April 12, 1776. [Ref: DA-39].

PAFVELSSON, Peder. Soldier. Arrived in New Sweden on the ship *Orn* in 1654. [Ref: DJ-721]. (First name also spelled "Per" or "Peter").

PALMER, Anthony. Second Lieutenant. Served in the War of Jenkins' Ear in 1739-1741 in a company which may have included soldiers from Delaware (muster rolls not extant). [Ref: DM-32].

PALMER, Mary, Joseph, and Daniel. See "John Miers," q.v.

PAPEGOJA, Johan. Captain. He served as lieutenant (*leutenampten*) at Fort Christina in New Sweden in 1643, and was still living there in 1654. He married Armegot Printz, the daughter of Gov. Johan Printz, circa 1645, and they had two girls (no names were given) and three boys (Bernt, Gustaf, and Goran). Johan was commander of the ship *Mercurius* during the twelfth expedition to New Sweden in 1655. He became captain in the Swedish Navy in 1661 and died at Ramstorp in 1667. Armegot Papegoja died on November 26, 1695. Their son Bernt Papegoja died circa 1720 "without children and with him that family became extinct." [Ref: DJ-686, DJ-687, DJ-690, DJ-700, DJ-710, DJ-716, DJ-761, DJ-762]. (Name was also spelled "Johan Paapegaia").

PARHAM, George. Private. Born 1741, Tyrone, Ireland. Laborer. Enlisted on May 6, 1759, in the French and Indian Wars, in Capt. James Armstrong's Company in Pennsylvania Regiment. [Ref: DA-26].

PARIS, Ferdinando John. Officer. English Agent for the Lower Counties [of Pennsylvania, now Delaware], informed the English Privy Council that 1,000 fighting men had been sent against the Spaniards in the War of Jenkins' Ear in 1741. About 300 men were raised at this time from the "Province of Pennsylvania and Three Lower Counties." (Delaware rolls not extant). [Ref: DM-34, 35].

PARK, James. Drummer and fifer. Served in Capt. Joseph Vaughan's Company in the Delaware Regiment of Continental Troops. Enlisted January 15, 1776, and was on duty (in barracks) at Dover on April 12, 1776. [Ref: DA-59].

PARKE, Thomas. Lieutenant. Served in Capt. John Vining's Company, Kent County, 1747-1748, in King George's War against Canada. [Ref: DA-8]. A Thomas Parke died intestate in Kent County and Jane Parke was named his administratrix on August 22, 1792. A later account mentioned his heirs Thomas, Ann, Susan, Samuel, Joshua, and Robert Parke. [Ref: DK-457].

PARKER, Anthony. Private. Born 1711, Ireland. Laborer. Enlisted in Capt. John Shannon's Company of Foot on July 8, 1746, during King George's War against Canada. He made his mark when he was paid for services on June 6, 1747. He was in winter quarters at Albany, New York, 1746-1747, and was discharged on October 31, 1747. [Ref: DA-5, DA-6, DM-40]. (Name also spelled "Parcker").

PARKER, John. Private. Served in Capt. Charles Pope's Company, Delaware Regiment of Continental Troops. Enlisted January 17, 1776, and was on duty (in quarters) at Lewis Town on April 11, 1776. [Ref: DA-51].

PARKER, Leah and John. See "Levin Cropper," q.v.

PARKER, Matthew. Private. Born 1718, Kent, Delaware. Occ: Smith. Enlisted in Capt. John Shannon's Company of Foot on July 20, 1746 and served in King George's War against Canada. He was in winter quarters at Albany, New York, during 1746-1747, and was discharged on October 31, 1747. [Ref: DA-5, 6]. (He is not listed in Source DM-40.) One Thomas Parker died testate in Kent County and his will was probated on September 25, 1750, naming a son Matthew Parker (among others). [Ref: DK-140].

PARLEN, Cathrine. See "Andrew Frauberg [Tranberg]," q.v.

PARMELA, Charles. Private. Born 1722, New England. Carpenter. Enlisted in Capt. John Shannon's Company of Foot on June 27, 1746, during King George's War against Canada. He was in winter quarters at Albany, New York, during 1746-1747, and was discharged October 31, 1747. [Ref: DA-5, DA-6]. (He is not listed in Source DM-40.)

PARR, James. Private. Born 1743, Chester, Pennsylvania). Laborer. Enlisted on May 9, 1759, in the French and Indian Wars, in Capt. James Armstrong's Company in Pennsylvania Regiment. [Ref: DA-26].

PARR, Zephaniah. Soldier. Enlisted May 19, 1759, during the French and Indian Wars, and his name appeared on a return of Capt. Henry Van Bibber's Company of the Lower Counties on Delaware Troops, at New Castle, on June 4, 1759. [Ref: DA-26].

PARRY, Thomas and Rachel. See "Matthew Crozier," q.v.

PASWATERS, David. Private. Served in Capt. Nathan Adams' Company, Delaware Regiment of Continental Troops. Enlisted January 20, 1776, and on duty (in barracks) at Dover on April 12, 1776. [Ref: DA-52].

PASWATERS, Ezekiel. Private. Served in Capt. Nathan Adams' Company, Delaware Regiment of Continental Troops. Enlisted January 15, 1776, and on duty (in barracks) at Dover on April 12, 1776. [Ref: DA-52].

PATTEN, John. First Lieutenant. Served in the 2nd Company, Delaware State Troops in Continental Service. Commissioned January 15, 1776. [Ref: DA-34, 36]. See "John Haslet" regarding Major John Patten.

PATTERSON, Samuel. Captain. Served in a company in White Clay Creek Hundred, Upper Regiment, in New Castle County, in 1756, during the French and Indian Wars. [Ref: DA-11, DM-45]. One Samuel Patterson, Esquire, died testate in White Clay Creek Hundred and his will was probated on May 12, 1785, naming the following: his father William; brothers John (now of Damarora, Merchant), William (a physician), Benjamin, and Joseph; sisters Rebecca and Deborth [sic] Patterson, Jane Rees, and Mary Gardner; daughters of sister Jane Rees, to wit: Mary Black (wife of James Black, Esquire), Catharine Rees, Martha Rees, and Elizabeth Rees; children of sister Mary Gardner, to wit: Mary Gardner, Hester Gardner, Elenor Gardner (who intermarried with a Gustavus Brown), Jane Gardner, William Gardner, and Elizabeth Gardner; cousin, Catharine Morgan; housekeeper, Jane Moran; and, cousin, Abiah McElray. [Ref: DN-106, DN-107].

PATTERSON, William. Captain. New Castle County Company, 1747-1748, and served in King George's War against Canada. [Ref: DA-7].

PATTERSON, William. Lieutenant Colonel. New Castle County Regiment, 1747-1748. Served in King George's War against Canada. [Ref: DA-7].

PATTERSON, William. Private. Served in Capt. Charles Pope's Company of the Delaware Regiment of Continental Troops. Enlisted on January 15, 1776, and was on duty (in quarters) at Lewis Town on April 11, 1776. [Ref: DA-51].

PATTIGREW, James. Corporal. Served in Capt. Charles Pope's Company, Delaware Regiment of Continental Troops. Enlisted January 16, 1776, and was on duty (in quarters) at Lewis Town on April 11, 1776. [Ref: DA-51].

PATTON, Robert. Private. Served in Capt. John Caton's Company, April 25, 1757, in the French and Indian Wars. [Ref: DA-13]. One "Robert Patton, yeoman," died testate in Kent County and his will was probated on May 17, 1783, naming his wife Mary, sons William, Andrew, and John, daughters Margaret Patton and Mary David, and grandson Robert Patton. A later account showed that Margaret Patton married ---- Muncy. [Ref: DK-350].

PAULSON, Benjamin. Sergeant. Born 1729, New Castle, Delaware. Farmer. Enlisted on April 25, 1759, during the French and Indian

Wars, in Capt. James Armstrong's Company in Pennsylvania Regiment. [Ref: DA-25].

PAULSON, Benjamin. Private. Born 1721, Ulster, Ireland). Laborer. Enlisted on April 25, 1759, in the French and Indian Wars, in Capt. James Armstrong's Company in Pennsylvania Regiment. [Ref: DA-26].

PAULSON, John. Private. Served in Capt. Joseph Stedham's Company, Delaware Battalion of Continental Troops. Enlisted on January 19, 1776, and was in quarters at Dover on April 12, 1776. [Ref: DA-39].

PAYNTER, Mary, and others. See "Rees Wolf," q.v.

PEACE, James. Private. Born 1726, London, England. Merchant. Enlisted on April 25, 1758, in the French and Indian Wars, by Capt. John McClughan "for the campaign in the lower counties." [Ref: DA-18]. (Name also spelled "Pease").

PEARCE, Esther. See "John Caton," q.v.

PEARL, Bryant. Artificer. Listed as being "of the thoroughfare to Duck Creek Hundred," he had died testate by April 18, 1706, in New Castle County, leaving a wife Jane and these children: Ann Slather, Margrett Pearl, William Pearl, Ralph Pearl, Benjamin Pearl, and Rachel Pearl. [Ref: DN-12].

PEASLEY, David. Private. Served in Capt. Nathan Adams' Company, Delaware Regiment of Continental Troops. Enlisted January 20, 1776, and was on duty (in barracks) at Dover on April 12, 1776, at which time he was reported to be "sick in quarters." [Ref: DA-52].

PEDDY, James. Land patentee and probable militiaman in Delaware in November, 1677. [Ref: DP-167, 168].

PEERY, Joshua. Private. Served in Capt. Samuel Smith's Company, Delaware Regiment of Continental Troops. Enlisted January 17, 1776, and on duty (in barracks) at Dover on April 12, 1776. [Ref: DA-54].

PEGG, John. Private. Served in Capt. Jonathan Caldwell's Company, Delaware Regiment of Continental Troops. Enlisted January 13, 1776, and on duty (in barracks) at Dover on April 12, 1776. [Ref: DA-41].

PEMBERTON, Thomas. Captain. In Sussex County he was named as an heir (no relationship given) in the will of Haward Knights that was probated on January 18, 1693. [Ref: DA-13]. He was also executor of the will of John Croutch (undated, no heirs) that was probated in February, 1697/8, in Sussex County. [Ref: DA-17]. He served as a Justice in Sussex County in 1697. [Ref: DC-41].

PENNINGTON, Wighland. Private. Enlisted May 1, 1759, in the French and Indian Wars, and his name appeared on a return of Capt. Henry

Van Bibber's Company of the Lower Counties on Delaware Troops, at New Castle, on June 4, 1759. [Ref: DA-26].

PENNINGTON, William. Private. Served in Capt. Henry Darby's Company of the Delaware Regiment of Continental Troops. Enlisted on March 3, 1776, and was on duty (in barracks) at Dover on April 12, 1776. [Ref: DA-46].

PENTLAND, Alexander. Private. Served in Capt. Samuel Smith's Company, Delaware Regiment of Continental Troops. Enlisted January 20, 1776, and on duty (in barracks) at Dover on April 12, 1776. [Ref: DA-54].

PEPPER, Isabell. See "Thomas Prettyman," q.v.

PEPPERAL, William. See "Francis Graham," q.v.

PERKINS, Benjamin. Private. Born 1739, Cedar Creek, Delaware. Farmer. Enlisted May 4, 1758, during the French and Indian Wars, as a private by Capt. John McClughan "for the campaign in the lower counties." [Ref: DA-18].

PERKINS, Hannah and Thomas. See "Benjamin Ford," q.v.

PERKINS, John. Second Lieutenant. Served in 8th Company, Delaware State Troops in Continental Service. Commissioned on January 21, 1776, and was on duty (in barracks) with Capt. Joseph Vaughan's Delaware Regiment of Continental Troops at Dover on April 12, 1776. [Ref: DA-34, 36, 57, 59].

PERKINS, William. Private. Enlisted on May 17, 1759, during the French and Indian Wars, and appeared on a return of Capt. Henry Van Bibber's Company of the Lower Counties on Delaware Troops at New Castle on June 4, 1759. [Ref: DA-26].

PERNON, Peter. Soldier. Planter in Delaware who paid his quit-rent to the governor in 1671, having received a patent to land near Duck Creek on June 17, 1671. [Ref: DP-29, DY-151].

PERRY, John. Private. Born 1733, Maryland. Laborer. Enlisted May 3, 1758, French and Indian War, by Capt. Benjamin Noxon. [Ref: DA-19].

PERRY, Samuel. Captain. Commissioned on June 4, 1746, during King George's War against Canada. He was in winter quarters at Albany, New York, during 1746-1747, and his company was discharged on October 31, 1747. [Ref: DA-6].

PERRY, William. Private. Served in Capt. Jonathan Caldwell's Company, Delaware Regiment of Continental Troops. Enlisted January 17, 1776, and on duty (in barracks) at Dover on April 12, 1776. [Ref: DA-41].

PERSSON, Hakan. Soldier. In New Sweden in 1654 and was paid various sums by Director Rising for his service. [Ref: DJ-726].

PERSSON, Johan. Soldier. Arrived in New Sweden on the ship *Orn* in 1654. [Ref: DJ-721].
PERSSON, Knut. Secretary (*skriffwaren*). Arrived in New Sweden in 1643 and was an "officer" at Fort Tinicum in 1643. He died in New Sweden "before the autumn of 1653." [Ref: DJ-705, DA-706, DA-713].
PERSSON, Lucas. Sailor. Arrived in 1641 on the ship *Charitas* and was a "sailor on the sloop" in New Sweden in 1648. By 1654 "Lucas Persson, or Peterson" was a freeman. [Ref: DJ-712, DJ-721, DH-45].
PERSSON, Mans. Soldier. He was in New Sweden in 1654 and was paid various sums by Director Rising for his services. [Ref: DJ-726].
PETER, Caja. Private. Born 1736, Pocomock, Maryland. Fiddle maker. Enlisted May 8, 1758, in the French and Indian Wars, by Capt. John McClughan "for the campaign in the lower counties." [Ref: DA-18].
PETERSON, Adam. Captain. Served in a company from St. George's Hundred, Lower Regiment, New Castle County, 1756, in the French and Indian Wars. He was probably a descendant of the Adam Peterson who arrived in the New World before 1671, settling in lower New Castle. [Ref: DA-11, DM-46, DF-28]. One Adam Peterson died testate in St. George's Hundred, having written his will on January 23, 1763 (but the date of probate was not indicated), naming his wife Veronica, cousins Richard and Lydia Cantwell, and a Dr. Jacob Peterson. [Ref: DN-60]. Another Adam Peterson died testate in St. George's Hundred and his will was probated November 26, 1773, naming only his wife Rachel. [Ref: DN-73].
PETERSON, Gabriel. Private. Born 1716, West Jersey. Laborer. Enlisted in Capt. John Shannon's Company of Foot on July 16, 1746 and served in King George's War against Canada. He was in winter quarters at Albany, New York, during 1746-1747, and was discharged October 31, 1747. [Ref: DA-5, DA-6]. (Not listed in Source DM-40.)
PETERSON, George Jr. Private. Served in Capt. Richard McWilliams' Company, New Castle County. Enlisted on December 28, 1757, during the French and Indian Wars. [Ref: DA-14].
PETERSON, Jacob. See "John Van Dyke" and "Adam Peterson," q.v.
PETERSON, John. Private. Served in Capt. Richard McWilliams' Company, New Castle County. Enlisted on December 28, 1757, during the French and Indian Wars. [Ref: DA-14].
PETERSON, John. Private. Served in Capt. Henry Darby's Company, Delaware Regiment of Continental Troops. Enlisted January 18, 1776, and on duty (in barracks) at Dover on April 12, 1776. [Ref: DA-46].

PETERSON, Peter. Trumpeter. An "officer" in New Sweden, having arrived there on the ship *Orn* in 1654. He was "probably the same person as Peter Petersson, the drummer." [Ref: DJ-716].

PETERSON, Peter. See "John Hendrickson," q.v.

PETERSON, Ruloff. Lieutenant. Served in Capt. John Almond's Company in New Castle County during 1747-1748, in King George's War against Canada. [Ref: DA-7].

PETERSON, William. Private. Served in Capt. Richard McWilliams' Company, New Castle County. Enlisted on December 28, 1757, during the French and Indian Wars. [Ref: DA-15].

PETTY, Phineas. Private. Served in Capt. Samuel Smith's Company, Delaware Regiment of Continental Troops. Enlisted January 15, 1776, and on duty (in barracks) at Dover on April 12, 1776. [Ref: DA-54].

PHILLIPS, Jacob. Major. Served in Sussex County militia regiment in 1756-1758, in French and Indian Wars. [Ref: DA-13, DA-15, DM-46]. One Jacob Phillips died testate in Sussex County and his will was probated on April 19, 1762, naming his wife Hester Phillips, nephew Phillip Kollock (son of Jacob Kollock), and his niece Hannah Nunez (wife of Daniel Nunez). [Ref: DS-74]. See "Jacob Kollock," q.v.

PHILLIPS, Thomas. Officer. His name appeared on a nomination list for officers for the Whorekill in Sussex County, Delaware circa 1675 (list was not dated). [Ref: DP-170].

PHILLIPS, Thomas. Ensign. Served in Capt. William Armstrong's Company, New Castle County, 1747-1748, in King George's War against Canada. [Ref: DA-7]. One Thomas Phillips died testate in Christiana Hundred, New Castle County, and his will was probated on April 26, 1755, naming his wife Mary, stepson Nathan Scothorn, nephew Thomas Phillips, and grandson John Scothorn. [Ref: DN-53].

PIERCE, Robert. Ensign. Served in Capt. Archibald Armstrong's Company, New Castle County, 1747-1748, in King George's War against Canada. [Ref: DA-7].

PIETERS, Dirck. Soldier. Planter in Delaware who paid his quit-rent to the governor in 1670, having received a patent to land at Whore Kill on May 25, 1670. [Ref: DP-29, DY-145].

PIETERS, Hans. Soldier. Planter in Delaware who paid his quit-rent to the governor in 1668, having received a patent to land at Wild Hook on November 14, 1668. [Ref: DP-28, DY-136].

PIETERSEN, Lambert. Skipper. Served on the ship *Swan* during the fifth expedition to New Sweden between 1642-1643. [Ref: DJ-759].

PIGGOT, John. Private. Served in Capt. Joseph Vaughan's Company, Delaware Regiment of Continental Troops. Enlisted January 16, 1776, and was on duty (in barracks) at Dover on April 12, 1776, at which time he was reported to be "under guard." [Ref: DA-57, DA-59]. (This same source spelled his name "John Pegot").

PIKE, Steven. Private. Served in Capt. Joseph Stedham's Company, Delaware Battalion of Continental Troops. Enlisted on February 3, 1776, and was in quarters at Dover on April 12, 1776, at which time he was reported sick. [Ref: DA-39].

PINDERGRASS, Antony. Private. Served in Capt. John Caton's Company, April 25, 1757, in the French and Indian Wars. [Ref: DA-13].

PIPER, Samuel. Private. Born 1724, Derry, Ireland. Tailor. Enlisted May 4, 1759, in the French and Indian Wars, Capt. James Armstrong's Company, Pennsylvania Regiment. [Ref: DA-26].

PLATT, Samuel. Lieutenant. Served in Capt. Rees Jones' Company, White Clay Creek Hundred, Upper Regiment, New Castle County, 1756, during the French and Indian Wars. [Ref: DA-11]. One Samuel Platt, Jr., M.D., died testate in Newark and his will, probated November 4, 1795, named his sisters Elizabeth Evans, Martha Duraghan (wife of John), nephew Samuel Anderson and nieces Mary and Ann Anderson (children of sister Ann Anderson), half brother George Platt, and half sisters Jane and Mary Platt. [Ref: DN-137]. One Samuel Platt, M.D., died testate in White Clay Creek Hundred and his will was probated on January 4, 1799, naming his wife Margery, daughters Dinah Worth, Margaret McCrea, Elizabeth Evans, Ann Anderson, Martha Durgan, Jane Platt, and Mary Platt, son George Platt, and granddaughter Ann Ross. [Ref: DN-147].

PLOWMAN, William. Private. Served in Capt. Jonathan Caldwell's Company, Delaware Regiment of Continental Troops. Enlisted January 13, 1776, and on duty (in barracks) at Dover on April 12, 1776. [Ref: DA-41].

PLUNKETT, Thomas. Private. Served in Capt. Joseph Vaughan's Company of the Delaware Regiment of Continental Troops. Enlisted on January 20, 1776, and wsa on duty (in barracks) at Dover on April 12, 1776. [Ref: DA-59].

PONDER, John. Private. Served in Capt. David Hall's Company of the Delaware Regiment of Continental Troops. Enlisted February 7, 1776, and was on duty (in barracks) at Lewis Town on April 11, 1776. [Ref: DA-43].

POOR, Comfort. See "Samuel Davis," q.v.

POPE, Charles. Captain. Served in the 5th Company of Delaware State Troops in Continental Service. Commissioned on January 18, 1776, and on duty (in quarters) with the Delaware Regiment of Continental Troops at Lewis Town on April 11, 1776. [Ref: DA-34, 36, 49, 51].

POPEGAY, Ufro. Soldier. Planter in Delaware who paid his quit-rent to the governor in 1669. [Ref: DP-27, 28].

POPHAM, William. Second Lieutenant. Served in 4th Company, Delaware State Troops in Continental Service. Commissioned January 17, 1776, and was on duty (in barracks) with Capt. Henry Darby at Dover on April 12, 1776. [Ref: DA-34, 36, 45].

PORTER, Alexander. Captain. Served in a New Castle County Company, during 1747-1748, in King George's War against Canada. [Ref: DA-7]. Another Alexander Porter was a lieutenant in Capt. Thomas Cooch's Company, Pencader Hundred, Lower Regiment, New Castle County, 1756, in the French and Indian Wars. [Ref: DA-12]. An Alexander Porter was a captain of a company in New Castle Hundred, Upper Regiment, New Castle County, 1756, also during the French and Indian Wars. [Ref: DA-11, DM-45]. One Alexander Porter, Esquire, died testate in New Castle Hundred, and his will was probated April 7, 1784, naming his sons Alexander and Jonas, daughter Mary, and his granddaughter Eleanor Porter Barclay. [Ref: DN-102].

PORTER, Betty and John. See "Robert Robinson," q.v.

PORTER, Thomas. Private. Served in Capt. Joseph Stedham's Company, Delaware Battalion of Continental Troops. Enlisted on March 11, 1776, and was in quarters at Dover on April 12, 1776. [Ref: DA-40].

POULSEN, Paul. Soldier. Planter in Delaware who paid his quit-rent to the governor in 1668. [Ref: DP-28]. Land patent at Christeen Kill on March 24, 1668 spelled his name "Paul Pousen," Pousen," and "Paul Poulsen," all in the same record. [Ref: DY-137].

POULSON, Wooley. Soldier. Planter in Delaware who paid his quit-rent to the governor in 1668. [Ref: DP-27, 28]. "Wooley Poulston," also spelled "Poulson," was granted a patent to a third of an island called Bread and Cheese Island in the Delaware River on August 3, 1668. [Ref: DY-134].

POUND, Samuel. Mariner. Died testate in Duck Creek Hundred in Kent County and his will was probated on November 30, 1730, naming his son James Pound and daughter Hannah Pound. [Ref: DK-61].

POWELL, William. Private. Served in Capt. John Caton's Company, April 25, 1757, in the French and Indian Wars. [Ref: DA-13]. One William

Powell was the brother-in-law of Richard Downham and one of the executors of his will probated on June 18, 1773. [Ref: DK-280].

POWELSON, Jacob. Captain. Served on ship *Fredenburg* which arrived in Delaware from Sweden on November 2, 1640, under the command of Jost van Bogardt, and whose passengers settled below Christiana in [now] St. George's Hundred of New Castle County. [Ref: DH-44].

PRATT, Abraham. Private. Served in Capt. Richard McWilliams' Company, New Castle County. Enlisted on December 28, 1757, during the French and Indian Wars. [Ref: DA-15].

PRATT, Jeremiah. Private. Served in Capt. Richard McWilliams' Company, New Castle County. Enlisted on December 28, 1757, during the French and Indian Wars. [Ref: DA-15].

PRENTICE, William. Land patentee and probable militiaman in Delaware in November, 1677. [Ref: DP-167, 168].

PRESTON, John. Private. Served in Capt. Nathan Adams' Company, Delaware Regiment of Continental Troops. Enlisted on March 17, 1776, and was on duty (in barracks) at Dover on April 12, 1776. [Ref: DA-53].

PRESTON, Joseph. Private. Served in Capt. Samuel Smith's Company, Delaware Regiment of Continental Troops. Enlisted January 25, 1776, and was on duty (in barracks) at Dover on April 12, 1776, at which time he transferred to Capt. Henry Darby's Company. [Ref: DA-54].

PRETTYMAN, Elenor and Robert. See "William Craig," q.v.

PRETTYMAN, Thomas. Ensign. Served in Capt. Cord Hazzard's Company, Northern District of Indian River Hundred, in the regiment of Sussex County, 1756, and ensign in the Angola District Company on March 18, 1758, during the French and Indian Wars. [Ref: DA-13, 15]. One "Thomas Prettyman, Esq.," died testate in Sussex County and his will was probated on January 22, 1765, naming his wife Comfort, and heirs Sarah Dobson, Mary Russel, and John Futcher (son of William). [Ref: DS-76]. One "Thomas Prettyman, planter," died testate in Sussex County and his will was probated on October 26, 1790, naming his wife Elizabeth, sons William, George, Burton, Robert, and Thomas, and daughters Hessy Prettyman, Comfort Rogers, Ann Morris, Tabitha Morris, Mary Ingram, Patience Noles, Sarah Marvel, Agnes Williams, and Isabell Pepper. A later account states the estate was settled on April 14, 1795 by Joseph Wharton and Elizabeth, his wife (late Elizabeth Prettyman). [Ref: DS-220].

PRETTYMAN, William. Ensign. Served in Capt. Burton Waples' Company in the Southern District, Indian River Hundred, in a regiment of

Sussex County, in 1756, and ensign in Capt. Waples' Indian River District Company on March 18, 1758, in the French and Indian Wars. [Ref: DA-13, 15]. One William Prettyman died in Sussex County and his will was probated on September 13, 1766, naming wife Sarah, son Burton, and daughters Sarah Prettyman, Magdalene Prettyman, Naomi Boyce, and Margaret Houston. [Ref: DS-79]. One "William Prettyman, yeoman," died intestate in Sussex County and estate administration was granted to Robert Prettyman on April 17, 1780. [Ref: DS-133].

PRICE, Daniel. Private. Born 1733, Elizabethtown, Jersey. Weaver. Enlisted on May 4, 1758, during the French and Indian Wars, as a private by Capt. John McClughan "for the campaign in the lower counties." [Ref: DA-18].

PRICE, Dudley. Private. Served in Capt. Charles Pope's Company, Delaware Regiment of Continental Troops. Enlisted January 16, 1776, and was on duty (in quarters) at Lewis Town on April 11, 1776. [Ref: DA-51].

PRICE, Solomon. Private. Served in Capt. Nathan Adams' Company, Delaware Regiment of Continental Troops. Enlisted February 26, 1776, and was on duty (in barracks) at Dover on April 12, 1776. [Ref: DA-53].

PRICE, William. Private. Served in Capt. David Hall's Company, Delaware Regiment of Continental Troops. Enlisted January 20, 1776, and was on duty (in barracks) at Lewis Town on April 11, 1776. [Ref: DA-43].

PRICHARD, Henry. Private. Served in Capt. John Caton's Company, April 25, 1757, in the French and Indian Wars. [Ref: DA-13].

PRIDE, Job. Private. Served in Capt. David Hall's Company, Delaware Regiment of Continental Troops. Enlisted February 3, 1776, and on duty (in barracks) at Lewis Town on April 11, 1776. [Ref: DA-43].

PRIDE, Luke. Private. Served in Capt. David Hall's Company, Delaware Regiment of Continental Troops. Enlisted January 17, 1776, and was on duty (in barracks) at Lewis Town on April 11, 1776. [Ref: DA-42].

PRIDE, Southy. Private. Born 1737, Sussex, Delaware. Planter. Enlisted on April 19, 1758, during the French and Indian Wars, by Capt. John McClughan "for the campaign in lower counties." [Ref: DA-18]. He was probably the same "Suthy Pride, private, born 1738, Sussex, Delaware," who had enlisted in Capt. John Wright's Company and appeared on the muster roll of May 11, 1759. [Ref: DA-25].

PRINGLE, Eleanor. See "John Ogle," q.v.

173

PRINTZ, Hans. Stone-cutter (*stenhuggate*). Soldier. He was hired in Stockholm in 1654, and he arrived in New Sweden on the ship *Orn* in 1654. He returned to Europe with Director Rising in 1655. [Ref: DJ-721, DJ-724]. (Name also spelled "Prentz," Preutz," or "Pryss").

PRINTZ, Gustaf. Lieutenant. Son of Governor Printz, he came to New Sweden and was an "officer" at Fort Tinicum in 1643. He was finally given the rank of a lieutenant. He returned to Sweden in 1652 and died in Skane in 1657. [Ref: DJ-687, DJ-688, DJ-705, DJ-710].

PRINTZ, Johan. Governor. Born in Bottnaryd in Smaland, Sweden, on July 20, 1592, and after a rather adventuresome youth, he entered the Swedish service in 1625. He became a cavalry captain in 1630 and then a major in 1635. He rose to the rank of lieutenant colonel and in 1642 he was requested to become governor (*governeuren*) in New Sweden, which he accepted. He was at Fort Tinicum from 1643 to 1653, and when he returned to Sweden he was promoted to colonel. In 1657 he became commandant at the castle of Jonkoping and in 1658 he became the governor. Johan married twice. His first wife, Elizabeth Bock, died in 1640 and his second wife was Maria von Linnestau. He had five girls (Armegot, Catharina, Christina, Elsa, and Gunilla) and one son (Gustaf). Johan Printz died on May 3, 1663. "He was in many ways a remarkable character (his adventures before entering Swedish service in 1630 border on romance) and deserves a prominent place among the early governors of the American settlements." [Ref: DJ-688, DJ-689, DJ-705, DJ-710, DH-44]. Pieterson De Vries observed "Captain Printz, who weighed 400 pounds, took three drinks at every meal," yet he lacked not of energy or decision of character. His alertness and aggressiveness made him a useful man for his time and place. [Ref: DH-48].

PRITCHARD, Henry. See "Henry Prichard," q.v.

PRITCHARD, Robert. See "Robert Hodgson," q.v.

PRITCHETT, Margaret. See "Robert Hodgson," q.v.

PROCTOR, Richard. Private. Born 1733, Lancaster, England. Weaver. Enlisted on April 29, 1759, in the French and Indian Wars, in Capt. James Armstrong's Company in Pennsylvania Regiment. [Ref: DA-26].

PUCKAM, Stephen. Private. Served in Capt. David Hall's Company, Delaware Regiment of Continental Troops. Enlisted February 3, 1776, and was on duty (in barracks) at Lewis Town on April 11, 1776. [Ref: DA-43].

PULLET, Richard. Private. Born 1730, Maryland. Enlisted in Capt. John Wright's Company and was on the muster roll of May 11, 1759, during the French and Indian Wars. [Ref: DA-25].

PURNELL, Esther. See "Peter Marsh," q.v.
PURSE, Alexander. Soldier. Enlisted May 19, 1759, during the French and Indian Wars, and his name appeared on a return of Capt. Henry Van Bibber's Company of the Lower Counties on Delaware Troops, at New Castle, on June 4, 1759. [Ref: DA-26].
PUSSEL, John. See "John Russel," q.v.
QUENOUAULT, Paul. Sergeant. Served in Capt. Nathan Adams' Company, Delaware Regiment of Continental Troops. Enlisted January 21, 1776, and on duty (in barracks) at Dover on April 12, 1776. [Ref: DA-52].
QUIGLEY, Edward. Private. Served in Capt. Henry Darby's Company, Delaware Regiment of Continental Troops. Enlisted January 18, 1776, and on duty (in barracks) at Dover on April 12, 1776. [Ref: DA-46].
QUIST, Pafwel. Soldier. Served in New Sweden and returned to Europe with Director Rising in 1655. [Ref: DJ-724]. (Name was also spelled "Pafvel Kvist").
RAHEW, Paul. Private. Served in Capt. Charles Pope's Company of the Delaware Regiment of Continental Troops. Enlisted January 16, 1776, and was on duty (in quarters) at Lewis Town on April 11, 1776. [Ref: DA-51].
RALSTON, Hugh. Private. Born 1731, Argyle, Scotland. Laborer. Enlisted on April 26, 1758, in the French and Indian Wars, by Capt. John McClughan "for the campaign in lower counties." [Ref: DA-18].
RAMBO, Peter Gunnarson. Soldier. Hired at Stockholm in 1653, he arrived in New Sweden on the ship *Orn* in 1654. [Ref: DJ-721]. One "Pieter Rambo" was a soldier and planter in Delaware who paid his quit-rent to the governor in 1669. [Ref: DP-27, DP-28].
RAMSEY, James. Private. Born 1738, Sussex, Delaware. Laborer. Enlisted on April 20, 1758, during the French and Indian Wars, as a private by Capt. John McClughan "for the campaign in the lower counties." [Ref: DA-18].
RAMSEY, Peter. Private. Born 1716, Scotland. Laborer. Enlisted in Capt. John Shannon's Company of Foot on July 9, 1746, and served in King George's War against Canada. He was also in winter quarters at Albany, New York, during 1746-1747, and was discharged on October 31, 1747. [Ref: DA-5, DA-6]. (He is not listed in Source DM-40.)
RAMSEY, Raynolds. Private. Served in Capt. Richard McWilliams' Company, New Castle County. Enlisted on December 28, 1757, during the French and Indian Wars. [Ref: DA-14].

RANDLE, Peter. Private. Born 1720, Inniskillen, Ireland. Laborer. Enlisted on May 4, 1759, in the French and Indian Wars, in Capt. James Armstrong's Company in Pennsylvania Regiment. [Ref: DA-26].
RANGER, Benjamin. Sergeant. Served in Capt. Samuel Smith's Company, Delaware Regiment of Continental Troops. Enlisted February 1, 1776, and on duty (in barracks) at Dover on April 12, 1776. [Ref: DA-53].
RAPPAY, Gabreel. Captain. He held this rank by 1693 when mentioned in an Action of Debt in Sussex County. [Ref: DC-862].
RASE, Olof. Soldier. Arrived in New Sweden on the ship *Orn* in 1654. [Ref: DJ-721].
RASH, John and Hannah. See "Renn Forkcum," q.v.
RASH, John Jr. Private. Served in Capt. John Caton's Company on April 25, 1757, in the French and Indian Wars. [Ref: DA-14]. One "John Rash" died testate in Kent County and his will was probated on January 3, 1761, naming his sons Joseph, James, and William, and daughters Elizabeth Swails, Mary Downham (wife of Thomas Downham), Sarah Smith (wife of David Smith), and Hannah Forkham (wife of Renn Forkham). [Ref: DK-192]. One "John Rash, Sr., farmer," died testate in Murderkill Hundred in Kent County and his will was probated on November 30, 1790, naming sons Daniel, Andrew, Martin, and Joseph, and daughters Sarah Shelton, Mary Rash, Easter Rash, Ann Rash, Letitia Rash, Ansley Rash, and Patience Rash. [Ref: DK-438].
RASH, Joseph. Private. Served in Capt. John Caton's Company, April 25, 1757, in the French and Indian Wars. [Ref: DA-14].
RATTLEDGE, James. Private. Served in Capt. John Caton's Company, April 25, 1757, in the French and Indian Wars. [Ref: DA-14]. One "John Rattledge, farmer," died testate in Kent County and his will was probated on July 26, 1773, naming wife Mary, sons John, Thomas, James, Moses, and William, and daughters Elizabeth Buckler, Ruth Rattledge, and Jemmimah Rattledge. A later account showed that Mary Rattledge married Jeremiah Calhoon. [Ref: DK-280].
RATTLEDGE, Moses. Private. Served in Capt. John Caton's Company, April 25, 1757, in the French and Indian Wars. [Ref: DA-14]. See information contained under "James Rattledge," q.v.
RATTLEDGE, Thomas. Private. Served in Capt. John Caton's Company, April 25, 1757, in the French and Indian Wars. [Ref: DA-14]. See information contained under "James Rattledge," q.v.
RAWLINS, Abel. Private. Served in Capt. David Hall's Company of the Delaware Regiment of Continental Troops. Enlisted January 28, 1776,

and was on duty (in barracks) at Lewis Town on April 11, 1776. [Ref: DA-43].

RAYANS, James. See "James Ryans (Rayans)," q.v.

RAYE, Christopher. Soldier. Enlisted on May 23, 1759, in the French and Indian Wars, and his name appeared on a return of Capt. Henry Van Bibber's Company of the Lower Counties on Delaware Troops at New Castle on June 4, 1759. [Ref: DA-26].

RAYMOND, Mary. See "George Martin," q.v.

REA, William. Corporal. Served in Capt. Charles Pope's Company, Delaware Regiment of Continental Troops. Enlisted January 18, 1776, and was on duty (in quarters) at Lewis Town on April 11, 1776. [Ref: DA-51].

READ, George. Esquire (attorney). Private. Served in Capt. Richard McWilliams' Company, New Castle County. Enlisted December 28, 1757, in the French and Indian Wars. [Ref: DA-15]. See "Caesar Rodney."

READ, John. Colonel. Born 1688 in Dublin, Ireland, and he was the first of his family to go to America. He settled in Cecil County, Maryland, and also owned land in Delaware. After a long period of single life he married Mary Howell (born 1711 in Wales) who had migrated to Delaware with her parents at a young age. John and Mary Read had three distinguished sons: George Read, the Signer; Colonel James Read; and, Commodore Thomas Read; and, only daughter Mary who married Gunning Bedford (lieutenant in the French and Indians Wars in 1755, lieutenant colonel in the Revolutionary War of 1776, and ultimately the Governor of Delaware). John Read died in 1756. [Ref: DH-186 to 202].

READ, John. Lieutenant. Served in Capt. William Patterson's Company in New Castle County in 1747-1748, and served in King George's War against Canada. [Ref: DA-7].

READ, William. Ensign. Served in Capt. Samuel Patterson's Company, White Clay Creek Hundred, Upper Regiment, New Castle County, 1756, during the French and Indian Wars. [Ref: DA-11].

REARDING, Darby. Private. Served in Capt. Samuel Smith's Company, Delaware Regiment of Continental Troops. Enlisted January 18, 1776, and on duty (in barracks) at Dover on April 12, 1776. [Ref: DA-54].

REECE, Evan. See "Evan Rees" and "Evan Rice," q.v.

REED, Walter. Private. Enlisted on May 19, 1758, in Capt. French Battell's Company of Lower County Provincials, during the French and Indian Wars. [Ref: DA-16].

REES, Evan. Captain. Served in a company in Mill Creek Hundred, Upper Regiment, New Castle County, 1756, during the French and Indian Wars. [Ref: DA-11, DM-45]. An "Evan Reece (Rice)," farmer, died in Mill Creek Hundred and his will was probated December 21, 1742, naming wife Katrina, sons Evan, William, and Thomas, daughter Sarah Wallace, and his granddaughter Rachel Wallace. [Ref: DN-33].

REES, John. Lieutenant. Served in Capt. Robert Blackshire's Company in Kent County, 1747-1748, and served in King George's War against Canada. [Ref: DA-8]. "John Reese" was a lieutenant in Capt. David Clark's Company in the upper part of Duck Creek Hundred, in Kent County, upon Delaware, in 1756, during the French and Indian Wars. [Ref: DA-12]. One "John Rees" died testate in Little Creek Hundred and his will was probated on June 4, 1769, naming his wife Esther, his sons John, Jeremiah, Thomas, and David, and his daughters Mary Griffith, Lydia Chance, and Sarah Rees. [Ref: DK-242].

REES, William. Ensign. Served in Capt. Robert Blackshire's Company, Kent County, 1747-1748, in King George's War against Canada. [Ref: DA-8]. One William Rees died intestate in Kent County and Martha Rees and James M. Gardiner were named as administrators on June 17, 1784. Later account showed Martha Rees married Thomas Skillington. [Ref: DK-359].

REF, Nils. Soldier. Served in New Sweden in 1654, and paid various sums by Director Rising. [Ref: DJ-726]. (Name also spelled "Raf").

REGESTER, John. Private. Served in Capt. John Caton's Company on April 25, 1757, during the French and Indian Wars. [Ref: DA-14]. One "Jeremiah Register" died testate in Murderkill Hundred, Kent County, and his will was probated April 11, 1774, naming a son John (among others). [Ref: DK-288].

RENCH, Sarah and James. See "Levin Cropper," q.v.

RENIERSE, Renier. Soldier. Planter in Delaware who paid his quit-rent to the governor in 1668. One "Reyner Reyniessen" received a patent to land on June 22, 1668. [Ref: DP-28, DY-132].

REYLIE, Matthew. Private. Served in Capt. Henry Darby's Company, Delaware Regiment of Continental Troops. Enlisted January 20, 1776, and on duty (in barracks) at Dover on April 12, 1776. [Ref: DA-46].

REYNERS, Herman. Soldier. Planter in Delaware who paid his quit-rent to the governor in 1669, having received a grant to a house and lot in New Castle, April 8, 1669. [Ref: DP-27, DY-158].

REYNOLDS, James. Private. Served in Capt. David Hall's Company, Delaware Regiment of Continental Troops. Enlisted February 20, 1776,

and was on duty (in barracks) at Lewis Town on April 11, 1776. [Ref: DA-43].

REYNOLDS, John. Soldier. He was probably a son of Daniel Reynolds (Reynals) and Grace Lowber, and the brother of Michael Reynolds. John enlisted in Capt. John Caton's Company on April 25, 1757, in the French and Indian Wars. He married, but had no children. One "John Reynalls" died in Kent County and his will was probated on October 2, 1773, naming wife Elizabeth and "John Reynalls, son of Michell Reynalls." A later account showed that his widow Elizabeth married James White. [Ref: DA-13, DF-32, DK-79, DK-282].

REYNOLDS, Michael. Soldier. He was probably a son of Daniel Reynolds (Reynals) and Grace Lowber, and brother of John Reynolds, Michael enlisted in Capt. John Caton's Company on April 25, 1757, in the French and Indian Wars. He married Miriam Blackshave and they had seven children: Robert, Michael, Thomas, Daniel, John, George, and Letitia. [Ref: DA-13, DF-32, DK-79].

REYNOLDS, William, Ann and Andrew. See "Andrew Caldwell," q.v.

RHEA, Mathew. Lieutenant. Served in Capt. George Gano's Company, Apoquinamink Hundred, Lower Regiment, New Castle County, in 1756, during the French and Indian Wars. [Ref: DA-12].

RHOADES, William. Captain. Served in a company of militia in lower part of Murder Kill Hundred, Kent County, upon Delaware, in 1756, in the French and Indian Wars. [Ref: DA-12, DM-46]. One "William Rhodes, Esquire," died in Kent County and his will was probated on January 9, 177,7 naming wife Mary and 3 children (no names given), plus his grandson William Gerrard. John Rhodes (son) was named one of his executors. Administrator *de bonis non* of one "Col. William Rhodes" on March 9, 1782, was Nehemiah Tilton. [Ref: DK-335, 338].

RHODES, John. Captain. Died intestate in Kent County and Mary Rhodes was named administratrix on December 29, 1781. Nehemiah Tilton was named administrator *de bonis non* on March 9, 1782. An account mentioned heirs William Jarrard and Mary Rhodes, and also mentioned brother James Rhodes, deceased. [Ref: DK-335, DK-338].

RIAL, George. Private. Served in Capt. Jonathan Caldwell's Company, Delaware Regiment of Continental Troops. Enlisted January 17, 1776, and on duty (in barracks) at Dover on April 12, 1776. [Ref: DA-41].

RICE, Evan. Captain. Served in a New Castle County Company, 1747-1748, in King George's War against Canada. [Ref: DA-7]. One Evan Rice died testate in Mill Creek Hundred, New Castle County, and his will was probated on November 29, 1783, naming his mother Elizabeth and his father Thomas (deceased), uncle Jeremiah Ball (deceased), wife Elizabeth and her father Francis Graham (deceased), daughter Mary, sons Thomas, Evan, William, Washington, Solomon, and John, and his (Evans') brother Jeremiah. [Ref: DN-101]. See "Evan Rees."

RICE, John David. Private. Born 1729, America. Carpenter. Enlisted on May 20, 1758, in the French and Indian Wars, by Capt. Benjamin Noxon. [Ref: DA-19].

RICE, Thomas. Private. Born 1737, Ware, Virginia. Laborer. Enlisted on May 12, 1758, during the French and Indian Wars, by Capt. John McClughan "for the campaign in the lower counties." [Ref: DA-18].

RICH, William. Private. Served in Capt. Nathan Adams' Company, Delaware Regiment of Continental Troops. Enlisted January 20, 1776, and on duty (in barracks) at Dover on April 12, 1776. [Ref: DA-53].

RICHARDSON, Benjamin. Private. Born 1727, New Castle, Delaware. Laborer. Enlisted in Capt. John Shannon's Company of Foot on July 21, 1746, and served in King George's War against Canada. He was in winter quarters at Albany, New York, 1746-1747, and was discharged October 31, 1747. [Ref: DA-5, DA-6]. (Not listed in Source DM-40.)

RICHARDSON, John. Private. Served in Capt. Joseph Vaughan's Company in Delaware Regiment, Continental Troops. Enlisted January 15, 1776 and on duty (in barracks) at Dover on April 12, 1776. [Ref: DA-59].

RICHARDSON, John. Private. Served in Capt. Charles Pope's Company, Delaware Regiment of Continental Troops. Enlisted January 15, 1776, and was on duty (in quarters) at Lewis Town on April 11, 1776. [Ref: DA-51].

RICHARDSON, Philip. Private. Served in Capt. Nathan Adams' Company, Delaware Regiment of Continental Troops. Enlisted January 31, 1776, and on duty (in barracks) at Dover on April 12, 1776. [Ref: DA-53].

RICHARDSON, Stephen. Private. Served in Capt. Charles Pope's Company, Delaware Regiment of Continental Troops. Enlisted January 18, 1776, and was on duty (in quarters) at Lewis Town on April 11, 1776. [Ref: DA-51].

RICHARDSON, Thomas. Private. Born 1734, Pennsylvania. Laborer. Enlisted on May 3, 1758, during the French and Indian Wars, by Capt. Benjamin Noxon. [Ref: DA-19].

RICHARDSON, William. Private. Born 1744, Ireland. Laborer. Enlisted in Capt. John Shannon's Company of Foot on July 2, 1746, and served in King George's War against Canada. He was in winter quarters at

Albany, New York, during 1746-1747, and was discharged on October 31, 1747. [Ref: DA-5, DA-6]. (He is not listed in Source DM-40.)

RICKARDS, Ann and Charles. See "John Newbold," q.v.

RIDDER, Peter Hollender. Commander. Of Dutch or low German origin, Peter entered the Swedish service circa 1635 and served in various capacities with the Admiralty in Finland and Sweden. In 1639 he was engaged to go to New Sweden (on the second expedition) where he was commander in 1640 and governor until February, 1643. He returned to Europe in 1643 and held the rank of lieutenant (which rank he held before going to America). He was made captain circa 1648, advanced to major in 1660, and in 1669 he became commander at the castle of Viborg in Finland. He was probably born in 1607, died in 1691 and married before going to New Sweden in 1640. He had two sons, Peter Peterson Ridder and Constantin Ridder, and four daughters (no names were given in this record). [Ref: DJ-691, DJ-692, DJ-699, DJ-700].

RIDGE, William. Private. Served in Capt. Charles Pope's Company, Delaware Regiment of Continental Troops. Enlisted January 20, 1776, and was on duty (in quarters) at Lewis Town on April 11, 1776. [Ref: DA-51].

RILEY, Mary and Isaac. See "Isaac Watson," q.v.

RILEY, Peter. Private. Enlisted on May 15, 1758, in Capt. French Battell's Company of Lower County Provincials, during the French and Indian Wars. [Ref: DA-16].

RISING, Johan Classon. Commander and Director. A son of Rev. Clas Botvidi, he was born in 1617 and entered the University of Upsala in 1635, after which he worked for the Swedish government. He was engaged to go to New Sweden as an assistant to Governor Printz, and was raised to the rank of a nobleman. He was commander on the ship *Orn* to New Sweden during the tenth expedition in 1654, and became director of New Sweden at that time. After the fall of New Sweden he returned to Europe and led a troubled life, both politically and financially. He died in April, 1672. [Ref: DJ-693, 694, 716, 761]. Also referred to as Governor Johan Classon Rising. [Ref: DC-6].

ROACH, John. Private. Served in Capt. Charles Pope's Company, Delaware Regiment of Continental Troops. Enlisted January 13, 1776, and was on duty (in quarters) at Lewis Town on April 11, 1776. [Ref: DA-51].

ROARK, Thomas. See "Thomas Boark," q.v.

ROBERTS, Bignal. Private. Enlisted on May 17, 1758, in Capt. French Battell's Company of Lower County Provincials, during the French and Indian Wars. [Ref: DA-16].

ROBERTS, Jeremiah. Private. Born 1736, Delaware. Laborer. Enlisted on April 29, 1758, during the French and Indian Wars, by Capt. Benjamin Noxon. [Ref: DA-19].

ROBERTS, John. Private. Born 1731, England). Laborer. Enlisted on May 9, 1758, in the French and Indian Wars, by Capt. John McClughan "for the campaign in the lower counties." [Ref: DA-18].

ROBERTSON, Charles. Sergeant. Born 1723, England. Cooper. Enlisted in Capt. John Shannon's Company of Foot on July 13, 1746, served in King George's War against Canada, and he was a sergeant by June 6, 1747. He signed his name when paid for his services, and he was in winter quarters at Albany, New York, 1746-1747. He was discharged on October 31, 1747. [Ref: DA-5, DA-6, DM-40].

ROBERTSON, Robert and Mary. See "John French," q.v.

ROBESON, George. Private. Served in Capt. Henry Darby's Company, Delaware Regiment of Continental Troops. Enlisted February 16, 1776, and was on duty (in barracks) at Dover on April 12, 1776. [Ref: DA-46].

ROBINET, Allen. Private. Served in Capt. Jonathan Caldwell's Company, Delaware Regiment of Continental Troops. Enlisted January 16, 1776, and on duty (in barracks) at Dover on April 12, 1776. [Ref: DA-41].

ROBINSON, Arcada and Hannah. See "Cord Hazzard," q.v.

ROBINSON, Daniel. Captain. Served in a company of militia in Murder Kill Hundred, Kent County, upon Delaware, 1756, in the French and Indian Wars. Resigned March 29, 1758. [Ref: DA-12, DA-15, DM-46].

ROBINSON, James. Mariner. Died testate in Duck Creek Hundred, Kent County and his will was probated on January 30, 1733. [Ref: DK-72].

ROBINSON, James. Private. Served in Capt. Jonathan Caldwell's Company, Delaware Regiment of Continental Troops. Enlisted January 15, 1776, and on duty (in barracks) at Dover on April 12, 1776. [Ref: DA-41].

ROBINSON, Joseph. Private. Served in Capt. John Caton's Company, April 25, 1757, in the French and Indian Wars. [Ref: DA-14]. One Joseph Robinson died in Kent County and the administration of his estate was granted to his widow Sarah on May 13, 1767. [Ref: DK-228]. Another Joseph Robinson died testate in Duck Creek Hundred in Kent County and his will was probated on October 9, 1798, naming his wife Elizabeth, sons George, John, and William, and daughters

Deborah, Rebecca, and Martha. A later account showed that Elizabeth Robinson subsequently married Ostend Tomlinson. [Ref: DK-542].

ROBINSON, Joseph. Private. Served in Capt. Jonathan Caldwell's Company, Delaware Regiment of Continental Troops. Enlisted January 13, 1776, and on duty (in barracks) at Dover on April 12, 1776. [Ref: DA-41].

ROBINSON, Magdalen. See "Andrew Frauberg [Tranberg?]," q.v.

ROBINSON, Mary and Charles. See "Matthew Crozier," q.v.

ROBINSON, Michael. Private. Served in Capt. David Hall's Company, Delaware Regiment of Continental Troops. Enlisted on March 4, 1776, and was on duty (in barracks) at Lewis Town on April 11, 1776. [Ref: DA-43].

ROBINSON, Peter. Lieutenant. Served in Capt. Cord Hazzard's Company in the Northern District of Indian River Hundred in the regiment of Sussex County, in 1756, during the French and Indian Wars, and was lieutenant in the Angola District Company on March 18, 1758. [Ref: DA-13, DA-15].

ROBINSON, Robert. Ensign. Served in Capt. Andrew Frauberg's [or Tranberg's?] Company, Christiana Hundred, Upper Regiment, in New Castle County, 1756, during the French and Indian Wars. [Ref: DA-11]. One Robert Robinson died in Christiana Hundred and his will was probated on March 10, 1787, naming his wife Ann, sons Aquilla, William, John, Thomas, and Ebenezer, and daughters Betty Porter (wife of John Porter), Rebecca Moore (wife of William Moore), and Sarah Robinson. [Ref: DN-112].

ROBINSON, Samuel. Private. Served in Capt. John Caton's Company on April 25, 1757, in the French and Indian Wars. [Ref: DA-13]. One "Samuel Robinson, Merchant," died testate in Kent County and his will was probated on November 28, 1774, naming his brother Daniel Robinson (executor) and other heirs, but no wife or children. [Ref: DK-293].

ROBINSON, William. Private. Born 1740, New York. Carpenter. Enlisted on May 8, 1758, in the French and Indian Wars, by Capt. Benjamin Noxon. [Ref: DA-19].

ROBNET, Alen. Private. Served in Capt. Joseph Stedham's Company, Delaware Battalion of Continental Troops. Enlisted February 9, 1776, and was in quarters at Dover on April 12, 1776. [Ref: DA-40].

RODGERS, James. Private. Born 1712, Ireland. Laborer. Enlisted in Capt. John Shannon's Company of Foot on July 5, 1746, and served in King George's War against Canada. He was in winter quarters at

Albany, New York, during 1746-1747, and was discharged on October 31, 1747. [Ref: DA-5, DA-6]. (He is not listed in Source DM-40.)

RODNEY, Caesar. Captain. Signer. Born October 7, 1728. Son of Caesar Rodeney and Elizabeth Crawford (and a grandson of William Rodeney, who came to America from Bristol, England circa 1681). Caesar was captain of a company of militia in Dover Hundred, Kent County, upon Delaware, in 1756, during the French and Indian Wars. He was a commissioner for Kent County in 1759 and was very involved in governmental affairs in Delaware. He was one of the Signers of the Declaration of Independence in 1776, and he died a bachelor on June 26, 1784. His will was probated on August 14, 1784, stating he was the eldest son of Caesar Rodney, deceased, naming these heirs: brothers William and Thomas Rodney; half-sister Sarah Wilson; half-brother John Wilson; nephew Caesar Augustus Rodney; nieces Lavinia Rodney (daughter of brother Thomas), Letitia Rodney (daughter of brother William Rodney), Elizabeth Gordon (daughter of sister Mary, deceased), Sarah Rodney (daughter of brother Daniel); Caesar Rodney Wilson (son of half-sister Sarah Wilson); children of sister Mary Gordon; Wardens of Christ Church in Dover; George Read, Esq.; and Finwick Fisher, Merchant (both of New Castle County). [Ref: DA-12, DM-46, DM-50, DF-36, DF-37, DK-361]. See Source DH-203 for details.

RODNEY, John. Esquire. Captain. Lived in Murder Kill Hundred, Kent County, was deceased by February 26, 1705, when a land warrant was assigned to William Rodney, attorney to John Rodeney's widow and administratrix. [Ref: DR-31]. (Name was also spelled "Rodeney").

RODNEY, William. Captain. Held that rank by September 26, 1701, when a special land grant was surveyed, and he was listed in the Kent County quit-rents (between 1701 and 1708). [Ref: DR-37, DR-38]. One "William Rodeney" died testate in Kent County and his will was probated October 4, 1708, naming his wife Sarah, sons William, Thomas, John, Anthony, George, and Caesar, daughter Sarah, mother Rachel, sisters Rachel and Elizabeth, and the orphans of Richard Willson (unnamed). [Ref: DK-29]. (See Source DF-36 for more data.) Also, Sarah Rodney, daughter of Capt. William and Sarah Rodney, is mentioned in the will of Simon Hirons, Sr., in 1706. [Ref: DK-28].

ROE, Richardson Thomas. Private. Born 1732, Maryland. Laborer. Enlisted on April 24, 1758, in the French and Indian Wars, by Capt. Benjamin Noxon. [Ref: DA-19]. (Name maybe "Thomas Richardson Roe").

ROEN, Thomas Richardson. Soldier. Enlisted on May 10, 1759, in the French and Indian Wars, and appeared on a return of Capt. Henry Van Bibber's Company of the Lower Counties on Delaware Troops, at New Castle, on June 4, 1759. [Ref: DA-26]. See "Thomas Richardson Roe."

ROGERS, Comfort. See "Thomas Prettyman," q.v.

ROGERS, Hugh. Private. Born 1739 (place not stated). Laborer. Enlisted on April 25, 1759, in the French and Indian Wars, in Capt. James Armstrong's Company in Pennsylvania Regiment. [Ref: DA-26].

ROGERS, William. Private. Born 1723, Pennsylvania. Laborer. Enlisted on April 24, 1758, during the French and Indian Wars, by Capt. Benjamin Noxon. [Ref: DA-19].

ROLAND, John. Private. Born 1733, Silver Point, Virginia. Farmer. Enlisted on April 22, 1758, during the French and Indian Wars, as a private by Capt. John McClughan "for the campaign in the lower counties." [Ref: DA-18].

ROLTON, Josiah. Private. Born 1736, Lewis Town, Delaware. Farmer. Enlisted on May 4, 1758, during the French and Indian Wars, as a private by Capt. John McClughan "for the campaign in the lower counties." [Ref: DA-18].

ROSBACK, Hans. Officer. Blacksmith (*smedenn*). An "officer" at Fort Christina in New Sweden in 1643, and returned to Sweden in 1648. [Ref: DJ-701, 715].

ROSEMAN, Marten. Officer. His name appeared on a nomination list of officers in New Castle circa 1675 (list not dated). [Ref: DP-170].

ROSS, Ann. See "Samuel Platt," q.v.

ROSS, David. Private. Served in Capt. Joseph Stedham's Company, Delaware Battalion of Continental Troops. Enlisted on March 19, 1776, and was in quarters at Dover on April 12, 1776. [Ref: DA-40].

ROSS, Jacob. M. D. Private. Served in Capt. Richard McWilliams' Company, New Castle County. Enlisted on December 28, 1757, during the French and Indian Wars. [Ref: DA-15].

ROSS, James. Private. Born 1741, Brandywine Hundred, Delaware. Miller. Enlisted on May 2, 1758, during the French and Indian Wars, as a private by Capt. John McClughan "for the campaign in the lower counties." [Ref: DA-18].

ROSS, Joseph. Private. Born 1738, Ireland. Enlisted in Capt. John Wright's Company and was on the muster roll of May 11, 1759, during the French and Indian Wars. [Ref: DA-25].

ROSSER, John. Private. Served in Capt. Charles Pope's Company, Delaware Regiment of Continental Troops. Enlisted January 18, 1776, and was on duty (in quarters) at Lewis Town on April 11, 1776. [Ref: DA-51].

ROTHWELL, Garrett. Ensign. Served in Capt. William Williams' Company, Apoquinamink Hundred, Lower Regiment, New Castle County, 1756, during the French and Indian Wars. [Ref: DA-11].

ROTHWELL, Isaac. Private. Served in Capt. Charles Pope's Company, Delaware Regiment of Continental Troops. Enlisted January 19, 1776, and was on duty (in quarters) at Lewis Town on April 11, 1776. [Ref: DA-51].

ROTHWELL, Jerrard. Ensign. Served in Capt. Henry Dyer's Company, New Castle County, 1747-1748, in King George's War against Canada. [Ref: DA-7].

ROWAN, John. Sergeant. Served in Capt. Jonathan Caldwell's Company, Delaware Regiment of Continental Troops. Enlisted January 13, 1776, and on duty (in barracks) at Dover on April 12, 1776. [Ref: DA-41].

ROWE, Elizabeth. See "James Barnes," q.v.

ROWELL, Constantine. Private. Born 1721, New England. Laborer. Enlisted in Capt. John Shannon's Company of Foot on July 15, 1746, and served in King George's War against Canada. He signed his name when paid for services on June 6, 1747. He was in winter quarters at Albany, New York, during 1746-1747, and was discharged October 31, 1747. [Ref: DA-5, DA-6, DM-40].

ROWLAND, David. Ensign. Served in Capt. Timothy Griffith's Company, New Castle County, 1747-1748, in King George's War against Canada. [Ref: DA-7]. A David Rowland was also an ensign in Capt. Thomas Cooch's Company, Pencader Hundred, Lower Regiment, in New Castle County, in 1756, during the French and Indian Wars. [Ref: DA-12]. One David Rowland died testate in Pencader Hundred and his will was probated on August 4, 1767, naming his wife Jean. [Ref: DN-65].

ROWLAND, John. Private. Born 1735, Virginia. Laborer. 5 ft. 5 in. tall. Enlisted at New Castle, Delaware on April 19, 1758, during the French and Indian Wars, by Capt. Paul Jackson, from "the three lower counties" to serve in the Pennsylvania Troops. [Ref: DA-27]. He was probably the John Rowland, born 1736, Virginia, who enlisted in Capt. John Wright's Company and appeared on the muster roll of May 11, 1759. [Ref: DA-25].

ROWLAND, Samuel. Pilot. Lived in Sussex County in Broadkill Hundred by December 6, 1764, at which time he sold the land of his deceased father, Samuel Rowland, who had died testate. [Ref: DD-120].

ROWLAND, Samuel, Sarah, Jane, and others. See "John Miers," q.v.

ROWLAND, Thomas. Pilot. Lived in Sussex County in the area of Pagan Creek by February 2, 1773, at which time he sold part of the land he had inherited from his father, William Rowland. [Ref: DD-75].

ROWLAND, Thomas. Private. Served in Capt. David Hall's Company, Delaware Regiment of Continental Troops. Enlisted January 16, 1776, and was on duty (in barracks) at Lewis Town on April 11, 1776. [Ref: DA-42].

RUDDIN, James. Private. Served in Capt. Samuel Smith's Company, Delaware Regiment of Continental Troops. Enlisted on February 27, 1776, and on duty (in barracks) at Dover, April 12, 1776, at which time he transferred to Capt. Henry Darby's Company. [Ref: DA-54].

RUDENIUS, Lars Jonsson. Soldier. Hired at Stockholm in 1653, he arrived in New Sweden on the ship *Orn* in 1654. [Ref: DJ-722].

RUMMEN, Thomas. Private. Served in Capt. Joseph Stedham's Company, Delaware Battalion of Continental Troops. Enlisted on February 28, 1776, and was in quarters at Dover on April 12, 1776. [Ref: DA-40].

RUNEY, Peter. Private. Served in Capt. John Caton's Company, April 25, 1757, in the French and Indian Wars. [Ref: DA-14].

RUSH, William. Ensign. Served in Capt. William Trent's Company on June 4, 1746, during King George's War against Canada. He was in winter quarters at Albany, New York, in 1746-1747, and his company was discharged on October 31, 1747. [Ref: DA-6].

RUSSEL, Elinor. See "Joseph Marrat," q.v.

RUSSEL, John. Private. Served in Capt. Charles Pope's Company, Delaware Regiment of Continental Troops. Enlisted January 20, 1776, and on duty (in quarters) at Lewis Town on April 11, 1776. [Ref: DA-51]. (Same source spelled his name "Pussel"). See "John Clowes."

RUSSEL, Mary. See "Thomas Prettyman," q.v.

RUSSELL, Jane. See "Rees Wolf," q.v.

RUSSELL, Levi. See "Ephraim Turner," q.v.

RUSSELL, Nicholas. Private. Born 1715, Ireland. Laborer. Enlisted in Capt. John Shannon's Company of Foot on June 26, 1746, in King George's War against Canada. He signed his name when paid for his services on June 6, 1747. He was in winter quarters at Albany, New

York, during 1746-1747, and was discharged on October 31, 1747. [Ref: DA-5, DA-6, DM-40].

RYAN, John. Private. Born 1742, Maryland. Tailor. Enlisted on May 2, 1758, in the French and Indian War, by Capt. Benjamin Noxon. [Ref: DA-19].

RYAN, Rachel. See "Joseph Marrat," q.v.

RYANS, James. Private. Born 1725, Kent, Delaware. Laborer. Enlisted in Capt. John Shannon's Company of Foot on July 17, 1746, in King George's War against Canada. "James Rayans" made his mark when paid for services on June 6, 1747. He was in winter quarters at Albany, New York, during 1746-1747, and was discharged on October 31, 1747. [Ref: DA-5, DA-6, DM-40].

RYNE, John. Private. Born 1737, Ireland. Laborer. Enlisted on May 2, 1758, during the French and Indian Wars, by Capt. Benjamin Noxon. [Ref: DA-19].

SAKRISSON, Anders. Soldier. Served in New Sweden in 1654, and paid various sums by Director Rising for his services. [Ref: DJ-726].

SALMONS, Robert. Private. Served in Capt. David Hall's Company, Delaware Regiment of Continental Troops. Enlisted January 17, 1776, and was on duty (in barracks) at Lewis Town on April 11, 1776. After his name is written "on guard." [Ref: DA-42].

SALTWELL, John. Private. Born 1728, England. Gardener. Enlisted on April 24, 1758, in the French and Indian Wars, by Capt. Benjamin Noxon. [Ref: DA-19].

SANDELIN, Jacob Everts. Sailor. Second Mate on ship *Kalmar Nyckel* on the first expedition to New Sweden in 1637-1639. [Ref: DJ-758].

SANDERS, Jabas. Private. Served in Capt. Joseph Vaughan's Company, Delaware Regiment of Continental Troops. Enlisted January 23, 1776, and on duty (in barracks) at Dover on April 12, 1776. [Ref: DA-59].

SANDERSON, Gerritt. Soldier. Planter in Delaware who paid his quit-rent to the governor in 1669, having received a land patent "at Delaware" on March 25, 1669. [Ref: DP-27, DY-157].

SANDERSON, James. Private. Born 1731, Ireland. Laborer. Enlisted on May 2, 1758, during the French and Indian Wars, by Capt. Benjamin Noxon. [Ref: DA-19].

SANDILANDS, James. Second Lieutenant. Served in the War of Jenkins' Ear in 1739-1741 in a company which likely included soldiers from Delaware (muster rolls not extant). [Ref: DM-32].

SANDYLANDS, James. Soldier. Planter in Delaware who paid his quit-rent to the governor in 1668. [Ref: DP-28].

SANKEY, Thomas. Private. Served in Capt. Richard McWilliams' Company, New Castle County. Enlisted on December 28, 1757, during the French and Indian Wars. [Ref: DA-14].

SAP, Benjamin. Private. Enlisted on May 20, 1758, in Capt. French Battell's Company of Lower County Provincials, during the French and Indian Wars. [Ref: DA-16].

SAPP, Daniel. Private. Served in Capt. Nathan Adams' Company, Delaware Regiment of Continental Troops. Enlisted on March 25, 1776, and was on duty (in barracks) at Dover on April 12, 1776. [Ref: DA-53].

SAUNDERS, William. Soldier. Enlisted on May 19, 1759, during the French and Indian Wars, and appeared on a return of Capt. Henry Van Bibber's Company of the Lower Counties on Delaware Troops, at New Castle, on June 4, 1759. [Ref: DA-26].

SAVAGE, Patrick. Private. Born 1721, Ireland. Laborer. Enlisted in Capt. John Shannon's Company of Foot on July 24, 1746, and served in King George's War against Canada. He was in winter quarters at Albany, New York, during 1746-1747, and was discharged on October 31, 1747. [Ref: DA-5, DA-6]. (He is not listed in Source DM-40.)

SAXTON, Andrew. See "Joseph Hodgson," q.v.

SCHABYMAN, Spicer. Private. Served in Capt. John Caton's Company on April 25, 1757, in the French and Indian Wars. [Ref: DA-13].

SCHALBRICK, Johan. Drummer. From Reval, he was an "officer" in New Sweden, having arrived on the ship *Orn* in 1654. [Ref: DJ-716].

SCHNEEWEISS, Jurgen. See "Joran Kyn Snohvit," q.v.

SCOTHORN, Nathan and John. See "Thomas Phillips," q.v.

SCOTT, John. Private. Served in Capt. Nathan Adams' Company of the Delaware Regiment of Continental Troops. Enlisted February 7, 1776, and was on duty (in barracks) at Dover on April 12, 1776. [Ref: DA-53]. One "John Scott, mariner," died testate in the town of Dover and his will was probated on February 27, 1778, naming his daughter Ann Martha Scott and brother-in-law William Carson, tavernkeeper, of New Castle County. [Ref: DK-316].

SCOTT, Mary. See "William Faries," q.v.

SCOTT, Robert. Private. Born 1735, Rye, Ireland. Spinner. Enlisted on May 12, 1758, during the French and Indian Wars, by Capt. John McClughan "for the campaign in the lower counties." [Ref: DA-18].

SCOTT, Robert. Soldier. Planter in Delaware who paid his quit-rent to the governor in 1669, having been granted land on Christina Creek on October 1, 1669. [Ref: DP-27, DP-28, DY-142].

SCOTT, Timothy. Private. Served in Capt. Henry Darby's Company, Delaware Regiment of Continental Troops. Enlisted January 25, 1776, and on duty (in barracks) at Dover on April 12, 1776. [Ref: DA-46].
SCOTT, William. Private. Born 1724, Ireland. Laborer. Enlisted on May 3, 1759, in the French and Indian Wars, in Capt. James Armstrong's Company with the Pennsylvania Regiment. [Ref: DA-26].
SCOTTON, Meriam. See "Amos Hindsley," q.v.
SEANY, John. Private. Served in Capt. John Caton's Company, April 25, 1757, in the French and Indian Wars. [Ref: DA-14]. One "John Seney" was a witness to the will of Richard Lewis in Kent County on January 31, 1777. [Ref: DK-310].
SENTILL, Christopher. Soldier. Planter in Delaware who paid his quitrent to the governor in 1671, having been granted land on west Delaware Bay on June 19, 1671. [Ref: DP-29, DY-153].
SETH, Jacob. Land patentee and probable militiaman in Delaware in November, 1677. [Ref: DP-167, DP-168, DY-175].
SHADWICK, John. Private. Served in Capt. Samuel Smith's Company, Delaware Regiment of Continental Troops. Enlisted January 15, 1776, and on duty (in barracks) at Dover on April 12, 1776. [Ref: DA-54].
SHADWICK, John. Private. Served in Capt. Samuel Smith's Company, Delaware Regiment of Continental Troops. Enlisted January 15, 1776, and on duty (in barracks) at Dover on April 12, 1776. [Ref: DA-56].
SHANKLAND, John. Captain. He died of syncope on August 28, 1774, as noted in the records of the Lewes and Coolspring Presbyterian Church in Lewes, Delaware. [Ref: DV-115].
SHANKLAND, John. Mariner. Married Sarah Simonton, daughter of James Simonton, in Sussex County, who wrote his will on May 29, 1751, and his only son John Simonton died about August 10, 1761, intestate, without issue, leaving these sisters, to wit: Jean Bailey (wife of Nathaniel Bailey, husbandman, of Sussex County), Sarah Shankland (wife of John Shankland, mariner, of the town of Lewes), and Mary Davison (wife of James Davison, mariner, of the Philadelphia. They sold some land to Noble Lewis on May 27, 1773. [Ref: DD-82, DD-83].
SHANNON, John. Captain. Commissioned on June 25, 1746, and served in King George's War against Canada, initially as the recruiting officer for the "lower counties" [now Delaware], in such places as Wilmington, New Castle, Grubbs, Christiana Bridge, Ogletown, St. George's, Dover, Red Lyon [Lion], Duck Creek, and Noxentown. He was in winter quarters at Albany, New York, 1746-1747, and his company was discharged October 31, 1747. [Ref: DM-39, DM-40, DM-41, DA-6]. One

John Shannon died in Christiana Hundred, New Castle County, and his will was probated on January 25, 1750, naming only his daughter Mary Shannon, but listing six executors: Richard Malone, Samuel Adams, Walter Dewison, Lawrance Hahan (in Jamaica), John Kinsey, and Dr. Reese Jones (in New Castle). [Ref: DN-47].

SHARP, Thomas. Corporal. Served in Capt. Henry Darby's Company, Delaware Regiment of Continental Troops. Enlisted January 25, 1776, and on duty (in barracks) at Dover on April 12, 1776. [Ref: DA-45].

SHARP, William. Private. Served in Capt. Henry Darby's Company, Delaware Regiment of Continental Troops. Enlisted January 25, 1776, and on duty (in barracks) at Dover on April 12, 1776. [Ref: DA-46].

SHEAHORN, David. Private. Served in Capt. John Caton's Company on April 25, 1757, in the French and Indian Wars. [Ref: DA-14]. "David Shahan (Shehorn)" died in Kent County and the administration of his estate was granted to "Levicee Shehorn" on April 27, 1786. A later account showed his heirs as John, David, George, Joshua, and Louisa Shahan, and "Louisa Shahan" later married Matthias Nowland. [Ref: DK-382].

SHEERMAN, James. Private. Born 1738, Dublin, Ireland. Enlisted on April 20, 1758, during the French and Indian Wars, by Capt. John McClughan "for the campaign in the lower counties." [Ref: DA-18].

SHELTON, Sarah. See "John Rash," q.v.

SHERON, John. Private. Served in Capt. Jonathan Caldwell's Company, Delaware Regiment of Continental Troops. Enlisted January 12, 1776, and on duty (in barracks) at Dover on April 12, 1776. [Ref: DA-41].

SHERRY, Roger. Private. Served in Capt. Henry Darby's Company, Delaware Regiment of Continental Troops. Enlisted January 27, 1776, and on duty (in barracks) at Dover on April 12, 1776. [Ref: DA-46].

SHERVIN, Thomas. Private. Served in Capt. Charles Pope's Company, Delaware Regiment of Continental Troops. Enlisted January 15, 1776, and was on duty (in quarters) at Lewis Town on April 11, 1776, at which time he was reported to be "on guard." [Ref: DA-51].

SHIPPEN, Joseph. Brigade Major. An officer "of lower government on Delaware" on June 7, 1758, during the French and Indian Wars, and served as a major to at least 1759. [Ref: DA-16, DA-22, DM-47].

SHIRKEE, Charles. Private. Served in Capt. Charles Pope's Company, Delaware Regiment of Continental Troops. Enlisted January 17, 1776, and was on duty (in quarters) at Lewis Town on April 11, 1776, at which time he was reportedly "on furlough." [Ref: DA-50, DA-51].

SHIRKEE, Cornelius. Private. Served in Capt. Charles Pope's Company of the Delaware Regiment of Continental Troops. Enlisted on January 20, 1776, and was on duty (in quarters) at Lewis Town on April 11, 1776. [Ref: DA-51].
SHOCKLEY, Richard. Private. Born 1727, Kent, Delaware. Laborer. Enlisted in Capt. John Shannon's Company of Foot on July 14, 1746, in King George's War against Canada. He was in winter quarters at Albany, New York, during 1746-1747, and was discharged on October 31, 1747. [Ref: DA-5, DA-6]. (He is not listed in Source DM-40.)
SHORTALL, Oliver. Private. Born 1712, Ireland. Laborer. Enlisted in Capt. John Shannon's Company of Foot on July 16, 1746, and served in King George's War against Canada. He was in winter quarters at Albany, New York, during 1746-1747, and was discharged on October 31, 1747. [Ref: DA-5, DA-6]. (He is not listed in Source DM-40.)
SHOULTER, Richard. See "Nathaniel Walker," q.v.
SHRIKA, Johan Matson. Soldier. Arrived in New Sweden on the ship *Orn* in 1654. [Ref: DJ-720]. "John Mattson Shrika" died testate in New Castle County, Delaware, and his will was probated on March 15, 1691, naming his wife (no name given), four sons (no names given), and daughters Annika and Mary. [Ref: DN-9]. See "Johan Mattson."
SIDHAM, Jonas. Private. Served in Capt. Richard McWilliams' Company in New Castle County. Enlisted on December 28, 1757, during the French and Indian Wars. [Ref: DA-14].
SIFVERTSON, Nils. Skipper. Served on the ship *Swan* during the eighth expedition to New Sweden between 1647-1648. [Ref: DJ-760]. (Name also spelled "Siversson").
SILL, Benjamin. Drummer and fifer. Enlisted January 16, 1776, Capt. Charles Pope's Company, Delaware Regiment, Continental Troops, and on duty (in quarters) at Lewis Town, April 11, 1776. [Ref: DA-51].
SILSBEE, John. Private. Served in Capt. Richard McWilliams' Company in New Castle County. Enlisted on December 28, 1757, during the French and Indian Wars. [Ref: DA-14].
SILSBEE, Nathaniel. Lieutenant. Served in Capt. Richard McWilliams' Company in New Castle Hundred, Upper Regiment, New Castle County, 1756, during the French and Indian Wars. [Ref: DA-11, spelled his name "Silsby."]. One Nathaniel Silsbee, bricklayer, died testate in New Castle County and his will was probated April 29, 1772, naming his son Nathaniel, daughters Ann and Mary, and brother-in-law Peter Jaquet. Another Nathaniel Silsbee, practitioner in physic, died in Red Lion Hundred, New Castle County, and his will was probated on

August 19, 1789, naming his wife Margaret and sisters Ann Mellar (wife of Andrew) and Mary Hunn (wife of John). [Ref: DN-70, 118].

SIM, John. Private. Born 1727, Ireland. Tailor. Enlisted in Capt. John Shannon's Company of Foot on July 23, 1746, and served in King George's War against Canada. He was in winter quarters at Albany, New York, during 1746-1747, and was discharged on October 31, 1747. [Ref: DA-5, DA-6]. (He is not listed in Source DM-40.)

SIMMONS, John. Private. Born 1737, Maryland. Laborer. Enlisted on May 23, 1758, during the French and Indian Wars, by Capt. Benjamin Noxon. [Ref: DA-19].

SIMMONS, John. Private. Served in Capt. Jonathan Caldwell's Company of the Delaware Regiment of Continental Troops. Enlisted on January 16, 1776, and was on duty (in barracks) at Dover on April 12, 1776. [Ref: DA-41].

SIMONTON, John. See "John Shankland," q.v.

SIMPLER, Jacob. Private. Born 1725, Germany. Laborer. Enlisted in Capt. John Shannon's Company of Foot on July 11, 1746, and served in King George's War against Canada. He was in winter quarters at Albany, New York, during 1746-1747, and was discharged on October 31, 1747. [Ref: DA-5, DA-6]. (He is not listed in Source DM-40.)

SIMPSON, Arthur. Private. Born 1716, Tyrone, Ireland. Schoolmaster. Enlisted on May 1, 1759, in the French and Indian Wars, in Capt. James Armstrong's Company in Pennsylvania Regiment. [Ref: DA-26].

SIMPSON, Benjamin. Private. Served in Capt. Joseph Vaughan's Company, Delaware Regiment of Continental Troops. Enlisted January 17, 1776, and on duty (in barracks) at Dover on April 12, 1776. [Ref: DA-59].

SIMPSON, James. Private. Born 1725, Ireland. Weaver. Enlisted in Capt. John Shannon's Company of Foot on July 21, 1746, and served in King George's War against Canada. He was in winter quarters at Albany, New York, during 1746-1747, and was discharged on October 31, 1747. [Ref: DA-5, DA-6]. (He is not listed in Source DM-40.)

SIMPSON, Thomas. Private. Served in Capt. Henry Darby's Company, Delaware Regiment of Continental Troops. Enlisted February 16, 1776, and was on duty (in barracks) at Dover on April 12, 1776. [Ref: DA-46].

SINCLEER, William. Soldier. Planter in Delaware who paid his quit-rent to the governor in 1671, having received land by patent on St. Jones Creek, June 19, 1671. [Ref: DP-29, DY-153].

SINGLETON, John. Captain. Recruited soldiers from "the three lower counties" [Delaware] to serve with the Pennsylvania Troops in 1758, during the French and Indian Wars. [Ref: DA-27].

SIPPLE, Caleb. Lieutenant. Served in Capt. Daniel James' Company in the Lower District of Mother Kill Hundred, Kent County, on March 29, 1758, in the French and Indian Wars. [Ref: DA-15]. One "Caleb Sipple, yeoman" died intestate in Kent County and his widow Sarah was named his administratrix on February 10, 1762. Administration account later indicated the widow Sarah Sipple had married David Lewis, and it also mentioned children Nancy, John, Caleb, Mary, Thomas, Elizabeth, and Garret Sipple. [Ref: DK-198].

SKEIR, Erick. Private. Born 1712, West Jersey. Laborer. Enlisted in Capt. John Shannon's Company of Foot on July 7, 1746, and served in King George's War against Canada. He was also in winter quarters at Albany, New York, during 1746-1747, and was discharged on October 31, 1747. [Ref: DA-5, DA-6]. (He is not listed in Source DM-40.)

SKELETON, Elijah. Sergeant. Served in Capt. Charles Pope's Company, Delaware Regiment of Continental Troops. Enlisted January 17, 1776, and was on duty (in quarters) at Lewis Town on April 11, 1776. [Ref: DA-51].

SKIDMORE, Edward. Private. Born 1737, Delaware. Laborer. Enlisted on April 29, 1758, in the French and Indian Wars, by Capt. Benjamin Noxon. [Ref: DA-19]. He was probably the same Edward Skidmore who enlisted on May 21, 1759, and appeared on a return of Capt. Henry Van Bibber's Company of the Lower Counties on Delaware Troops, at New Castle, on June 4, 1759. [Ref: DA-26].

SKIDMORE, Thomas. Private. Served in Capt. David Hall's Company, Delaware Regiment of Continental Troops. Enlisted January 20, 1776, and was on duty (in barracks) at Lewis Town on April 11, 1776. [Ref: DA-43].

SKILLINGTON, Thomas. See "William Rees," q.v.

SKINNER, George. Private. Served in Capt. Nathan Adams' Company, Delaware Regiment of Continental Troops. Enlisted January 24, 1776, and on duty (in barracks) at Dover on April 12, 1776. [Ref: DA-53].

SKINNER, Robert. Private. Served in Capt. Charles Pope's Company, Delaware Regiment of Continental Troops. Enlisted January 18, 1776, and was on duty (in quarters) at Lewis Town on April 11, 1776. [Ref: DA-51].

SKINNER, William. Private. Served in Capt. John Caton's Company, April 25, 1757, in the French and Indian Wars. [Ref: DA-14]. One William Skinner died testate in Kent County and his will written on March 27, 1792 [no date of probate given, but it appears to have been in April, 1792], naming his wife Rebecca Skinner, sons John, Thomas, Daniel, and Stephen Skinner, daughters Nelly Skinner and Betsey Skinner, and daughter-in-law Mary Cole. [Ref: DK-454].

SKOG, Jonas. Soldier. Arrived in New Sweden on the ship *Orn* in 1654, along with Jan Mansson Skog. [Ref: DJ-722].

SKUTE, Sven. Captain. Officer in New Sweden. "Schwenn Schuute" came to New Sweden with Johan Printz in 1643 and served as a lieutenant (*leutenampten*) at Fort Elfsborg. He was still living there in 1654, by which time he was a captain. "Johan Skute, son of Capt. Skute," was born September 4, 1654, in New Sweden. [Ref: DJ-703, DJ-710, DJ-716, DJ-722]. He was also referred to as "Commander Sven Schute" in the capture of Fort Casimir in May, 1654. His name has also been spelled "Swenn Skuuta." [Ref: DH-47]. See "Elias Gyllengren," q.v.

SLATHER, Ann. See "Bryant Pearl," q.v.

SLEVAN, John. Private. Born 1722, Ireland. Weaver. Enlisted in Capt. John Shannon's Company of Foot on July 15, 1746, and served in King George's War against Canada. He was in winter quarters at Albany, New York, during 1746-1747, and was discharged on October 31, 1747. [Ref: DA-5, DA-6]. (He is not listed in Source DM-40.)

SLOAN, John. Private. Born 1733, Tyrone, Ireland. Weaver. Enlisted on May 4, 1758, during the French and Indian Wars, by Capt. John McClughan "for the campaign in the lower counties." [Ref: DA-18].

SLUBEY, William. Private. Served in Capt. Richard McWilliams' Company, New Castle County. Enlisted on December 28, 1757, during the French and Indian Wars. [Ref: DA-15].

SMAAL, Pafvel. Soldier. Served as a common soldier (*saldater*) after arriving in New Sweden from Stockholm in 1643. He returned home to Sweden on the *Fama* on June 20, 1644. [Ref: DJ-709, DH-45]. (Name also spelled "Pafuell Smal" or "Pal Smal").

SMITH, Alexander. Private. Born 1723, Scotland. Laborer. Enlisted in Capt. John Shannon's Company of Foot on July 19, 1746, and he served in King George's War against Canada. He made his mark when he was paid for his services on June 6, 1747. He was in winter quarters at Albany, New York, during 1746-1747, and was discharged on October 31, 1747. [Ref: DA-5, DA-6, DM-40].

SMITH, George. Private. Served in Capt. Samuel Smith's Company, Delaware Regiment of Continental Troops. Enlisted on February 16, 1776, and was on duty (in barracks) at Dover on April 12, 1776. [Ref: DA-54].

SMITH, Henrietta. See "Richard Gallaway," q.v.

SMITH, Henry. Captain. His name appeared on a nomination list for officers for the Whorekill in Sussex County, Delaware circa 1675 (list not dated). [Ref: DP-170]. He was also mentioned in an Action of Debt Due in Sussex County as "Capt. Henery Smith" in 1683. [Ref: DC-233, 238]. The will of Luke Wattson, Sr. was probated in Sussex County on November 6, 1705, and among the heirs was one "daughter Mary Wattson, by former wife Margery, daughter of Capt. Henry Smith." [Ref: DS-20].

SMITH, James. Private. Born 1725, Ireland. Laborer. Enlisted in Capt. John Shannon's Company of Foot on July 12, 1746, and served in King George's War against Canada. He was in winter quarters at Albany, New York, during 1746-1747, and was discharged on October 31, 1747. [Ref: DA-5, DA-6]. (He is not listed in Source DM-40.)

SMITH, James. Private. Born 1725, Sussex, Delaware. Planter. Enlisted in Capt. John Shannon's Company of Foot on July 13, 1746 and served in King George's War against Canada. He was in winter quarters at Albany, New York, during 1746-1747, and was discharged October 31, 1747. [Ref: DA-5, DA-6]. (Not listed in Source DM-40.)

SMITH, James. Private. Served in Capt. David Hall's Company, Delaware Regiment of Continental Troops. Enlisted January 20, 1776, and was on duty (in barracks) at Lewis Town on April 11, 1776. [Ref: DA-43].

SMITH, James. Private. Served in Capt. Henry Darby's Company, Delaware Regiment of Continental Troops. Enlisted January 30, 1776, and on duty (in barracks) at Dover on April 12, 1776. [Ref: DA-46].

SMITH, Janet. See "James Caldwell," q.v.

SMITH, John. Private. Served in Capt. David Hall's Company of the Delaware Regiment of Continental Troops. Enlisted January 21, 1776, and was on duty (in barracks) at Lewis Town on April 11, 1776. [Ref: DA-43].

SMITH, John. Private. Served in Capt. David Hall's Company of the Delaware Regiment of Continental Troops. Enlisted January 17, 1776, and was on duty (in barracks) at Lewis Town on April 11, 1776. [Ref: DA-42].

SMITH, Joseph. Private. Served in Capt. John Caton's Company on April 25, 1757, in the French and Indian Wars. [Ref: DA-13]. One Joseph

Smith died in Kent County and his will was probated on September 30, 1767, naming his wife Mary, sons Henry and James, and daughter Mary. [Ref: DK-230]. Another "Joseph Smith, yeoman," died testate in the Duck Creek Hundred of Kent County and his will was probated on July 17, 1775, naming his wife Mary, son Charles, and daughters Elizabeth Stevenson, Sophiah Craigh, and Mary Smith, plus an orphan named John Matthews. [Ref: DK-298]. And, another "Joseph Smith, blacksmith," died in Kent County and administration of his estate was granted to Mary Smith, November 14, 1793. [Ref: DK-470].

SMITH, Margaret. See "Peter Ganthony," q.v.

SMITH, Nancy and William. See "James Moore," q.v.

SMITH, Richard. Private. Served in Capt. Charles Pope's Company, Delaware Regiment of Continental Troops. Enlisted January 15, 1776, and was on duty (in quarters) at Lewis Town on April 11, 1776. [Ref: DA-51].

SMITH, Samuel. Captain. Served in the 7th Company, Delaware State Troops in Continental Service. Commissioned January 20, 1776, and was on duty (in barracks) with the Delaware Regiment of Continental Troops at Dover on April 12, 1776. [Ref: DA-34, DA-36,DA- 53].

SMITH, Samuel. Sergeant. Served in Capt. Henry Darby's Company, Delaware Regiment of Continental Troops. Enlisted January 22, 1776, and on duty (in barracks) at Dover on April 12, 1776. [Ref: DA-45].

SMITH, Sarah and David. See "John Rash," q.v.

SMITH, Solomon. Private. Served in Capt. Joseph Stedham's Company, Delaware Battalion of Continental Troops. Enlisted on January 26, 1776, and was in quarters at Dover on April 12, 1776. [Ref: DA-39].

SMITH, William. Private. Born 1731, Bellyshannon, Ireland. Baker. Enlisted on May 9, 1758, during the French and Indian Wars, as a private by Capt. John McClughan "for the campaign in the lower counties." [Ref: DA-18].

SMITH, William. Corporal. Served in Capt. Joseph Stedham's Company, Delaware Battalion of Continental Troops. Enlisted on January 23, 1776, and was in quarters at Dover on April 12, 1776. [Ref: DA-39].

SMITH, William Jr. Private. Served in Capt. Joseph Vaughan's Company, Delaware Regiment of Continental Troops. Enlisted February 8, 1776, and on duty (in barracks) at Dover on April 12, 1776. [Ref: DA-59].

SMITH, William. Private. Served in Capt. Nathan Adams' Company, Delaware Regiment of Continental Troops. Enlisted January 16, 1776, and on duty (in barracks) at Dover on April 12, 1776. [Ref: DA-52].

SMITH, William Sr. Private. Served in Capt. Joseph Vaughan's Company, Delaware Regiment of Continental Troops. Enlisted January 19, 1776, and on duty (in barracks) at Dover on April 12, 1776. [Ref: DA-59].

SNEED, George. Private. Served in Capt. Joseph Vaughan's Company, Delaware Regiment of Continental Troops. Enlisted on March 5, 1776, and on duty (in barracks) at Dover on April 12, 1776. [Ref: DA-60].

SNOHVIT, Joran Kyn. Soldier (*saldater*). One of the men "who daily followed and served the governor" [Johan Printz] at Fort Tinicum in 1643. [Ref: DJ-705, 706]. (Footnote within this source states that "*Snohvit*" means "*Snow-white*," probably so-called on account of his complexion. Also, "*Goran*" is the same as "*George*"). One "Jurgen Schneeweiss" (or "Goran Kyn Snohvit") was a soldier who arrived in New Sweden in 1643. [Ref: DJ-713]. "Joran Kyn Snohvit" became the chief colonist at Upland and was a soldier in 1644. [Ref: DH-47]. (Name also spelled "Jorann Kyn Snohuitt").

SOLWAY, Robert. Private. Served in Capt. Jonathan Caldwell's Company, Delaware Regiment of Continental Troops. Enlisted January 12, 1776, and on duty (in barracks) at Dover on April 12, 1776. [Ref: DA-41].

SOUTHREN, Edward. Officer. His name appeared on a nomination list for officers for the Whorekill, Sussex County, Delaware circa 1675 (list was not dated). [Ref: DP-170]. Administration of his estate in Sussex County was granted to "Mary Southrin, widow," on January 24, 1684. [Ref: DS-10].

SOWARD, Daniel. Private. Served in Capt. John Caton's Company on April 25, 1757, in the French and Indian Wars. [Ref: DA-13].

SOWARD, Isaac. Private. Served in Capt. John Caton's Company on April 25, 1757, in the French and Indian Wars. [Ref: DA-13].

SPANIOL, Jacob. Officer. Served at Fort Tinicum in New Sweden in 1643. [Ref: DJ-705].

SPEAR, Charles. Private. Born 1734, Faughboyne, Ireland. Enlisted in April or May, 1758 [exact date not given] as a private, by Capt. John McClughan "for the campaign in the lower counties" during the French and Indian Wars. [Ref: DA-18].

SPENCER, Richard and Elizabeth. See "Richard McWilliams," q.v.

SPENCER, Thomas. Private. Served in Capt. Charles Pope's Company, Delaware Regiment of Continental Troops. Enlisted January 13, 1776, and was on duty (in quarters) at Lewis Town on April 11, 1776, at which time he was reported "on guard." [Ref: DA-50, DA-51].

SPENCER, William. Private. Served in Capt. Richard McWilliams' Company, New Castle County. Enlisted on December 28, 1757, during the French and Indian Wars. [Ref: DA-15].

SPENCER, William Jr. Private. Served in Capt. Richard McWilliams' Company, New Castle County. Enlisted on December 28, 1757, during the French and Indian Wars. [Ref: DA-14].

SPENCER, William Sr. Major. Died testate in Sussex County and his will was probated on May 2, 1688, naming his wife Frances Spencer, son William Spencer, daughter Margarett Spencer, and other children [not named], plus his servant Black Will. [Ref: DS-12, DC-560]. In 1692 the administrator of his estate was Thomas May. [Ref: DC-814].

SPICER, Robert. Second Lieutenant. Served in the War of Jenkins' Ear in 1739-1741 in a company which may have included soldiers from Delaware (muster rolls not extant). [Ref: DM-32].

SPRING, John. Private. Served in Capt. Jonathan Caldwell's Company, Delaware Regiment of Continental Troops. Enlisted January 15, 1776, and on duty (in barracks) at Dover on April 12, 1776. [Ref: DA-41].

SPRINGER, Charles. Private. Served in Capt. Richard McWilliams' Company, New Castle County. Enlisted on December 28, 1757, during the French and Indian Wars. [Ref: DA-15].

SPRINGER, Gabriel and Elizabeth. See "Andrew Frauberg [Tranberg]."

SPRINT, Jacob. Soldier. From Nyland in northern Sweden, he was hired by Mans Kling as a farm hand in 1641 and arrived in New Sweden that year. He was later appointed a soldier. [Ref: DJ-711].

SPROUL, Thomas. Private. Served in Capt. Richard McWilliams' Company, New Castle County. Enlisted on December 28, 1757, during the French and Indian Wars. [Ref: DA-14].

SQUIRES, Richard. Drummer. Born 1734, Bristol, Pennsylvania. Served in Capt. John Wright's Company on May 11, 1759, during the French and Indian Wars. [Ref: DA-25].

STACY, Richard. Private. Served in Capt. Jonathan Caldwell's Company, Delaware Regiment of Continental Troops. Enlisted April 2, 1776 and was on duty (in barracks) at Dover on April 12, 1776. [Ref: DA-41].

STAKE, Lars Ericksson. Soldier. Hired in Stockholm in 1653, he was on the ship *Haj* to New Holland and he "may have gone to New Sweden after 1655." [Ref: DJ-723].

STAKE, Mans. Provost-marshal. Arrived in New Sweden on the ship *Orn* in 1654, along with Mans Persson Stake. [Ref: DJ-716, DJ-722].

STALCOP, Johan Andersson. Gunner. Arrived in New Sweden on the ship *Orn* in 1654. [The name "*Stalkofta*" was later changed to "Stalcop"

(Stalcup, or Stalkup). It meant "*steel coat or jacket.*"] [Ref: DJ-717]. One "John Anderson, alias Stalcup" died testate in New Castle County, Delaware and his probated will on July 20, 1686 named "wife Christina Carlos, son-in-law Lucas Stiddom, eldest son Auchin, and children Charlos [sic], John, Peter, Mary, and Jonas." [Ref: DN-8]. (Name also spelled "Stalkofta").

STALCUP, Israel. Private. Served in Capt. Richard McWilliams' Company in New Castle County. Enlisted on December 28, 1757, in the French and Indian Wars. [Ref: DA-14]. One "John Stalcop, yeoman" died testate in Christiana Hundred, in New Castle County, and his will was probated on July 1, 1751, naming his wife Mary and his son "Israll Stalcop" (among others). [Ref: DN-49].

STANDINGS, James. Soldier. He was reported to be a deserter from the company of Capt. John Shannon in 1747 during King George's War against Canada. [Ref: DM-40].

STANT, Elizabeth and Easter. See "Thomas Bedwell," q.v.

STANT, Joseph. Private. Enlisted on May 10, 1758, in Capt. French Battell's Company of Lower County Provincials, during the French and Indian Wars. [Ref: DA-17].

STARLAND, William. Private. Born 1729, South Carolina. Mariner. Enlisted in Capt. John Shannon's Company of Foot on June 26, 1746, in King George's War against Canada. He was in winter quarters at Albany, New York, during 1746-1747, and was discharged on October 31, 1747. [Ref: DA-5, DA-6]. (He is not listed in Source DM-40.)

STARRET, Alexander. Private. Served in Capt. Samuel Smith's Company of the Delaware Regiment of Continental Troops. Enlisted on January 15, 1776, and was on duty (in barracks) at Dover on April 12, 1776. [Ref: DA-54].

STATON, Robert. Private. Served in Capt. David Hall's Company of the Delaware Regiment of Continental Troops. Enlisted January 17, 1776, and on duty (in barracks) at Lewis Town on April 11, 1776. [Ref: DA-42].

STATON, Thomas. Private. Served in Capt. David Hall's Company of the Delaware Regiment of Continental Troops. Enlisted January 23, 1776, and on duty (in barracks) at Lewis Town on April 11, 1776. [Ref: DA-43].

STEARS, Richard. Drummer and fifer. Served in the company of Capt. Joseph Vaughan in the Delaware Regiment of Continental Troops. He enlisted on January 15, 1776, and was on duty (in barracks) at Dover on April 12, 1776. [Ref: DA-59].

STEDHAM, Joseph. Captain. Commissioned January 13, 1776. Served in 1st Company, Delaware State Troops, Continental Service. [Ref: DA-34, DA-36]. (Same source spelled his name "Stidman" and "Stidham").
STEDHAM, Timon. See "Timon Stidden," q.v.
STEDHAM, Lucas. See "Johan Andersson Stalcop," q.v.
STEEL, Andrew. Private. Enlisted on May 20, 1759, during the French and Indian Wars, and his name appeared on a return of Capt. Henry Van Bibber's Company of the Lower Counties on Delaware Troops, at New Castle, on June 4, 1759. [Ref: DA-26].
STEEL, Arthur. Private. Born 1736, Kent, Delaware. Enlisted in Capt. John Wright's Company and was on the muster roll of May 11, 1759, during the French and Indian Wars. [Ref: DA-25].
STEEL, Hugh. Private. Born 1731, Ireland. Laborer. Enlisted May 1, 1758, in the French and Indian Wars, by Capt. Benjamin Noxon. [Ref: DA-19].
STEEL, James. Private. Enlisted on May 24, 1758, in Capt. French Battell's Company of Lower County Provincials, during the French and Indian Wars. [Ref: DA-17].
STEEL, Nancy and James. See "Thomas Tilton," q.v.
STENSON, James. Corporal. Served in Capt. Joseph Stedham's Company, Delaware Battalion of Continental Troops. Enlisted on January 17, 1776, and was in quarters at Dover on April 12, 1776. [Ref: DA-39].
STEPHENS, John. Private. Served in Capt. Joseph Vaughan's Company, Delaware Regiment of Continental Troops. Enlisted on March 8, 1776, and was reported to have "deserted" on March 11, 1776. [Ref: DA-58, DA-60]. (This same source also spelled his name "John Stevens").
STEPHENS, William. Colonel. He held this rank by 1684 when he was mentioned in an action in Sussex County court. [Ref: DC-277, 288].
STEPHENSON, George. Private. Served in Capt. David Hall's Company, Delaware Regiment of Continental Troops. Enlisted January 20, 1776, and was on duty (in barracks) at Lewis Town on April 11, 1776. After his name is written "on guard." [Ref: DA-43].
STEPHENSON, Joseph. Corporal. Served in Capt. David Hall's Company, Delaware Regiment of Continental Troops. Enlisted January 20, 1776, and was on duty (in barracks) at Lewis Town on April 11, 1776. [Ref: DA-42].
STEUART, John. Private. Served in Capt. Richard McWilliams' Company in New Castle County. Enlisted on December 28, 1757, during the French and Indian Wars. [Ref: DA-14].

STEVENS, James. Ensign. Served in the 2nd Company of Delaware State Troops in Continental Service. Commissioned on January 15, 1776. [Ref: DA-34, 36].

STEVENS, John. Land patentee and probable militiaman in Delaware in November, 1677. [Ref: DP-167, 168].

STEVENS, Nathan, Henry, and Ann. See "Jonathan Caldwell," q.v.

STEVENSON, Elizabeth. See "Joseph Smith," q.v.

STEVENSON, James. Private. Born 1725, Ireland. Laborer. Enlisted in Capt. John Shannon's Company of Foot on July 13, 1746, and served in King George's War against Canada. He was in winter quarters at Albany, New York, during 1746-1747, and was discharged on October 31, 1747. [Ref: DA-5, DA-6]. (He is not listed in Source DM-40.)

STEVENSON, James. Ensign. Served in Capt. Samuel Perry's Company on June 4, 1746, in King George's War against Canada. He was in winter quarters at Albany, New York, during 1746-1747, and his company was discharged on October 31, 1747. [Ref: DA-6].

STEWARD, David. Captain. New Castle County Company, 1747-1748, and served in King George's War against Canada. [Ref: DA-7].

STEWART, Alexander Jr. Second Lieutenant. Served in 5th Company of Delaware State Troops in Continental Service. Commissioned January 18, 1776, and was on duty (in quarters) with Capt. Charles Pope at Lewis Town on April 11, 1776. [Ref: DA-34, 36, 49, 51]. (Source spelled his name "Alexander Steward" and also "Alexander Stuart").

STEWART, Robert. Ensign. Served in Capt. John Edwards' Company, New Castle County in August, 1748, in King George's War against Canada. [Ref: DA-7].

STEWART, William. Private. Enlisted on May 23, 1758, in Capt. French Battell's Company of Lower County Provincials, during the French and Indian Wars. [Ref: DA-17].

STEWART, William. Mariner. Lived in Sussex County in Indian River Hundred by February 1, 1772, at which time he purchased land on the west side of the road from Lewes Town to the sawmill. [Ref: DD-64].

STIDDEN, Timon. Barber-surgeon (*balberenn*). An "officer" in New Sweden in 1643, he returned home to Sweden in 1644. (His mother lived at Stockholm in 1641.) "Timon Stidden from Hammel, north of Sundsvall, Sweden, barber-surgeon," returned to New Sweden on the ship *Orn* in 1654. [Ref: DJ-709, 716]. "Timon Stedham (Stiddom)" died testate in Christiana Hundred, New Castle County, Delaware, and his will was probated on April 24, 1686, naming wife Christina Stiddom,

daughter Ingabor Stiddom, and "little daughter" Magdolena Stiddom, and sons Lucas Stiddom and Erasmus Stiddom. [Ref: DN-8].
STIDDOM, Lucas. See "Johan Andersson Stalcop," q.v.
STILL, Richard. Private. Served in Capt. John Caton's Company, April 25, 1757, in the French and Indian Wars. [Ref: DA-13].
STOAKLEY, Soloman. Private. Born 1736, Sussex, Delaware. Enlisted in Capt. John Wright's Company and was on the muster roll of May 11, 1759, during the French and Indian Wars. [Ref: DA-25].
STOOP, Christopher. Private. Served in Capt. Richard McWilliams' Company, New Castle County. Enlisted on December 28, 1757, during the French and Indian Wars. [Ref: DA-14].
STOOP, John Jr. Private. Served in Capt. Richard McWilliams' Company, New Castle County. Enlisted on December 28, 1757, during the French and Indian Wars. [Ref: DA-14].
STOREY, Jereboam. Private. Served in Capt. Joseph Vaughan's Company of the Delaware Regiment of Continental Troops. Enlisted on January 27, 1776, and was on duty (in barracks) at Dover on April 12, 1776, at which time he was reported "absent on furlow." [Ref: DA-58, 59].
STORREY, James. Private. Served in Capt. Joseph Vaughan's Company, Delaware Regiment of Continental Troops. Enlisted March 12, 1776, and was on duty (in barracks) at Dover on April 12, 1776, at which time he had transferred from Capt. Adams' Company. [Ref: DA-58, DA-60]. (This same source spelled his name "James Stoary").
STORY, James. Private. Served in Capt. Nathan Adams' Company of the Delaware Regiment of Continental Troops. Enlisted March 21, 1776, and on duty (in barracks) at Dover on April 12, 1776, at which time he had transferred to Capt. Joseph Vaughan's Company. [Ref: DA-53].
STOUT, Jacob. Lieutenant. Served in Capt. Charles Hillyard's Company in the lower part of Duck Creek Hundred, Kent County, upon Delaware, 1756, during the French and Indian Wars. [Ref: DA-12].
STRADLY, Edward and Nanny. See "Thomas Craig," q.v.
STRAGHAN, John. Private. Born 1734, Derry, Ireland. Laborer. Enlisted on April 18, 1758, in the French and Indian Wars, by Capt. John McClughan "for the campaign in lower counties." [Ref: DA-18].
STREEP, William. Private. Served in Capt. John Caton's Company, April 25, 1757, in the French and Indian Wars. [Ref: DA-13]. One William Streep died in Kent County and administration of his estate was granted to his widow Rachel on January 9, 1771. [Ref: DK-255].

STREET, David. Private. Born 1736, Sussex, Delaware. Enlisted in Capt. John Wright's Company and was on the muster roll of May 11, 1759, during the French and Indian Wars. [Ref: DA-25].
STREET, Ezekiel. Private. Born 1736, Black Swamp, Delaware. Planter who enlisted on April 10, 1758, in the French and Indian Wars, by Capt. John McClughan, "for the campaign in the lower counties." [Ref: DA-18].
STREET, Hannah. See "Richard Manwaring," q.v.
STRETCHER, Henry. Land patentee and probable militiaman in Delaware in November, 1677. [Ref: DP-167, 168].
STRINGER, William. Private. Born 1736, England. Laborer. Enlisted on May 29, 1758, in the French and Indian Wars, by Capt. Benjamin Noxon. [Ref: DA-19]. He was probably the same William Stringer who enlisted on May 1, 1759, and appeared on a return of Capt. Henry Van Bibber's Company of the Lower Counties on Delaware Troops, at New Castle, on June 4, 1759. [Ref: DA-26].
STROUD, Jacob. Private. Born 1725, New Castle, Delaware. Laborer. Enlisted in Capt. John Shannon's Company of Foot on July 20, 1746, and served in King George's War against Canada. He was in winter quarters at Albany, New York, during 1746-1747, and was discharged October 31, 1747. [Ref: DA-5, DA-6]. (Not listed in Source DM-40.)
STUART, David. Private. Born 1738, Sussex, Delaware. Enlisted in Capt. John Wright's Company and was on the muster roll of May 11, 1759, in the French and Indian Wars. [Ref: DA-25]. Administration of the estate of one David Stuart was granted to Sophia Stuart in Sussex County on June 8, 1785. A later account mentioned a minor daughter, Sarah Stuart. [Ref: DS-166].
STURGIS, Stokely. Ensign. Served in Capt. John Brinckle's Company, lower part of Little Creek Hundred, Kent County, upon Delaware, in 1756, during the French and Indian Wars. [Ref: DA-12]. A "Stokely Sturgis, yeoman," died testate in Little Creek Hundred and his will was probated on May 14, 1787, naming his son Stokly [sic], daughter Sarah, and grandchildren (no names given). [Ref: DK-392].
STUYVESANT, Peter. Governor. Born circa 1602 in Frieland, entered the military service soon after leaving school, lost a leg at St. Martin in 1644, and he was appointed director of New Netherland in 1646. He took charge of this American colony in May, 1647, and was an active governor. He also erected a new fort on the Delaware and eventually captured New Sweden. Both New Sweden and New Netherland (essentially Delaware and New York) passed into the hands of the

English in 1664. He died in New York in 1682. Facts about him can be found in all the histories of New York and he is mentioned here because of the impact he had on the Delaware area. [Ref: DJ-696].

STYLES, Samuell. Land patentee and probable militiaman in Delaware in November, 1677. [Ref: DP-167, 168].

SULAVIN, John. Private. Served in Capt. Joseph Vaughan's Company, Delaware Regiment of Continental Troops. Enlisted February 16, 1776, and was on duty (in barracks) at Dover on April 12, 1776. [Ref: DA-58, DA-59]. (Same source spelled his name "John Sulovan").

SUTLIFF, Michael. Private. Born 1723, Ireland. Laborer. Enlisted in Capt. John Shannon's Company of Foot on July 29, 1746, and served in King George's War against Canada. He was in winter quarters at Albany, New York, during 1746-1747, and was discharged on October 31, 1747. [Ref: DA-5, DA-6]. (He is not listed in Source DM-40.)

SUTTON, John. Private. Born 1730, Wilts, England. Weaver. Enlisted on April 30, 1758, during the French and Indian Wars, by Capt. John McClughan, "for the campaign in the lower counties." [Ref: DA-18].

SVENSSON, Jacob. Soldier. From Sarestad in Askerad, he arrived in New Sweden in 1643 and served as a common soldier (*saldater*) at Fort Elfsborg and then as a gunner (*constaple*) at Fort Christina. He was assistant commissary by 1654. [Ref: DJ-703, DJ-714, DJ-716]. (This same source also spelled his name "Jacob Swensonn").

SVENSSON, Johan. Sailor. Served on the ship *Kalmar Nyckel* during the first expedition to New Sweden between 1637-1639. He was dead by 1640, leaving a widow in Stockholm. [Ref: DJ-758].

SVENSSON, Nils. Boatswain. Served on the ship *Fama* in the fifth expedition to New Sweden between 1642-1643. [Ref: DJ-760].

SWAILS, Elizabeth. See "John Rash," q.v.

SWALES, Benjamin. Private. Served in Capt. Nathan Adams' Company, Delaware Regiment of Continental Troops. Enlisted on February 13, 1776, and was on duty (in barracks) at Dover on April 12, 1776. [Ref: DA-53].

SWAMPSTEAD, Hutchins. Private. Served in Capt. Joseph Vaughan's Company, Delaware Regiment of Continental Troops. Enlisted January 17, 1776, and on duty (in barracks) at Dover on April 12, 1776. [Ref: DA-59].

SWART, Antoni. Sailor. Also known as Anthony the Negro, or Anthony the Black. He was "one of the laboring people at Fort Tinicum who was appointed to cut hay for the cattle and also in the meantime follow the governor [Johan Printz] on the little sloop" in 1643. [Ref: DJ-706].

"Anthony, a Morian (negro) or Angoler (i.e., someone from Angola, the Portuguese Colony in West Africa near the Kunene River), was a purchased slave brought to New Sweden on the ship *Grip* in 1639." [Ref: DJ-710]. "Antoni Swartz (Black), Anthony the Negro, the slave, made several purchases from the company in 1654 and may have been a freeman at this time." [Ref: DJ-722].

SWENSSON, Anders. Sailor. Arrived in New Sweden on the ship *Orn* in 1654. [Ref: DJ-722]. There was an "Anders Swennson, boatswain," on the ship *Haj* to New Holland and he "may have gone to New Sweden after 1655." [Ref: DJ-723].

SWIFT, Magdelan and Mary. See "Jacob Kollock," q.v.

SYBRANTSE, Jan. Soldier. Planter in Delaware who paid his quit-rent to the governor in 1669. [Ref: DP-27, DP-28]. One "Jan Sibrantsen" received land patent on March 26, 1669. [Ref: DY-139].

SYKES, James. Lieutenant. Served in Capt. Caesar Rodney's Company, Dover Hundred, Kent County, upon Delaware, 1756, during the French and Indian Wars. One James Sykes died testate in Kent County and his will was probated on April 16, 1792, naming his wife Agnes, sons James, Stephen, George, and Nathaniel, and daughters Mary Whethered and Ann, Lucy Matilda, and Harriott Sykes. [Ref: DA-12, DK-454]. Also see "Andrew Caldwell," q.v.

SYMONSZEN, Michel. Sailor. First Mate on the ship *Kalmar Nyckel* in first expedition to New Sweden in 1637-1638. [Ref: DJ-758]. (Name also spelled "Simonzs").

TABIN, Thomas. See "Thomas Tobin," q.v.

TAGE, Thomas. Private. Served in Capt. Charles Pope's Company, Delaware Regiment of Continental Troops. Enlisted January 17, 1776, and was on duty (in quarters) at Lewis Town on April 11, 1776. [Ref: DA-51].

TALBOURT, John. Private. Served in Capt. John Caton's Company, April 25, 1757, in the French and Indian Wars. [Ref: DA-14].

TALKINTON, Stephen. Private. Born 1738, Pennsylvania. Cooper. Enlisted on April 29, 1758, in the French and Indian Wars, by Capt. Benjamin Noxon. [Ref: DA-19]. He was probably the same "Stephen Talkington" who enlisted on May 19, 1759, and his name appeared on a return of Capt. Henry Van Bibber's Company of the Lower Counties on Delaware Troops at New Castle on June 4, 1759. [Ref: DA-26].

TATLOW, Joseph. Private. Served in Capt. Richard McWilliams' Company, New Castle County. Enlisted on December 28, 1757, during the French and Indian Wars. [Ref: DA-14].

TATT, Erick Akesson. Soldier (*saldater*). Served at Fort Christina in New Sweden from 1643 until April 1, 1648, and then returned to Sweden. [Ref: DJ-701, DJ-715]. (Also spelled "Erich Akesson Taat").

TAYLOR, John. Private. Enlisted on May 10, 1758, in Capt. French Battell's Company of Lower County Provincials, during the French and Indian Wars. [Ref: DA-17].

TAYLOR, Mary. See "Thomas Bennett," q.v.

TAYLOR, Richard. Private. Served in Capt. Joseph Stedham's Company, Delaware Battalion of Continental Troops. Enlisted on January 25, 1776, and was in quarters at Dover on April 12, 1776. [Ref: DA-39].

TAYLOR, Robert. Private. Served in Capt. Henry Darby's Company, Delaware Regiment of Continental Troops. Enlisted February 6, 1776, and on duty (in barracks) at Dover on April 12, 1776. [Ref: DA-46].

TAYLOR, Stephen. Private, Capt. Joseph Vaughan's Company, Delaware Regiment of Continental Troops. Enlisted January 19, 1776, and was on duty (in barracks) at Dover on April 12, 1776. [Ref: DA-59].

TAYLOR, Thomas. Private. Born 1710, England. Cooper. Enlisted in Capt. John Shannon's Company of Foot on July 23, 1746, and served in King George's War against Canada. He made his mark when paid for services on June 6, 1747, and he was in winter quarters at Albany, New York, during 1746-1747. He was discharged on October 31, 1747. [Ref: DA-5, DA-6, DM-40].

TEAT, Joseph. Private. Enlisted on May 10, 1758, in Capt. French Battell's Company of Lower County Provincials, during the French and Indian Wars. [Ref: DA-17].

TEUNISSE, Leendert. Soldier. Planter in Delaware who paid his quit-rent to the governor in 1671. [Ref: DP-29]. One land grant at Whorekill on June 1, 1671, spelled his name as "Leendert Teunijssen" and also "Leedert Teunijsse Van Lier." [Ref: DY-148].

THARP, Henry. Private. Born at Kent on Delaware (date not given). Laborer. 5 ft. 6 in. tall. Enlisted at Philadelphia, Pennsylvania on May 15, 1758, by Capt. John Blackwood, from "the three lower counties" to serve with the Pennsylvania Troops during the French and Indian Wars. [Ref: DA-27].

THARP, Ruth. See "Thomas Clarke," q.v.

THATCHER, Edith. See "Emanuel Grubb," q.v.

THINN, William. Captain. Served in the War of Jenkins' Ear in 1739-1741. His company may have included soldiers from Delaware (muster rolls not extant). [Ref: DM-32].

THOMAS, Benjamin. Private. Served in Capt. John Caton's Company, April 25, 1757, in the French and Indian Wars. [Ref: DA-14].

THOMAS, Henry. Private. Served in Capt. Henry Darby's Company, Delaware Regiment of Continental Troops. Enlisted February 23, 1776, and was on duty (in barracks) at Dover on April 12, 1776. [Ref: DA-46].

THOMAS, James. Private. Served in Capt. Nathan Adams' Company, Delaware Regiment of Continental Troops. Enlisted January 25, 1776, and on duty (in barracks) at Dover on April 12, 1776. [Ref: DA-53].

THOMAS, James. Private. Served in Capt. John Caton's Company on April 25, 1757, in the French and Indian Wars. [Ref: DA-13].

THOMAS, Joseph Bush. Private. Served in Capt. Henry Darby's Company of the Delaware Regiment of Continental Troops. Enlisted on January 19, 1776, and was on duty (in barracks) at Dover on April 12, 1776. [Ref: DA-46].

THOMAS, Lewis. Captain. Served in a company in Pencader Hundred in the Lower Regiment of New Castle County in 1756, during the French and Indian Wars. [Ref: DA-12, DM-46].

THOMAS, Micha. Private. Born 1727, Pennsylvania. Carpenter. Enlisted on May 13, 1758, during the French and Indian Wars, by Capt. Benjamin Noxon. [Ref: DA-19].

THOMAS, Rees. Private. Born 1712, Wales. Laborer. Enlisted in Capt. John Shannon's Company of Foot on July 11, 1746, and served in King George's War against Canada. He was in winter quarters at Albany, New York, during 1746-1747, and was discharged on October 31, 1747. [Ref: DA-5, DA-6]. (He is not listed in Source DM-40.)

THOMAS, Richardson. See "Thomas Richardson," q.v.

THOMAS, Samuel. Private. Served in Capt. Samuel Smith's Company, Delaware Regiment of Continental Troops. Enlisted January 19, 1776, and on duty (in barracks) at Dover on April 12, 1776. [Ref: DA-54].

THOMAS, Thomas. Private. Served in Capt. John Caton's Company on April 25, 1757, in the French and Indian Wars. [Ref: DA-13].

THOMASSON, Lars. Sailor. From Weddinge, he arrived in New Sweden on the ship *Charitas* in 1641 and he was "appointed to be on the sloop" (i. e., the governor's yacht) at Fort Christina in 1643. One "Lars Thomasson, or Thomson" was a freeman by 1654. [Ref: DJ-701, DJ-712, DJ-722]. "Lars Thompson, from Vedding, was a sailor on the sloop" in 1648." [Ref: DH-45]. (Name was also spelled "Lars Tommesonn").

THOMASSON, Marthen. Soldier (*saldater*). From Osterbotten, he served in New Sweden. Along with soldier Martin Bagge, he was "killed by the savages between Christina and Elfsborg" on March 4, 1643. [Ref: DJ-707, 708]. (He was also known as "Martin Thomasson, the Finn").

THOMPSON, Benjamin. Private. Served in Capt. Joseph Vaughan's Company, Delaware Regiment of Continental Troops. Enlisted February 9, 1776, and was on duty (in barracks) at Dover on April 12, 1776. [Ref: DA-59].

THOMPSON, James. Private. Born 1740, Ireland. Linen printer. Enlisted on April 28, 1758, in the French and Indian Wars, by Capt. Benjamin Noxon. [Ref: DA-19].

THOMPSON, John. Private. Served in Capt. Richard McWilliams' Company, New Castle County. Enlisted on December 28, 1757, during the French and Indian Wars. [Ref: DA-14].

THOMPSON, Joseph. Private. Served in Capt. Henry Darby's Company, Delaware Regiment of Continental Troops. Enlisted February 16, 1776, and was on duty (in barracks) at Dover on April 12, 1776. [Ref: DA-46].

THOMPSON, Lars. See "Lars Thomasson," q.v.

THOMPSON, Richard. Private. Enlisted on May 12, 1758, in Capt. French Battell's Company of Lower County Provincials, during the French and Indian Wars. [Ref: DA-17].

THOMPSON, Robert. Drummer and fifer. Served in Capt. Jonathan Caldwell's Company, Delaware Regiment of Continental Troops. Enlisted on January 27, 1776, and was on duty (in barracks) at Dover on April 12, 1776. [Ref: DA-41].

THOMPSON, Robert. Private. Enlisted on May 15, 1758, in Capt. French Battell's Company of Lower County Provincials, during the French and Indian Wars. [Ref: DA-17].

THOMPSON, Thomas. Private. Served in Capt. Joseph Vaughan's Company of the Delaware Regiment of Continental Troops. Enlisted February 16, 1776 and was on duty (in barracks) at Dover on April 12, 1776. [Ref: DA-59].

THOMPSON, William. Soldier. Enlisted May 1, 1759, during the French and Indian Wars, and his name appeared on a return of Capt. Henry Van Bibber's Company of the Lower Counties on Delaware Troops at New Castle on June 4, 1759. [Ref: DA-26].

THOMSON, William. See "William Cullen," q.v.

THORNE, Sydenham and Betty. See "Levin Cropper," q.v.

THORSSON, Olof. Sailor. Laborer. Arrived in New Sweden as a midshipman on the ship *Kalmar Nyckel* in 1641. [Ref: DJ-712]. In 1644 he cultivated tobacco for the company at Christina and in 1648 he was a freeman. [Ref: DH-45]. (Name also spelled "Roff Toorsson").

THORSSON, Bengt. Sailor. Appointed to serve on the sloop (i. e., the governor's yacht) continually at Fort Christina in New Sweden in 1643. [Ref: DJ-701]. (Name was also spelled "Bengt Torsonn").

THORSSON, Alexander. Sword cutler (*svardfejare*), bladesmith, and furbisher. Hired in 1653, he arrived in New Sweden on the ship *Orn* in 1654. [Ref: DJ-722]. (His first name was also spelled "Sander").

THROP, Samuel. Private. Enlisted on May 16, 1758, in Capt. French Battell's Company of Lower County Provincials, during the French and Indian Wars. [Ref: DA-17].

TILL, Thomas. Captain. Served in a company in regiment of Sussex County, Southern District of Cedar Creek Hundred, 1756, during the French and Indian Wars, and became captain in the Slaughter Neck District Hundred on March 18, 1758. [Ref: DA-13, DA-15, DM-46].

TILLINGER, George. Private. Born 1740, Germany. Saddler. Enlisted on May 6, 1759, during the French and Indian Wars, in Capt. James Armstrong's Company in the Pennsylvania Regiment. [Ref: DA-26].

TILTON, James. Surgeon. Served in Delaware Battalion of Continental Troops. Commissioned on January 13, 1776. [Ref: DA-35].

TILTON, Nehemiah. See "William Rhoades" and "John Rhodes," q.v.

TILTON, Thomas. Ensign. Served in Capt. Charles Hillyard's Company, lower part of Duck Creek Hundred, Kent County, upon Delaware, in 1756, in the French and Indian Wars. [Ref: DA-12]. A Thomas Tilton died testate in Duck Creek Hundred and his will was probated on November 9, 1789, naming his wife Sabrah, sons James, Abraham, and Thomas, and daughter Rachel. His brother Nehemiah Tilton was one of the executors. [Ref: DK-416]. Sabrah Tilton, widow of Thomas, died testate and her will was probated on November 28, 1797, naming her sons James, Abraham, and Thomas, and daughters Sarah Allee (wife of Abraham Allee), Nancy Steel (widow of James Steel). [Ref: DK-531].

TIMS, John. Private. Served in Capt. Jonathan Caldwell's Company, Delaware Regiment of Continental Troops. Enlisted January 27, 1776, and on duty (in barracks) at Dover on April 12, 1776. [Ref: DA-41].

TOBIN, Thomas. Lieutenant. Served in Capt. Jacob Gooding's Company, Red Lyon [Lion] Hundred, Lower Regiment, New Castle County, 1756, in the French and Indian Wars. [Ref: DA-12]. Rachel Tobin died in

Red Lion Hundred and her will was probated July 15, 1775, naming a son Thomas (and others). [Ref: DN-80]. (Name also spelled "Tabin").

TOM, William. Soldier. Land patentee at Whorekill. Planter who paid his quit-rent to the governor in 1665, and also received a land patent for land at Whorekill on August 3, 1668. His name appeared on a nomination list for officers in New Castle circa 1675 (list not dated). [Ref: DP-27, 28, 29, 170, DY-135]. He owned an island on the west side of Delaware Bay about seven miles south of New Castle, which was recorded in a resurvey on March 6, 1679, as being "land lately to Mr. William Tom, deceased." [Ref: DY-32].

TOMLINSON, Ostend. See "Joseph Robinson," q.v.

TORKILLUS, Reorus. Reverend. Military preacher (*predikanten*) and religious teacher. An "officer" in New Sweden, 1640-1643, he died September 7, 1643, at Fort Christina. [Ref: DJ-699, DJ-707, DH-42].

TORRSEN, Olle. Soldier. Land patentee. Planter who paid his quit-rent to the governor in 1669. His name also appeared on a nomination list for officers in New Castle circa 1675 (list was undated). [Ref: DP-170, DY-157]. (Name also spelled "Olla Towson").

TOWLAND, William. Private. Born 1736, New Castle County, Delaware. Laborer. Enlisted on April 25, 1758, during the French and Indian Wars, as a private by Capt. John McClughan "for the campaign in the lower counties." He was probably the same William Towland. Private. Born 1736, Delaware). Laborer, who was enlisted on April 25, 1758, by Capt. Benjamin Noxon. [Ref: DA-18, 19].

TOWNEY, Archibald. Lieutenant. Served in the "Lower County," May 22, 1759. [Ref: DA-20]. (This name probably has been spelled in error in the aforementioned source as one "Archibald Finig" was commissioned on the same day in the same company. It appears that the actual person in question is one "Archibald Finney," q.v.).

TOWNSEND, Ephraim. Private. Served in Capt. Jonathan Caldwell's Company, Delaware Regiment of Continental Troops. Enlisted January 17, 1776, and was on duty (in barracks) at Dover on April 12, 1776. [Ref: DA-41]. Charles Townsend died testate in Kent County and his will was probated on August 12, 1772, naming his wife Mary, sons Solomon, Ephraim, William and Charles, and daughters Mary, Meriam, Sarah, Ansley, Rachel, and Elizabeth Townsend. [Ref: DK-269].

TOWNSEND, Solomon. Private. Served in Capt. Jonathan Caldwell's Company, Delaware Regiment of Continental Troops. Enlisted on April 3, 1776, and on duty (in barracks) at Dover on April 12, 1776. [Ref: DA-41]. See information under "Ephraim Townsend," q.v.

TOWNSON, John. Private. Served in Capt. John Caton's Company on April 25, 1757, during the French and Indian Wars. [Ref: DA-13]. One "John Townsend" died testate in Kent County and his will was probated January 8, 1781, naming his mother Febey Morris, brother William, and sisters Elizabeth, Rachel, and Mary. [Ref: DK-328].

TOY, Cornelius. Private. Served in Capt. Samuel Smith's Company, Delaware Regiment of Continental Troops. Enlisted January 17, 1776, and was reported as "deserted" on February 1, 1776. [Ref: DA-54].

TRACEY, Thomas. Private. Served in Capt. Henry Darby's Company, Delaware Regiment of Continental Troops. Enlisted on March 4, 1776, and on duty (in barracks) at Dover on April 12, 1776. [Ref: DA-46].

TRAIN, Hamilton. Private. Served in Capt. John Caton's Company, April 25, 1757, in the French and Indian Wars. [Ref: DA-13]. One Hamilton Train died intestate in Kent County and the administration of his estate was granted to Alice Train and James Train, who were referred to as his "next-of-kin," on May 19, 1768. [Ref: DK-235].

TRAIN, Mary. See "Jacob Kollock, Jr.," q.v.

TRAIN, Thomas. Private. Served in Capt. Nathan Adams' Company of the Delaware Regiment of Continental Troops. Enlisted February 12, 1776, and was on duty (in barracks) at Dover on April 12, 1776. [Ref: DA-53].

TRANBERG, Andrew, and family. See "Andrew Frauberg [or Tranberg?]."

TRAYLEY, Robert. Land patentee and probable militiaman in Delaware in November, 1677. [Ref: DP-167, 168].

TRENT, William. Captain. Commissioned on June 4, 1746, during King George's War against Canada. He was in winter quarters at Albany, New York, during 1746-1747, and his company was discharged October 31, 1747. [Ref: DA-6].

TRIPPIT, Daniel. Private. Served in Capt. John Caton's Company on April 25, 1757, in the French and Indian Wars. [Ref: DA-14]. One "Daniel Trippet, yeoman," died intestate in Kent County and the administration of his estate was granted to an "Ann Trippett" on November 26, 1761. [Ref: DK-197].

TRISER, Emanuel. Private. Served in Capt. Nathan Adams' Company, Delaware Regiment of Continental Troops. Enlisted on March 20, 1776, and was on duty (in barracks) at Dover on April 12, 1776. [Ref: DA-53].

TRUE, William. Land patentee and probable militiaman in Delaware in November, 1677. [Ref: DP-167, 168].

TRUET, Lodwick. Private. Served in Capt. John Caton's Company on April 25, 1757, in the French and Indian Wars. [Ref: DA-14].
TRUET, Rouns. Private. Served in Capt. John Caton's Company on April 25, 1757, in the French and Indian Wars. [Ref: DA-14].
TRUETT, Newbold. Private. Served in Capt. Joseph Vaughan's Company, Delaware Regiment of Continental Troops. Enlisted January 17, 1776, and on duty (in barracks) at Dover on April 12, 1776. [Ref: DA-59].
TRUETT, Phillip. Private. Served in Capt. Joseph Vaughan's Company, Delaware Regiment of Continental Troops. Enlisted February 3, 1776, and was on duty (in barracks) at Dover on April 12, 1776. [Ref: DA-58, DA-59]. (This same source spelled his name "Phillip Truitt").
TRUITT, George, Esq. See "Robert Hodgson," q.v.
TRUITT, Joseph. First Lieutenant. Served in 8th Company, Delaware State Troops in Continental Service. Commissioned January 21, 1776, and was on duty (in barracks) with Capt. Joseph Vaughan's Delaware Regiment of Continental Troops at Dover on April 12, 1776. [Ref: DA-34, DA-36, DA-59]. (One list had misspelled his name "Frint").
TRUMP, John. Private. Served in Capt. Charles Pope's Company of the Delaware Regiment of Continental Troops. Enlisted January 17, 1776, and was on duty (in quarters) at Lewis Town on April 11, 1776. [Ref: DA-51]. (This same source spelled his name "John Frump").
TUCKFIELD, William. Soldier. He was listed as a deserter from the company of Capt. John Shannon in 1747 during King George's War against Canada. [Ref: DM-40].
TUFFREY, Simon. Soldier. Enlisted on May 21, 1759, in the French and Indian Wars, and his name appeared on a return of Capt. Henry Van Bibber's Company of the Lower Counties on Delaware Troops at New Castle on June 4, 1759. [Ref: DA-26].
TURNER, Barnaby. Private. Served in Capt. Samuel Smith's Company, Delaware Regiment of Continental Troops. Enlisted January 17, 1776, and reported to have "deserted" on February 1, 1776. [Ref: DA-54].
TURNER, Edward. Private. Enlisted on May 26, 1758, in Capt. French Battell's Company of Lower County Provincials, during the French and Indian Wars. [Ref: DA-17].
TURNER, Ephraim. Private. Born 1741, Sussex, Delaware. Enlisted in Capt. John Wright's Company and was on the muster roll of May 11, 1759, in the French and Indian Wars. [Ref: DA-25]. Administration of the estate of one Ephraim Turner was granted to Levi Russell in Sussex County and date of the bond was May 31, 1785. [Ref: DS-166].

TURNER, Henry. Private. Served in Capt. Joseph Vaughan's Company, Delaware Regiment of Continental Troops. Enlisted January 16, 1776, and was on duty (in barracks) at Dover on April 12, 1776. [Ref: DA-57, DA-59]. (This same source spelled his name "Henry W. Turner").

TURNER, James. Private. Served in Capt. Charles Pope's Company, Delaware Regiment of Continental Troops. Enlisted January 15, 1776, and was on duty (in quarters) at Lewis Town on April 11, 1776. [Ref: DA-51].

TURNER, Samuel. Private. Born 1724, Ireland, stocking weaver. Enlisted in Capt. John Shannon's Company of Foot on July 14, 1746, and served in King George's War against Canada. He was in winter quarters at Albany, New York, during 1746-1747, and was discharged October 31, 1747. [Ref: DA-5, DA-6]. (Not listed in Source DM-40.)

TURNER, Samuel Bevens. Ensign. Served in Capt. Robert Killen's Company, in middle part of Mispillim [Mispillion] Hundred, Kent County, upon Delaware, 1756, during the French and Indian Wars. [Ref: DA-12]. "Samuel Bevans Turner" died testate in Mispillion Hundred and his will was probated on August 31, 1793, naming his wife Jean Huet Turner, sons Benjamin, Samuel, George, Jesse and Elias, daughters Polly Turner, Levicy Turner, Nicy Fisher, and Sally Langrel, and granddaughter Polly Fisher. [Ref: DK-467].

TURNER, Thomas. Private. Served in Capt. Jonathan Caldwell's Company, Delaware Regiment of Continental Troops. Enlisted February 8, 1776, and on duty (in barracks) at Dover on April 12, 1776. [Ref: DA-41].

TURNER, Thomas. Private. Served in Capt. David Hall's Company, Delaware Regiment of Continental Troops. Enlisted January 20, 1776, and was on duty (in barracks) at Lewis Town on April 11, 1776. [Ref: DA-43].

TUSEY, Stephen. Private. Born 1732, Brandywine Hundred, Delaware. Laborer. Enlisted on April 24, 1758, during the French and Indian Wars, as a private by Capt. John McClughan "for the campaign in the lower counties." [Ref: DA-18].

TYBOUT, James. Lieutenant. Served in Capt. John Barnes' Company, upper part of Little Creek Hundred, Kent County, upon Delaware, 1756, during the French and Indian Wars. [Ref: DA-12].

TYSK, Rutkiert. Soldier (*saldater*). Served in New Sweden and died on August 3, 1643, at Fort Christina. [Ref: DJ-707]. (Name also spelled "Rother Tijck").

ULF, Lars Anderson. Cook. Engaged in cultivating tobacco for the company at Christina in 1644, and then became "a cook on the sloop" (i. e., on the governor's yacht) in 1648. [Ref: DH-45].

UTTER, Nils Matsson. Soldier. Hired at Stockholm in 1653, he arrived in New Sweden on the ship *Orn* in 1654. [Ref: DJ-722].

VAN BIBBER, Henry. Captain. Served as first lieutenant under Capt. Benjamin Noxon on April 21, 1758, during the French and Indian Wars and was promoted to adjutant "of the lower government on Delaware" under Major Richard Wells on June 4, 1758. He was then promoted to first lieutenant under Capt. Jacob Gooding on June 13, 1758. "Henry Vanbeber" was captain of one of the three companies of "the lower counties" [Delaware] of the 3rd Battalion of Pennsylvania Regiment under Col. Hugh Mercer, May 23, 1759. [Ref: DA-16, 20, DM-47, 49].

VAN BIBBER, Jacob. Lieutenant. In Capt. John Gooding's Company, New Castle County, 1747-1748, and served in King George's War against Canada. He was promoted to major of a New Castle County Regiment, 1747-1748. He was colonel of the Lower Regiment, New Castle County, 1756, during the French and Indian Wars. [Ref: DA-7, DA-11, DM-45]. (Source DA-7 also spelled his named "Jacob Vanbidder"). One Jacob Van Bebber [sic] died testate in Red Lion Hundred and his will was probated on April 28, 1768, naming his wife Mary, son William, and daughter Sarah. [Ref: DN-65].

VAN BOGAERT, Joost. Commander. Served on the ship *Kalmar Nyckel* during the third expedition to New Sweden in 1640-1641. [Ref: DJ-759, DH-44].

VAN DE WAETER, Jan H. See "Jan van de Waeter Hindrickson," q.v.

VAN DIKE, Andrew. Private. Born 1738, Delaware. Laborer. Enlisted on May 2, 1758, in the French and Indian Wars, by Capt. Benjamin Noxon. [Ref: DA-19].

VAN DYCK, Gregorius. Assistant Commissary. He was in New Sweden between 1640-1642, and served as head guard (*wachmesteren*) at Fort Elfsborg, 1643. He returned to Europe in 1642 and came back to New Sweden with Governor Printz in 1642 [sic]. He served as sheriff from 1644 until 1661. [Ref: DH-47, DJ-699, DJ-703, DJ-710, DJ-716]. (Name also spelled "Van Dicke").

VAN DYKE, John. Lieutenant. Served in Capt. John Vance's Company, New Castle County, 1747-1748, in King George's War against Canada. He was a lieutenant in Capt. John Vance's Company in St. George's Hundred, Lower Regiment, New Castle County, in 1756, in the French and Indian Wars. [Ref: DA-7, 11]. One "John Vandike" died in St.

George's Hundred and his will was probated on December 26, 1759 naming his wife Margaret, son Isaac, daughter Ann, brothers James, David, and Isaac (executor), sisters Jemima, Mary, and Elizabeth, and brother-in-law Jacob Peterson (executor). [Ref: DN-57].

VAN EISSEN, Isack. Corporal. From Stockholm, he arrived in New Sweden in 1643. He served as a common soldier (*saldater*) at Fort Elfsborg until August, 1643, "when he was made corporal at a wage of 6 *riksdalers* a month." [Ref: DJ-703, DJ-714]. "Isack van Eysen" was a soldier at Fort Elfsborg in 1644-1648. [Ref: DH-47]. (Name also spelled "Isaac von Eyssen").

VAN WINKLE, John. Ensign. Served in Capt. George Martin's Company, Kent County, 1747-1748, in King George's War against Canada. [Ref: DA-8]. One "Simon Vanwinkle" died testate in Kent County and his will was probated on January 23, 1752, naming his wife Jane and sons Jacob, John, and Simon, and daughter Susannah. [Ref: DK-147].

VAN WINKLE, Peter. Private. Served in Capt. Charles Pope's Company, Delaware Regiment of Continental Troops. Enlisted January 20, 1776, and was on duty (in quarters) at Lewis Town on April 11, 1776. [Ref: DA-51]. (Name also spelled "Vanwincle").

VANCE, John. Captain. Served in a New Castle County Company, 1747-1748, in King George's War against Canada. He was a captain of a company in St. George's Hundred, Lower Regiment, New Castle County, 1756, in the French and Indian Wars. [Ref: DA-7, DA-11, DM-46].

VANCE, John. Sergeant. Served in Capt. Samuel Smith's Company, Delaware Regiment of Continental Troops. Enlisted January 17, 1776, and on duty (in barracks) at Dover on April 12, 1776. [Ref: DA-53].

VANDERFORD, Charles. Private. Served in Capt. John Caton's Company, April 25, 1757, in the French and Indian Wars. [Ref: DA-13]. Thomas Vanderford died in Kent County and administration of his estate was granted to Charles Vanderford, next-of-kin, on April 7, 1767. [Ref: DK-226].

VANDERFORD, Vincent. Private. Enlisted on May 15, 1758, in Capt. French Battell's Company of Lower County Provincials, during the French and Indian Wars. [Ref: DA-17].

VANDERVERE, Jacob. Soldier. Planter in Delaware who paid his quit-rent to the governor in 1669, having received a patent to "a small island at Delaware lying beyond Christeen Kill." [Ref: DP-27, DP-28, DY-156]. One "Jacob Vandeveer" died testate in New Castle County and his will was probated on March 30, 1699, naming his wife

Katharine and his sons John, Cornelius, William, and "my fourth son Jacob." [Ref: DN-12].

VANDEVER, Andrew. Private. Served in Capt. Joseph Stedham's Company, Delaware Battalion of Continental Troops. Enlisted January 22, 1776, and was in quarters at Dover on April 12, 1776, at which time he was sick. He was reported to be "dead by October 20, 1776, at Brunswick." [Ref: DA-37, 39].

VANDIKE, John. See "John Van Dyke," q.v.

VANDIVER, Jacob. Private. Born 1741, Wilmington, Delaware. Laborer. Enlisted on May 2, 1759, in the French and Indian Wars, in Capt. James Armstrong's Company in Pennsylvania Regiment. [Ref: DA-26].

VANHOY, Ann and John. See "Wilson Buckmaster," q.v.

VANLANGDONK, Joost. Commissary. In New Sweden, 1640, he returned to Europe in 1642 upon the arrival of Hendrick Huygen. [Ref: DJ-699].

VANLEUVENIGH, Philip. Private. Served in Capt. Richard McWilliams' Company, New Castle County. Enlisted on December 28, 1757, in the French and Indian Wars. [Ref: DA-14]. "Philip Vanluveneigh" died in New Castle County and his will was probated on June 5, 1745, naming his wife Eleanor and a son Philip (among others). [Ref: DN-34, 35].

VANLEUVENIGH, Samuel. Private. Served in Capt. Richard McWilliams' Company, New Castle County. Enlisted on December 28, 1757, during the French and Indian Wars. [Ref: DA-14]. One "John Vanlewveneigh, shopkeeper" died testate in New Castle and his will was probated on December 31, 1754, naming his wife (no name was given) and his sons John, Zachariah, and Samuel (executor). [Ref: DN-53]. One "Samuel Vanleuveneigh, shopkeeper," died in New Castle and his will was probated on December 27, 1759, naming his nieces Rebecca and Mary Vanleuveneigh, daughters of his brother Zachariah; nieces Catharine and Elizabeth Vanleuveneigh, daughters of brother John (deceased); and, an Eliakim Garretson. The executor was his brother Zachariah Vanleuveneigh. [Ref: DN-57].

VANLEUVENIGH, Zachariah. Ensign. Served as ensign in Capt. Richard McWilliams' Company in New Castle Hundred, Upper Regiment, New Castle County, 1756, in the French and Indian Wars. [Ref: DA-11, which spelled his name "Vanlunanigh."]. A "Zachariah Vanleuvenigh, tanner," died in New Castle County and his will was probated on March 13, 1789, naming his wife Ann, sons George, John, William, and George [sic], daughters Elizabeth, Rebecca McWilliams, and Mary, granddaughters Ann McWilliams, Sarah ----, Rebecca ----, Louisa ----, and niece Catharine Vanleuvenigh. [Ref: DN-117]. Also, one "John Vanlewveneigh, shopkeeper," died in New Castle and his will was probated on December 31, 1754, naming wife (no name given) and sons John, Zachariah, and Samuel Vanleuvenigh. [Ref: DN-53].

VANLOODEN, Cornelius. Private. Served in Capt. Samuel Smith's Company, Delaware Regiment of Continental Troops. Enlisted January 24, 1776, and was on duty (in barracks) at Dover on April 12, 1776. [Ref: DA-54, 56]. (This same source spelled his name "Vandlooden").

VANSANDT, John. Private. Served in Capt. Joseph Stedham's Company, Delaware Battalion of Continental Troops. Enlisted February 29, 1776, and was in quarters at Dover on April 12, 1776. [Ref: DA-40].

VASA, Knut Martensson. Sailor. Arrived in New Sweden in 1644. He was engaged in cultivating tobacco for the company at Christina and by 1648 was a freeman. [Ref: DH-45].

VASHAN, Michael. Private. Born 1729, Armagh, Ireland. Laborer. Enlisted on May 7, 1759, in the French and Indian Wars, in Capt. James Armstrong's Company in Pennsylvania Regiment. [Ref: DA-26].

VASS, Sven. Gunner (*constaple*). "Officer in charge" of the small copper cannon at Fort Tinicum" in 1643. [Ref: DJ-705]. (Name also spelled "Swenn Waass").

VAUGHAN, Betty. See "Burton Waples," q.v.

VAUGHAN, Joseph. Captain. Served in the 8th Company, Delaware State Troops in Continental Service. Commissioned January 21, 1776, and was on duty (in barracks) with the Delaware Regiment of Continental Troops at Dover on April 12, 1776. [Ref: DA-34, 36, 57, 59].

VAUGHAN, William. Ensign. Served in 8th Company, Delaware State Troops, Continental Service. Commissioned January 21, 1776, and on duty (in barracks) with Capt. Joseph Vaughan, Delaware Regiment of Continental Troops at Dover, April 12, 1776. [Ref: DA-35, 36, 57].

VERHOOFE, Cornelius. Land patentee and probable militiaman in Delaware in November, 1677. [Ref: DP-167, 168].

VICTOR, Elijah. Private. Served in Capt. David Hall's Company, Delaware Regiment of Continental Troops. Enlisted on April 7, 1776, and was on duty (in barracks) at Lewis Town on April 11, 1776. After his name is written "on furlow." [Ref: DA-45].

VINING, John. Captain. Served in a Kent County Company, 1747-1748, and served in King George's War against Canada. He was colonel of a regiment of militia for Kent County, upon Delaware, 1756, in the French and Indian Wars. [Ref: DA-8, DA-12, DM-46]. One John Vining died testate in Kent County and his will was probated on November 22, 1770, naming his wife Pheebe, daughter Mary, and sons Benjamin, Nicholas, and John. [Ref: DK-254]. Also see "James Barnes," q.v.

VINNEY, Peter. Private. Born 1734, Newport, Delaware. Shoemaker. Enlisted on April 24, 1758, during the French and Indian Wars, as a private by Capt. John McClughan "for the campaign in the lower counties." [Ref: DA-18].

VINYARD, John. Drummer and fifer. Served in Capt. Nathan Adams' Company, Delaware Regiment of Continental Troops. Enlisted January 27, 1776, and was on duty (in barracks) at Dover on April 12, 1776. [Ref: DA-52].

VIRDEN, Hugh. Private. Served in Capt. David Hall's Company of the Delaware Regiment of Continental Troops. Enlisted January 21, 1776, and was on duty (in barracks) at Lewis Town on April 11, 1776. [Ref: DA-43].

VIRDEN, Levi. Private. Served in Capt. David Hall's Company of the Delaware Regiment of Continental Troops. Enlisted January 20, 1776, and was on duty (in barracks) at Lewis Town on April 11, 1776. [Ref: DA-43].

VIRDEN, Marnit. Corporal. Served in Capt. David Hall's Company of the Delaware Regiment of Continental Troops. Enlisted on January 16, 1776, and was on duty (in barracks) at Lewis Town on April 11, 1776. [Ref: DA-42].

VIRDIN, Daniel and Elizabeth. See "Joseph Jackson," q.v.

VIRDIN, William. See "Matthew Lowber," q.v.

VON ELSWICK, Hendrick. Commissary. Arrived in New Sweden in 1654 on the ship *Orn*. [Ref: DJ-716]. A "Hendrick Elswick" was commander of the ship *Gyllene Haj* during the eleventh expedition to New Sweden in 1654, but "did not reach New Sweden." [Ref: DJ-761].

VON EYSSEN, Isack. See "Isack Van Eissen," q.v.

WAILY, William. Private. Served in Capt. Jonathan Caldwell's Company, Delaware Regiment of Continental Troops. Enlisted on March 1, 1776, and was on duty (in barracks) at Dover on April 12, 1776. [Ref: DA-41].

WAINRIGHT, James. Private. Served in Capt. Henry Darby's Company, Delaware Regiment of Continental Troops. Enlisted February 3, 1776, and on duty (in barracks) at Dover on April 12, 1776. [Ref: DA-46].

WALDRAVEN, Tobias. Private. Born 1739, New Castle, Delaware. Tanner. Enlisted April 26, 1759, during the French and Indian Wars, in Capt. James Armstrong's Company in the Pennsylvania Regiment. [Ref: DA-26].

WALKER, James. Lieutenant. Served in Capt. Evan Rice's Company in New Castle County, 1747-1748, in King George's War against Canada. He was lieutenant in Capt. Evan Rees' [sic] Company in Mill Creek Hundred, Upper Regiment of New Castle County, 1756, in the French and Indian Wars. [Ref: DA-7, DA-11].

WALKER, Jesse. Private. Served in Capt. David Hall's Company of the Delaware Regiment of Continental Troops. Enlisted January 20, 1776, and was on duty (in barracks) at Lewis Town on April 11, 1776. [Ref: DA-42].

WALKER, Nathaniel. Captain. Received a land survey for tract called *Walkers Purchase* on the west side of Delaware Bay [Rehoboth Hundred in Sussex County] on June 16, 1681, and the tract *Walkers Choyse* on June 17, 1681. [Ref: DR-50, DY-76, DY-78, DC-79]. He was also an heir of Richard Shoulter in 1683. [Ref: DS-9]. One "Capt. Nathaniel Walker, formerly of New England, late of Northampton County in the Province of Virginia," died in Sussex County and William Dyer was administrator *cum testamento annexo* on July 20, 1685. [Ref: DS-10].

WALKER, Robert. Private. Served in Capt. David Hall's Company, Delaware Regiment of Continental Troops. Enlisted January 25, 1776, and was on duty (in barracks) at Lewis Town on April 11, 1776. [Ref: DA-43].

WALKER, Thomas. Private. Served in Capt. Samuel Smith's Company, Delaware Regiment of Continental Troops. Enlisted January 20, 1776, and on duty (in barracks) at Dover on April 12, 1776. [Ref: DA-54].

WALKER, William. Corporal. Served in Capt. Nathan Adams' Company, Delaware Regiment of Continental Troops. Enlisted January 26, 1776, and on duty (in barracks) at Dover on April 12, 1776. [Ref: DA-52].

WALKER, William. Private. Served in Capt. Richard McWilliams' Company, New Castle County. Enlisted on December 28, 1757, during the French and Indian Wars. [Ref: DA-14].

WALLACE, Rachel and Sarah. See "Evan Rees," q.v.

WALLACE, Reuben. Corporal. Served in Capt. Nathan Adams' Company, Delaware Regiment of Continental Troops. Enlisted January 29, 1776, and on duty (in barracks) at Dover on April 12, 1776. [Ref: DA-52].

WALLACE, Richard Jr. Private. Served in Capt. John Caton's Company on April 25, 1757, in the French and Indian Wars. [Ref: DA-13].

WALLACE, Ruben. See "Caleb Luff," q.v.

WALLACE, William. Private. Served in Capt. John Caton's Company, April 25, 1757, in the French and Indian Wars. [Ref: DA-14]. One William Wallace died in Kent County and the administration of his estate was granted to Hannah Wallace and Layton Jones on August 27, 1779. An administration account on May 31, 1781, by Layton Jones, Mentioned heirs Mary Jones, William David, Elizabeth Wallace, and Solomon Wallace. [Ref: DK-322, 331]. Another William Wallace died in Kent County and the administration of his estate was granted to Jonathan Clampit on October 2, 1783. [Ref: DK-353]. And a William Wallace died in Kent County and administration of his estate was granted to Elizabeth Wallace on December 8, 1789. [Ref: DK-419].

WALLIAM, James. Officer. His name appeared on a nomination list for officers in New Castle, Delaware circa 1675 (list was not dated). [Ref: DP-170, DY-95]. (Name also spelled "Wallems").

WALLINGTON, Abram. Private. Served in Capt. Charles Pope's Company, Delaware Regiment of Continental Troops. Enlisted January 15, 1776, and was on duty (in quarters) at Lewis Town on April 11, 1776. [Ref: DA-51].

WALRAVEN, William. Private. Served in Capt. Joseph Stedham's Company, Delaware Battalion of Continental Troops. Enlisted January 26, 1776, and in quarters at Dover on April 12, 1776. [Ref: DA-39].

WALTON, Elizabeth, and children. See "Bethuel Watson," q.v.

WAPLES, Burton. Captain. Served in a company in regiment of Sussex County, Southern District of Indian River Hundred, 1756, during the French and Indian Wars, and captain of the Indian River District Company on March 18, 1758. [Ref: DA-13, DA-15, DM-46]. One Burton Waples died in Sussex County and his will was probated September 14, 1796, naming heirs: daughters Agnes Waples, Comfort King, and Anne Hall; grandsons Woolsey Waples, Wallace Waples, Burton West, Jacob Bounds, Wiliam Bounds, William Vaughan; granddaughters Betty Vaughan, Neala Waples, and Comfort Burton Waples; brothers William, deceased, and Peter Waples; and, uncle Paul Waples. [Ref: DS-275].

WARD, Edward. Major. Served during the French and Indian Wars in the 3rd Battalion of the Pennsylvania Regiment under Col. Hugh Mercer, which included the three companies "of the lower counties" [Delaware] on April 26, 1759. [Ref: DA-20].

WARD, Henry. Officer, His name appeared on a nomination list for officers in New Castle circa 1675 (list not dated). [Ref: DP-170].

WARD, James. Private. Served in Capt. Henry Darby's Company of the Delaware Regiment of Continental Troops. Enlisted January 22, 1776, and on duty (in barracks) at Dover on April 12, 1776. [Ref: DA-46].

WARD, John. Private. Born 1719, Jersey. Enlisted in Capt. John Wright's Company and was on the muster roll of May 11, 1759, during the French and Indian Wars. [Ref: DA-25].

WARD, John. Private. Born 1739, Donegal, Ireland. Miller. Enlisted on May 6, 1759, in the French and Indian Wars, in Capt. James Armstrong's Company in the Pennsylvania Regiment. [Ref: DA-26].

WARE, William. Mariner. Lived in Sussex County on Lewis Creek by January 1, 1770, at which time he purchased land. [Ref: DD-17].

WARRAN, Elizabeth. See "William Jackson," q.v.

WARREN, Benjamin Jr. Ensign. Served in Capt. Daniel Robinson's Company, Murder Kill Hundred, Kent County, upon Delaware, in 1756, during the French and Indian Wars. He resigned on March 29, 1758. One "Benjamin Warren, yeoman," died in "Murtherkill Hundred" and administration of his estate was granted to his widow, Elizabeth Warren, on April 21, 1772. [Ref: DA-12, DA-15, DK-266].

WARREN, William. Land patentee and probable militiaman in Delaware in November, 1677. [Ref: DP-167, 168].

WARRINGTON, Jacob. Private. Served in Capt. David Hall's Company, Delaware Regiment of Continental Troops. Enlisted on March 8, 1776, and was on duty (in barracks) at Lewis Town on April 11, 1776. [Ref: DA-43].

WARRINGTON, John. Private. Served in Capt. David Hall's Company, Delaware Regiment of Continental Troops. Enlisted January 20, 1776, and was on duty (in barracks) at Lewis Town on April 11, 1776. [Ref: DA-43].

WARRINGTON, William. Corporal. Served in Capt. David Hall's Company in the Delaware Regiment of Continental Troops. Enlisted on January 16, 1776, and was on duty (in barracks) at Lewis Town on April 11, 1776. After his name is written "on command." [Ref: DA-42].

WARRINGTON, Zachariah. Private. Born 1740, Angola Hundred, Delaware. Planter. Enlisted on April 20, 1758, during the French and Indian Wars, by Capt. John McClughan "for the campaign in the lower counties." [Ref: DA-18].

WASA, Knut Martensson. Sailor. A freeman, "probably from Vasa in Finland," he arrived in New Sweden as a sailor on the ship *Charitas* in 1641. [Ref: DJ-712]. (Name also spelled "Knut Martensson Vasa").

WATKINS, James. Private. Born 1732, England. Laborer. Enlisted on May 3, 1758, during the French and Indian Wars, by Capt. Benjamin Noxon. [Ref: DA-19].

WATSON, Bethuel. Lieutenant. Served in Capt. Benjamin Wyncoop's Company, Northern District of Cedar Creek Hundred, in the regiment of Sussex County, in 1756, during the French and Indian Wars, and lieutenant in Capt. Wynkoop's [sic] Cedar District Company on March 18, 1758. [Ref: DA-13, DA-15]. One "Bethuel Wattson, Sr.," farmer, Cedar Creek Hundred, died testate in Sussex County and his will was probated on September 12, 1797, naming his sons Jesse Wattson and Bethuel Wattson, daughters Hester Metcalf, Mary Collins (widow of John), and Naomi Herrington, and grandchildren Esther, Elizabeth, Jesse, John, and Bethuel (children of deceased son David Wattson), and Luke, Nehemiah, John, Wattson, Mary, Betty, and Zipporah Walton (children of deceased daughter Elizabeth Walton). [Ref: DS-284].

WATSON, Isaac. Lieutenant. Served in Capt. Thomas Till's Company, Southern District of Cedar Creek Hundred, in the regiment of Sussex County, in 1756, during the French and Indian Wars, and lieutenant in the Slaughter Neck District Company on March 18, 1758. [Ref: DA-13, DA-15]. One "Isaac Wattson" died testate in Sussex County and his will was probated March 24, 1773, naming wife Mary, sons Joseph and Isaac Watson, daughter Elizabeth Draper, and his grandchildren Isaac Riley and Mary Riley. [Ref: DS-94].

WATSON, Luke. Captain. He held that rank by 1692 when he served as a Justice in Sussex County. [Ref: DC-38].

WATSON, Thomas. Private. Served in Capt. David Hall's Company of the Delaware Regiment of Continental Troops. Enlisted on February 2, 1776, and was on duty (in barracks) at Lewis Town on April 11, 1776. [Ref: DA-43].

WATSON, Thomas. Private. Served in Capt. Joseph Stedham's Company, Delaware Battalion of Continental Troops. Enlisted on February 7, 1776, and was in quarters at Dover on April 12, 1776. [Ref: DA-40].

WATTSON, Isaac. See "John Curwithen," q.v.

WATTSON, Luke, Mary, and Margery. See "Henry Smith," q.v.

WATTSON, Susanna and Thomas. See "David John," q.v.

WEALE, George Sr. Soldier. Planter who paid his quit-rent to the governor in 1671. [Ref: DP-29]. See "George Whale."

WEAVER, Isaac. See "William Hay," q.v.

WEBB, John. Private. Served in Capt. Charles Pope's Company of the Delaware Regiment of Continental Troops. Enlisted January 15, 1776, and was on duty (in quarters) at Lewis Town on April 11, 1776, at which time he was reported to have been "on guard." [Ref: DA-51].

WEBB, John. Private. Served in Capt. John Caton's Company on April 25, 1757, in the French and Indian Wars. [Ref: DA-14]. One John Webb died testate in Kent County and his will was probated on December 1, 1760, naming his wife Ann, sons Caleb and Daniel, and daughters Elizabeth and Sarah. A later account showed that Ann Webb had married James Howell. [Ref: DK-191].

WELCH, Tamer. See "Joseph Marrat," q.v.

WELDON, Daniel. Ensign. Served in Capt. Alexander Chance's Company, Apoquinamink Hundred, Lower Regiment, New Castle County, in 1756, during the French and Indian Wars. [Ref: DA-11].

WELDON, Isaac. Private. Served in Capt. Charles Pope's Company, Delaware Regiment of Continental Troops. Enlisted January 18, 1776, and was on duty (in quarters) at Lewis Town on April 11, 1776. [Ref: DA-51].

WELLS, George. Ensign. Served as private in Capt. Benjamin Noxon's Company, and was promoted to ensign in Capt. Jacob Gooding, Jr.'s Company on June 16, 1758, during the French and Indian Wars. [Ref: DA-16, DM-47].

WELLS, James. Private. Born 1727, Kent, Delaware. Laborer. Enlisted in Capt. John Shannon's Company of Foot on July 18, 1746 and served in King George's War against Canada. He was in winter quarters at Albany, New York, during 1746-1747, and was discharged on October 31, 1747. [Ref: DA-5, DA-6, DM-40]. However, Source DM-40 stated that he was listed as a deserter in Capt. Shannon's record book.

WELLS, James. Ensign. Served in Capt. John Clayton's Company, Town of Dover, Kent County, upon Delaware, 1756, during the French and Indian Wars. [Ref: DA-12].

WELLS, James. First Lieutenant. Served in 5th Company, Delaware State Troops in Continental Service. Commissioned on January 18, 1776, and was on duty (in quarters) with Capt. Charles Pope at Lewis Town on April 11, 1776. [Ref: DA-34, DA-36, DA-49, DA-51].

WELLS, James. Land patentee and probable militiaman in Delaware in November, 1677. Was appointed Justice of the Peace at the Whorekill and Dependency, Delaware, by Gov. Edmund Andros on October 8, 1678, and was a member of the First Assembly under the new charter for Pennsylvania in 1684. He died in Kent County by January 20,

1684, when Mary Wells was recorded as his "relict." Their children were John, James, and Catherine. [Ref: DP-167, DP-168, DF-39, DF-40].

WELLS, Joseph. Private. Born 1728, Maryland. Laborer. Enlisted in Capt. John Shannon's Company of Foot on July 14, 1746, and served in King George's War against Canada. He was in winter quarters at Albany, New York, during 1746-1747, and was discharged on October 31, 1747. [Ref: DA-5, DA-6]. (He is not listed in Source DM-40.)

WELLS, Richard. Major. Served as an ensign in Capt. John Vining's Company, Kent County, in 1747-1748, in King George's War against Canada. He became a captain on April 17, 1758, and was promoted to a major "of the lower government on Delaware" in June, 1758, during the French and Indian Wars. [Ref: DA-8, 16]. One "Richard Wells, Esq." died testate in Kent County and his will was probated on May 20, 1767, naming Catherine Buckmaster and her four children, John Wells Buckmaster, James Wells Buckmaster, Mary Wells Buckmaster and Sarah Wells Buckmaster, as his heirs. A subsequent administration account also showed son Thomas Wells, a minor. [Ref: DK-228].

WELLS, Richard. Mariner. Lived in Lewes Town in Sussex County by August 28, 1771, at which time he purchased a lot. He conveyed this same lot to Jacob Kollock on August 29, 1771. [Ref: DD-47, DD-48].

WELSH, Robert. Private. Enlisted on May 12, 1758, in Capt. French Battell's Company of Lower County Provincials, during the French and Indian Wars. [Ref: DA-17].

WENDEL, Peder Hansson. Ensign. Arrived in New Sweden on the ship *Orn* in 1654 and returned to Europe with Director Rising in 1655. [Ref: DJ-722, DJ-724]. (Name also spelled "Peder Hansson Vendel").

WESSELLS, Marie. See "Pieter Alricks," q.v.

WEST, ----. Colonel. He held that rank in 1686 when mentioned in an Action of Debt in the court of Sussex County. [Ref: DC-373].

WEST, Alexander. Private. Served in Capt. David Hall's Company, Delaware Regiment of Continental Troops. Enlisted January 17, 1776, and was on duty (in barracks) at Lewis Town on April 11, 1776. [Ref: DA-42].

WEST, John. Major. He held that rank by 1693 when mentioned in Sussex County as being "of Accomack in Verginia." [Ref: DC-865].

WEST, Burton. See "Burton Waples," q.v.

WEST, Luke. Private. Served in Capt. David Hall's Company, Delaware Regiment of Continental Troops. Enlisted January 22, 1776, and was on duty (in barracks) at Lewis Town, April 11, 1776. [Ref: DA-43].

WEST, William. Pilot. Lived in Lewes, Sussex County, by August 3, 1770 at which time he purchased a lot on Mulberry St. [Ref: DD-26].

WESTCOTT, Thomas. Private. Born 1735, Indian River, Maryland. Farmer. Enlisted May 4, 1758, in the French and Indian Wars, by Capt. John McClughan, "for the campaign in the lower counties." [Ref: DA-18].

WESTLEY, Richard. Pilot. Died in Lewes, Sussex County, intestate, and the administration of his estate was granted to Ann Westley in March, 1784. A later account mentions minor children Mary, George, and Richard Westley. [Ref: DS-155].

WHALE, George. Soldier. Planter who paid his quit-rent to the governor in 1667, having been granted along with George Moore "a tract called by the name of the old Minquas plantation at Delaware" on January 19, 1667. [Ref: DP-27, DY-128].

WHARTON, Walter. Officer. He was in Delaware as an "officer" by 1671. His name appeared on a nomination list for officers in New Castle circa 1675 (list was not dated). [Ref: DP-170, DY-34].

WHEELER, Owen. Private. Served in Capt. John Caton's Company on April 25, 1757, in the French and Indian Wars. [Ref: DA-13]. One "Owen Wheelor" died in Kent County and administration of his estate was granted to widow "Anne Wheelor" on May 11, 1774. [Ref: DK-289].

WHEELER, Samuel. See "William Jackson," q.v.

WHEELER, William. Private. Served in Capt. John Caton's Company on April 25, 1757, during the French and Indian Wars. [Ref: DA-14]. One "William Wheeler, shoemaker," died testate in Kent County and his will was probated on November 9, 1774, naming wife Elizabeth and sons William, Joseph, and Jesse. [Ref: DK-292]. Another William Wheeler died in Kent County and the administration of his estate was granted to "Alice Wheeler" on August 28, 1782. A later account showed that Alice Wheeler married John Gregg. On November 28, 1783, the administrators were James Craig and James Jones, and an account showed the heirs as follows: Alice Wheelor, the widow (had married John Gregg), daughter Sarah Wheelor (had married Thomas Cavendar), and daughter Mary Wheelor (who was deceased). [Ref: DK-344, 355].

WHELLAN, Luke. Private. Born 1723, Waterford, Ireland. Miller. Enlisted on April 22, 1758, in the French and Indian Wars, by Capt. John McClughan "for the campaign in lower counties." [Ref: DA-18].

WHETHERED, Mary. See "James Sykes," q.v.

WHITE, James and Elizabeth. See "John Reynolds," q.v.

WHITE, Richard. Private. Served in Capt. John Caton's Company on April 25, 1757, in the French and Indian Wars. [Ref: DA-14]. One "Richard White, the younger" died in Kent County and administration of his estate was granted to his widow, Rebecca White, on February 15, 1777. [Ref: DK-309]. Another Richard White died testate in Kent County in Murderkill Hundred, and his will was probated on January 20, 1794, naming his sons William and Thomas, and daughters Martha White, Lydia White, Sarah Hatfield, Mary Hatfield, Rachel Craige, and Elizabeth Craige. A later account showed that Lydia White had married ---- Knotts. [Ref: DK-474].

WHITE, William. Private. Born 1734, Cedar Creek, Delaware. Farmer. Enlisted on May 4, 1758, in the French and Indian Wars, by Capt. John McClughan "for the campaign in lower counties." [Ref: DA-18].

WHITE, William. Private. Served in Capt. John Caton's Company on April 25, 1757, in the French and Indian Wars. [Ref: DA-14]. One William White died in Kent County and administration of his estate was granted to Sarah White on November 1, 1762. [Ref: DK-203]. A William White died in Kent County and administration of his estate was granted to John Darrach on February 28, 1778. [Ref: DK-316]. A William White died and the administration of his estate was granted to Deborah White on February 16, 1793. [Ref: DK-461].

WHITE, William. Sergeant. Served in Capt. Henry Darby's Company, Delaware Regiment of Continental Troops. Enlisted January 19, 1776, and on duty (in barracks) at Dover on April 12, 1776. [Ref: DA-45].

WHITEFIELD, Richard. Soldier. Applied from New Castle County in June, 1776, stating he desired to take an active part in the Flying Camp of the Third Pennsylvania Battalion. [Ref: DA-65].

WHITEHEAD, John. Private. Served in Capt. John Caton's Company, April 25, 1757, in the French and Indian Wars. [Ref: DA-13].

WHITFORD, John. Private. Enlisted on May 13, 1758, in Capt. French Battell's Company of Lower County Provincials, during the French and Indian Wars. [Ref: DA-17].

WHITTEL, William. Lieutenant. Served in Capt. Adam Peterson's Company, St. George's Hundred, Lower Regiment, New Castle County, 1756, during the French and Indian Wars. [Ref: DA-11].

WHITTENTON, Thomas. Private. Served in Capt. Nathan Adams' Company, Delaware Regiment of Continental Troops. Enlisted February 1, 1776, and on duty (in barracks) at Dover on April 12, 1776. [Ref: DA-53].

WHITTILO, David. Private. Served in Capt. Richard McWilliams' Company, New Castle County. Enlisted on December 28, 1757, during the French and Indian Wars. [Ref: DA-15].

WHITTLY, Daniell. Land patentee and probable militiaman in Delaware in November, 1677. [Ref: DP-167, 168].

WIAT, Ann and Thomas. See "Robert North," q.v.

WILDBANK, Harmanes. Officer. His name appeared on a nomination list for officers for Whorekill in Sussex County, Delaware, circa 1675 (list undated). [Ref: DP-170]. One "Halmanius [Hermanis] Wiltbanck" died in Sussex County, intestate, and administration of his estate was granted to "Jane Wiltbanck, widow," [no date given]. His estate was settled in December, 1693, and it mentioned that the widow Jane had married ---- Hoskins. Also named were sons Cornelius, Abraham, and Isaac Wiltbanck, daughter ---- Williams (wife of John) and John Hill (guardian of son Isaac "Wiltbanck"). [Ref: DS-14]. "Hermanus Frederick Wiltbanck" was granted a parcel of land at the Whorekill on July 1, 1671, and "Helmanus Wiltbanck" received a land survey for a tract called *Hopewell* on the west side of Delaware Bay on March 3, 1680/1. [Ref: DY-61, DY-147].

WILDGOOSE, Robert. Private. Served in Capt. David Hall's Company, Delaware Regiment of Continental Troops. Enlisted January 20, 1776, and was on duty (in barracks) at Lewis Town, April 11, 1776. [Ref: DA-43]. (Name also spelled "Wildgoos" and possibly even "Wildgus").

WILDGOOSE, Thomas Blades. Private. Capt. Joseph Vaughan's Company, Delaware Regiment of Continental Troops. Enlisted January 20, 1776, and was on duty (in barracks) at Dover on April 12, 1776. [Ref: DA-59]. (Name also spelled "Wildgoos" and possibly even "Wildgus").

WILDT, John. Lieutenant. Served in Capt. John Deimer's Company on June 4, 1746, during King George's War against Canada. He was in winter quarters at Albany, New York, in 1746-1747, and his company was discharged on October 31, 1747. [Ref: DA-6].

WILEY, Hugh. Private. Served in Capt. Henry Darby's Company of the Delaware Regiment of Continental Troops. Enlisted on February 13, 1776, and was on duty (in barracks) at Dover on April 12, 1776. [Ref: DA-46].

WILKINS, Richard. Private. Born 1721, England. Laborer. Enlisted in Capt. John Shannon's Company of Foot on July 28, 1746, and served in King George's War against Canada. He was in winter quarters at Albany, New York, during 1746-1747, and was discharged on October 31, 1747. [Ref: DA-5, DA-6]. (He is not listed in Source DM-40.)

WILKINS, Truett. Private. Served in Capt. Joseph Vaughan's Company, Delaware Regiment of Continental Troops. Enlisted January 18, 1776, and was on duty (in barracks) at Dover on April 12, 1776. [Ref: DA-57, DA-59]. (This same source spelled his name "Truitt Wilkens").

WILLCOX, Peter. Private. Served in Capt. Jonathan Caldwell's Company, Delaware Regiment of Continental Troops. Enlisted January 28, 1776, and on duty (in barracks) at Dover on April 12, 1776. [Ref: DA-41].

WILLEMSEN, Steffen. Captain. Served on the ship *Swan* during the eighth expedition to New Sweden between 1647-1648. [Ref: DJ-760]. (This same source also spelled his name "Stephen Williamsson").

WILLEMSON, Herman. Sailor. Mate on the ship *Kalmar Nyckel* in the second expedition to New Sweden between 1638-1640. [Ref: DJ-759].

WILLET, Christ. Private. Served in Capt. Charles Pope's Company, Delaware Regiment of Continental Troops. Enlisted January 19, 1776, and was on duty (in quarters) at Lewis Town on April 11, 1776. [Ref: DA-51].

WILLIAMS, Agnes. See "Thomas Prettyman," q.v.

WILLIAMS, Derrick. Lieutenant. Served in Capt. William Williams' Company, Apoquinamink Hundred, Lower Regiment, New Castle County, 1756, during the French and Indian Wars. [Ref: DA-11].

WILLIAMS, John. Private. Born 1739, Wales. Laborer. Enlisted May 5, 1759, in the French and Indian Wars, in Capt. James Armstrong's Company in the Pennsylvania Regiment. [Ref: DA-26].

WILLIAMS, John. Soldier. Cooper. Enlisted in Wilmington Township in 1758 by Capt. Samuel Grubb to serve in the Pennsylvania Troops during the French and Indian Wars. [Ref: DA-27].

WILLIAMS, John. Private. Served in Capt. Joseph Stedham's Company, Delaware Battalion of Continental Troops. Enlisted on January 24, 1776, and was in quarters at Dover on April 12, 1776. [Ref: DA-39].

WILLIAMS, Lambert. Private. Served in Capt. Jonathan Caldwell's Company, Delaware Regiment of Continental Troops. Enlisted January 27, 1776, and on duty (in barracks) at Dover on April 12, 1776. [Ref: DA-41].

WILLIAMS, Solomon. Private. Served in Capt. Joseph Vaughan's Company, Delaware Regiment of Continental Troops. Enlisted February 15, 1776 and on duty (in barracks) at Dover on April 12, 1776. [Ref: DA-59].

WILLIAMS, Thomas. Private. Served in Capt. Nathan Adams' Company, Delaware Regiment of Continental Troops. Enlisted January 20, 1776, and on duty (in barracks) at Dover on April 12, 1776. [Ref: DA-53].

WILLIAMS, William. Captain. Served in a company in Apoquinamink Hundred, Lower Regiment, New Castle County, 1756, during the French and Indian Wars. [Ref: DA-11, DM-46].

WILLIAMSON, Cuthbert. Private. Served in Capt. David Hall's Company Delaware Regiment of Continental Troops. Enlisted on January 20, 1776, and on duty (in barracks) at Lewis Town on April 11, 1776. [Ref: DA-43].

WILLIAMSON, Jacob. Private. Served in Capt. John Caton's Company on April 25, 1757, in the French and Indian War. [Ref: DA-13]. A Jacob Williamson died in Kent County and administration of his estate was granted to William Manlove on September 22, 1773. [Ref: DK-282].

WILLIAMSON, John and Sampson. See "John Caton," q.v.

WILLIAMSON, Thomas. Ensign. Served in Capt. Rees Jones' Company, White Clay Creek Hundred, Upper Regiment, New Castle County, 1756, during the French and Indian Wars. [Ref: DA-11].

WILLIS, Thomas. Private. Born 1742, Sussex, Delaware. Enlisted in Capt. John Wright's Company and was on the muster roll of May 11, 1759, during the French and Indian Wars. [Ref: DA-25].

WILLISS, Henry. Private. Served in Capt. Joseph Vaughan's Company, Delaware Regiment of Continental Troops. Enlisted January 21, 1776, and was on duty (in barracks) at Dover on April 12, 1776. [Ref: DA-57, DA-59]. (This same source spelled his name "Henry Willess").

WILLS, Caleb. Private. Born 1738, Sussex, Delaware. Enlisted in Capt. John Wright's Company and was on the muster roll of May 11, 1759, during the French and Indian Wars. [Ref: DA-25].

WILLS, Lawrence. Private. Born 1738, Sussex, Delaware. Enlisted in Capt. John Wright's Company and was on the muster roll of May 11, 1759, during the French and Indian Wars. [Ref: DA-25].

WILLSON, Hosea. Private. Served in Capt. Jonathan Caldwell's Company, Delaware Regiment of Continental Troops. Enlisted January 18, 1776, and was on duty (in barracks) at Dover on April 12, 1776. [Ref: DA-41].

WILLSON, Jacob. Private. Served in Capt. Jonathan Caldwell's Company, Delaware Regiment of Continental Troops. Enlisted January 13, 1776, and was on duty (in barracks) at Dover on April 12, 1776. [Ref: DA-41].

WILLSON, John. Private. Served in Capt. Joseph Stedham's Company, Delaware Battalion of Continental Troops. Enlisted on January 26, 1776, and reportedly "deserted" on February 13, 1776. [Ref: DA-40].

WILLSON, John. Private. Served in Capt. Jonathan Caldwell's Company of the Delaware Regiment of Continental Troops. Enlisted on January 16, 1776, and was on duty (in barracks) at Dover on April 12, 1776. [Ref: DA-41].

WILLSON, John. Private. Served in Capt. John Caton's Company on April 25, 1757, in the French and Indian Wars. [Ref: DA-13]. One "John Wilson" died in Duck Creek Hundred in Kent County and his will was probated on February 13, 1767, naming his wife Martha and sons Jesse, Thomas, Samuel, Jonathan, and David. [Ref: DK-226]. A "John Willson" died in Murderkill Hundred in Kent County and his will was probated on July 30, 1781, naming his wife Susannah, son Nathan, and daughters Mary, Susannah, Hannah, Sarah, Ruth, Rachel, Elizabeth, Mariam, Margaret, Ann, and Lutisi. [Ref: DK-332]. One "John Wilson, captain, late of the Delaware Regiment, tanner" died in Murderkill Hundred in Kent County and the administration of his estate was granted to Simon Wilmer Wilson on November 23, 1786. [Ref: DK-386]. One "John Wilson, blacksmith" died in Kent County and administration of his estate was granted to Eleanor Wilson on January 5, 1792. [Ref: DK-451].

WILLSON, Richard. See "William Rodney," q.v.

WILLSON, Thomas. Private. Served in Capt. Joseph Stedham's Company, Delaware Battalion of Continental Troops. Enlisted on February 2, 1776, and was in quarters at Dover on April 12, 1776. [Ref: DA-39].

WILLY, Waitman. Private. Born 1734, Maryland. Enlisted in Capt. John Wright's Company and was on the muster roll of May 11, 1759, during the French and Indian Wars. [Ref: DA-25].

WILSON, John. Ensign. Served in the 5th Company of Delaware State Troops in Continental Service. Commissioned on January 18, 1776, and was on duty (in quarters) with Capt. Charles Pope at Lewis Town on April 11, 1776. [Ref: DA-35, DA-36, DA-49, DA-51]. (Name also spelled "Willson").

WILSON, Allan. Private. Served in Capt. Richard McWilliams' Company in New Castle County. Enlisted on December 28, 1757, during the French and Indian Wars. [Ref: DA-14].

WILSON, Richard. Corporal. Served in Capt. Samuel Smith's Company, Delaware Regiment of Continental Troops. Enlisted January 19, 1776, and on duty (in barracks) at Dover on April 12, 1776. [Ref: DA-54].

WILSON, Samuel. Private. Born 1743, Kennett, Pennsylvania. Laborer. Enlisted on May 12, 1758, in the French and Indian Wars, by Capt. John McClughan "for the campaign in lower counties." [Ref: DA-18].

WILSON, Samuel. Private. Served in Capt. John Caton's Company on April 25, 1757, in the French and Indian Wars. [Ref: DA-14]. One "Samuel Wilson, farmer," died tetstate in Duck Creek Hundred in Kent County and his will was probated on July 28, 1787, naming his wife Mary, sons John, Thomas, Samuel, and Gustavus, and daughters Ann and Lydia. [Ref: DK-394].

WILSON, Sarah and Caesar. See "Caesar Rodney," q.v.

WILSON, Simon Wilmer. See "John Willson," q.v.

WILSON, Solomon. Private. Born 1740, Chester River, Maryland. Laborer. Enlisted on May 1, 1758, during the French and Indian War, by Capt. John McClughan "for the campaign in the lower counties." [Ref: DA-18].

WILTBANK, Abraham. Pilot. Lived in Lewes, Sussex County, by January 1, 1769, at which time he (and others) conveyed a lot on 2nd Street to Nehemiah Field. He also sold land on Lewes Creek on February 13, 1771, "which he had purchased from the estate of his brother Jacob Wiltbank and on land belonging to John Wiltbank, Esq., and the same land that Abraham Wiltbank had died seized of." [Ref: DD-1, DD-36]. Also see "Jacob Kollock," q.v.

WILTBANK, Catherine. See "Jacob Kollock," q.v.

WILTBANK, Halmanius, and others. See "Harmanes Wildbank," q.v.

WILTBANK, Isaac. See "Harmanes Wildbank" and "John Hill," q.v.

WIMBERO, Elijah. Private. Served in Capt. David Hall's Company, Delaware Regiment of Continental Troops. Enlisted January 21, 1776, and was on duty (in barracks) at Lewis Town on April 11, 1776, when he was reported to have "deserted, April 11." [Ref: DA-43].

WISE, John. Private. Served in Capt. Charles Pope's Company of the Delaware Regiment of Continental Troops. Enlisted January 16, 1776, and was on duty (in quarters) at Lewis Town on April 11, 1776. [Ref: DA-51].

WITHERSPOON, David. Lieutenant Colonel. Served as a captain in a New Castle County Company, 1747-1748, in King George's War against Canada. He was lieutenant colonel of the Lower Regiment of New Castle County, 1756, in the French and Indians Wars. [Ref: DA-7, DA-11, DM-45].

WITHERSPOON, Robert. Private. Born 1737, Down, Ireland. Weaver. Enlisted on May 1, 1759, in the French and Indian Wars, in Capt. James Armstrong's Company in Pennsylvania Regiment. [Ref: DA-26].

WITTINGTON, John. Private. Served in Capt. Jonathan Caldwell's Company, Delaware Regiment of Continental Troops. Enlisted March

29, 1776, and on duty (in barracks) at Dover on April 12, 1776. [Ref: DA-41].

WOLF, Rice. Lieutenant. Served in Capt. John Newbold's Company, Southern District of Lewis and Rehoboth Hundred, in the regiment of Sussex County, in 1756, in the French and Indian Wars. "Rees Woolf, Sr." was a lieutenant in Capt. Newbold's Rehoboth District Company in March, 1758. [Ref: DA-13, 15]. One "Rees Woolf, innholder," died testate in Lewes, Delaware and his will was probated April 21, 1773 naming his daughter Mary Paynter and grandsons Rees, Richard, and Samuel Paynter. [Ref: DS-94]. "Reece Wolfe" died testate in Sussex County and his will was probated on May 10, 1797, naming his wife Mary, his sons Reece, William, Daniel, Harry, George, Benjamin, and David, plus children of deceased daughter Comfort Orr, the children of daughter Sarah Marriner, and one Jane Russell. [Ref: DS-283].

WOLLASTON, Elizabeth. See "John Ogle," q.v.

WOLLASTON, Thomas. Soldier. Planter in Delaware who paid his quitrent to the governor in 1668, having received a grant "for a certain house and back side in the Towne of New Castle upon Delaware" on January 19, 1667. [Ref: DP-27, DP-28, DY-127]. He was referred to as "Serjeant Tho. Wollaston" when he was granted land on White Clay Kill [Creek] on August 1, 1668. [Ref: DY-133].

WOOD, John. Private. Served in Capt. Samuel Smith's Company of the Delaware Regiment of Continental Troops. Enlisted February 1, 1776, and on duty (in barracks) at Dover on April 12, 1776. [Ref: DA-54].

WOOD, Richard. Private. Born 1724, Long Island. Tanner. Enlisted in Capt. John Shannon's Company of Foot on June 26, 1746, and served in King George's War against Canada. He was in winter quarters at Albany, New York, during 1746-1747, and was discharged on October 31, 1747. [Ref: DA-5, DA-6, DM-40]. However, Source DM-40 stated that he was listed as a "deserter" in Capt. Shannon's record book.

WOODS, John. Mariner. Lived in Sussex County in the town of Lewes by October 28, 1773, at which time he purchased a lot on 2nd Street from Dormon Lofland, sheriff. [Ref: DD-118].

WOOLF, Rees Sr. See "Rice Wolf," q.v.

WOOTTERS, James. Private. Served in Capt. Nathan Adams' Company, Delaware Regiment of Continental Troops. Enlisted on February 17, 1776, and was on duty (in barracks) at Dover on April 12, 1776. [Ref: DA-53].

WORK, Patrick. Lieutenant Colonel. Served in the 3rd Battalion of the Pennsylvania Regiment under Col. Hugh Mercer, which included three companies "of the lower counties" [Delaware], on April 24, 1759. [Ref: DA-20].

WORTH, Dinah. See "Samuel Platt," q.v.

WRIGHT, Ezekiel. Soldier. Enlisted on May 10, 1759, in the French and Indian Wars, and his name appeared on a return of Capt. Henry Van Bibber's Company of the Lower Counties on Delaware Troops, at New Castle, on June 4, 1759. [Ref: DA-26].

WRIGHT, James. Private. Served in Capt. Joseph Vaughan's Company, Delaware Regiment of Continental Troops. Enlisted January 20, 1776, and on duty (in barracks) at Dover on April 12, 1776. [Ref: DA-59].

WRIGHT, John. Private. Born 1736, Maryland. Laborer. Enlisted on May 2, 1758, during the French and Indian Wars, by Capt. Benjamin Noxon. [Ref: DA-19].

WRIGHT, John. Captain. Served as a first lieutenant in Capt. John McClughan's Company on April 19, 1758, during the French and Indian Wars, and became a captain of one of the three companies "of the lower counties" [Delaware] in the 3rd Battalion of the Pennsylvania Regiment under Col. Hugh Mercer in May, 1759. [Ref: DA-16, DA-20, DA-25, DM-47, DM-49].

WRIGHT, Thomas. Private. Served in Capt. Nathan Adams' Company, Delaware Regiment of Continental Troops. Enlisted January 25, 1776, and on duty (in barracks) at Dover on April 12, 1776. [Ref: DA-53].

WRIGHT, William. Private. Served in Capt. Joseph Vaughan's Company, Delaware Regiment of Continental Troops. Enlisted February 16, 1776 and on duty (in barracks) at Dover on April 12, 1776. [Ref: DA-59].

WYNKOOP, Benjamin. Captain. Served in a company in the regiment of Sussex County in the Northern District of Cedar Creek Hundred, in 1756, in the French and Indian Wars. "Benjamin Wynkoop" was captain of the Cedar Creek District Company on March 18, 1758. [Ref: DA-13, DA-15, DM-46]. An Abraham Wynkoop died testate in Sussex County and his will was probated January 3, 1754, naming a son Benjamin (and others). A later account showed that the estate was settled May 10, 1783, by Benjamin Wynkoop, acting executor. [Ref: DS-62]. (Name was also spelled "Wyncoop").

WYNHART, Cornelis. Soldier. Planter in Delaware who paid his quit-rent to the governor in 1671, having received a land patent at Whorekill on June 1, 1671. [Ref: DP-29, DY-148].

YORKSON, John. Private. Born 1738, Maryland. Carpenter. Enlisted on May 2, 1758, during the French and Indian Wars, by Capt. Benjamin Noxon. [Ref: DA-19].

YOUNG, David. Private. Served in Capt. Joseph Stedham's Company, Delaware Battalion of Continental Troops. Enlisted February 2, 1776, and was in quarters at Dover on April 12, 1776. [Ref: DA-39].

YOUNG, Goodman. Private. Born 1736, Ireland. Weaver. Enlisted on May 3, 1758, during the French and Indian Wars, by Capt. Benjamin Noxon. [Ref: DA-19].

YOUNG, Isaac. Private. Born 1739, Down, Ireland. Laborer. Enlisted on May 7, 1759, during the French and Indian Wars, in Capt. James Armstrong's Company in the Pennsylvania Regiment. [Ref: DA-26].

YOUNG, James. "Commiss. of the Musters." Served in this capacity on June 13, 1759, in the French and Indian Wars, for the 3rd Battalion of the Pennsylvania Regiment under Col. Hugh Mercer, including the three companies "of the lower counties" [Delaware]. [Ref: DA-20].

YOUNG, James. Private. Born 1738, New England. Weaver. Enlisted on May 15, 1758, during the French and Indian Wars, by Capt. Benjamin Noxon. [Ref: DA-19].

YOUNG, James. Soldier. Enlisted on May 23, 1759, in the French and Indian Wars, and appeared on a return of Capt. Henry Van Bibber's Company of the Lower Counties on Delaware Troops, at New Castle, on June 4, 1759. [Ref: DA-26].

YOUNG, John. Private. Born 1739, Ireland. Weaver. Enlisted in Capt. John Wright's Company and was on the muster roll of May 11, 1759, during the French and Indian Wars. [Ref: DA-25].

YOUNG, John. Private. Enlisted on May 15, 1758, in Capt. French Battell's Company of Lower County Provincials, during the French and Indian Wars. [Ref: DA-17].

YOUNG, Thomas. Soldier. Planter in Delaware who paid his quit-rent to the governor in 1671, having received a patent to land on St. Jones Creek on June 17, 1671. [Ref: DP-29, DY-150].

YOUNGE, Jacob. Officer. His name appeared on a nomination list for officers in New Castle, Delaware, circa 1675 (list was not dated). [Ref: DP-170, DY-102].

ZAKARIASSON, Anders. Soldier. Arrived in New Sweden on the ship *Orn* in 1654. [Ref: DJ-722]. (Name also spelled "Anders Zachariezon").

ZIM, Mester. Barber-surgeon (*balberenn*). An "officer" in New Sweden in 1643, he returned home to Sweden in 1644. [Ref: DJ-709].

Other books by the author:

A Closer Look at St. John's Parish Registers [Baltimore County, Maryland], 1701-1801
A Collection of Maryland Church Records
A Guide to Genealogical Research in Maryland: 5th Edition, Revised and Enlarged
Abstracts of the Ledgers and Accounts of the Bush Store and Rock Run Store, 1759-1771
Abstracts of the Orphans Court Proceedings of Harford County, 1778-1800
Abstracts of Wills, Harford County, Maryland, 1800-1805
Baltimore City [Maryland] Deaths and Burials, 1834-1840
Baltimore County, Maryland, Overseers of Roads, 1693-1793
Bastardy Cases in Baltimore County, Maryland, 1673-1783
Bastardy Cases in Harford County, Maryland, 1774-1844
Bible and Family Records of Harford County, Maryland Families: Volume V
Children of Harford County: Indentures and Guardianships, 1801-1830
Colonial Delaware Soldiers and Sailors, 1638-1776
*Colonial Families of the Eastern Shore of Maryland
Volumes 5, 6, 7, 8, 9, 11, 12, 13, 14, and 16*
Colonial Maryland Soldiers and Sailors, 1634-1734
Dr. John Archer's First Medical Ledger, 1767-1769, Annotated Abstracts
Early Anglican Records of Cecil County
*Early Harford Countians, Individuals Living in Harford County, Maryland in Its Formative Years
Volume 1: A to K, Volume 2: L to Z, and Volume 3: Supplement*
Harford County Taxpayers in 1870, 1872 and 1883
Harford County, Maryland Divorce Cases, 1827-1912: An Annotated Index
Heirs and Legatees of Harford County, Maryland, 1774-1802
Heirs and Legatees of Harford County, Maryland, 1802-1846
Inhabitants of Baltimore County, Maryland, 1763-1774
Inhabitants of Cecil County, Maryland, 1649-1774
Inhabitants of Harford County, Maryland, 1791-1800
Inhabitants of Kent County, Maryland, 1637-1787
*Joseph A. Pennington & Co., Havre De Grace, Maryland Funeral Home Records:
Volume II, 1877-1882, 1893-1900*
Maryland Bible Records, Volume 1: Baltimore and Harford Counties
Maryland Bible Records, Volume 2: Baltimore and Harford Counties
Maryland Bible Records, Volume 3: Carroll County
Maryland Bible Records, Volume 4: Eastern Shore
Maryland Deponents, 1634-1799
Maryland Deponents: Volume 3, 1634-1776
*Maryland Public Service Records, 1775-1783: A Compendium of Men and Women of
Maryland Who Rendered Aid in Support of the American Cause against
Great Britain during the Revolutionary War*
*Marylanders to Carolina: Migration of Marylanders to
North Carolina and South Carolina prior to 1800*

Marylanders to Kentucky, 1775-1825
Methodist Records of Baltimore City, Maryland: Volume 1, 1799-1829
Methodist Records of Baltimore City, Maryland: Volume 2, 1830-1839
Methodist Records of Baltimore City, Maryland: Volume 3, 1840-1850 (East City Station)
More Maryland Deponents, 1716-1799
More Marylanders to Carolina: Migration of Marylanders to North Carolina and South Carolina prior to 1800
More Marylanders to Kentucky, 1778-1828
Outpensioners of Harford County, Maryland, 1856-1896
Presbyterian Records of Baltimore City, Maryland, 1765-1840
Quaker Records of Baltimore and Harford Counties, Maryland, 1801-1825
Quaker Records of Northern Maryland, 1716-1800
Quaker Records of Southern Maryland, 1658-1800
Revolutionary Patriots of Anne Arundel County, Maryland
Revolutionary Patriots of Baltimore Town and Baltimore County, 1775-1783
Revolutionary Patriots of Calvert and St. Mary's Counties, Maryland, 1775-1783
Revolutionary Patriots of Caroline County, Maryland, 1775-1783
Revolutionary Patriots of Cecil County, Maryland
Revolutionary Patriots of Charles County, Maryland, 1775-1783
Revolutionary Patriots of Delaware, 1775-1783
Revolutionary Patriots of Dorchester County, Maryland, 1775-1783
Revolutionary Patriots of Frederick County, Maryland, 1775-1783
Revolutionary Patriots of Harford County, Maryland, 1775-1783
Revolutionary Patriots of Kent and Queen Anne's Counties
Revolutionary Patriots of Lancaster County, Pennsylvania
Revolutionary Patriots of Maryland, 1775-1783: A Supplement
Revolutionary Patriots of Maryland, 1775-1783: Second Supplement
Revolutionary Patriots of Montgomery County, Maryland, 1776-1783
Revolutionary Patriots of Prince George's County, Maryland, 1775-1783
Revolutionary Patriots of Talbot County, Maryland, 1775-1783
Revolutionary Patriots of Worcester and Somerset Counties, Maryland, 1775-1783
Revolutionary Patriots of Washington County, Maryland, 1776-1783
St. George's (Old Spesutia) Parish, Harford County, Maryland: Church and Cemetery Records, 1820-1920
St. John's and St. George's Parish Registers, 1696-1851
Survey Field Book of David and William Clark in Harford County, Maryland, 1770-1812
The Crenshaws of Kentucky, 1800-1995
The Delaware Militia in the War of 1812
Union Chapel United Methodist Church Cemetery Tombstone Inscriptions, Wilna, Harford County, Maryland

www.ingramcontent.com/pod-product-compliance
Lightning Source LLC
Chambersburg PA
CBHW071710160426
43195CB00012B/1632